LEADERSHIP
FOR CATHOLIC
YOUTH
MINISTRY

Dedication

In celebration of thirty years of partnership with ministry leaders, the staff of the Center for Ministry Development would like to dedicate this book to all of the leaders who have journeyed with us over these three decades. Thank you for letting us be part of your ministry.

Leadership *for* Catholic Youth Ministry

A Comprehensive Resource

Thomas East *with*

Alejandro Aguilera-Titus ❧ Carolyn Coll, RSM
Ann Marie Eckert ❧ Leif Kehrwald
Sean T. Lansing ❧ Mariette Martineau
John Roberto ❧ Cheryl M. Tholcke

TWENTY
THIRD 23rd
PUBLICATIONS

Contributing Authors

Thomas East

with

Alejandro Aguilera-Titus

Carolyn Coll, RSM

Ann Marie Eckert

Leif Kehrwald

Sean Lansing

Mariette Martineau

John Roberto

Cheryl M. Tholcke

Sixth Printing 2016

TWENTY-THIRD PUBLICATIONS
A Division of Bayard
One Montauk Avenue, Suite 200
New London, CT 06320
(860) 437-3012 or (800) 321-0411
www.twentythirdpublications.com

ISBN 978-1-58595-732-3
Library of Congress Catalog Card Number: 2008940046
Printed in the U.S.A.

Contents

SECTION III
Promoting Personal and Spiritual Growth of Youth

SECTION IV
Planning and Leadership for Youth Ministry

Foreword

LIVING THE VISION FOR CATHOLIC YOUTH MINISTRY

Leadership for Catholic Youth Ministry was published in 2008 for parish leaders who strive to provide vibrant and dynamic ministry for adolescents. As authors, we are delighted that the insights and practical guidance provided has struck a chord. This book has become a foundational resource for parish teams as well as for training programs provided by dioceses, universities, and ministry centers. The heart of this book is the lived practice of ministry with youth as inspired and guided by *Renewing the Vision—A Framework for Catholic Youth Ministry*.

Renewing the Vision was approved and published in November 1997 by the United States Catholic bishops. Since that time, this document has sold over 126,000 copies in print form in addition to hundreds of thousands of downloads. More importantly, the insights of this document have spread to parishes small and large throughout the United States and to most English-speaking nations around the world. Many people credit *Renewing the Vision* with strengthening and transforming Catholic youth ministry. This document provides a compelling vision for ministry with youth and for parish life that includes youth as full members of the community. It also provides a common language and framework for envisioning and building a ministry with youth that is responsive, inclusive, and comprehensive.

It is striking how enduring the document has become. Many documents of the bishops' conference are received by the field with initial enthusiasm but receive little attention after the first few years of implementation. *Renewing the Vision* continues to be a driving force in leadership training, resource development, and parish renewal of ministry. This document is also the focus of dialogue and debate, conversations that point toward the growing edges of the vision for Catholic youth ministry.

As we present this second edition of *Leadership for Catholic Youth Ministry*, it seems fitting to recall the past sixteen years of *Renewing the Vision*, analyze our current context, and look ahead to future ministry opportunities. Let's look together at areas of ministry that are challenging and chart a path for continued growth in our pastoral ministry with youth.

The Growing Edges of Renewing the Vision

Evangelization—Identity of Church and Component of Youth Ministry

> Evangelizing is in fact the grace and vocation proper to the Church, her deepest identity. She exists in order to evangelize, that is to say, in order to preach and teach, to be the channel of the gift of grace, to reconcile sinners with God, and to perpetuate Christ's sacrifice in the Mass, which is the memorial of His death and glorious resurrection. *EVANGELI NUNTIANDI, N. 14.*

In *Renewing the Vision*, evangelization is a component of youth ministry. Within this description, readers are told that evangelization is "the energizing core of everything we do" in youth ministry. Still, some readers of the document would not fully appreciate the importance of evangelization. Evangelization is the deepest identity of the Church and should be given this sense of priority. Even though evangelization is present within all of the components, describing it as a component does remind leaders that it is important to attend to evangelization in an intentional way and to include elements of evangelization that are distinct from other aspects of the ministry. As we continue to

ISSUE:
Evangelization is described by Church documents as the "deepest identity" of the Church, yet it is described as a component of ministry within *Renewing the Vision.*

explore the context and direction for evangelization of youth and their families, it will be essential that our vision for youth ministry is communicated with both of these concepts in mind: first, all of youth ministry is evangelization, which means we should be evangelizing through every aspect of our ministry, every interaction, every relationship, and every contact; second, evangelization should be intentional and have distinctive elements within youth ministry so that we continually reach out to youth and families beyond those who present themselves.

Recognition of the Cultural Context for Youth Ministry in the United States

In many ways, *Renewing the Vision* was pioneering in its inclusion of multiculturalism and the practical ways that cultural diversity is integrated within the document. The document was published in English and Spanish and provides a solid direction for ministry with youth of diverse cultures:

> Effective youth ministry should help all young people to feel comfortable and welcome so that they can develop their identity by affirming and utilizing the values and traditions of their unique culture, and the gifts and talents they offer to the entire faith community.
>
> **RENEWING THE VISION, P. 23**

ISSUE: Though *Renewing the Vision* includes a theme of multiculturalism and provides numerous references to cultural diversity and the eradication of the evil of racism, the treatment of cultural diversity within the document does not reflect the current reality of the context for ministry with youth in the United States.

The references in *RTV* are intended to help parishes address important questions: How do we include youth of different cultures within youth ministry? How do we minister to youth from diverse cultural groups? It is clear that the questions addressed by the document are different now than they were in 1997. The ministry context and paradigm of *RTV* comes largely from suburban, white, middle class parishes and does not fully reflect the significant history, tradition, resources, challenges, and opportunities provided by the many cultures within the United States, especially considering that youth from diverse cultures now constitute the majority of Catholic young people rather than a minority group.

The current pastoral situation now goes beyond considerations of inclusion and context. In this moment, how do we foster a genuine national dialogue that considers not just the contributions of individual youth but the contributions of ethnic communities with long-standing traditions of ministering with youth? How can we empower parishes that have more than one ethnic community to develop ministry with youth that reflects the possibilities for connection and the needs of each community? How do we work to ensure that leaders are formed with the cultural competencies needed for leadership of communities that include more than one cultural group?

These questions lead to an essential conversation where communities can share their strengths and challenges and find ways to build ministry with youth in shared parishes with leaders who have the skills and openness needed to engage and minister with diverse communities.

Role and Priority of Catechesis

In the earlier description of the history of the document, it was noted that CCD or religious education was one of the three main ways that the Church ministered to youth prior to the naming of a description of youth ministry within *A Vision of Youth Ministry*. This is part of our history and part of what distinguishes Catholic youth ministry from the ministry provided by mainline and evangelical churches. Studies of effective youth ministry and research with youth indicate the importance of catechesis as the heart of youth ministry. In addition, the *National Directory for Catechesis* describes the placement of catechesis:

ISSUE: For many bishops, pastors, diocesan leaders, and parishes, the priority in ministering with youth is catechesis, faith identity, and knowledge of the Catholic faith. In practice, many parishes put most of their emphasis on confirmation preparation programs that are primarily catechetical. In *Renewing the Vision*, catechesis, like evangelization, is one component of eight.

> "…adolescent catechesis is most effective when situated within a comprehensive program of youth ministry that includes social, liturgical, and catechetical components as well as opportunities for service."
>
> **NATIONAL DIRECTORY FOR CATECHESIS, P. 264**

This directive reminds us that youth ministry is broader than catechesis, even if catechesis is provided in a way that includes many dimensions. In other words, it isn't enough for parishes to provide catechesis or confirmation preparation in a youth ministry style. To be truly effective and responsive to youth, catechesis should be provided as a priority component within a ministry that has many dimensions. Parish communities across the United States have demonstrated that effective adolescent catechesis relies on the context of comprehensive youth ministry and the intentionality of a systematic approach. When asked about effective youth ministry, pastors, parents, parish leaders, and youth agree that learning and growing in faith is at the heart of ministry with young people. This experience matches with the direction provided by national documents for catechesis and youth ministry, which converge around two important insights.

First, youth ministry is effective when evangelization and catechesis are at the core of all pastoral efforts. Second, catechesis for youth happens most effectively in the context of broader youth ministry efforts. Within this context, informal catechetical moments help youth to make the connections between faith and life. Systematic, intentional catechesis helps youth develop as followers of Christ who grow to know, love, and live their Catholic faith. It leads them to ongoing conversion. Working together, these elements forge a connection for youth where faith becomes their compass for life, and formation in the faith becomes a lifelong journey.

Pastoral Care and Catholic Identity—General Good versus Specific Good

Many pastoral leaders feel that the formation of authentic Catholic identity is the highest priority for ministries with youth and consequently see all other initiatives as a distraction. Other leaders see the promotion of healthy adolescent development as recommended in *Renewing the Vision* to be a natural and important way to stand with youth and their families in the important transition to adulthood. These efforts flow

ISSUE: *Renewing the Vision* highlights the resources provided by the Search Institute that promote healthy youth development. Some leaders question the importance of these efforts in comparison with the urgency of forming Catholic faith identity in youth. Parishes who utilize community resources such as the Assets approach provide helpful service to youth and families by promoting healthy development, but do these efforts sacrifice or hinder our intentions to evangelize and catechize youth?

from the directives in the Advocacy, Justice and Service, and Pastoral Care components and provide a practical witness within our evangelization efforts.

This is a tension that deserves thoughtful reflection, which could lead to renewed practices that are intentional about evangelization as we provide pastoral care for youth and support for families. The relationships of trust that are built through this support could lead to greater participation and formation as youth and families rely more and more on parishes as a source of support, community, and faith growth.

An Ecclesiology of Parish Life—An Idealized Parish Community

In many ways, this issue is the shadow side of a great strength of *Renewing the Vision*, which provides a profound and compelling vision for parish life that is nearly unparalleled among Church documents. Many trainers and leaders have applied the insights of *RTV* far beyond youth ministry by suggesting that this vision with its pattern of responsiveness, goals, settings for ministry, themes, and components could describe all of parish life. However, this positive view of parish life can lead to frustration because the challenge of providing youth ministry in parishes who are struggling is clearly a different challenge than providing for youth ministry in a parish where ministries are flourishing.

These differences were highlighted in *Effective Practices for Dynamic Youth Ministry*, which pointed out that the challenge for parishes with vibrant

ISSUE: The description of parish life provided within *Renewing the Vision* is very positive and does not acknowledge the challenges many parishes face in leadership, vibrancy, and effective programming. Some who may read RTV without any knowledge of parish life in the United States could have the impression that all parishes are flourishing communities with robust pastoral ministry whose greatest challenge is the inclusion of youth within the ministries and life of the community.

ministry is to include youth in the parish and to continually reach out to youth and families in the community (*Winona, MN: Saint Mary's Press, 2004, pages 75-76*). For parishes with developing ministry, there is a much greater responsibility to provide the spiritual support and nurture that is not found within parish life as a whole. For these parishes, the first priority is the spiritual formation of team members and families of youth. These insights were also found in the dialogue of the symposium for the *Effective Practices* project, during which many leaders suggested that the spiritual formation of the leaders and teams who work with youth should be considered the first goal of youth ministry because leaders can't give what they don't have.

Looking at *Renewing the Vision* through the lens of the New Evangelization

> (Evangelization is to be) "new in its ardor, methods and expression" (#6)....
> **POPE JOHN PAUL II, ECCLESIA IN AMERICA**

The New Evangelization provides an opportunity for youth ministry leaders to stand back and consider how our pastoral ministry with youth invites them into a deep relationship with our loving God and empowers them as witnesses. With new ardor, we embrace new methods and new expressions all aimed at helping youth to feel reconciled, embraced, loved, and called.

Embracing this new energy and direction calls us to reach out to youth and families who are practicing in a marginal way or who have fallen away from their practice of the faith. At the same time, we are called to equip those who are faithful to be bold and compassionate witnesses of their faith.

> Today, we need a Church capable of walking at people's side, of doing more than simply listening to them; a Church which accompanies them on their journey; a Church able to make sense of the "night" contained in the flight of so many of our brothers and sisters from Jerusalem; a Church which realizes that the reasons why people leave also contain reasons why they can eventually return. **POPE FRANCIS, IN HIS ADDRESS TO BRAZILIAN BISHOPS PRIOR TO WORLD YOUTH DAY, JULY 27, 2013**

Where do We Grow from Here?

We are currently in an amazing moment to lead and support ministry with youth. Pope Francis brings a new energy in the Catholic Church, including her youth ministry, through his direct call to link all evangelization with love, joy, and reconciliation. He proposes this as the pastoral foundation for all that we do.

> Spreading the Gospel means that we are the first to proclaim and live the reconciliation, forgiveness, peace, unity and love which the Holy Spirit gives us. Let us remember Jesus' words: "by this all men will know that you are my disciples, if you have love for one another" (John 13:34-35).
>
> *EXCERPT FROM THE GENERAL AUDIENCE WITH POPE FRANCIS,*
> *WEDNESDAY, MAY 22, 2013*

Sharing Christ's love is a personal mandate and is the mission for the pastoral work of all of the institutions of the Church. Youth ministry as proposed by *Renewing the Vision* is a ministry directed outward that seeks, includes, and empowers young people as disciples. This vision is very much in synch with and appropriate to this moment as we see in Pope Francis's comments to the Argentinean youth prior to World Youth Day:

> What do I expect as a consequence of the Youth Day? I expect a mess. There will be one. … But I want a mess in the dioceses! I want people to go out! I want the Church to go out to the street! I want us to defend ourselves against everything that is worldliness… that is comfortableness, that is clericalism….The parishes, the schools, the institutions, exist to go out!
>
> *POPE FRANCIS, JULY 26, 2013*

As we celebrate, acknowledge, and reflect upon the sixteen years since the publication of *Renewing the Vision*, leaders of youth ministry from parishes, organizations, schools, and universities should see this moment as an opportunity to name a common framework, language, and direction as we embrace new possibilities in our ministry with youth and their families. *Renewing the Vision* is a living document that continues to develop as leaders implement pastoral ministry with youth. As leaders, we continue to write this document through our leadership actions, our innovations, and our continued discernment of the movement of the Spirit. We work together within the Church to help youth encounter Christ and proclaim his love to the world.

Introduction

 ## Youth Ministry as Encounter and Adventure

> In the sixth month, the angel Gabriel was sent from God to a town of Galilee
> called Nazareth, to a virgin betrothed to a man named Joseph, of the house
> of David, and the virgin's name was Mary. And coming to her, he said, "Hail,
> favored one! The Lord is with you." But she was greatly troubled at what was
> said and pondered what sort of greeting this might be. Then the angel said
> to her, "Do not be afraid, Mary, for you have found favor with God. Behold,
> you will conceive in your womb and bear a son, and you shall name him
> Jesus. He will be great and will be called Son of the Most High, and the Lord
> God will give him the throne of David his father, and he will rule over the
> house of Jacob forever, and of his kingdom there will be no end."
>
> LUKE 1:26-33 (NAB)[1]

Youth ministry provides an encounter with the love of Christ and supports
youth in the adventure of discipleship. We see this pattern in the exchange between the angel Gabriel and the teenage Mary. Gabriel is speaking on God's
behalf and telling Mary that she is beautiful, she is beloved, and God has a plan
for her life. All of us, as leaders in youth ministry, are like Gabriel. We speak on
God's behalf and share God's love and longing for youth as we invite youth to
follow God's plan as young disciples.

To be messengers of God's love and invitation, we need to see youth in the
way that God sees them. At World Youth Day in Sydney (2008), Pope Benedict
XVI warned youth about those who see them in a narrow, opportunistic way:

> Do not be fooled by those who see you as just another consumer in a market
> of undifferentiated possibilities, where choice itself becomes the good, nov-
> elty usurps beauty, and subjective experience displaces truth.[2]

1

We see youth as God's beloved and treat them as treasured members of the community as well as coworkers in our mission. This means that we look beyond any singular role of a young person. Dr. Christian Smith, Director for the Study of Religion and Society at the University of Notre Dame, recently wrote to youth workers on this topic:

> Young people, especially in view of the gospel, are fundamentally persons, not students.…We should…push back on society's labels by insisting that teenagers are referenced by the full depth, richness, and complexity of their personhood. They should be hearing from us: "Unlike most of the rest of society, we understand and value you in the fullness of who you are. Here among God's people we know you as real human persons—you don't have to perform to be accepted here. Please be your real selves."[3]

To become a sign of God's love, we also need to see ourselves as a faith community, as revealing the face of Christ to youth.

> Part of the vision of youth ministry is to present to youth the richness of the person of Christ, which perhaps exceeds the ability of one person to capture, but which might be effected by the collective ministry of the many persons who make up the Church.[4]
>
> *A VISION OF YOUTH MINISTRY*

Throughout the documents, and teachings of over three decades of Catholic youth ministry, we see this essential pattern for ministry with young people: provide an encounter with Christ and support youth in their "yes" to the invitation to the adventure of discipleship. This encounter and invitation strengthen the ways that God has walked with young people and their families through childhood and prepares youth for the questions, challenges, and opportunities of adult faithful living. We support youth and their families along this distinctive path that their journey takes during the adolescent years.

To be faithful in our part of facilitating God's encounter and communicating God's invitation will take the full breadth of our commitment and resources:

- We need to **cast a wide net**. Viewing all youth as God's beloved means we go beyond serving just those youth who present themselves. We look at the full spectrum of youth in our community from those in need of healing and outreach to the youth who are ready for engagement in witness, ministry, and service.
- We need to **go deep**. The vision for Catholic youth ministry as presented by the United States Catholic Bishops in *Renewing the Vision: A Frame-*

work for Catholic Youth Ministry and in the *National Directory for Catechesis* focuses on the call to youth in the adventure of discipleship. The consistent messages to young people by Pope John Paul II and Pope Benedict XVI at World Youth Days have been about challenge and going beyond the expectations of popular culture. Youth are hungry for the challenge of discipleship. They long to experience an invitation that is bold and big enough for their life's dreams and visions. Our efforts in youth ministry should feed that hunger and help youth to grow deeply in their faith.

- We need to *make it personal*. Youth long to experience God in a personal way and to feel personally invited and connected to the faith community. To be personal does not mean that we organize ministries around our personality. Making it personal means that, as a community, we strive to make a personal connection with youth as we help them know Jesus in a variety of ways.

- We need to *put all of our oars in the water, going the same direction*. When faith communities bicker over methodologies and compete for perceived limitations in resources, facilities, and time, we end up going in circles in our efforts for pastoral ministry with youth. Effective youth ministry requires the concerted, collaborative, and coordinated efforts of a faith community that longs to become Christ's love incarnate in the lives of young people today.

The encounter and adventure that God has planned for young people in our communities is within our means. This book is designed to guide leaders as they recall the vision for Catholic youth ministry and seek to make this vision a reality for youth in their parish, school, diocese, and youth-serving agency.

Reading This Book

This book is a group project by the core staff and key adjunct staff of the Center for Ministry Development. Three decades of training, research, and developing resources lead us to provide this book to leaders in Catholic youth ministry. We envision leaders engaging with the chapters of this book in ways that match their individual starting points and leadership needs. Pastors, parish council members, Directors of Religious Education, Youth Ministry Coordinators, youth ministry volunteers, youth leaders, and parents will all find information and practical ideas.

Each of the four sections of this book provides a different vantage point for viewing the dimensions of Catholic youth ministry. Let your journey with this book begin with the topics you need most and lead you to further explore the growing resources available for leaders in Catholic youth ministry.

Section I: Foundations for Youth Ministry

This section examines the history and context for Catholic youth ministry while looking at young people today, providing a summary of the vision for ministry, exploring the cultural context for youth ministry, and applying the latest research in viewing practical models and elements in effective youth ministry.

Section II: Communities Nurturing Youth

This section examines three essential communities that nurture youth: the peer community, the family, and the parish.

Section III: Promoting Personal and Spiritual Growth of Youth

This section explores several of the components for youth ministry that comprise the foundations for gathered and non-gathered ministry programs and strategies.

Section IV: Planning and Leadership for Youth Ministry

This section provides practical ways to develop leaders and engage in visioning and planning for dynamic ministry with youth.

We're Here to Help with Support on the Web

The Center for Ministry Development has over thirty years of experience helping parishes get started and enhance their ministry efforts. We are supporting this book with planning guides, meeting outlines, power point presentations, and practical tips that will be available to you online as part of your book purchase.

These materials will be provided at a special website designed for this book. Go to: www.cmdnet.org/leadingyouthministry.

Where Should I Start?

In implementing youth ministry, parish communities and leaders have a variety of situations and hopes that guide the place where each needs to start. Each perspective may have a different path through the chapters of this resource. Below you will find a sample for starting points and paths through the chapters that get you started. The remaining chapters will be a resource for the growth for which you are hoping.

We are just getting started in youth ministry.

Start with Chapter 1: A Vision for Comprehensive Youth Ministry, Chapter 3: Understanding Youth Today, and Chapter 5: Models for Effective Youth Ministry. This will give you the big picture. Next, go to Chapter 14: Youth Ministry Leadership, and Chapter 15: Visioning and Planning for Youth Ministry. These chapters will help you organize and begin planning with a leadership team. The remaining chapters will be there to help you continue to grow.

We have a good youth ministry, but we're ready to grow.

Start with Chapter 5: Models for Youth Ministry. Use these ideas to assess your current model and to identify strengths and areas to grow. Use Chapter 14: Youth Ministry Leadership, and Chapter 15: Visioning and Planning for Youth Ministry, to begin a process of including new leaders and planning for enhanced youth ministry efforts. Once you identify the places you need to grow, the remaining chapters will help you.

We want to learn about how to include more youth in our ministries.

Start with Chapter 10: Evangelization of Youth. This chapter will put your outreach and invitation into the context of the vision of Church. Continue with Chapter 1: A Vision for Comprehensive Youth Ministry, Chapter 3: Understanding Youth Today, Chapter 4: Ministry with Youth in a Culturally Diverse Church, and Chapter 5: Models for Effective Youth Ministry. These chapters will help identify the diverse starting points and needs of youth in your community. Consider Chapter 6: Building community with Youth, Chapter 7: Connecting with Families, and Chapter 8: Connecting Youth with the Parish Community. These chapters will help provide practical starting points for inviting and responding to youth and their families.

We want to improve our adolescent catechesis efforts.

Start with Chapter 10: Evangelization of Youth, and Chapter 9: Catechesis with Youth. These chapters present the vision for evangelizing and catechizing youth. Continue with Chapter 3: Understanding Youth Today, Chapter 7: Connecting with Families, and Chapter 8: Connecting Youth with the Parish Community to explore the settings for faith learning and the needs of youth and families today. Use Chapter 14: Youth Ministry Leadership, and Chapter 15: Visioning and Planning for Youth Ministry to plan for renewed efforts and include additional leaders.

We Are On This Journey with You

This book is a summary of what we know so far and we hope it provides the beginning of continued exploration and searching. We also hope you find yourself in the questions, ideas, and insights of this book. After all, the direction for this book came from conversations with you, the leaders of Catholic youth ministry. Read the book and talk about it with colleagues. Continue your own searching in this shared quest to bring our best leadership in this shared mission of helping youth encounter Christ and engage in active discipleship.

— ENDNOTES —

1. Confraternity of Christian Doctrine. Board of Trustees. 1996, 1986. *The New American Bible: Translated from the original languages with critical use of all the ancient sources and the revised New Testament* (Lk 1:26–33).

2. Pope Benedict XVI, Message to Youth, World Youth Day 2008, Sydney, Australia. http://www.vatican.va/holy_father/benedict_xvi/speeches/2008/july/documents/hf_ben-xvi_spe_20080717_barangaroo_en.html (accessed October 23, 2008).

3. Smith, Dr. Christian. "Stop Calling Kids 'Students,'" *Group Magazine*, Volume 34, No. 6. September-October 2008 (Loveland, Colorado: Group Publications), p. 8.

4. *A Vision of Youth Ministry* (Washington, DC: United States Conference of Catholic Bishops), 1976, p. 24.

Foundations for Youth Ministry

The challenge of discipleship—of following Jesus— is at the heart of the Church's mission. All ministry with adolescents must be directed toward presenting young people with the Good News of Jesus Christ and inviting and challenging them to become his disciples....If we are to succeed, we must offer young people a spiritually challenging and world-shaping vision that meets their hunger for the chance to participate in a worthy adventure.

United States Catholic Conference of Bishops,
Renewing the Vision: A Framework for Catholic Youth Ministry, p. 10

CHAPTER ONE

A Vision for Comprehensive Youth Ministry

Thomas East

Editor's Note

This chapter explores the vision of Catholic Youth Ministry through the lens of our essential identity as Church. Christ's presence in the Eucharist gathers us and sends us out to respond to and include young people as we continue our mission. *Renewing the Vision: A Framework for Catholic Youth Ministry* guides this ministry and directs us to be goal-centered, comprehensive, and intentional as we strive to respond to and include youth in our communities.

As Jesus with the disciples of Emmaus, so the Church must become today the traveling companion of young people.

POPE JOHN PAUL II,
WORLD YOUTH DAY 1995,
IN *RENEWING THE VISION: A FRAMEWORK FOR CATHOLIC YOUTH MINISTRY*[1]

As a Church, we are asked to travel with today's young people. The process of youth ministry is described within the Gospel story of Jesus walking with the disciples on the road to Emmaus. We meet youth in the midst of their questions. We walk with them and present the fullness of the faith. We stay with them. Together, we break bread and experience Jesus in our midst. Transformed by his presence, we walk with youth as they journey to the upper room and spread the message of their experience of the risen Christ.

To be Church with young people means that we help youth to fully participate in the community that is gathered in

8

Christ's name. We evangelize youth and share the Good News with them in the context of their life and relationships. We catechize youth and help them grow in active faith. We include youth in worship and sacraments. We empower youth to minister to others and to witness to their faith.

 ## The Church as Sacrament

The *Catechism of the Catholic Church* offers several images of Church that help explain the task of youth ministry. One of these images describes the Church as the sacrament of Christ's presence in the world. (See #770–776.) William Shannon explains that "a sacrament is a visible sign of God's presence and action in the world. Christ, because he is precisely that, is the Great Sacrament. The Church is the visible post-Resurrection sign (sacrament) of Christ's presence among his people, leading them to holiness of life and toward the fullness of the Kingdom."[2]

Making the Connection

Renewing the Vision describes youth ministry as a response to youth's needs and the inclusion of their gifts.

- *In your experience of youth, what are their needs?*
- *What gifts could young people bring to your community?*

Simply put, the Church is a sacrament because it makes Christ present in our world. Through what we believe and how we live as Catholics, we reveal that Christ is present in us and the Church, and Christ acts through us to bring his Good News to the world. Christ works through us, his followers, to continue his mission in the world today.

The *Catechism of the Catholic Church* describes this image of Church as sacrament in this way: "Christ himself is the mystery of salvation: 'For there is no other mystery of God, except Christ.' The saving work of Christ's holy and sanctifying humanity is the sacrament of salvation, which is revealed and active in the Church's sacrament. The Seven Sacraments are the signs and instruments by which the Holy Spirit spreads the grace of Christ the Head throughout the Church, which is his Body. The Church, then, both contains and communicates the invisible grace she signifies. It is in this analogical sense, that the Church is called a sacrament."[3]

The following diagram helps to explain sacrament.[4] God sent Jesus into the world. Jesus encircled a people in love, called Church. Jesus' love, challenge, and presence transformed lives and drew them to his teachings and to the community gathered in his name. Jesus instructed the community to rely upon the Holy Spirit and to celebrate his presence. He charged them to go and make disciples. (See Matthew 28:19–20.) He told them to go and be his hands and feet and word of love.

SACRAMENT
God Encircles a People in Love

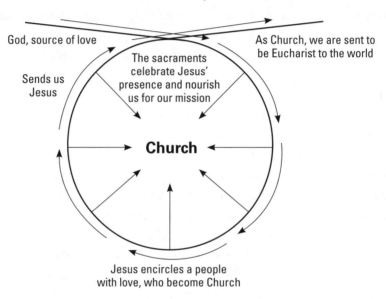

Jesus encircles a people
with love, who become Church

In this diagram, Jesus gathers a people as Church and sends them in mission to continue his saving work. Within the circle, the Church celebrates Jesus' presence through the seven sacraments. These sacraments are intended to strengthen the community gathered in Christ's name and nourish it for the mission of spreading Christ's Word, healing, and transforming love.

Our communion with Christ compels us to go to others and share his love. In *God Is Love*, the encyclical letter of Pope Benedict XVI, we are reminded that the sacrament of Eucharist radically joins us to all whom Christ calls to himself:

Union with Christ is also union with all those to whom he gives himself. I cannot posses Christ just for myself; I can belong to him only in union with all those who have become, or who will become, his own. Communion draws me out of myself toward him, and thus also toward unity with all Christians.[5]

The implications of this image for youth ministry are rich. First, one must reach out to young people and help them to be drawn to community, to Eucharist, and to the sacraments. One must love young people in Christ's name and share the Good News of the Gospel message with them. The Good News that Jesus shared was practical and transforming. For those who hunger, it is food. For those who are lonely, it is love and friendship. For those who are hurting, it is healing and forgiveness. One must share this kind of practical and transforming ministry to youth through simple presence and through a variety of ministry programs and strategies.

Once youth are part of a community, surround them with love and care and help them to celebrate the sacraments that strengthen everyone for mission. Encourage youth to participate in the life of the community and to join in full participation in the liturgical and service life of the parish. Send youth out to witness to their faith with their families, their peers, and people of all ages throughout the community. Empower youth as Christian leaders and involve youth in serving those most in need in the community. Encourage youth to become advocates for the poor and marginalized and to witness by their lives and lifestyle the life of a disciple. This is what it means to be sent out as sacrament.

Two distinct elements of this understanding of sacrament are (1) staying connected to God as the source and (2) being sent out into the world. To become Christ's love incarnate for adolescents, be sure that we are connected to God as the source of our love. Through prayer, participation in the sacraments, and authentic participation in the community, we remain rooted in God's love. When we lose our connection with God, we become like a lake that has lost its source of life. The lake dries up and everything within it dies. As leaders in youth ministry, we must attend to our own spiritual formation and prayer life to be nourished for our ministry with youth. To be faithful, we must also be attentive to our mission out in the wider community. There are Seven Sacraments designed to strengthen and nourish the community, but the Church itself is called to be the sacrament of Christ's presence for the world. As a community gathered in Christ's name, we are a sign of God's love in our neighborhood and our world. To be authentic as Church, we must reach out and be present in the lives of those who need God's love and healing touch. We must be sent out into the world. Otherwise, we could become like a lake that has no outlets, which dies because there is no release for the water. The lake becomes stagnant, as can our church. We could be selfishly hoarding the love of God rather than responding to our call to share. Youth ministry describes this process: we love youth in Jesus' name, and we send them out to walk with us and be witnesses and disciples.

A clear implication of this image is our call to minister to youth who are in a variety of situations and starting points. Some youth are right in the middle of the circle; they are involved and experiencing ministry in the community. Some youth are also sharing their faith and sharing their time and talents in service and ministry. Some youth are far from the community. They have not experienced the love and care; they have not been included and evangelized. Other youth are right on the line, trying to decide if they belong. Youth ministry is for all of these youth, not just the ones who attend programs. We have a clear call to reach out to those who furthest away from the love and care of the parish community.

Renewing the Vision

Comprehensive youth ministry describes a way for parishes and communities to minister to youth by reaching out to them, inviting them into the circle of community, and sending them out to share their gifts. This pattern of responding to needs and involving young people's gifts is at the heart of the vision statement for Catholic youth ministry. In 1997, the United States Conference of Catholic Bishops published a pastoral plan for youth ministry: *Renewing the Vision: A Framework for Catholic Youth Ministry*. In this plan they describe a ministry that empowers youth as disciples, promotes the full participation of youth in the community, and provides for the personal and spiritual growth of young people. The bishops wrote this document to provide direction for the continued development of effective ministry with young people, recognizing the tremendous growth of youth ministry in previous decades. This document affirmed the 1976 document, *A Vision for Youth Ministry*, and called communities to address current challenges and make youth ministry a central concern.[6]

Renewing the Vision expands our vision for ministry with youth in several important ways. First, this vision for ministry involves the whole community and calls parishes, schools, and dioceses to help youth to take their place as active members of the community. Youth ministry flows from the gifts, resources, and charisms of a local community. Communities will find different ways to organize ministry, which is why *Renewing the Vision* is a framework, not a prescriptive plan or outline. A second emphasis of *Renewing the Vision* is the calling of youth to personal discipleship. Communities need to intentionally invite youth, form them in the faith, and empower them for mission. Throughout the document, communities are challenged to trust youth to join with the adult community as disciples.

> What is needed today is a Church which knows how to respond to the expectations of young people. Jesus wants to enter into dialogue with them and, through his body which is the Church, to propose the possibility of a choice which will require a commitment of their lives.[7]

To inspire communities to serve and include youth, *Renewing the Vision* provides a practical framework for utilizing the resources of the community and developing youth ministry. This framework has the following dimensions:

- A definition for Catholic youth ministry that focuses upon response to the needs of youth and inclusion of their gifts.
- Three goals for youth ministry that promote the empowerment of youth for discipleship, the full participation of youth in the community, and the personal and spiritual growth of each young person.
- Seven themes for youth ministry that act as continuous threads to guide all ministry efforts with youth. These describe ministry that is developmentally appropriate, family friendly, intergenerational, multicultural, and collaborative—both within the parish and within the wider community.
- Eight components of youth ministry describe how the Church's ministries work together to include, form, and empower youth. These components are: advocacy, catechesis, community life, evangelization, justice and service, leadership development, pastoral care, and prayer and worship.

Definition of Catholic Youth Ministry

The definition for Catholic youth ministry describes our role as leaders and as a community: "Youth ministry is the response of the Christian community to the needs of young people, and the sharing of the unique gifts of youth with the larger community."[8]

When Jesus encountered someone in need, he did not see them only as someone needy. He healed them, fed them, transformed their life, and challenged them to join in healing, feeding, and transforming others for the Kingdom of God. Similarly, this definition calls us to respond to the needs of youth, not because they are broken or needy, but because of who we are: we are a community gathered in Jesus' name. We love youth and respond to their needs by joining in the healing, pastoral, and teaching mission of Jesus. We see in youth not just their needs but also the incredible gifts they have to share with our community today.

To live out this definition, we need to know young people and become aware of their needs so that we can help our community reach out and respond. We also need to learn the gifts of youth and work to make room for young people throughout the life of our parish by including them in leadership committees, ministries, and opportunities to be involved in service and advocacy. There is a beautiful mutuality described in this relationship between youth and the community. The community has resources to offer young people; youth have gifts that our communities need today. Some of these gifts—such as enthusiasm, creativity, new ideas, and hospitality—are exactly the gifts needed by our communities so that we can become truly vibrant signs of God's love in our community. As the Church strives to be the sacrament of Christ's presence in the world, young disciples join with adults in this witness of love.

Goals

Three goals provide direction for youth ministry. The image of church as sacrament presented in the diagram helps to explain the dimensions of these goals.

Goal 1: To empower young people to live as disciples of Jesus Christ in our world today.[9] The first goal is to empower youth as disciples. In the image, this goal describes those youth who are in the circle and are ready to be sent out as sacrament for the world. Our ministry sends youth out into the community to witness to their faith and share their gifts in service. Youth are also empowered for ministries and leadership within the community.

To empower young disciples, we begin by presenting the Good News in the context of their life and relationships. We help youth to develop their relationship with Jesus and experience the call to discipleship. As a community, we are challenged to present this call to youth as a "worthy adventure." Youth are asked to commit themselves totally to Christ. Youth are ready to invest their lives in a cause that captures their imagination. As a community, our task is to present the mission of following the gospel in all of its fullness so that youth can join us with enthusiasm. This goal also includes catechesis so that youth can be equipped for discipleship. Ultimately, youth are invited to explore vocations and discern from the variety of ways that God calls us to live as disciples.

Goal 2: To draw young people to responsible participation in the life, mission, and work of the Catholic faith community.[10] The second goal is about promoting participation in community. In the image of church as sacrament, this goal focuses on drawing youth into the circle and helping them to belong deeply to the communities of which they are an important part.

Youth want to belong and want to be part of a community within which they are accepted, valued, and cherished. Four faith communities are described within this goal: families, parishes (including the youth ministry program), Catholic schools, and other organizations that serve youth. Youth are encouraged to enhance their families with their love and their faith. Parishes are encouraged to welcome youth and to become "youth friendly" by providing practical ways for youth to belong and share their gifts. Catholic schools are resources for youth and their families as youth grow in faith. Parishes, schools, and families are called to work in partnership to be stewards of these resources. Youth serving organizations are noted for their ability to reach youth who may be outside of other church structures.

Goal 3: To foster the total personal and spiritual growth of each young person.[11] In the image of church as sacrament, this goal is concerned with helping the youth within the community to experience the love, care, nurture, encouragement, and practical help of the community of faith.

The aim of these efforts is to develop "healthy, competent, caring, and faith-filled Catholic young people."[12] We seek to help youth experience the growth and develop the strengths that they need to be ready for adulthood as young disciples. To help youth grow, we address their spiritual needs in the context of their everyday life. This includes helping youth to address the obstacles that so many youth face, such as poverty and discrimination. We also help youth to grow in the midst of the conflicting values presented in our media culture and consumer society. Within this goal, we aim to promote healthy adolescent growth, Catholic identity, and Christian discipleship.

Themes

There are seven themes provided in this vision for youth ministry. These themes "…provide a continuous thread that ensures that ministry with adolescents utilizes all available resources and is all-inclusive."[13]

Developmentally Appropriate Our human development is part of the way God created us. Adolescents journey through an important and dynamic period of

---

THEMES IN THIS BOOK

The following themes of youth ministry are treated in greater detail in the noted subsequent chapters:

Developmentally Appropriate *Chapter 3: Understanding Youth Today*

Family Friendly *Chapter 7: Connecting with Families of Youth*

Intergenerational *Chapter 8: Connecting with the Parish*

Multicultural *Chapter 4: Ministry with Youth in a Culturally Diverse Church*

Leadership *Chapter 14: Youth Ministry Leadership*

Flexible and Adaptable Programming *Chapter 15: Visioning and Planning for Effective Youth Ministry*

---

change in their development. To respond to youth from a developmental perspective, we begin by recognizing the growth that has occurred in childhood and the milestones yet to come as adults. Youth ministry recognizes two distinct ministries based upon differing developmental needs. Young adolescent ministry is aimed at youth who are 11/12 to 14/15 years of age. This ministry is also referred to as Junior High Youth Ministry or Middle School Ministry. High school youth ministry is aimed at youth who are 14/15 to 18 years of age. The differences in maturity require different responses, which is why it is important to offer two distinct ministry strategies for these age groups. The developmental perspective also reminds us that it is important to tailor the content and processes of ministry events and strategies to the developmental readiness of the young person. An adolescent's developmental needs will suggest program responses. For instance, knowing that a young adolescent's world is expanding in terms of their relationships provides an opportunity to offer a meeting or retreat day focusing on relationships that are guided by faith. Throughout youth ministry, we must be sure that the activities we use and the content we choose to include are a good match for the young people we are serving.

Family Friendly Youth ministry leaders are challenged to make sure that all ministry efforts are family-friendly. This direction recognizes the Church's long standing belief in the holiness present within families. Families can and do make a profound difference in shaping the faith lives of their children. Youth ministry should support families in their role of sharing and celebrating faith at home. Parents of adolescents face lots of challenges with little support from society in general. Church can be the place that supports parents by providing good communication, helpful resources, and practical programs of parent education. An important way to be family-friendly is to avoid competing with families for the time and attention of their children by scheduling events in a way that is sensitive to family time. It is about working together and empowering families to share faith.

Intergenerational From studies, we know that youth benefit from intergenerational relationships, and yet most of their lives (school, work, and recreation) are age-segregated. Church is one of the few places where youth experience an intergenerational community intact. Within the parish, there are rich opportunities for involving youth in the intergenerational community as a place to learn the Catholic faith story and to share in leadership. Youth can experience adults as mentors and can provide leadership for children and younger teens. Age-specific programming can sometimes be replaced with intergenerational events that allow for relationship building and celebrations with people of all ages.

Multicultural In the rich cultural context here in the United States, leaders do not need to make the church more multicultural. We do need to recognize the diversity that is in our midst. Begin with the conviction that God is present in the many cultures that comprise our Church and society. Each culture has a piece of the Good News, which is communicated through the traditions, ethos, and cultural norms of that community. When we approach another culture, we "take off our shoes," recognizing that we are on holy ground—for our God has already been with the people we are encountering. In ministry with youth, leaders have a tremendous opportunity to build upon the openness and appreciation for diversity that is present in this generation in order to promote awareness, skills, and sensitivity towards the many cultures that comprise our community. Ministry in a multicultural church utilizes the rich and profound resources of these cultures to form faith and spread the Good News of Jesus Christ. Being inclusive of diversity also includes the ways that we address the needs of youth in the context of their culture and the ways that we promote appreciation of all cultures throughout the ministry.

Community-Wide Collaboration In youth ministry, some of the ways that we would like to respond to youth's needs and include their gifts go beyond our parish community's resources. Effective ministry promotes collaboration with leaders, agencies, and congregations in the wider community as a way to join together in serving youth. Collaboration can include sharing information, co-sponsoring programs, and developing advocacy efforts.

Leadership Youth and adults are called to share in leadership to help make youth ministry happen. It is not just about the programs, events, or strategies of youth ministry. It is also the life of the parish community. The coordinator of youth ministry has an important role in facilitating the gifts of the community on behalf of young people. This leader empowers youth and adults to share gifts in a variety of roles within the ministry. An important aspect of all ministry efforts is cooperation; leaders work to make sure that all parish ministry efforts are connected with each other. This ensures that programs are not in competition with each other and do not exist in isolation.

Flexible and Adaptable Programming Communities are directed to create "flexible and adaptable program structures that address the changing needs and life situations of today's young people and their families...."[14] Youth's lives are often filled with competing commitments and demands on their time. The family schedule for the week is complicated and sometimes overwhelming. Youth ministry can work with youth and families to provide different ways to be involved. These differences can include the timing, schedule, or group size. Some programs can be offered as individualized or family-based approaches. Others can be offered as part of a weekly gathering or on a retreat weekend. Some can be geared to large groups; others can be designed for small groups. The key is to have a variety of ways that youth and their families can be involved.

Components

The components describe specific areas of the mission of the Church that work together to provide ministry with adolescents. "These components provide a framework for the Catholic community to *respond* to the needs of young people and to *involve* young people in sharing their unique gifts with the larger community."[15] The components describe the ministries of the Church and are not necessarily individual programs or strategies; in fact most youth ministry events include many components working together. Communities are challenged to work toward balance in providing these eight components within their ministry efforts over the course of a season or a year of ministry.

COMPONENTS IN THIS BOOK

The components of youth ministry are each treated with more detail in other chapters of this book. See:

Advocacy *Chapter 8: Connecting with the Parish*
Catechesis *Chapter 9: Catechesis with Youth*
Community *Chapter 6: Building Community with Youth*
Evangelization *Chapter 10: Evangelization of Youth*
Justice and Service *Chapter 11: Justice and Service*
Leadership Development *Chapter 14: Youth Ministry Leadership*
Pastoral Care *Chapter 12: Pastoral Care of Youth*
Prayer and Worship *Chapter 13: Prayer and Worship*

These components are essential within the Church's mission to evangelize and catechize young people.

> The most effective catechetical programs for adolescents are integrated into a comprehensive program of pastoral ministry for youth that includes catechesis, community life, evangelization, justice and service, leadership development, pastoral care, and prayer and worship.
> UNITED STATES CATHOLIC BISHOPS, *NATIONAL DIRECTORY FOR CATECHESIS*[16]

Advocacy The component of advocacy is speaking up for the needs of youth and their families within the parish community and the wider community. This also includes helping youth to speak for themselves and giving them a voice in leadership structures.[17]

Catechesis The component of catechesis is the deepening of the faith of young people through teaching and reflection. Catechesis is about faithfully lifting each other up; it is working towards the transformation of our lives.[18]

Community Life The component of community life focuses upon building community on a variety of levels: between young people, with their families, and engaging youth in the broader parish community.[19]

Evangelization The component of evangelization is proclaiming the Good News and inviting youth into relationship with Jesus Christ through ongoing witness. Evangelization is the energizing core of all that we do in youth ministry and also refers to specific programs of outreach and witness.[20]

Justice and Service The component of justice and service is engaging young people in helping and serving other people, and understanding the Gospel call to justice through education and reflection.[21]

Leadership Development The component of leadership development is inviting, training, and supporting adults and young people for leadership in youth ministry and the broader parish community.[22]

Pastoral Care The component of pastoral care is providing prevention programs for youth and families, caring for those in crisis, and providing guidance during times of decisions and moral choices.[23]

Prayer and Worship The component of prayer and worship helps youth to participate in the Liturgy of the Eucharist and the sacramental life of the Church, provides youth with a variety of communal prayer experiences, and helps youth to develop their personal prayer life.[24]

A Comprehensive Youth Ministry Mindset

This chapter began with an explanation of church as sacrament. In this image, church is the community gathered by God's love and sent into the world as a sign of God's presence. Youth ministry is an expression of church that focuses on adolescents and their families. This image of church as gathered and sent is bigger than a single program or strategy. It is not the actions of an individual leader. It is not about a particular group of young people. It is the description of all of the efforts that serve youth through the life of the parish or community. If you were to picture youth ministry in your parish, where would the picture take place? Is it a particular room or building where youth often meet? Comprehensive youth ministry describes a ministry that takes place in the parish hall and the worship space. It includes the ministry that happens in family homes and in the schools, on the sidewalks and within the gathering places of the community.

> …the comprehensive approach is a framework for integration rather than a specific model. The comprehensive approach is not a single program or recipe for ministry. Rather, it provides a way for integrating ministry with

adolescents and their families into the total life and mission of the Church, recognizing that the whole community is responsible for this ministry.[25]

Settings for Youth Ministry

Many parishes will choose to have a youth community or youth group as an important strategy within the ministry. This community can become a central strategy that serves as a focus for developing broader youth ministry efforts. It is important that we do not mistake this one part of the ministry for the larger picture. Parishes that are effectively living out this renewed vision for youth ministry have a variety of ways for youth and their families to belong. To minister to the diverse needs of youth and include their gifts, we need to take stock of the different means and settings for ministry with youth. Essentially, youth will experience ministry in four settings:

Youth Setting Ministry directed towards youth as individuals and within their peer group. This includes

- Gathering with youth to provide programs of ministry.
- Being present to youth by going where they are and being part of sporting events or concerts.
- Delivering ministry to youth by providing resources, individualized programs, and small group settings for ministry.

Family Setting Ministry to youth that is provided through their families. This includes

- Supporting families in their ministry with youth at home.
- Providing for strategic gatherings or events with families of adolescents.
- Supporting parents of adolescents with resources and programs, and by connecting parents with each other.

Parish Setting Ministry to youth through the life of the parish. This includes

- Involving youth in parish events in a meaningful way.
- Empowering youth to share their gifts in a variety of leadership and ministry roles.
- Aligning the programming of youth ministry to the events of the Church year and parish life.

Wider Community Setting Ministry to youth that utilizes the resources of the wider community. This includes

- Collaborating with the wider community by connecting youth and their families with the resources of neighboring churches and community agencies.
- Connecting with other congregations and civic agencies to advocate on behalf of youth and their families.
- Participating in inter-parish, inter-church, diocesan, and national programs designed for young people.
- Involving youth in service roles within the wider community.

A Church for Young People

To be responsive and inclusive it will take resources, vision, and leadership. To create comprehensive youth ministry, we will need to be a community that is connected to God's love as our source, that allows Christ's love to encircle us. To be faithful as we help build the Kingdom of God, we must feast upon Christ's presence in the Eucharist and the other sacraments. To be a Church with young people is to draw them deeply to the center of this love and empower them to share their gifts as leaders and witnesses in our community and in our world.

> This is what is needed: A Church for young people, which will know how to speak to their heart and enkindle, comfort and inspire enthusiasm in it with the joy of the gospel and the strength of the Eucharist; a Church which will know how to invite and to welcome the person who seeks a purpose for which to commit his whole existence; a Church which is not afraid to require much, after having given much; which does not fear asking from young people the effort of a noble and authentic adventure, such as that of the following of the Gospel.
>
> John Paul II, *World Day of Prayer for Vocations*, 1995 [26]

— RECOMMENDED RESOURCES —

Bass, Dorothy C. and Don C. Richter (eds.). *Way to Live: Christian Practices for Teens*. Nashville: Upper Room Books, 2002.

Black, Wesley, Chap Clark, Malan Nal, and Mark Senter (general ed.). *Four Views of Youth Ministry and the Church*. Grand Rapids, MI: Zondervan Publishing, 2001.

Celebrate Youth—Becoming a Youth-Friendly Church. Naugatuck, CT: Center for Ministry Development, 1998. (Available online through Youth Ministry Access: www.youthministryaccess.org.)

Dean, Kenda Creasy. *Practicing Passion: Youth and the Quest for a Passionate Church*. Grand Rapids, MI: Wm. B. Eerdmans Publishing Co., 2004.

Dean, Kenda Creasy, Chap Clark, and Dave Rahn (eds.). *Starting Right: Thinking Theologically about Youth Ministry*. Grand Rapids, MI: Zondervan Publishing, 2001.

Dean, Kenda Creasy, and Ron Foster. *The Godbearing Life: The Art of Soul Tending for Youth Ministry*. Nashville: Upper Room Books, 1998.

East, Thomas. *Total Faith Initiative Coordinators Manual*. Winona, MN: Saint Mary's Press, 2004.

East, Thomas. *Effective Practices for Dynamic Youth Ministry*. Winona, MN: Saint Mary's Press, 2004.

Jones, Tony. *Postmodern Youth Ministry*. Grand Rapids, MI: Zondervan Publishing, 2001.

Kielbasa, Marilyn. *Total Youth Ministry: Ministry Resources for Pastoral Care*. Winona, MN: Saint Mary's Press, 2004.

McCarty, Robert (general ed.). *The Vision of Catholic Youth Ministry: Fundamentals, Theory, and Practice*. Winona, MN: Saint Mary's Press, 2005.

Renewing the Vision: A Framework for Catholic Youth Ministry. Washington, DC: United States Conference of Catholic Bishops, 1997.

Rice, Wayne, Chap Clark, et al. *New Directions for Youth Ministry*. Loveland, CO: Group Books, 1998.

Semmel, Christina. *No Meeting Required: Strategies for Nongathered Ministry with Young People*. Winona, MN: Saint Mary's Press, 2007.

Strommen, Merton P., Karen Jones, and Dave Rahn. *Youth Ministry that Transforms*. Grand Rapids, MI: Zondervan Publishing, 2001.

Yaconelli, Mark. *Growing Souls: Experiments in Contemplative Youth Ministry*. Grand Rapids, MI: Zondervan Publishing, 2007.

YouthWorks. Naugatuck, CT: Center for Ministry Development, 1994, 1996. (Available online through Youth Ministry Access: www.youthministryaccess.org.)

Youth Ministry Access (subscription Web site). Naugatuck, CT: Center for Ministry Development. www.youthministryaccess.org

— ENDNOTES —

1. *Renewing the Vision: A Framework for Catholic Youth Ministry* (Washington, DC: United States Conference of Catholic Bishops, 1997), p. 2.

2. Shannon, William H. *Exploring the Catechism of the Catholic Church* (Cincinnati: St. Anthony Messenger Press, 1995), p. 42.

3. *Catechism of the Catholic Church*, paragraph 774. See also paragraphs 770–776.

4. This diagram of Church as sacrament is based on the work of Kenan B. Osborne, OFM. For further explanation, see:

> Kenan B. Osborne, OFM, *Sacramental Theology* (New York: Paulist Press, 1988), especially Chapter 6: The Church as the Basic Sacrament.
> Kenan B. Osborne, OFM, *Christian Sacraments in a Postmodern World: A Theology for the Third Millenium* (New York: Paulist Press, 1999), Chapter 5: The Church as the Foundational Sacrament.

5. Pope Benedict XVI, *God Is Love*, Vatican translation (Boston: Pauline Books and Media, 2006), p. 19.

6. See RTV, pp. 1-2.

7. Pope John Paul II, "Youth: Sent to Proclaim True Liberation," World Youth Day 1995, Philippines, as cited in RTV, pp. 1-2.

8. *Vision of Youth Ministry*, 1976, p. 6 as cited in *Renewing the Vision*, p. 1.

9. RTV, p. 9.

10. RTV, p. 11.

11. RTV, p. 15.

12. RTV, p. 15.

13. RTV, p. 20.

14. RTV, p. 25.

15. RTV, p. 26.

16. *National Directory for Catechesis* (Washington, DC: United States Conference of Catholic Bishops, Publication #5-443, 2005), p. 201.

17. See RTV, pp. 26-28.

18. See RTV, pp. 28-34.

19. See RTV, pp. 34-36.

20. See RTV, pp. 36-37.

21. See RTV, pp. 37-40.

22. See RTV, pp. 40-42

23. See RTV, pp. 42-44.

24. See RTV, pp. 44-47.

25. RTV, p. 19.

26. RTV, p. 10.

CHAPTER TWO

History of Catholic Youth Ministry

John Roberto

Editor's Note

We have come this far by faith. In this chapter, John Roberto weaves together the common themes of some of the central figures in the history of ministry and service to youth. These insights form the basis for exploring the development of youth ministry from the 1976 document, *A Vision of Youth Ministry*, to the renewed vision and efforts today.

There is a rich tradition of ministry with young people throughout the history of the Church. In every era, individuals and communities have responded to the unique needs of young people and guided them toward faith in Jesus Christ. There is a thread of continuity that we can see in the faithfulness of those who continued the mission and ministry of Jesus with young people. Yet every era had to find ways to minister with young people in the midst of a particular social and cultural setting.

Several stories from our tradition will help to illustrate the continuity *and* the unique response necessary to address the lives of young people in a particular social setting.

France 1600 France in the 1600s was a country divided into two classes of people: the very poor and the very rich. Only the very rich could afford to send their children to school. With a doctorate in theology, John Baptist de la Salle had prepared himself for a powerful position in the church. Urged on by an acquaintance, he founded a school for poor children, began teaching them, and trained teachers to plan lessons and keep order in classrooms. Soon his community of teachers became the "Brothers of the Christian Schools." They were the first religious group whose special mission was to teach the poor.

Back in those days, classes were taught in Latin. If you did not understand Latin, you could not learn. The brothers began to teach in French so ordinary students could understand. What de la Salle wanted to do—teach poor children— was revolutionary. His belief was that if poor children were given a practical education, they could better support themselves and their families and climb out of the poverty that spawned so much crime and despair. While receiving an education, the children could also learn how to live in the world as Christians. To reach poor children, de la Salle developed much of the approach that has since become standard in schools worldwide. At this time, students were taught, for the most part, one at a time by tutors; this was practical only for the rich and the few. To accommodate the large number of poor children, de la Salle created classrooms with rows of students. A fixed daily schedule of a variety of courses was required in his schools. De la Salle also created commercial or business courses, which had not been offered before. He opened the first teachers' college, as well as industrial schools for boys. Today, John Baptist de la Salle is considered one of the founders of modern education. He is a patron saint of teachers.[1]

United States of America 1700s The United States in the late 1700s and early 1800s did not have the educational system and social services that are widespread today. After the death of her husband and without financial support for her five children, Elizabeth Ann Bayley Seton was invited by the rector of St. Mary's Seminary in Baltimore to establish a school for young girls from poor families. The school she founded in 1808, near Baltimore, Maryland, was the first Catholic school in the United States. With eighteen other dedicated women, Elizabeth went on to organize the first group of women religious in the United States, the Daughters (or Sisters) of Charity. She started from scratch in the work of building Catholic education. That meant not only starting more schools but also training teachers and writing textbooks herself. Elizabeth Ann Seton accomplished all this in a very short life. She died when she was in her late 40s. Everywhere her community of sisters went they opened schools and taught in orphanages. She and her community are credited with laying the foundation for the Catholic school system in the United States. Elizabeth Ann Seton is the first person to be declared a saint who was born in the United States.[2]

Italy 1800s In the 1800s, Italy was experiencing the beginning of the industrial revolution. Teenage boys would leave their poor families in the countryside and come into town searching for work. In the city, these teenagers lived in terrible conditions. Even before his ordination, John Bosco began taking a group of boys out to the country every Sunday for sports, a picnic, songs, and prayer. No one else cared about them. After John became a priest, he housed boys who had nowhere else to live. Then he began programs to train them as shoemakers, tailors, and printers. The training protected them from a harsh world they were too young to face. Many of the boys and young men John assisted were troubled. Often they had experienced abuse or neglect. Somehow John called forth the best in them by affirming them and treating them kindly. Many young people learned about God because of the care they received from John.

The number of young people in John's care grew ever larger. He had trouble finding assistants who understood his gentle teaching methods. Eventually he founded the Salesian Order (named after St. Francis de Sales). He also started a group of laypeople called Cooperators. All were trained especially for this work. By the time of his death, there were some sixty-four Salesian foundations in Europe and the Americas and about 800 Salesian priests. He also founded the Daughters of Our Lady, Help of Christians, to provide the same care and education for poor and neglected girls. Today, these orders serve in schools, colleges, seminaries, hospitals, and missions all over the world.[3]

United States of America 1800s There was great poverty on Native American reservations in the 1800s. Katharine Drexel was shocked by the poverty she saw. Born into a wealthy Philadelphia family, she was encouraged by Pope Leo XIII to devote her fortune and her life to the poor. In 1891, with thirteen other women, she founded the Sisters of the Blessed Sacrament. They worked to provide for the needy, and, over time, Katharine donated $12 million of the fortune she had inherited. Katharine and her sisters first opened a boarding school for Pueblo Indian students in Santa Fe, New Mexico. In time, they founded missions for Indians in sixteen states and nearly a hundred missions for African American children in rural areas and the inner cities of the South. In 1915, she founded a teachers' college that would eventually grow to become the first and only Catholic university for African Americans, Xavier University in New Orleans. Despite poor health in her later years, she continued to fight for and fund civil rights causes. Katharine Drexel died in 1955 at the age of 96. People of all races from across the United States journeyed to Philadelphia to attend her funeral. She is the second American-born saint.[4]

Chicago 1930 Chicago in the 1930s was in the midst of the Great Depression. Many families experienced unemployment, financial hardships, and poverty. Young people, without jobs or meaningful activities, turned to the streets, and often to delinquency. Starting with a boxing program to get teenage boys off the streets, auxiliary bishop Bernard J. Sheil eventually launched an organized youth program, which became known as the Catholic Youth Organization (CYO). CYO sought to solve the "youth problem" by offering young people worthwhile activities. The original charter states that CYO was created to "promote among Catholic youth a recreational, educational, and religious program that adequately meets their physical, mental, and spiritual needs in their after-school hours; and without regard to race, creed, or color, to assist those people who are in need; to inspire, direct, and guide the natural creative instincts of young people into those worthwhile channels, which permit the widest expression of personality, individually or in groups, while instilling in the minds and hearts a true love of God and Country."[5] The CYO offered a wide-ranging system of social services, community centers, and vacation schools; but its greatest publicity resulted from an extensive and comprehensive sports program that claimed the world's largest basketball league (430 teams) and an international boxing team. Such CYO ventures included American Indians, African Americans, Asians, and Jews, which catapulted Bishop Sheil to national prominence as a social activist.[6]

What do all these stories have in common? First, we can see that ministry with youth transforms their lives—personally, academically, socially, and spiritually. Second, ministry begins with the reality of young people's lives and their social-cultural situation. In each story, we see recognition, analysis, and response to the society of the day and its impact on young people. Third, trusting, loving relationships form the foundation for the entire ministry. Fourth, ministry requires great flexibility and adaptability—tailoring programs and activities to the lives of young people. Lastly, we can see that the invitation to follow Jesus and to live as a disciple is situated within a holistic response to the total life of the young person.

In many ways we see reflected in these stories the definition of youth ministry offered in the documents by the United States Catholic Bishops that guide our pastoral ministry with youth, *A Vision of Youth Ministry* and *Renewing the Vision: A Framework for Catholic Youth Ministry*: "Youth ministry is the response of the Christian community to the needs of young people, and the sharing of the unique gifts of youth with the larger community."[7] This pattern of presence and listening, relationship building, attention to the context, response to the needs of young people, invitation into faith and community, and empowerment for ministry is repeated throughout the tradition. It is also clear in the most recent history of youth ministry.

 **Making the Connection**

Heroes and guides in youth ministry have led the way and shaped our vision.

- *Who do you consider to be a model for ministry with youth?*
- *What values and qualities do they exemplify?*

Pastoral Ministry with Youth from 1930 to 1970

From the 1930s through the 1960s, ministry with young people took three distinct forms: Catholic schools (elementary and secondary), the Catholic Youth Organization (CYO), and the Confraternity of Christian Doctrine (CCD).

In most parishes, CYO, which was founded in the 1930s, developed into a weekly program of religious, cultural, social, and athletic activities, adding service to the program mix in the 1960s. An essential component of CYO was leadership training for youth and the adults who worked with them. CYO also pioneered the development of youth retreats in the 1960s through the Search retreat program. Many dioceses developed annual CYO manuals containing program outlines and organizational materials for the weekly meetings.

CCD dates back to the period of Catholic reform in the late sixteenth century, and was the official "agency" for the catechetical instruction of Catholic laity. Pope Pius X in 1905 called for a renewed approach to religious instruction and the establishment of CCD in every Catholic parish. In the United States, CCD was established as an independent apostolate in 1935 with a national director and a publishing division. CCD was seen as the means of instructing youth (and their parents) who did not have the advantage of attending Catholic school. In most parishes, CCD was organized in weekly one-hour classes of religious instruction. Many parishes had one hour of CCD followed by a CYO program every week during the school year.

This more instructional, programmatic, and organizational approach to ministry with young people was situated within a "Catholic culture" that supported the development of a Catholic way of life in young people. Most Catholic youth grew up in practicing Catholic families where the Catholic faith was lived at home. Youth had more contact with extended family. They attended Mass on Sunday and participated in a wide array of festivals and social gatherings. The home and the parish provided the primary contexts for faith growth. The sense of neighborhood and community played a large role in reinforcing the faith values of the family. The programs of CYO and CCD complemented and extended what was already happening at home and in the parish. They were not replacements.

Youth Ministry in the 1970s and 1980s

The tremendous changes within young people, their families, and the broader society during the late 1960s and 1970s had a tremendous impact on the programs of CYO and CCD. As a result, parishes saw declining participation in CYO and CCD programs. In the statistical survey, *Where Are the 6.6 Million?*, the United States Conference of Catholic Bishops found "the number of Catholic elementary and secondary age children and youth not receiving formal religious instruction had grown from 3.1 to 6.6 million in the ten years between 1965 and 1974." Of the total of 6.6 million there were 3.2 million high school age youth not receiving formal religious instruction.[8]

As one approach to parish youth ministry—CYO and CCD—was in decline due to the changing context of ministry, a new approach was being born. Guided by the spirit, theology, and pastoral vision of Vatican II, a new generation of youth ministry leaders began to experiment with new approaches and techniques for working with young people. These leaders worked in parishes, Catholic high school campus ministries, retreat movements such as Search and TEC (Teens Encounter Christ), and in diocesan youth departments. The renewed and expanded ecclesiology of Vatican II provided a solid foundation for constructing a new model of Catholic youth ministry. Changing the language from CYO, CCD, and the youth apostolate to *youth ministry* signaled a significant shift in the paradigm for the Church's ministry with youth.

The work of this new generation of youth ministry leaders led to the forming of a national task force to write a vision for youth ministry that "reaffirms and re-casts the Church's ministry with youth." Commissioned by the USCC National Advisory Board for Youth Activities in 1974, the writing team created a first draft of this new vision, which was widely circulated for review and feedback. Utilizing the feedback from the field, the Department of Education published *A Vision of Youth Ministry* in 1976, which "offers a focus for the work of youth ministry, and sets forth an outline of its major components."[9]

What is truly amazing is that the document contained no guidelines, no pro-gram models, no program ideas, or activities. *A Vision of Youth Ministry* called for a new direction in ministry with youth by blending the best of past efforts with emerging ideas from leaders all across the country. *A Vision of Youth Ministry* articulated the philosophy, goals, principles, and components of a contem-porary approach to the Church's ministry with youth. By presenting a vision, or framework, for the development of ministry with youth, rather than specific program models, it gave focus and direction while allowing local creativity in addressing the needs of young people.

A Vision of Youth Ministry initiated a transformation in the Church's thinking and practice of youth ministry. Its key insights became the basis for new ways of ministering to young people.

Youth ministry must be theologically and pastorally sound. *A Vision of Youth Ministry* was first and foremost a statement about church and ministry, theo-logically applicable to all church ministries. The pastoral, integrated vision of Church, as expressed through the seven components, was grounded in a con-temporary understanding of the mission and ministry of Jesus Christ and his Church. *A Vision of Youth Ministry* made it quite clear that youth ministry is inte-gral to the life of the Church. Far from peripheral to the Church's concern, youth ministry is *essential* for helping the Church realize its mission with its young members. Youth ministry focuses the ministries of the Church upon this unique stage of life with its distinct life tasks and social context *and* actively engages young people as disciples in the mission of Jesus Christ and the Church.

Youth Ministry is relational. *A Vision of Youth Ministry* re-affirmed that effec-tive ministry with youth was built on relationships. The importance of relation-ships in ministry was captured by utilizing the Emmaus Story (Luke 24:13–35) as the central image for ministry with youth. Jesus' encounter with the disciples on the road to Emmaus after the Resurrection provided clues to ministry with youth: presence and listening, questioning and responding, interpreting experiences in the light of faith, and celebrating faith at Eucharist.

Youth ministry is focused around specific goals. *A Vision of Youth Ministry* proposed two goals to guide a comprehensive, multifaceted ministry with youth: "Youth ministry works to foster the total personal and spiritual growth of each young person. Youth ministry seeks to draw young people to responsible participation in the life, mission and work of the faith community."[10] These two goals gave specific direction while encouraging leaders in local communities to create a variety of ways to reach their goals. There was not just *one* way to do youth ministry.

Youth Ministry is comprehensive and balanced. One of the most important breakthroughs in *A Vision of Youth Ministry* was the comprehensive framework of seven components: Word (evangelization and catechesis), Worship, Creating Community, Guidance and Healing, Justice and Service, Enablement, and Advocacy. This overcame the fragmented approach to ministry with youth that separated catechetical programs from other youth programs. This comprehensive and balanced approach was an antidote to social-only, athletics-only, or religious education-only youth programming, which had characterized much of parish youth ministry in the 1970s. *A Vision of Youth Ministry* clearly stated that an effective youth ministry demonstrated balance among the seven components and program activities so that the needs of all of the young people could be addressed and the resources of the community wisely used.

Youth ministry promotes the holistic growth of young people in developmentally appropriate ways. *A Vision of Youth Ministry* proposed an approach that attended to a wide spectrum of youth needs and that was also attuned to the distinct developmental, social, and cultural needs of adolescents.

Youth ministry is people-centered and needs-focused. *A Vision of Youth Ministry* put young people first. It emphasized throughout its pages that *programs are made for people; people are not made for programs.* It encouraged a flexible, adaptable approach to youth ministry that was designed to address the real needs and life situations of today's young people in a particular community setting. In not recommending program models or activities, *A Vision of Youth Ministry* recognized that the day had passed when a single program structure could respond to all the needs of youth.

Youth ministry is family and community-centered. Central to A *Vision of Youth Ministry* was the incorporation of young people into all aspects of church life. One of the two goals in the document focused on drawing young people into responsible participation in the life, mission, and work of the faith community. The concept of ministry with families of youth was introduced in *A Vision of Youth Ministry*, beginning the move toward a family perspective in youth ministry.

Inherent in this more inclusive and multidimensional approach to youth ministry was the recognition of the need for collaboration.

> No one aspect of youth ministry is independent of others; they are all interdependent elements of a unified total vision. The multifaceted nature of youth ministry requires a process of collaboration among all persons involved in it, rather than fragmentation or competition....Part of the vision of youth ministry is to present to youth the richness of the person of Christ, which perhaps exceeds the ability of one person to capture, but which might be effected by the collective ministry of the many persons who make up the Church.
>
> UNITED STATES CATHOLIC BISHOPS, *A VISION OF YOUTH MINISTRY*[11]

In 1979, the *National Catechetical Directory, Sharing the Light of Faith*, affirmed the comprehensive, holistic approach of *A Vision of Youth Ministry*: "Youth catechesis is most effective within a total youth ministry."[12] It went on to say:

> Total ministry to youth includes catechetical activities in which the message is proclaimed, community is fostered, service is offered, and worship is celebrated. There is need for a variety of models integrating message, community, service, and worship and corresponding to the stages of development and levels of perception of the young. Guidance and healing, involvement of youth in ministry, and interpretation and advocacy of their legitimate interests and concerns also have catechetical dimensions.[13]

A Vision of Youth Ministry provided the foundation for a dramatic increase in new and innovative pastoral efforts, youth programming, training programs, and resource materials. Over the next two decades, the Church in the United States experienced a tremendous growth of comprehensive parish youth ministries throughout the country, the emergence of the roles of parish coordinators of youth ministry and Catholic high school campus ministers, the development and widespread availability of high quality youth ministry training programs and youth leadership training programs, an increase in the number of effective youth ministry resources, attention to the needs of families with adolescents, and expansion of the scope of ministry to include young adolescents and older adolescents.

A Vision of Youth Ministry also gave birth to two other important documents that developed the Ministry of the Word component of youth ministry: *The Challenge of Adolescent Catechesis* (NFCYM, 1986), which developed catechetical principles and faith themes for designing curriculum and teaching young people, and *The Challenge of Catholic Youth Evangelization* (NFCYM, 1993), which developed the principles and methods for evangelizing young people.

A variety of other developments continued to expand the vision and practice of Catholic youth ministry. The 1980s and early 1990s witnessed an emphasis on family ministry and two important documents from the United States Conference of Catholic Bishops: *A Family Perspective in Church and Society* (1988) and *Follow the Way of Love* (1994). Catholic youth ministry began to develop a more intentional focus on the parents of youth and on developing a family perspective in youth ministry. The 1980s also saw the increased importance of justice, peace, and service within the Church's ministry. The United States Catholic Bishops issued two landmark pastoral letters: *The Challenge of Peace* (1983) and *Economic Justice for All* (1986), as well as a number of pastoral letters on 100 years of Catholic social teaching and social ministry in parishes. Youth ministry responded by making justice education programs, service projects, and week-long service/mission trips central to a comprehensive youth ministry. Through the 1980s and 1990s, there was a growing awareness of the need to be inclusive of the cultural diversity of young people and to address the specific cultural needs of youth.

All of these developments gave rise to the next stage in the development of Catholic youth ministry.

The New Generation of Youth Ministry: 1990s to 2000s and Beyond

The changing social context for young people in the 1990s meant that youth ministry needed to adapt and respond to new challenges. Society's neglect of young people made the healthy growth of adolescents into adulthood a "troubled journey." Many communities across the United States lacked the social support infrastructure for promoting strong families and positive adolescent development. This dramatic decrease in the social support network was documented by research by the Search Institute. Their research identified forty developmental assets that described building blocks for positive adolescent development and highlighted the significance of the community—family, school, church, and organizations—in promoting positive growth. According to their research, the vast majority of the nation's young people lacked the requisite number of assets for healthy growth into adulthood.[14]

The new generation of young people, born in the 1980s and 1990s, presented a new set of challenges for all those in ministry with youth. Many of their perspectives, attitudes, and values were fresh and new, and different from previous generations. They brought a different set of needs and expectations. One of their important needs was for a spiritually challenging vision that gave meaning and purpose to their lives and presented a worthy adventure to which they could commit their lives. One of their expectations was for a faith community worthy of their allegiance or loyalty, in which they could become active members. They expected active roles in the ministerial life of the faith community—liturgy, leadership, and service to name only a few. They were looking to be the church of today!

Through his pastoral letters to young people, biennial World Youth Days, and continuous advocacy on their behalf, Pope John Paul II raised the profile of young people in the Church. His emphasis on discipleship and the active participation of young people in the ecclesial community were constant themes in his writing and homilies. These emphases would be reflected in the second generation vision of youth ministry.

> As leaders in the field of the youth apostolate, your task will be to help your parishes, dioceses, associations, and movements to be truly open to the personal, social, and spiritual needs of young people. You will have to find ways of involving young people in projects and activities of formation, spirituality, and service, giving them responsibility for themselves and their work, and taking care to avoid isolating them and their apostolate from the rest of the ecclesial community. Young people need to be able to see the practical relevance of their efforts to meet the real needs of people, especially the poor and neglected. They should also be able to see that their apostolate belongs fully to the Church's mission in the world.
> POPE JOHN PAUL II, *LISTEN TO THE TRUE WORD OF LIFE*, 1993[15]

> This is what is needed: a Church for young people, which will know how to speak to their heart and enkindle, comfort, and inspire enthusiasm in it with the joy of the Gospel and the strength of the Eucharist; a Church which

will know how to invite and to welcome the person who seeks a purpose for which to commit his whole existence; a Church which is not afraid to require much, after having given much; which does not fear asking from young people the effort of a noble and authentic adventure, such as that of the following of the Gospel.

POPE JOHN PAUL II, *WORLD DAY OF PRAYER FOR VOCATIONS*, 1995[16]

The blueprint for the next generation of youth ministry is found in the pastoral plan of the United States Conference of Catholic Bishops, *Renewing the Vision: A Framework for Catholic Youth Ministry*. Building on the 1976 national document, *A Vision of Youth Ministry*, and reflecting over twenty years of experience in developing effective approaches and strategies for ministry with adolescents, *Renewing the Vision* deepened the vision and expanded the scope of Catholic youth ministry. In November of 1997, the assembly of Catholic bishops approved *Renewing the Vision* as their pastoral plan for the future of Catholic youth ministry.

A Vision of Youth Ministry focused attention on youth and new ways to minister with them. *Renewing the Vision* focused attention on the power of community—the church community, the family community, and the wider community—for promoting healthy adolescent development and faith growth. *Renewing the Vision* re-affirmed the truth that youth ministry is the work of the entire Church and that youth ministry is to draw upon the faith, the gifts, the talents, the energies, and the resources of the entire church community.

Several key characteristics gave shape and form to the framework for ministry presented in *Renewing the Vision*:

Youth ministry is focused on young and older adolescents. *Renewing the Vision* broadened the scope of youth ministry to encompass younger adolescents (ages 11-14/15) and older adolescents (ages 14/15 to 18.) Up until this point much of youth ministry was focused on high school youth.[17]

Youth ministry is goal-directed. *Renewing the Vision* embraced and enhanced the two goals from *A Vision of Youth Ministry*—identifying assets for healthy faith development and providing direction on the role of families, the parish, the Catholic school, and youth-serving organizations in promoting faith growth. *Renewing the Vision* added a third goal specifically designed to focus youth ministry on promoting active discipleship in the lives of young people, "a spiritually challenging and world-shaping vision that meets their hunger for the chance to participate in a worthy adventure."[18]

"Goal 1: To empower young people to live as disciples of Jesus Christ in our world today."[19]

"Goal 2: To draw young people to responsible participation in the life, mission, and work of the Catholic faith community."[20]

"Goal 3: To foster the total personal and spiritual growth of each young person."[21]

Youth ministry is comprehensive in scope, integrating diverse activities into a larger, integrated framework. *Renewing the Vision* fully developed the comprehensive approach suggested in *A Vision of Youth Ministry*. "[T]he comprehensive approach is a framework for integration rather than a specific model. The comprehensive approach is not a single program or recipe for ministry. Rather, it provides a way for integrating ministry with adolescents and their families into the total life and mission of the Church, recognizing that the whole community is responsible for this ministry. The comprehensive approach uses all of our resources as a faith community—people, ministries, programs—in a common effort to promote the three goals of the Church's ministry with adolescents."[22]

Renewing the Vision presented eight components of a comprehensive ministry: advocacy, catechesis, community life, evangelization, justice and service, leadership development, pastoral care, and prayer and worship. The presentation of each component was grounded in Church teachings and provided specific directions for the development of that component. The catechetical component integrated the faith themes for younger and older adolescents, found in *The Challenge of Adolescent Catechesis*, with the content themes from the *Catechism of the Catholic Church* to provide the basis for an adolescent catechetical curriculum within youth ministry.

Renewing the Vision presented a framework which integrated the eight ministries of the Church with four essential elements or settings for ministry with adolescents: youth, family, church community, and wider community. This is the heart of the comprehensive approach developed in *Renewing the Vision*:

- utilize each of the Church's ministries—advocacy, catechesis, community life, evangelization, justice and service, leadership development, pastoral care, prayer and worship—in an integrated approach to achieving the three goals for ministry with adolescents;
- provide developmentally appropriate programs and activities that promote personal and spiritual growth for young and older adolescents;

- enrich family life and promote the faith growth of families with adolescents;
- incorporate young people fully into all aspects of Church life and engage them in ministry and leadership in the faith community;
- create partnerships among families, schools, churches, and community organizations in a common effort to promote positive youth development.[23]

Renewing the Vision proposed flexible and adaptable program structures for developing ministry with youth, including:

- a diversity of program settings: age-specific programs, family-centered programs, intergenerational parish programs, and community-wide programs
- a balanced mix of programs, activities, and strategies that address the eight components of comprehensive ministry
- a variety of approaches to reach all adolescents and their families including large-group gathered programs, small-group programs, home-based programs, one-on-one/mentoring programs, and independent programs
- a variety of scheduling options and program settings to respond to the reality of the busy lives and commitments of adolescents and their families.[24]

Youth ministry partners with parents in developing the faith life of adolescents by empowering families to share, celebrate, and live the Catholic faith at home and in the world. *Renewing the Vision* moved the family to the center of youth ministry efforts. Reflecting the teachings of the Vatican and the United States Conference of Catholic Bishops, it affirmed the home as the primary context for sharing, celebrating, and living the Catholic faith, and that parents are partners with youth ministry leaders in developing the faith life of adolescents. *Renewing the Vision* challenged youth ministry leaders to develop a family perspective in the policies, programs, and activities, and to be of service to the family at home.[25]

Youth ministry engages the power and resources of the intergenerational community of faith. *Renewing the Vision* advocated for a community and intergenerational focus for ministry with adolescents. The whole community—by its way of learning together, living together, serving together, praying together, and celebrating together—helps young people become disciples of Jesus Christ and members of the Catholic community. Comprehensive ministry integrates youth ministry and young people into the larger faith community and focuses energy on building intergenerational relationships between young people and the community.[26]

Youth ministry cooperates with community leaders and organizations to promote positive adolescent development and create healthier communities for all young people. *Renewing the Vision* advocated for a collaborative approach between the Church and community organizations. Promoting healthy adolescent development is not only the work of families, parishes, and schools. It requires an entire community. This approach involves advocacy on behalf of young people and their families, connecting with other congregations, and networking with leaders in public schools, youth-serving agencies, and community organizations.

Youth ministry empowers everyone in the faith community to utilize their gifts, talents, and resources in ministry with adolescents. *Renewing the Vision* challenged the entire faith community to assume responsibility for ministry with adolescents. Every member of the faith community has a role to play and special skills, gifts, talents, and resources that can enrich and expand ministry with adolescents.

The relationship between young disciples and their Lord in the Emmaus story was the guiding image for ministry in *A Vision of Youth Ministry*. While still an essential guide image for ministry with youth, *Renewing the Vision* proposed a second image—young people empowered for mission. Just as Jesus sent out the twelve (Lk 9:1–6) and seventy-two (Lk 10:1–12) to carry out his mission, ministry with adolescents empowers young people to proclaim the Good News and to build a world that is more just, more peaceful, and more respectful of human life and creation. "We must ensure that young people are well equipped for their special mission in the world. All of our efforts to promote an active Christian discipleship and growth in Catholic identify must lead toward mission."[27]

Promoting discipleship is central as youth ministry embraces a call for renewal of efforts in catechesis. In 2008, the Committee on Evangelization and Catechesis of the United States Conference of Catholic Bishops provided guidance in developing a curriculum within systematic catechesis with older adolescents in their document, *Doctrinal Elements of a Curriculum Framework for the*

Development of Catechetical Materials for Young People of High School Age. Yet, catechesis remains a part of the larger framework for Catholic youth ministry as we were reminded in the 2005 document, the *National Directory for Catechesis*, which affirms the importance of a comprehensive approach for the effectiveness of catechesis with young people:

> The most effective catechetical programs for adolescents are integrated into a comprehensive program of pastoral ministry for youth that includes catechesis, community life, evangelization, justice and service, leadership development, pastoral care, and prayer and worship.* Such programs aim to empower young people to live as disciples of Jesus Christ in our world today; to draw young people to responsible participation in the life, mission, and work of the Catholic faith community; and to foster the total personal and spiritual growth of each young person.**[28]

 Conclusion

Continuity and newness. Faithfulness and adaptability. Care and challenge. Social reality and hope-filled vision. Formation and transformation. Comfort and empowerment. The tradition of Catholic youth ministry has demonstrated the ability to balance what might seem like opposing tendencies into a comprehensive and holistic response to the total life of the young person. While the Church's ministry must address the newness of each historical event, we have seen the pattern of effective ministry repeated in each era. It is a rich tradition that continues to grow and develop. The foundation is set for the next generation of Catholic youth ministry.

— DOCUMENTS REFERENCED —

The Challenge of Peace. Washington, DC: United States Conference of Catholic Bishops, 1983.

The Challenge of Adolescent Catechesis. Washington, DC: National Federation for Catholic Youth Ministry, 1986.

Economic Justice for All. Washington, DC: United States Conference of Catholic Bishops, 1986.

A Family Perspective in Church and Society. Washington, DC: United States Conference of Catholic Bishops, 1988.

The Challenge of Catholic Youth Evangelization. Washington, DC: National Federation for Catholic Youth Ministry, 1993.

Follow the Way of Love. Washington, DC: United States Conference of Catholic Bishops, 1994.

Libreria Editrice Vaticana. Catechism of the Catholic Church. Washington, DC: United States Conference of Catholic Bishops, 1997.

Renewing the Vision: A Framework for Catholic Youth Ministry. Washington, DC: United States Conference of Catholic Bishops, 1997.

National Directory for Catechesis. Washington, DC: United States Conference of Catholic Bishops, 2005.

Committee on Evangelization and Catechesis. *Doctrinal Elements of a Curriculum Framework for the Development of Catechetical Materials for Young People of High School Age.* Washington, DC: United States Conference of Catholic Bishops, 2008.

— FOR FURTHER READING —

Articles on the History of Youth Ministry

Warren, Michael. "A Vision of Youth Ministry in Retrospect." *The Living Light,* October 1986 (Washington, DC: USCC Department of Education).

Warren, Michael. "Youth Ministry in Transition." *Youth and the Future of the Church.* New York: Seabury Press, 1982.

Warren, Michael. "Youth and the Churches: A Historical Survey." *Youth, Gospel, Liberation.* San Francisco: Harper and Row, 1987.

Weldgen, Francis. "A Brief Look at the Growth of Catholic Youth Work in the United States." *Hope for the Decade.* Washington, DC: USCC National Catholic Youth Organization Federation, 1980.

Zanzig, Thomas. "Youth Ministry: Reflections and Directions." *Readings and Resources in Youth Ministry.* Winona, MN: Saint Mary's Press, 1987.

Other Sources for History of Youth Ministry

Dean, Kenda Creasy, and Ron Foster. *The Godbearing Life: The Art of Soul Tending for Youth Ministry.* Nashville: Upper Room Books, 1998. See Appendix A, pp. 211-13.

McCorquodale, Charlotte. *The Emergence of Lay Ecclesial Youth Ministry as a Profession.* Washington, DC: National Federation for Catholic Youth Ministry, 2002.

Strommen, Merton P., and Richard A. Hardel. *Passing on the Faith: A Radical New Model For Youth and Family Ministry.* Winona, MN: Saint Mary's Press, 2000, pp. 189-200.

— ENDNOTES —

1. For additional information about St. John Baptist de la Salle, consult these sources:
    Cowan, Tom. *The Way of the Saints: Prayers, Practices, and Meditations*. New York: Putnam, 1998, pp. 227-28.
    Hynes, Mary Ellen. *Companion to the Calendar*. Chicago: Liturgy Training Publications, 1993, p. 65.
    McBrien, Richard. *Lives of the Saints*. San Francisco: HarperSanFrancisco, 2001, pp. 156-57.

2. For additional information about St. Elizabeth Ann Seton, consult these sources:
    Cowan, Tom. *The Way of the Saints: Prayers, Practices, and Meditations*. New York: Putnam, 1998, pp. 146-47.
    Hynes, Mary Ellen. *Companion to the Calendar*. Chicago: Liturgy Training Publications, 1993, pp. 29-30.

3. For additional information about St. John Bosco, consult these sources:
    Cowan, Tom. *The Way of the Saints: Prayers, Practices, and Meditations*. New York: Putnam, 1998, pp. 229-230.
    Hynes, Mary Ellen. *Companion to the Calendar*. Chicago: Liturgy Training Publications, 1993, pp. 40-41.
    McBrien, Richard. *Lives of the Saints*. San Francisco: HarperSanFrancisco, 2001, p. 94.

4. For additional information about St. Katharine Drexel, consult these sources:
    Ellsberg, Robert. *All Saints: Daily Reflections on Saints, Prophets, and Witnesses for Our Time*. New York: Crossroad Publishing, 1997, p. 99-100.
    Hynes, Mary Ellen. *Companion to the Calendar*. Chicago: Liturgy Training Publications, 1993, pp. 53-54.
    McBrien, Richard. *Lives of the Saints*. San Francisco: HarperSanFrancisco, 2001, pp. 122-23.

5. *Hope for the Decade: A Look at the Issues Facing Catholic Youth Ministry*. Washington, DC: National Catholic Youth Organization Federation, 1980, p. 2.

6. For additional information about Bishop Bernard. J. Sheil, consult the Sheil Catholic Center Web site: www.sheil.northwestern.edu/index.html (accessed on April 17, 2006.) and the Encyclopedia of Chicago Web site: www.encyclopedia.chicagohistory.org/pages/220.html (accessed May 16, 2006).
    See also: McBrien, Richard P. (general ed.). *Encyclopedia of Catholicism*. San Francisco: HarperSanFrancisco, 1995, pp. 288-89.

7. *A Vision of Youth Ministry*.Washington, DC: United States Conference of Catholic Bishops, 1976, p. 6.
    See also: *Renewing the Vision: A Framework for Catholic Youth Ministry*. Washington, DC: United States Conference of Catholic Bishops, 1997, p. 1.

8. Paradis, Wilfrid, and Andrew Thompson. *Where Are the 6.6 Million?* Washington, DC: United States Conference of Catholic Bishops, 1976, p. 9. This study noted that "these figures are very likely the most optimistic possible and probably minimize the

true dimensions of the problem" (p. 9) due to the self-reporting of participation numbers by parishes and the undetermined number of non-Catholic students in Catholic schools.

9. *A Vision of Youth Ministry*, p. 1.

10. ibid, p. 7.

11. ibid, p. 24.

12. *Sharing the Light of Faith*. Washington, DC: United States Conference of Catholic Bishops, 1979), #228.

13. ibid.

14. Benson, Peter L. *The Troubled Journey: A Portrait of 6th to 12th Grade Youth*. Minneapolis: Search Institute, 1993. This book was the first document in the Search Institute's research on developmental assets in young people. For more information about developmental assets go to: www.search-institute.org.
    See also: Benson, Peter L. *All Kids Are Our Kids: What Communities Must Do to Raise Caring and Responsible Children and Adolescents*. San Francisco: Jossey-Bass, 1998.

15. Pope John Paul II. *Listen to the True Word of Life*, 1993, as cited in *Renewing the Vision*, p. 9.

16. Pope John Paul II, *World Day of Prayer for Vocations*, 1995, as cited in *Renewing the Vision*, p. 10.

17. *Renewing the Vision: A Framework for Catholic Youth Ministry*. Washington, DC: United States Conference of Catholic Bishops, 1997, p. 20.

18. ibid., 10.

19. ibid., 9.

20. ibid., 11.

21. ibid., 15.

22. ibid., 19-20.

23. ibid., 20.

24. See RTV, 25.

25. See RTV, 21.

26. See RTV, 22.

27. RTV, 51.

28. *National Directory for Catechesis*, p. 201. Asterisks make reference to these references: *Renewing the Vision, p. 26; **Renewing the Vision, pp. 9-17.

CHAPTER THREE

Understanding Youth Today

Cheryl M. Tholcke

Editor's Note

To respond to youth and include them in our community, we need to know something about their journey through adolescence. In this chapter, Cheryl M. Tholcke explores the developmental changes and the generational attributes of youth. She also shares practical approaches for supporting youth and connecting them to the faith community.

They gather at shopping centers, skate parks, movie theatres, homes, schools, coffee houses, and church. They sport tattoos, piercings, and dyed hair. They listen to rap, country, classical, rock, alternative, and Christian music. They carry backpacks, purses, skate boards, iPods®, Blackberrys®, and laptop computers. Their modes of transportation are cars, bicycles, motorcycles, public transit, and walking. They play sports, perform in plays, and play musical instruments. They study. They have jobs. They are religious; they are searching for God. They have siblings; they are only children. They are being raised by parents; some are raising their parents. They live in small towns, urban centers, and suburban developments. They live in apartments, condos, juvenile halls, townhouses, houses, motel rooms, and in shelters. They know everything. They know almost nothing. They want to be like everyone else. They pride themselves on their individuality.

These are today's young people—boys and girls in grades six through twelve. Today's adolescents are leaving the experience of childhood and rushing toward adulthood. These young people are the focus of youth ministry.

So what do youth ministers need to know about the development of adolescents? The third goal in *Renewing the Vision: A Framework for Catholic Youth Ministry* (RTV)—"to foster the total personal and spiritual growth of each young person"—states that "ministry with adolescents promotes the growth of healthy, competent, caring, and faith-filled Catholic young people."[1]

This is a tall order! Everything about a young person is taken into account in youth ministry. This chapter will address the following areas:

- Adolescent development
- Generational characteristics of young people
- Connecting with young people
- Young people and the Church

 Making the Connection

Were you ever their age? Youth today share common challenges and unique perspectives.

- *What do you remember as the high points and challenges of your adolescence?*
- *How did adults and communities help and support you?*

Adolescent Development

A Historical Perspective

The notion of adolescence as a specific period in a young person's life is relatively new. Only in the last 100 years or so has the period between childhood and adulthood—now known as adolescence—become part of societal structure, "although it was not until 1960 that there was common agreement among developmental psychologists that adolescence was a legitimate phase of the life span."[2]

The term "adolescence" comes from the Latin *adolescere*, "to grow up." During this time span—usually beginning at ten to twelve years of age and continuing to the early twenties—boys and girls grow and change from children to young men and women. This is a wide span of years because no two people go through adolescence in exactly the same way. However, there are common elements to all young people in their development from children to young adults. Of adolescence, developmental psychologist John Santrock said, "Adolescence begins in biology and ends in culture."[3]

The beginning of adolescence is marked by entry into puberty. Developmental experts agree that the onset of puberty is slowly dropping. In girls, for example, puberty is "dropping from as late as an average of 14.5 years old a century and more ago, to as early as eleven years old today."[4] Other changes in addition to physical ones are also occurring. A young person's ability to think and reflect on issues and topics and the ability to make decisions about behavior are considered psychological changes. The ability to form and maintain mutual relationships with others is part of the sociological change that occurs during adolescence.[5]

When does adolescence end? Culture is the indicator for when adolescence is over and adulthood begins. In some cultures, adolescence continues until the person is married—even if that means to age thirty. In other cultures, once young people have taken on adult roles in the society, their adolescence is finished.

What markers are there for young people in the United States? In current civic society, the age for voting is eighteen, ostensibly the age of majority or adulthood. However, the drinking age is twenty-one. With many insurance companies, auto insurance costs will drop once the age of twenty-five is attained. More recently, the judicial system in the United States has lowered the age of who may be considered an adult in criminal proceedings, and children as young as eleven have been tried as adults.

Age does not seem to be the indicator of when adolescence is completed. If, however, the process of adolescence itself "has become the marker distinguishing youth from adulthood," young people need to be provided with an understanding of what the end goal of adolescence actually is.[6]

The expression, "He's his own person" is an acknowledgment that the person knows who he is and lives by a set of values and standards that he believes in. The person is a distinct entity from others, an individual unlike others, a unique person. This sense of being, knowing, and understanding oneself as a unique individual is a key goal in adolescence known as *individuation*. As boys and girls grow and develop and mature from childhood to adulthood, they become the person God calls them to be—there's no one else exactly like them. They may have the physical traits of their parents, similar interests to their friends, and hold common beliefs of their faith community, but the sum total is a unique person.

An adolescent is a person on a journey, learning to own one's identity, exploring the ability to be autonomous, and reconnecting with family, friends, and community in a new way. In this process of developing a distinct identity, adolescents confront the questions of "Who am I?", "Do I matter?", and "How do I relate to others?"[7] When they have successfully addressed these three tasks, then one can say adolescence is finished.

This chapter will take a look at the developmental process of younger (10/11 years to 14/15 years) and older (14/15 years to 18 years) adolescents. These two groups of young people, in these two stages of development, are the focus of youth ministry.

Younger Adolescents

Younger adolescents are typically in middle school—grades six, seven, and eight. Sometimes called "tweeners" because they are between being a child and being a teenager, younger adolescents are bridging two worlds as they grow toward maturity. On the one hand, they are children who still like to kiss mom or dad goodnight, who are consoled by sitting in dad's lap or having milk and cookies with mom, and who play with Legos® and Barbies®. On the other hand, they are growing up. Girls experiment with make-up, have crushes on teen idols (or the boy sitting next to them in class), and become new best friends with the phone (or the computer). Boys pay attention to their hair (to gel or not to gel?), and notice the girls around them. Their voices are changing—cracking or squeaking—and they hang out in groups with their friends. Younger adolescents are physically changing at the same time their bodies are seemingly out of control—perhaps it's the onset of acne or a growth spurt—which can lead to a sense of awkwardness and confusion as they grapple with all the changes going on around and in them.

From the time they are about ten to fifteen years old, younger adolescents experience great changes in six areas: physical, intellectual, identity-related, moral, interpersonal, and faith-based.

Developmental Characteristics of Younger Adolescents

PHYSICAL DEVELOPMENT
- Secondary sex characteristics and the capacity to reproduce
- Sensitivity about physical changes and confusion about emerging sexuality
- Incorporation of bodily changes into self image as male or female

INTELLECTUAL DEVELOPMENT

- Move from concrete thinking (what is) to abstract thinking or formal operations (what might be true)
- Questioning/testing of adults' statements and evaluation of adults' values
- Painful self-consciousness and critical, idealistic, argumentative, self-centered behaviors
- Expanding interests; intense, short-term enthusiasm

IDENTITY DEVELOPMENT

- Requirement of time to reflect upon new reactions received from others and to build consistent self-image from the different mirrors in which they see themselves
- Discovery of who they are as unique persons with abilities, interests, and goals
- Pursuit of limited independence and autonomy from parents and adults

MORAL DEVELOPMENT

- Engagement in more complex decision-making processes
- Resolution of moral dilemmas in terms of outside expectations—family, friends, or other significant persons or the law or the system of good order

INTERPERSONAL DEVELOPMENT

- Reliance on parents and families for setting values and giving affection
- Stronger identification with peer group for belonging and friendships
- Entrance into broader social world of middle school, peer groups, and activity groups
- Ability to consider feelings and needs of others in a relationship
- Growing knowledge of how to relate to the opposite sex (what to say and how to behave)

FAITH DEVELOPMENT

- Acquisition of faith from parents and family
- Development of faith and identity
- Establishment of a set of religious beliefs, attitudes, and values through the experiences of participation and belonging in a caring faith community

Participating in organized sports helps many girls and boys adjust to the physical changes in their bodies. Young adolescents begin to think differently, moving from thinking in concrete terms—such as how to combine, or how to organize—

to abstract thinking. Examples of abstract thinking include thinking about possibilities, considering different points of view, and thinking about thinking. Young adolescents begin to form opinions about which TV shows are better or which peer group is the best one. Adolescents learn to make independent decisions about values, attitudes, and personal beliefs. Young adolescents will "try on" different identities as they seek to find out who they are. It is during the young adolescent years that friendship-making skills are critical; the ability to forge relationships with others sets the stage for success in the later adolescent years.

During this time of changes in a young adolescent's life, eight developmental needs arise.

Developmental Needs of Younger Adolescents

OPPORTUNITIES FOR SELF-DEFINITION
- To better understand, define, and accept selves as individuals
- To explore widening social world and to reflect upon the meaning of new experiences in order to consider selves as participants in society
- For young adolescents of ethnic cultures to achieve positive orientation toward their own culture
- To affirm ethnicity through observation of ceremonies, retention of native language, and reinforcement of specific attitudes, beliefs, and practices

OPPORTUNITIES FOR COMPETENCE AND ACHIEVEMENT
- To discover skills and learn that skills are valued by others
- To encourage the practice of new skills, public performance and recognition, and reflection on personal and group accomplishments

OPPORTUNITIES FOR POSITIVE SOCIAL INTERACTION WITH ADULTS AND PEERS
- To develop interpersonal skills
- To learn how to develop a relationship with parents that reflects growing autonomy and utilizes new patterns of communicating
- To form positive peer relationships and support, especially through structured programs
- For caring relationships with respectful adults who share experiences, views, values, and feelings, and who serve as role models and advisors

OPPORTUNITIES FOR PHYSICAL ACTIVITY
- To utilize energy and growing bodies through activities which require physical movement or expression

OPPORTUNITIES FOR MEANINGFUL PARTICIPATION IN FAMILIES, SCHOOLS, CHURCHES, AND COMMUNITY ORGANIZATIONS

- To participate in making decisions about life-shaping activities as active leaders or participants making a viable contribution to the success of the activities
- To participate as valued members of a faith community and as leaders in church ministries and programs
- For exposure to situations in which to use skills to solve real-life problems and affect the world, such as community service programs

OPPORTUNITIES FOR CREATIVE EXPRESSION

- To express the internal to the external world (feelings, interests, abilities, thoughts) through a variety of activities (music, writing, sports, art, drama, cooking)
- Activities that allow the experience and testing of new and different forms of self-expression

PROVISION OF STRUCTURE AND CLEAR LIMITS

- Guidance for young adolescents in making decisions about behavior that involves young people in the process of decision-making
- Structure that permits focus on a task, perseverance in various efforts, and success leading to an increase in self-esteem
- Structure and clear limits that ensure feelings of safety in activities and the possibility of living with joy and confidence

OPPORTUNITIES FOR PERSONAL RELIGIOUS EXPERIENCE

- To explore "the big questions" in life whose answers can only be comprehended within the context of faith and religion
- For a deeper and more personal relationship with God

Let young adolescents find out what they're good at and let them do it! Help them develop peer friendships and provide caring adults to be role models and mentors. Incorporate creative activities in sessions that allow young adolescents to express themselves. Let them know they are safe by providing clear rules and limits.

Young adolescents are growing in new ways. They need the security that boundaries and structure provide, but they also need some freedom to figure things out on their own. Just as a newly fledged bird tests its wings in the presence of its parents, young adolescents need to test their newly developing independence, skills, and understanding in the presence of parents and other caring adults. The support of youth and their parents and a parish's ministry offerings provide opportunities for these young people to grow and to succeed as they leave childhood behind for the great adventure of adolescence.

Older Adolescents

Older adolescents are typically in high school—grades nine through twelve. These youth are looking forward to making their own decisions, growing up, deciding on a future direction, figuring out life's questions, and flexing their independence. In many ways, these young people have a foot in two worlds—the teenage world and the young adult/adult world. Youth have begun to take on some of the responsibilities of adults—jobs, driver's licenses, duties to help maintain the family home, schedules of activities, meetings, appointments, etc. They are expected to behave as grown-ups. In the teenage world, young people are still accountable to mom and dad for their behavior, school grades, where they go, and with whom. Consequences for failing to meet expectations are meted out—being grounded or losing driving privileges and computer access— by parents or other authority figures. Young people want to hang out with friends, they come to mom and dad when cash flow is low, and they expect the refrigerator to be full when they are hungry!

During the high school years, older adolescents (fifteen to nineteen years of age) experience growth in five developmental areas: intellect, identity, morality, interpersonal skills, and faith. These adolescents spend time contemplating their thoughts and feelings on various topics and issues. As they continue to forge their own self-identity, they look to other authorities in their life (peers, other caring adults) for direction. Older adolescents review the moral values they have received in an effort to develop a code based on integrity and beliefs that will guide their behavior. Deeper personal relationships develop with friends and significant others. They begin the process of owning their faith as theirs and integrating it more deeply into their lives.

Developmental Characteristics of Older Adolescents

INTELLECTUAL DEVELOPMENT

- The ability to engage in reflective thinking ("What do I think?" "Why do I think that?"), making it possible to develop personal identity, personal value system, and personal faith
- Thinking about and planning for the future

IDENTITY DEVELOPMENT

- The process of establishing personal identity, which includes acceptance of one's sexuality, decision-making regarding the future, and commitment to a personally held system of values and religious beliefs
- Shift from authority of family to self-chosen authority, often by establishing an identity that is shaped by significant others (peers and adults)
- A period of questioning, re-evaluation, and experimentation
- Increasing autonomy in making personal decisions, assuming responsibility for oneself, and regulating one's own behavior

MORAL DEVELOPMENT

- Exercise of moral judgments in matters of much greater complexity as steps to establishing a more personal form of moral reasoning
- Re-evaluation of moral values received from family, church, and significant others
- Search for a moral code that preserves personal integrity and provides the basis for developing an internalized moral value system to guide behavior

INTERPERSONAL DEVELOPMENT

- Movement toward greater personal intimacy and adult sexuality
- Capability for more mutual, trusting, deep, and enduring personal friendships with members of the same sex and opposite sex, which provide acceptance, love, affirmation, and the opportunity to honestly share deepest selves
- Expansion of social perspective to encompass the larger world

FAITH DEVELOPMENT

- Exploration and questioning of the faith which has been handed down by family and church; search for a style of faith and belief which is more personal
- Beginning of the process of taking responsibility for one's own faith life, commitments, lifestyle, beliefs, and attitudes
- Exploration of a personal relationship with God, who knows, accepts, and confirms the individual, and with Jesus Christ through his teaching, example, and presence

Older adolescents have eight developmental needs during this period in their lives: exploration and experimentation, adult sexuality, interpersonal relationships, adult mentors, meaningful roles in community and society, preparation for the future, personal value systems and decision-making skills, and personal faith.

Developmental Needs of Older Adolescents

OPPORTUNITIES FOR EXPLORATION AND EXPERIMENTATION

- To experiment with a wide array of behaviors, roles, attitudes, relationships, ideas, and activities in developing own identity and faith identity
- To explore personal identity by reflecting on self in relation to others
- For youth of ethnic cultures to achieve positive orientation toward own culture, to affirm ethnicity through observation of ceremonies, retention of native language, and reinforcement of specific attitudes, beliefs, and practices

ADULT SEXUALITY

- Opportunities to understand sexual growth and integrate sexuality into own personality in a holistic way
- Opportunities to develop healthy values and attitudes regarding own sexuality

OPPORTUNITIES FOR INTERPERSONAL RELATIONSHIPS

- To form positive relationships and experiences with peers in a comfortable and secure environment and to develop friendship-making and friendship-maintaining skills
- To learn how to develop a relationship with parents that is reflective of growing autonomy and that utilizes new patterns of communicating

ADULT MENTORS

- To develop relationships with adult Christians who affirm the journey and struggles, explore sensitive issues, listen to stories and questions, share their own faith journey, and ask questions that encourage critical thinking and reflection

OPPORTUNITIES FOR MEANINGFUL ROLES IN COMMUNITY AND SOCIETY

- To participate with other older adolescents as full members and leaders in the community, society, and church
- To explore, discuss, and act on local and global justice issues; to develop an active responsibility for what happens in the community and world, and to be involved in meaningful community service
- To participate in the decision-making, planning, and implementation of programs that serve young people

Preparing for the Future
- To acquire necessary competencies for adult roles, such as goal-setting, problem-solving, time management, and decision-making
- To explore life options and plan futures (education, career) and to help acquire the skills, knowledge, and experience for chosen fields; to link more closely the worlds of school and work

Personal Value System and Decision-Making Skills
- Opportunities to discuss conflicting values and formulate their own value system
- Opportunities to gain knowledge and experience in making decisions, and to apply Christian moral values in making moral judgments

Opportunities for Personal Faith
- To explore and question the faith gifts from family and the faith community and to develop own faith identity
- To explore what it means to be and live as a person of faith today
- To develop a more personal relationship with Jesus Christ

Provide opportunities to affirm and celebrate the teen's ethnic culture. Assist them in understanding and living their sexuality from a Christian perspective. Help them learn new ways of maintaining relationships—especially for seniors who move on to university or college. Invite caring adults to serve as faith mentors with older adolescents. Involve teens as leaders in parish or community-wide programs or projects. Link older adolescents to professionals for career or education planning. Teach decision-making skills and how to apply them to life situations. Offer retreats that help adolescents explore their faith and deepen their relationship with Jesus.

Older adolescents start looking outward as they contemplate the next phase of their lives. They begin exerting their independence, not from family or community, but for the opportunity to make their own decisions and forge their own paths. These emerging young adults are thinking independently and setting their own goals. Caring adults and ministry leaders journey with these young men and women as they make their way in the world. The life of the faith community, the programs offered, and the relationships shared with these young people and their families provide a foundation upon which they can grow.

Adolescents and Brain Development

In recent years, scientists have learned a great deal about brain development. Some of these findings help us to understand what a child and adolescent retains and what they lose in the learning process. You may have heard the saying, "It's like riding a bike; it just comes back to you." It seems that it would depend on when you last rode a bike.

Around ages 11-13, youth are experiencing growth in their frontal cortex which is helping them develop the ability to have more control over impulses and make better judgments. This growth is accompanied by a period of "pruning" in which unused areas of the brain are cut off to strengthen the paths for areas that are used frequently.

This pruning and growth is an important stage in brain development. What youth choose to do or not do could impact them for life. Dr. Jay Giedd, of the National Institute of Mental Health in Bethesda, Maryland, calls this the "use it or lose it principle," and explained further, "If a teen is doing music or sports or academics, those are the cells and connections that will be hardwired. If they're lying on the couch or playing video games or MTV, those are the cells and connections that are going to survive."

What does "use it or lose it" means to us as we share faith with adolescents? Well, it sounds like if you rode a bike as a child but didn't ride a bike as a young adolescent, you would lose that ability and memory. This makes this period of time all the more important for sharing faith and engaging youth in the practices of faith so that faithful living is an experience that is remembered and practiced for life.[8]

In an interview with Brad Griffin for Fuller Youth Institute, Dr. Kelly Schwartz, an adolescent psychology specialist, addressed cognitive development and its effect on teens. Science now can see the brain function in "real" time. Previously, static images were taken of the brain and scientists made logical leaps as to what was happening and how it impacted various parts of the brain. While what is seen now is "descriptive"—we can see what the brain does and how it does it—there is still a lot of work to be done to make reliable predictions on the findings.

Schwartz suggested two things we can do to foster healthy brain development in adolescents. First, allow for cognitive dissonance. We need to allow young people to struggle with things that don't make sense and allow this struggle to be open-ended. Being able to say "I don't know" helps young people learn it is okay to struggle with the answer. Work through issues in a supervised manner with young people so they can develop the ability to think critically and to know that there isn't always an easy answer to a complex problem or idea.

Second, connect the emotional and cognitive experiences of young people. Many times we do not spend as much time debriefing an experience as we do planning for it. Young people need to unpack the experience, deal with the dissonance they may have experienced (lack of harmony between what they learned in preparation and what they experienced). Using a service learning experience (aka mission trip) as an example, perhaps a young person did not feel compassion toward those they served or they could see no relief to the problem. Let them wrestle with this and think through it. There's a definite payoff when hard cognitive work is united with the emotional experience. Allow the young people (and yourself!) to work together and not just come up with easy solutions to tough problems such a hunger, unemployment, and homelessness.[9]

Family Changes during Adolescence

As adolescents transition from being children to their new roles, families are changing and growing too. When a family with young children becomes a family with adolescents, many aspects of family life are renegotiated. Typically, a family will adopt new ways of recreating together, dividing chores, disciplining, communicating, supporting homework, and monitoring media.

At the same time that adolescents are experiencing growth and changes, parents may also be in transition. The changes within adolescents and parents cause changes in the ways that families interact. Physical, intellectual, and emotional changes during this stage of life can result in temporary disruptions in family interaction as relationships shift between parents and adolescents. Intellectually, adolescents begin to think abstractly, to question and test adults' statements, and to evaluate adults' values. The adolescent world expands with new possibilities, ideas, and dreams. The new ability to think abstractly can improve family communication, but there is often tension because the adolescents are questioning parental authority and testing parental values. Many adolescents are self-conscious and sensitive to criticism. At the same time, many parents feel less control over their children, which can result in more critical attitudes toward their adolescents. Parents and adolescents both have a mutual need for respect, reassurance, and approval, which can be threatened by the changes at this stage of the life cycle.

Throughout this stage, parent-child relationships move from greater to less control, with adolescents gradually gaining more independence—with limits. Conflict often exists between "letting go" too early or "hanging on" too late. In the youth ministry publication, *YouthWorks*, John Roberto describes the challenge and opportunity present within this time of change:

> The task for most families with adolescents—and it is by no means an easy one—is to maintain emotional involvement, in the form of concern and caring, while gradually moving toward a relationship characterized by greater behavioral autonomy.[10]

Developmental Assets

In *Renewing the Vision*, the bishops refer to the work done by the Search Institute in the area of healthy adolescent development.[11] The Search Institute identified forty essential building blocks or assets for positive adolescent development. These forty assets offer faith communities realistic and specific ways to encourage the healthy development of their younger members. Assets are positive experiences and qualities that young people need to grow up healthy. Assets are factors that prevent risky behavior and promote positive attitudes and activities. The assets are divided into external assets—the supports that young people need in their lives and internal assets—the capacities and abilities that young people need to develop in themselves.

Focusing on helping teens grow and becoming the best they can be is a marked difference from mainstream culture, which usually focuses on adolescence as a troubling and problematic time in young peoples' lives.

Asset-builders see young people as a work in progress. Ministry leaders—indeed entire faith communities—can be asset-builders. Parents are potentially the most influential asset builders, a circumstance which presents youth ministry with rich opportunities to provide support and resources. Asset-building is not about adding more programs to ministry but about what already exists and being intentional about the expected outcomes.

External assets include support, empowerment, boundaries and expectations, and time use. Examples of external asset-building include

- Providing gathered youth events
- Involving adults as mentors and role models
- Providing parents with information and resources on parenting, sharing faith, etc.

Internal assets include educational commitment, positive values, social competencies, and positive identity.

Examples of internal asset-building include
- Teaching youth life skills such as conflict resolution, decision-making, and planning
- Building self-esteem and integrity among young people
- Encouraging their efforts in school

Developmental Assets from the Search Institute[12] The forty developmental assets, identified through national research by the Search Institute, are powerful shapers of young people's behavior. Assets help to inoculate youth from high-risk behaviors (e.g., use of alcohol and drugs, antisocial behavior, sexual activity). As assets increase, the incidence of high-risk behaviors decreases. Developmental assets also promote positive outcomes. As assets increase, so do school success, the affirmation of diversity, educational aspirations, and prosocial behavior. Young people with a greater number of assets are more likely to grow up caring, competent, healthy, and responsible. This important relationship between developmental assets and choices made has been documented for all types of youth, regardless of age, gender, geographic region, town size, or race/ethnicity.

These forty developmental assets have been identified through research by the Search Institute as forming a foundation for healthy development in children and adolescents.

External Assets

SUPPORT

Family support Family life provides high levels of love and support.

Positive family communication Young person and her or his parent(s) communicate positively, and young person is willing to seek advice and counsel from parents.

Other adult relationships Young person receives support from three or more non-parent adults.

Caring neighborhood Young person experiences caring neighbors.

Caring school climate School provides a caring, encouraging environment.

Parent involvement in schooling Parent(s) are actively involved in helping young person succeed in school.

EMPOWERMENT

Community values youth Young person perceives that adults in the community value youth.

Youth as resources Young people are given useful roles in the community.

Service to others Young person serves in the community one hour or more per week.

Safety Young person feels safe at home, at school, and in the neighborhood.

BOUNDARIES AND EXPECTATIONS

Family boundaries Family has clear rules and consequences and monitors the young person's whereabouts.

School boundaries School provides clear rules and consequences.

Neighborhood boundaries Neighbors take responsibility for monitoring young people's behavior.

Adult role models Parent(s) and other adults model positive, responsible behavior.

Positive peer influence Young person's best friends model responsible behavior.

High expectations Both parent(s) and teachers encourage the young person to do well.

TIME USE

Creative activities Young person spends three or more hours per week in lessons or practice in music, theater, or other arts.

Youth programs Young person spends three or more hours per week in sports, clubs, or organizations at school and/or in the community.

Religious community Young person spends one or more hours per week in activities in a religious institution.

Time at home Young person is out with friends "with nothing special to do" two or fewer nights per week.

Internal Assets

EDUCATIONAL COMMITMENT

Achievement motivation Young person is motivated to do well in school.

School engagement Young person is actively engaged in learning.

Homework Young person reports doing at least one hour of homework every school day.

Bonding to school Young person cares about her or his school.

Reading for pleasure Young person reads for pleasure three or more hours per week.

Positive Values

Caring Young person places high value on helping other people.

Equality and social justice Young person places high value on promoting equality and reducing hunger and poverty.

Integrity Young person acts on convictions and stands up for her or his beliefs.

Honesty Young person "tells the truth even when it's not easy."

Responsibility Young person accepts and takes personal responsibility.

Restraint Young person believes it is important not to be sexually active or to use alcohol or other drugs.

Social Competencies

Planning and decision-making Young person knows how to plan ahead and make choices.

Interpersonal competence Young person has empathy, sensitivity, and friendship skills.

Cultural competence Young person has knowledge of and comfort with people of different cultural/racial/ethnic backgrounds.

Resistance skills Young person can resist negative peer pressure and dangerous situations.

Peaceful conflict resolution Young person seeks to resolve conflict nonviolently.

Positive Identity

Personal power Young person feels he or she has control over "things that happen to me."

Self-esteem Young person reports having a high self-esteem.

Sense of purpose Young person reports that "my life has a purpose."

Positive view of personal future Young person is optimistic about her or his personal future.

Asset-building supports the work of youth ministry by involving all members of the faith community. Assets attract people's energy and commitment because they are

- shared by all
- hopeful
- effective in promoting positive adolescent development
- manageable

- able to empower communities to make a positive difference in the lives of their young people
- capable of empowering young people to take some responsibility for their lives

Implications of Developmental Changes for Ministry

Employing a developmental perspective in ministry with adolescents means that youth ministry is organized into two distinct categories: one for younger adolescents (junior high/middle school), and one for older adolescents (high school). Each of these stages has its own unique needs. Different program content, process, formats, and schedules are just a few of the implications.

A developmental perspective also means that the content and processes within these two age groups must connect to their needs and interests. For example, develop a program for younger adolescents that includes plenty of time for physical activity and opportunities for hands-on learning. For older adolescents, offer special-interest or small group opportunities, and leadership opportunities for the young people to help vision, plan, implement, and lead various aspects of the ministry.

Generational Characteristics of Young People

Even experts on adolescent development and observers of generational change among young people cannot agree on everything, but they do share some common insights about today's young people.

> They are the young navigators. They doubt that traditional institutions can provide them with the good life and take personal responsibility for their lives. They do value material goods, but they are not self-absorbed. They are more knowledgeable than any previous generation, and they care deeply about social issues. They believe strongly in individual rights such as privacy and rights to information. But they have no ethos of individualism, thriving, rather, from close interpersonal networks and displaying a strong sense of social responsibility.[13]
>
> Don Tapscott

Who Is a Post-Modern?

Postmodernism is a worldview—a way of looking at life. "It emerged from philosophical ideas (mostly French) that over time distilled into common cultural expressions (e.g., from the disjointedness of music videos and Internet hyperlinks to interactive learning to common sayings like, "That works for me" or "Get real")."[14] Postmodernism is best understood when contrasted with modernism—the belief that traditional understandings (of everything) were outdated and that only change and embracing new ways of thinking and doing would advance the human condition (economic, social, political).

> The term postmodern ("pomo" for short) is used to denote a 40-year transition from an Information Age to a Bionomic Age that will begin no later than 2020. My generation (the Boomers) and our children (Gen-Xers and Net-Gens) are the transitional generations to this new world. The Net-Gens (those born after 1981) will be the first ones to really live the majority of their time in the new world. We Boomers will make it to the river, but we won't cross over. The crossover to a post-postmodern world will be made by the generations that follow ours.[15]
>
> LEONARD SWEET

Many people are products of the modern culture, raised in a society that holds beliefs such as

- The individual is most important.
- Progress is always positive—things will always get better
- Reason is the "be all and end all" of finding truth
- Humans have dominion over creation (called "progress")

It takes little imagination to recognize that many of today's adolescents do not view progress as always positive because they believe that many of the problems in the world are the result of initiatives begun in the name of progress. Adolescents also have few illusions about the future always being brighter. Young people are products of a post-modern culture.

What sets a post-modern outlook apart from modernism? In his book, *Post-Modern Pilgrims*, Leonard Sweet says the characteristics most appealing to post-moderns form the acronym EPIC:[16]

Experiential. Post-moderns are on a quest to experience, not just talk or read about things. They want to "experience life for themselves. ... They don't want their information straight—they want it laced with experience (hence edutainment)."[17]

Participatory. "[I]nteractivity is hard-wired into the post-modern brain itself."[18] Post-moderns are not content to be spectators or to have decisions made for them—a characteristic of modernism; they want to be involved in every aspect of their lives from customizing their cars to choosing how food is prepared in a restaurant. They want to transform the culture they have been handed. "People want to make their own decisions and have multiple choices."[19]

Image-driven. Modern culture was word-based; post-modern culture is image-driven. "Images come as close as human beings will get to a universal language.... Propositions are lost on postmodern ears, but metaphors they will hear; images they will see and understand."[20] They access and process information through an intricate, interwoven web of metaphors, symbols, pictures, and stories.

Connectedness. In a culture that prizes individuality, where it is easy to become isolated in our digital world, post-moderns seek connection and community with others. They are looking for deeply personal and communal experiences of the divine.[21] "There is a deepening desire for a life filled with friends, community, service, and creative and spiritual growth."[22] "Relationship issues stand at the heart of postmodern culture."[23]

Implications for Ministry with Today's Young People

> Postmodern evangelism is recognizing that God is already at work in people's lives before we arrived on the scene, and that our role is helping people to see how God is present and active in their lives, calling them home. Postmodern evangelism is not "I have Jesus, and you don't. How can I get you here so that I can give you my Jesus?" but "you already know Jesus, even if you don't think you know Jesus. How can I help you see and know what you already know, and how can I know and meet your Jesus?"[24]
>
> LEONARD SWEET, *SOUL TSUNAMI*

Today's young people are Catholics from after the Second Vatican Council. They have never experienced the Church as it was before the Council. Many adults remember the advent of Mass in English, missalettes, lay leadership, and receiving Communion in the hand—fruits of the Council. What will today's young people look back on as "new" in their experience of Church? How will their life in the Church be EPIC?

More than ever before, paying attention to the experience of young people is key to ministry. The assumptions that all young people are the same, think the same, believe the same, and develop the same no longer apply. Youth are not empty vessels waiting to be filled to the brim. They come with their life experience, their enthusiasm and energy, and their need to develop into the people God has called them to be. As society has become more culturally, economically, and educationally diverse, young people reflect that diversity.

Ministry to and with the young Church, includes some key implications:

- *Deepening the relationship with Jesus.* Accompanying young people on their faith journey throughout adolescence requires more than teaching about Jesus. Provide opportunities for them to meet the one who loves them completely and unconditionally through experiences of community, worship, prayer, and relationships. How will youth ministry help the young experience and deepen their relationship with Jesus?

- *Being grounded in Tradition, Scripture, and Church teaching.* How do adults continue to learn and grow as Catholics? What opportunities are available—and utilized—to study theology, Scripture, ecclesiology, or morality? Mature Christians know there is always something to be learned about their faith and how to live it everyday. A commitment to lifelong learning is a powerful message to the young that growth in faith takes a lifetime and does not stop with Confirmation. How will youth ministry invite young people into meaningful participation in lifelong learning?

- *An understanding of multiple intelligences.* This includes: linguistic (word smart), logical-mathematical (number/reasoning smart), spatial (picture smart), bodily-kinesthetic (body smart), musical (music), interpersonal (people smart), intrapersonal (self smart), and naturalistic (nature smart). In programs, activities, and events, consider the various learning styles of the young people. How are youth ministry efforts developed to meet the diverse needs of young people? How will youth ministry incorporate technology to help the Church tell its story and to help young people tell their story?

- *Broadening methodology to embrace the various ways young people learn.* In *Growing Up Digital*, Don Tapscott lists eight shifts from broadcast learning (in which the teacher has the information and "broadcasts" it to the leaner) to interactive learning:

  ▷ From linear and sequential (beginning to end) to hypermedia learning (interactive and nonsequential, like the way young people surf the Internet)

  ▷ From instruction to construction and discovery (allowing the young person to learn by doing—experiential learning)

▷ From teacher-centered (interests and background of the teacher) to learner-centered (what are they interested in, how they learn)

▷ From absorbing materials to learning how to learn (gathering various pieces of information, analyzing, and synthesizing)

▷ From school to lifelong (that learning does not end with formal education)

▷ From one-size-fits-all to customized (people learn in different ways so utilize different learning methods to include everyone)

▷ From school as torture to school as fun (learning can be entertaining and challenging)

▷ From teacher as transmitter to teacher as facilitator (teachers provide the framework and process for the learning, the learners determine the knowledge to gain)[25]

Connecting with Young People

> Primarily our task in youth ministry is to approach each adolescent as a uniquely designed and gifted masterpiece of the Creator. While it is important to understand the broad developmental differences between genders and across age groups, what every child, adolescent, and young adult needs far more is the personal touch of a loving community.[26]
>
> CHAP CLARK

Youth ministry today provides young people with myriad opportunities for spiritual growth, leadership development, participation in the Christian community, and understanding of how the Catholic faith guides and influences their lives. As articulated by the bishops of the United States in *Renewing the Vision*, youth ministry provides young people and their families with the necessary programs, activities, and events to grow as young Catholics. This comprehensive approach to ministry reminds us that there is more to a young person than just spiritual development or intellectual needs because all aspects of a human person are in need of nurturing, growth, and development.

Connect with youth using technology and the digital world:

• Stay connected to them through a parish youth ministry Web site, chat room, or online learning opportunities.

• Use e-mail for program reminders, deadlines, and invitations to participate.

• Offer online registrations for programs and events.

- Highlight interesting, fun, and interactive Web sites that promote healthy adolescent development and growth in faith.
- Set up a chat room facilitated by an adult to discuss a topic of interest.
- Create a digital scrapbook of youth ministry using photos taken by youth at various activities and events.
- Design a daily, weekly, or monthly prayer or a seasonal retreat that can be done online.
- Train youth leaders using online learning sessions they can do at home or on their own time.

Gathered youth events are another way to connect with young people because they address the immediate needs of building a community of young people and addressing topics of general interest to youth. Such gatherings include food, community-building and socializing, prayer and reflection, content-rich learning and discussion of various topics, and action steps—ways to live out the learning in the coming week or month. Special events such as retreats, service learning experiences, and participation in regional or national conferences provide another way to connect with young people.

Non-gathered strategies also connect with youth. Stay connected by

- Sending birthday cards
- Attending events where youth are present
- Providing resources for youth to use at home
- Placing announcements in the parish bulletin
- Offering a drop-in center or office hours for drop-ins
- Encouraging their participation in the events of the parish community

Young People and the Church

No pope in history called such attention to the young Church as did John Paul II. Early in his pontificate (1984), John Paul II called the youth of the world together to celebrate their identity as young Catholics and to challenge them to live as disciples of Jesus Christ. These international meetings of youth with the Holy Father became known as World Youth Day.

> Dear young people, the Church needs genuine witnesses for the new evangelization: men and women whose lives have been transformed by meeting with Jesus, men and women who are capable of communicating this experience to others.[27]
>
> JOHN PAUL II, 2004

Not only was John Paul II a believer in the power of young people and their relationship with Jesus Christ, the Holy Father put the challenge to the adult Church as well:

> You will have to find ways of involving young people in projects and activities of formation, spirituality, and service, giving them responsibility for themselves and their work, and taking care to avoid isolating them and their apostolate from the rest of the ecclesial community. Young people need to be able to see the practical relevance of their efforts to meet the real needs of people, especially the poor and neglected. They should also be able to see that their apostolate belongs fully to the Church's mission in the world.[28]

Members of the faith community are invited to reach out to the young people in their midst. Invite them into a deeper relationship with God and the parish community, support them through prayer, and celebrate who they are and what they are becoming.

The attraction of popular culture is strong. Young people are bombarded daily with promises of happiness, success, material goods, and recognition—if only they would buy this article of clothing, behave this way, or spend time with this type of person. Whose voice is getting the attention of the young? To whom are they listening? In the absence of hearing and experiencing and being challenged by the Good News of Jesus, young people will be drawn to what is available. Ministry leaders—adults who care about young people—must provide an alternate voice.

Youth hunger for God and the promise of eternal life. They may not be able to articulate this hunger, but young people are searching for something more— relationships, intimacy, a connection with the divine. They are searching for meaning *in* their life and *for* their life. In his 2004 message to young people on the occasion of the 19th World Youth Day, John Paul II said

> My dear young people, I want you too to imitate those "Greeks" who spoke to Philip, moved by a desire to "see Jesus." May your search be motivated not simply by intellectual curiosity, though that too is something positive, but be stimulated above all by an inner urge to find the answer to the question about the meaning of your life. Like the rich young man in the Gospel, you too should go in search of Jesus to ask him: "What must I do to inherit eternal life?" (Mk 10:17).[29]

Help youth in their hungers. Know them and understand what they are going through. Seek a developmental perspective in ministry work with young people as an important step to understanding the broader vision of youth ministry. Youth ministry is not just for an individual young person, or just for the Church; it is for the world. Understanding young people and the developmental process of adolescence means that youth ministry's three goals in *Renewing the Vision*—empowering young disciples, calling youth to participation in the faith community, and promoting the spiritual and personal growth of adolescents—can become a reality!

— RECOMMENDED RESOURCES —

Bradley, Michael C. *Yes, Your Teen Is Crazy: Loving Your Kid Without Losing Your Mind*. Gig Harbor, WA: Harbor Press, 2002.

Clark, Chap, and Kara Powell. *Deep Ministry in a Shallow World: Not-So-Secret Findings about Youth Ministry*. Grand Rapids, MI: Zondervan/Youth Specialties, 2006.

Clark, Chap. *Hurt: Inside the World of Today's Teenagers*. Grand Rapids, MI: Baker Publishing Group, 2004.

Clark, Chap, and Dee Clark. *Disconnected: Parenting Teens in a MySpace World*. Grand Rapids, MI: Baker Publishing Group, 2007.

Clark, Chap, Kenda Creasy Dean, Dave Rahn (eds.). "The Changing Face of Adolescence: A Theological View of Human Development" in *Starting Right*. Grand Rapids, MI: Zondervan Publishing, 2001, pp. 41-61.

Kehrwald, Leif. *Youth Ministry and Parents*. Winona, MN: Saint Mary's Press, 2004.

Kelcourse, Felicity B. (ed.). *Human Development and Faith: Life-Cycle States of Body, Mind, and Soul*. St. Louis, MO: Chalice Press, 2004.

National Institute of Mental Health. "Teenage Brain: A Work in Progress." http://www.nimh.nih.gov/health/publications/teenage-brain-a-work-in-progress.shtml.

Renewing the Vision: A Framework for Catholic Youth Ministry. Washington, DC: United States Conference of Catholic Bishops, 1997.

Search Institute. Minneapolis. www.search-institute.org

Smith, Timothy. *The Seven Cries of Today's Teens*. Brentwood, TN: Integrity Publishers, 2003.

Sweet, Leonard. *Post-Modern Pilgrims: First Century Passion for the 21st-Century World*. Nashville: Broadman & Holman, 2000.

Sweet, Leonard. *Soul Tsunami: Sink or Swim in New Millennium Culture*. Grand Rapids, MI: Zondervan, 1999.

Sylwester, Robert. *The Adolescent Brain: Reaching for Autonomy.* Thousand Oaks, CA: Corwin Press, 2007.

Tapscott, Don. *Growing Up Digital: The Rise of the Net Generation.* New York: McGraw-Hill, 1998.

Walsh, David. *Why Do They Act That Way? A Survival Guide to the Adolescent Brain for You and Your Teen.* New York: Simon and Schuster (Free Press), 2004.

— ENDNOTES —

1. *Renewing the Vision: A Framework for Catholic Youth Ministry.* Washington, DC: United States Conferences of Catholic Bishops, 1997, p. 15.

2. Dean, Kenda Creasy, Chap Clark, and Dave Rahn (eds). *Starting Right: Thinking Theologically about Youth Ministry.* Grand Rapids, MI: Zondervan Publishing, 2001, p. 44.

3. Santrock, J.W. *Adolescence,* 4th ed. Dubuque: William C. Brown, 1990, p. 29.

4. *Starting Right,* p. 45.

5. ibid., p. 46.

6. ibid., p. 47.

7. ibid., p. 55.

8. From "Adolescent Brains are Works in Progress—Here's Why" by FRONTLINE Producer Sarah Spinks. http://www.pbs.org/wgbh/pages/frontline/shows/teen-brain/works/adolescent.html

9. From an interview conducted by Brad Griffin of Fuller Youth Institute with Dr. Kelly Schwartz, adolescent psychology specialist. http://fulleryouthinstitute.org/2008/05/kelly-schwartz-interview/

10. Roberto, John, and Michael Moseley, "Adolescents Today" in *YouthWorks.* Naugatuck, CT: Center for Ministry Development, 1994, revised 1998, p. 12.

11. *Renewing the Vision,* p. 55.

12. Search Institute. www.search-institute.org

13. Tapscott, Don. *Growing Up Digital: The Rise of the Net Generation.* New York: McGraw-Hill, 1998, p. 9.

14. Mercadante, Frank. "The Millennial Generation, Postmodernism, and the Changing Face of Catholic Youth Ministry." *Youth Ministry Access.* Naugatuck, CT: Center for Ministry Development, 2008, p. 10.

15. Sweet, Leonard. *Soul Tsunami: Sink or Swim in New Millennium Culture.* Grand Rapids, MI: Zondervan, 1999, pp. 17-18.

16. Sweet, Leonard. *Post-Modern Pilgrims: First Century Passion for the 21st-Century World.* Nashville: Broadman & Holman, 2000, p. 28.

17. ibid., p. 33.

18. ibid., p. 56.

19. ibid., p. 60.

20. ibid., p. 86.

21. ibid., p. 112.

22. *Soul Tsunami*, p. 221.

23. *Post-Modern Pilgrims*, p. 113.

24. *Soul Tsunami*, pp. 53-54.

25. *Growing Up Digital*, pp. 142-48.

26. *Starting Right*, p. 49.

27. Pope John Paul II. *Message to the Youth of the World on the Occasion of the 20th World Youth Day*, #7, August 6, 2004.

28. RTV, p. 9, citing John Paul II, *Listen to the True Word of Life*, 1993.

29. John Paul II. *Message to the Youth of the World on the Occasion of the 19th World Youth Day*, #2.

CHAPTER FOUR

Ministry with Youth in a Culturally Diverse Church

Alejandro Aguilera-Titus

Editor's Note

Church leaders and guiding documents direct us to respond to the cultural diversity in our communities and provide an ecclesial home for all young people. To do this, we need to understand and learn from the leaders and communities who are leading the way. Alejandro Aguilera-Titus guides us from the history of diversity in the United States through the journey that leads to the empowerment and inclusion of all young people. This chapter is longer than the others because of the many perspectives, voices, and resources that are here to help us get started.

In the United States today, adolescents grow up in an unprecedented culturally diverse society. Such diversity is even more present in the Church: new waves of Catholic immigrants—representing many races, languages, and cultures—live and celebrate their faith under one roof and share the same spiritual home with post-immigrant Catholic communities in parishes across the country.

American Catholics today number more than sixty-five million and most live in culturally diverse parishes. In youth ministry, "The perceived image of the United States has shifted from a melting pot to a multihued tapestry."[1] The images of a "pizza supreme," a salad, or even a stew also illustrate this shift in cultural differences as a gift that enriches the whole in transforming and unifying ways. On the other hand, the temptation

→ **Making the Connection**

Ministry with youth from diverse cultures begins by reflecting on the God-given gifts of each community.

- *What is a gift that you admire in a culture other than your own?*
- *How did you come to know of this gift?*

to expect adolescents from different cultural backgrounds to simply assimilate into a one-size-fits-all program, group, or activity continues to linger in a number of parishes.

God-given human diversity challenges all Catholics to achieve ecclesial integration—to discover ways in which Catholic communities can be one Church, yet come from diverse cultures and ethnicities.[2] Keenly aware of this challenge, the bishops of the United States have called upon all Catholics to recognize and celebrate cultural and ethnic diversity as a gift from God.

In a statement titled *Many Members, One Body* (1994), the bishops of the Diocese of Galveston-Houston wrote,

Faithful to the teachings of Jesus Christ, the Church affirms the dignity of everyone and presents the diversity of races, cultures and languages as a gift from God, not as a problem.[3]

At the convocation of the *Encuentro 2000* national event celebrated in Los Angeles, the bishops spoke of the need to acknowledge and embrace the cultural, ethnic, and linguistic diversity and God's unique presence in each other's lives, histories, and cultures.[4] This two-fold commitment to unity in diversity is highlighted in various pastoral statements, marking the beginning of the twenty-first century. The common thread in all of them is a call for a ministry that requires the commitment to welcome and foster the specific cultural identity of each the many faces in the Church, while building a profoundly Catholic identity that strengthens the unity of the one body of Christ.[5]

In *Renewing the Vision* this call emphasizes the need to focus on a "specialized ministry" to, with, and from youth of "particular racial and ethnic cultures" and, at the same time, promote mutual "awareness and unity" among all young people.[6]

This chapter offers ministry leaders insights, pastoral principles, and practical recommendations to help them achieve unity in diversity among all Catholic young people in their parishes. The first part of the chapter provides a historical understanding of how parish models have emerged to respond to the needs and aspirations of different cultural and ethnic groups. The second part explores concepts in pastoral theology and pastoral approaches that have shaped youth ministry, such as ecclesial integration, inculturation, multicultural ministry, and intercultural ministry. The third part includes pastoral principles and practices for an effective intercultural youth ministry. It also proposes a developmental understanding of youth ministry based on nine practical steps that build a solid Catholic identity amid culturally diverse parish communities.

PART I: Understanding Cultural Diversity in the Parish Context

A Glance at the Diverse Catholic Experience

Looking at the experience of previous generations of Catholics and at parish development in response to particular needs and aspirations is helpful to discern the best ways of achieving true ecclesial integration that shares unity in diversity for today and in the future. Such ecclesial integration is of particular importance among adolescents as they face the generational challenge of building the Church of tomorrow by renewing the Church today.

Immigration is not new to the Catholic experience in the United States. In fact, immigration is the beginning and the historical context of the Catholic Church in the United States. Ecclesial integration is a fundamental principle of its growth. The right of people to migrate to support themselves and their families is strongly defended by the Church. This right is deeply rooted in the history of the United States as a country of immigrants.[7]

When the massive European Catholic immigrations took place in the late 1800s and early 1900s, the Church allowed the establishment of national parishes in many dioceses to welcome them. Such a model of ecclesial integration provided these communities with the ecclesial space they needed to live their faith, to pray, and to worship in the context of their own culture, language, and traditions. The viability of this model was possible because European immigrants came in great numbers, within specific times, and with their own priests. The establishment of national parishes was instrumental in helping new immigrants adapt to life in the United States from a position of strength. Catholic schools in these faith communities were started to provide Catholic children a familiar environment for learning and to keep them from being sucked into a culture often times unwelcoming of Catholic immigrants.

African American Catholics also had their own ecclesial spaces in parishes established for Black Catholics, or they gathered in the basement of existing parishes. However, coming from an experience of slavery and imposed segregation, these faith communities were less a national parish model than a way of separating Black Catholics from mainstream life and culture. While national parishes for Italians, Poles, Germans, and other European immigrants were located just blocks from each other, parishes for Black American Catholics were located in Black neighborhoods and depended on clergy of European descent, since Blacks were not allowed in seminaries at the time.

Despite these limitations, Black Catholics developed their own sense of cultural identity and belonging to the Church. In fact, African American Catholics still take pride in the story of how they remained faithful to the Church despite overt and covert racism.

The Native American Catholic experience was similar to that of Black Catholics. Native Americans had their own parishes—within the confines of their reservations—and depended on religious priests of European American descent for their sacramental needs, which made it difficult for the natives to develop native ministers and ministries.

Early immigration from Asia was primarily from China. In the mid to late 1800s, laborers were enlisted to help build the railroads, primarily in the western states. Few of the early Asian immigrants were Catholic. Today there are significant Chinese Catholic communities in San Francisco and Los Angeles who can trace their roots to these first immigrants.

The case of the Hispanic American Catholic community was quite different. After the annexation of the southwestern states, Mexican Americans were expected to assimilate into the new reality; they did not, therefore, benefit from the national parish model. Hispanic Americans did not bring their priests with them, which made it even more difficult to have the ecclesial space needed to live the faith, to pray, and to worship in the context of their own culture, language, and traditions.

The same expectation to assimilate was placed on subsequent generations of new immigrants from Mexico and other Latin American countries. In contrast with the European new immigrant experience, Hispanic Americans had a long-standing presence and a steady and robust immigration flow, which continues to the present and into the foreseeable future.

The New Waves of Catholic Immigrants

At the conclusion of World War II, a big push for cultural assimilation took hold in a diverse nation seeking a new sense of unity. Within the Church, the national parish model was phased out as immigration from Europe dwindled. The European new immigrant population aged and its children moved out of ethnic neighborhoods. This exodus gave way to generations of post-immigrant Catholics—mostly of European descent—who came to constitute the bulk of what may be called mainstream Catholic Americans. The move of Blacks and other non-European immigrant groups into the old ethnic neighborhoods also motivated flight to the suburbs.

When the Civil Rights Movement started the desegregation process under the banner of social integration, African American Catholics were expected to assimilate into mainstream culture. This expectation created tension among Black Catholics, as issues of exclusion and discrimination remained clearly present. In 1979, the bishops of the United States once more denounced the problem of racism in their pastoral letter *Brothers and Sisters to Us,*

> Racism is a sin: a sin that divides the human family, blots out the image of God among specific members of that family, and violates the fundamental human dignity of those called to be children of the same Father.[8]

Even though some African American Catholics moved out of their neighborhoods and into the suburbs, most remained in their neighborhoods and parishes. Native American Catholics were even more resistant to cultural assimilation and very few ventured outside their reservations.

The 1950s and 1960s witnessed a major increase in immigration from Mexico, Puerto Rico, Cuba, and Central America. Immigrants from Mexico came under the labor agreement called the Bracero Program. Many Puerto Ricans left the island seeking better job opportunities in a time of great demand for labor in the United States. The Cuban revolution of 1959 drove thousands of Cubans—including many Catholic priests—into exile. Central Americans—especially those from Nicaragua, El Salvador, and Guatemala—began fleeing from homelands that were immersed in civil war. While the population coming from Latin American countries shared a common cultural heritage, religion, and two related languages (Spanish and Portuguese), the dramatic influx of new immigrants from Latin American countries began to challenge the assumptions that all Hispanics spoke English, and that they had already assimilated into mainstream culture.

The Vietnam War generated massive immigration from that country. The Korean War generated a significant immigration flow from Korea and other countries in Asia and the Pacific Islands, which were impacted by these wars.

The immigration experience of Vietnamese and Korean Catholics was similar to the European experience: the Asians came in significant numbers during a well-defined time span and brought their priests with them. Despite the phasing out of the national parish model, this may be why Vietnamese and Korean Catholics show a preference to gather in personal parishes that are quite similar to the national parishes of the European experience. In contrast, immigrants from the Philippines had a smaller yet steadier immigration flow. Given their cultural ties to the United States and the lack of native priests among them, Filipino immigrants were expected to assimilate into mainstream Catholic life. It is worth noting that immigrants from Asia and the Pacific Islands represent many different languages and religious traditions among themselves.[9]

The number of Catholic immigrants from Africa, Brazil, and the Caribbean has increased significantly over the past twenty years according to the Offices for Pastoral of Migrants and Refugees at the USCCB. Ministry leaders working with immigrant communities are trying to find ways to connect with these newly arrived groups. A growing number of clergy in the United States are coming from these areas.[10]

PART II: Promoting Intercultural Awareness and Understanding

The Shift from Cultural Assimilation to Ecclesial Integration

By the time the Second Vatican Council concluded in 1965, the new landscape for parish life in the United States was in place. With the national parish model behind, and the new waves of Catholic immigrants coming from Latin America, Asia, and the Pacific Islands, the territorial parish shared by culturally diverse members emerged as the new reality of the Catholic Church in the United States.

This new reality generated a shift in pastoral ministry from a policy of cultural assimilation prevalent after World War II to one of ecclesial integration. Through a policy of assimilation, the bishops said in 1987:

> New immigrants are forced to give up their language, culture, values and traditions. ... This attitude alienates new Catholic immigrants from the Church. ... By [ecclesial] integration, we mean that our Hispanic people [and Catholics from all cultures] are to be welcomed to our church institutions at all levels. They are to be served in their language when possible, and their cultural values and religious traditions are to be respected. Beyond that, we must work toward mutual enrichment through interaction among all cultures.[11]

This concept of ecclesial integration generated the emergence of Hispanic ministry and the renewal of Black Catholic ministry in the early seventies, and more recently in ministry among Asian Pacific Islanders and others in parishes across the country. Ten years later, *Renewing the Vision* echoed this call for ecclesial integration by stating that effective youth ministry should help all young people to feel comfortable and welcome so that they can "develop their identity by affirming and utilizing the values and traditions of their ethnic cultures," and the gifts and talents they offer to the entire faith community.[12]

A Missed Opportunity to Minister among Adolescents from Diverse Cultures

Ministry among adolescents found definition in 1976 when the bishops issued the pastoral statement *A Vision of Youth Ministry*. Since then, youth ministry has experienced a tremendous growth, becoming a sophisticated and professionalized ministry among mainstream Catholic adolescents. Ministries within the Black, Hispanic, Native American, and Asian and Pacific Island Catholic communities have successfully welcomed and developed ministers and ministries among adults, following an ecclesial integration model within culturally diverse parishes.

Unfortunately, adolescents from these ethnic communities only benefited marginally from the impressive growth of youth ministry or culturally specific ministries for adults. The unspoken assumption that children of new immigrants knew English, or were in the process of learning English, made the development of culturally specific catechetical programs for them quite difficult. This assumption was even more prevalent in youth ministry as adolescents from these communities were simply expected to assimilate into the existing mainstream parish youth group, programs, and activities.[13] This assumption is now questioned. A large segment of the young ethnic population outside of mainstream Catholicism has gone without appropriate pastoral attention, which is evidenced by their absence at mainstream diocesan, national youth, and young adult ministry gatherings. In the document *Encuentro and Mission: A Renewed Pastoral Framework for Hispanic Ministry*, the bishops of the United States explained why Catholic adolescents from ethnic and cultural communities had been falling through the cracks between successful youth ministry and culturally specific ministries.

In the case of Hispanic ministry, the principle of ecclesial integration versus cultural assimilation was only consistently applied to ministry with adults, leaving adolescents in a kind of cultural and ministerial limbo. In the area of youth ministry, the bishops wrote that

> The traditional [mainstream] model of parish youth ministry does not, for the most part, reach Hispanic adolescents because of economic, linguistic, cultural, age, and educational differences.[14]

The bishops noted that the majority of parish youth ministry programs served adolescents from well-established families of mostly European descent. They were part of mainstream culture, English-speaking, and middle class or upper-middle class. Many of them lived in the suburbs, were more likely to attend Catholic schools, and were college-bound. On the other hand, Hispanic adolescents were monolingual in Spanish or English, or bilingual. They could be American-born of many generations or new immigrants; working class, middle class, white, Black, or brown. Most of them went to public schools, a significant number had a low educational attainment, and fewer than twenty percent were college-bound.[15]

Such contrasting economic, linguistic, cultural, racial, and educational differences explain part of the reason why most Hispanic adolescents living in culturally diverse parishes do not participate in mainstream youth ministry. Additional factors include a lack of outreach to Hispanic families and a misunderstanding between cultures.

One area of misunderstanding is in the contrast between cultural value systems. In mainstream culture in the United States, individualism is highly valued. Youth ministry often undertakes the task of helping youth to establish their individual identity. In Hispanic culture, the individual exists as part of a community. This understanding of individual needs apart from communal affiliations is a foreign concept for Hispanic young people and their families. These values sometimes clash if youth ministry leaders believe Hispanic parents are stifling their child's emerging sense of self, or if Hispanic parents believe youth ministry leaders are encouraging disrespectful behavior and rebelliousness. These factors also help explain the emergence of alternative youth groups and apostolic movements for Hispanics and by Hispanics to fill the pastoral void created by a policy of assimilation.

A similar situation faces adolescents from Black, Native American, Asian and Pacific Islander families living in culturally diverse parishes; they often find themselves without the ecclesial space to be themselves.

Inculturation of the Gospel

In 1987, Pope John Paul II met with more than 10,000 Native Americans in Phoenix, Arizona. During the gathering, the pope encouraged Native American Catholics to "keep alive your cultures, your languages, the values and customs which have served you well in the past and which provide a solid foundation for the future." The Catholic faith, he added, can thrive in any culture. The pope spoke in response to the desire of Native Americans to "seek to follow Jesus in languages and cultures which God has given us."[16]

These words evoke the image of each culture as holy ground, for God dwells in each culture and in each person in a unique and amazing way. The words are also a clear example of what the Church understands by inculturation of the Gospel. The *General Directory for Catechesis* (GDC) says

> The Word of God became man, a concrete man, in space and time and rooted in a specific culture: "Christ by his incarnation committed himself to the particular social and cultural circumstances of the men [and women] among whom he lived." This is the original "inculturation" of the word of God and is the model of all evangelization by the Church, "called to bring the power of the Gospel into the very heart of culture and cultures."[17]

In the context of a culturally diverse parish, inculturation comprises all the riches of the different cultural and ethnic communities given to Christ as an inheritance. Inculturation is a profound process that touches every culture deeply, going to the very center and roots of each culture, taking from each what is compatible with Gospel values while seeking to purify and transform beliefs, attitudes, and actions which are contrary to the Reign of God.[18]

The challenge to inculturate the Gospel is part of the most fundamental mission of the Church—to evangelize and bring the Good News of Christ to every human situation.[19] John Paul II called for a New Evangelization that would renew the commitment of the Church, and of each believer, to denounce all things that go against the dignity of the human person, and to build a culture of life inspired by Gospel values. The New Evangelization serves as a bridge between faith and culture, proving that a faith that does not generate and transform culture is a sterile faith.[20]

The Difference between Multicultural Ministry and Intercultural Ministry

The inculturation of the Gospel involves following Jesus' example to become "Gracious hosts for one another, as we acknowledge and embrace our cultural, ethnic, and linguistic diversity and God's unique presence in each other's lives, histories, and cultures." Inculturation describes "a truly Catholic understanding" of ministry among diverse communities that focuses less on how mainstream culture looks at and relates to minority communities and more on how to have meaningful conversations and build meaningful relationships among all the culturally and racially diverse members of the parish community.[21]

This subtle and yet powerful difference can be captured in the concepts of *multicultural* ministry and *intercultural* ministry respectively. The following examples may help illustrate the differences between the two approaches.

Example A At St. Joseph's Parish, the primary expression of youth ministry is a youth group. Despite the youth group's open-door policy, the pastoral leadership is concerned with the lack of cultural and racial diversity in the parish youth group and its activities. The leadership decides to reach out to adolescents from the other two cultural groups that are present in the parish in significant numbers. The goal is to increase these adolescents' participation by having them join the youth group and participate in its activities. After a good amount of effort, a handful of adolescents join the youth group, and the leadership is grateful for the new members and the fact that the youth group is closer to becoming multicultural. However, the lack of response from the two minority communities to get involved is disappointing to them. On the other hand, the leadership from these minority communities remains distant because it feels excluded from the decision-making process.

Example B The leadership of the youth ministry in the neighboring church, St. Luke, shares the same concern and seeks to achieve the same goal of increasing the participation of adolescents from the two ethnic and cultural communities present in the parish. The youth ministry program at St. Luke is comprehensive and already allows for the convening of a variety of groups of youth around interests, ministries, and needs. To address its concern about the participation of youth, the leadership decides to meet with the leaders of the two communities to study the situation and identify the best way of reaching out to these young Catholics. After reflection and discernment, everyone decides together to develop youth groups for each one of these two communities in the context of one parish, which will be coordinated under one united but diverse youth ministry. After a few months, both of these new youth groups are bursting at the seams with adolescents, and activities between the three youth groups begin to take place in the context of an "intercultural" youth ministry. This does not discourage adolescents from joining the already-established youth community or other activities, but it gives them a choice.

The second example is representative of a pastoral approach which has proven to be successful in bringing young people from different cultural and ethnic groups into active participation in the life and mission of the Church. Anecdotal evidence shows that a growing number of parishes are welcoming adolescents from diverse cultures and successfully ministering among them in the context of their particular lived experience. Some parishes have several youth groups and many different strategies within youth ministry. Some have also developed events, activities, and programs to bring all Catholic young people together as one young and diverse Church.

Renewing the Vision affirms this effort when it says that "Ministry with adolescents creates flexible and adaptable program structures that address the changing needs and life situations of today's young people and their families within a particular community." A flexible response allows for a variety of programs, communities, and strategies, which can respond to the particular needs and aspirations of particular groups. This idea of flexible ministry responses is often described as comprehensive youth ministry.[22]

Envisioning a New Pentecost

The existence of different youth groups and apostolic movements bring parishes face to face with the contrasting realities of middle class/working class, post-immigrant/new immigrant, citizen/foreigner, mainstream white/Black, Hispanic/Latino, Native American, Asian and Pacific Islander cultures; and black/white/brown/yellow faces and realities. Bringing these very different realities to the one table of the Lord is the great challenge of building the Reign of God beginning right at home. These diverse groups and ministries are fertile ground in which to foster the total personal and spiritual growth of each Catholic adolescent. These groups are also the first step toward interaction and ecclesial integration of adolescents within culturally diverse parishes.

Interactions between culturally diverse adolescents are transformational opportunities that bear the fruits of Christian unity in the spirit of a new Pentecost. As it did two thousand years ago, the Feast of Pentecost today "offers a redeeming vision of human diversity. It is a vision of unity among peoples that goes far beyond their differences and in which all share the same human dignity."[23]

The Holy Spirit empowered the Apostles to preach to people of many nations and different languages, creating among them a new community united by the same Spirit. The communion of the Church, rooted in God's love, is called to offer all Catholic young people the sense of identity, purpose, and community they seek. Claimed by Christ and baptized into the Holy Spirit, all Catholic adolescents from all generations, immigration statuses, or social situations are full members of the Church—worthy of the love, the respect, and the support of the entire Christian community. Faced by a society that is increasingly diverse and to some extent divided, it is urgent to proclaim with joy and firm faith that through communion with Christ, Catholics enter into living communion with all believers.[24]

Learning from past pastoral experiences and reclaiming the universal roots of the Catholic faith provides youth ministry today with new opportunities to achieve unity in diversity. Building upon the openness and appreciation for diversity that is present in this generation of Catholics is the opportunity to bring together the many faces of Catholic young people in a new yet old way. "The power of the Holy Spirit and the intimate connection of the members of the faith community give unity to the body, and in this way, stimulate and produce love between the believers."[25]

PART III: Effective Ministry to, with, and from Youth of Cultural/Ethnic Communities

A Renewed Vision of Youth Ministry and Ministers among Young People

Striking a balance between the needs and aspirations of adolescents from different cultural and ethnic communities is not an easy task. Equally challenging is accepting each other's differences and confronting each case of prejudice, cultural stereotype, and expression of racism present in society even today. It is in this context that pastoral leaders working with young people ask: How can the Church provide a healthy environment and a sense of community for all adolescents in culturally diverse parishes today and in the future? According to *Renewing the Vision*, the answer to this question is not only found in "*what* we do (activity), but *who* we are (identity) and *how* we interact (relationships).[26]

The deepest of these dimensions is who the leaders are as persons and as ministers with all adolescents. Ministry involves a spirituality of discipleship and a human maturity that allows people to grow in welcoming others, embracing them, and journeying with them—leaving behind *we-they* language and moving into *all-of-us-together* language. This way of being fosters growth in respect and in love for each adolescent, "not so much the love of a teacher [or minister] as of a father, or rather of a mother. It is the Lord's wish that every preacher of the Gospel, every builder up of the Church should have this love."[27] The Church must be "the home and the school of Communion."[28]

What leaders do and teach should be rooted in their double commitment as ministers to the message of Christ and to the adolescents to whom they minister. This commitment requires solid knowledge of Christ and his message, as well as interpersonal knowledge of all adolescents in the parish, and the cultural, religious, social, and economic context in which they live. Such knowledge is born from efforts to be good listeners—sensitive and authentically interested in people's lives, needs, aspirations, and ideas. Commitment also requires an ability to relate beyond cultural boundaries, to engage in dialogue, and to promote collaboration with a constructive spirit.

How leaders do things is as important as what they do. Knowing how to communicate and relate to others—particularly to parents and young people from other cultures—is the key to building relationships and ministries. Ministers need to be effective communicators of the message of Christ among people speaking different languages. Effectiveness includes knowing how different communities make decisions, how they learn, and how they organize and come together with other groups.

Such awareness and commitment helps welcome and empower all young people to develop and exercise their leadership and contribute their unique perspectives. The youth can develop groups, activities, and program contents that are culturally appropriate and relevant to the needs and aspirations of adolescents within each culture, while affirming their sense of belonging to the universal Church and the local parish community in the spirit of unity in diversity.[29]

Pastoral Principles for Youth Ministry in Culturally Diverse Parishes

Renewing the Vision emphasizes the importance of helping young people "develop their identity by affirming and utilizing the values and traditions of their ethnic cultures."[30] The following pastoral principles stem from ministry experiences and Church teachings gathered together in a wealth of pastoral statements and published by the bishops of the United States. These principles have served parishes well in the development of ministries and ministers within cultural/ ethnic groups, and in relationship with the broader parish community.

1. Articulate a vision of youth ministry based on ecclesial integration.

- Be willing to listen to the stories, perspectives, and preferences of youth and families from the different cultures and ethnicities present in the parish.
- Build relationships of trust and respect with parents of youth from the cultural communities in the parish. Take the time to listen and be present to families prior to promoting a particular program or activity.
- Recognize and affirm cultural, linguistic, and racial differences as a gift from God, not a problem to be solved.
- Promote the right of each Catholic cultural/ethnic group to have its own space to live and practice the faith in the context of the one parish community.
- Avoid the temptation to expect others to assimilate into a one-size-fits-all youth group, program, or activity.
- Commit to achieve unity in diversity, not uniformity.

2. Foster the practice of inculturation of the Gospel in all cultures.

- Be aware of one's own cultural heritage and relate to people from other cultures with respect and appreciation of differences and commonalities.
- Use the concept of inculturation of the Gospel as a point of reference in all ministry efforts.
- Be willing to be a bridge-builder between people from other cultures rather than a gate-keeper of one's own culture.
- Avoid the tendency to see one's own culture as better or more valuable than the cultures of others; avoid we-they language.
- Commit to the spirit of mission of the New Evangelization and its ongoing transformation of all cultures by Gospel values.

3. Plan *with* people not *for* people.

- First listen and welcome the unique perspectives of the different cultural/ethnic communities in the parish.
- Include the various communities, from the beginning, in the development of plans, programs, and activities.
- Provide ministry that is "to, with, by, and for" young people from the unique cultures and ethnicities present in the parish. In *A Vision of Youth Ministry*, this type of ministry is not imposed on youth, but instead arises from relationships and empowerment of youth.[31]

- Avoid planning for others and judging them when they do not attend an activity.
- Build community in everything within each cultural/ethnic group and between all of them as one Body of Christ.

4. Broaden understanding of youth ministry groups, programs, and structures, and cast a bigger net.

- Recognize the unique lived experiences, needs, and aspirations of adolescents from each cultural/ethnic community in the parish.
- Understand the existence of more than one youth group in the parish as a blessing, and as the first step towards ecclesial integration among all of them.
- Promote the formation of culturally specific youth groups and apostolic movements for youth as effective means of evangelization and community-building.
- Avoid the perception that allowing the formation of culturally specific youth groups creates division or separation.
- Commit to creating welcoming spaces for all Catholic young people living in the parish.

5. Empower young people and adults from different cultures/ethnicities into leadership positions.

- Understand the way in which different groups view leadership, organize themselves, and make decisions.
- Identify young leaders and family members, and mentor them into ministry in their own cultural community and in the parish as a whole.
- Advocate for inclusion of young people and their families in leadership positions within youth ministry and in the parish.
- Avoid a mentality of scarcity when growth in ministry generates demands for more resources.
- Commit to the awesome mission of weaving a new diverse parish community by helping shape the leadership of Catholic young leaders today.

Pastoral Stages for Building Effective Youth Ministry in Culturally Diverse Parishes

The following pastoral stages are offered to develop intercultural youth ministry in parishes and other Catholic institutions and organizations. The three stages follow a developmental sequence, which empowers young people from different cultural and ethnic groups to a) develop a sense of belonging; b) develop intercultural relationships; and c) achieve ownership and stewardship. The three stages are grounded in nine steps that provide a roadmap for promoting ecclesial integration and active participation of young people in the life and mission of the Church. Such processes also transform youth ministry and an entire parish into missionary and evangelizing faith communities that embrace all the baptized in their God-given human diversity.

Developing a Sense of Belonging
The first three steps focus on welcoming and supporting young people in ways that strengthen their cultural identity.

1. Meet young people where they are. Catholic adolescents from different ethnic groups are very receptive when the Church, particularly other Catholic young people, reach out to them by:
   a) Visiting them with good news. This involves a missionary action of going to them in schools, neighborhoods, homes, gathering places for young people of different ethnic backgrounds, and workplaces like labor camps. Keep in mind that the vast majority of Catholic adolescents from cultural/ethnic communities have not been reached by mainstream youth ministry and are not enrolled in Catholic schools.
   b) Affirming their gifts and contributions. Affirmation involves engaging young people in dialogue, getting to know who they are, what is unique about them and their culture, and how they live, express, and celebrate their Catholic faith. Be ready to identify and affirm who they are as African Americans, Asian Americans, Latinos/Hispanic Americans, Native Americans, or Pacific Islander Americans. Do not be color-blind or culture-light, but see different colors, accents, and ways of being in a spirit of human equality and Christian fraternity.
   c) Inviting them to live their baptism in the faith community. Specifically invite them to participate in parish youth groups, and in programs and activities designed for young people.

2. Make young people feel at home. Catholic adolescents feel welcomed when they:
   a) Have room to develop their own sense of identity. This involves creating

opportunities for young people from specific cultures/ethnic communities to gather by themselves in the context of their culture, language, traditions, and lived experiences. Music, sports, cultural celebrations, religious practices, civic events, and recreational activities can vary significantly from one culture to another. Give young people the room to be and to express who they are to strengthen the sense of identity of all Catholic young people and make them feel welcome.

b) Have the ecclesial space to develop their leadership. Young people from different cultural/ethnic groups can be found in limited numbers in the mainstream youth ministry of specific parishes. Typically, they join the youth group as individuals who feel comfortable in that environment. This is good news and needs to be encouraged in every parish. However, when the number of young people from a specific cultural community is present in the parish in significant numbers, experience shows that the best way of ministering among them is to create a culturally specific youth group. In doing so, young people from different communities have the ecclesial space to strengthen their Catholic identity and organize themselves in a way that is more culturally relevant. Hundreds of such groups have been formed in parishes across the country and they generate vibrant ministries.

c) Adapt to a different culture from a position of strength. Studies show that Latino/Hispanic American young people involved in parish life and activities have a better chance to succeed educationally and economically.[32] Just as national parishes and Catholic schools helped Catholic immigrants to better adapt to life in the United States in the past, culturally specific youth groups are helping young people from new immigrant families to adapt to life in the United States today from a position of strength. Graduating from high school, receiving encouragement and support to go to college, finding a better job, and dealing with racism, poverty, and/or immigration issues are often challenges faced by young people in these youth groups.

3. Develop ministries and ministers.

a) Young people are empowered when they provide for their own ministerial needs and aspirations. It is quite different to be a recipient of ministry than to be a minister. *Renewing the Vision* emphasized the importance to develop leaders and to include young people from cultural/ethnic communities and their families on advisory councils.[33] Such goals should be pursued aggressively. However, empowerment should also include supporting ministry models and structures that, within the context of the parish and the unity of the Church, empower an entire segment of the faith community into ministry.

Many examples exist of culturally specific youth groups and apostolic movements that empower dozens of young people into inactive ministry. Such ministries can benefit hundreds of young people who would not otherwise be reached by a parish. Vocations to the priesthood and religious life, healthy marriages, and Christian maturity are the visible fruit of these youth groups and apostolic movements.

b) Young people are empowered when parish staff and leaders work with them to develop a comprehensive ministry. The leadership in culturally specific youth groups seeks the support and collaboration of parish staff, specifically the youth minister and youth ministry committee. Young leaders often need help with materials, formation, skill development, and other resources. They do not see themselves as separated from the parish. On the contrary, they want to be recognized as a parish youth group and to be included in the structure of the parish's youth ministry and the faith community as a whole.

c) "They devoted themselves to the teaching of the apostles and to the communal life, to the breaking of bread and to the prayers" (Acts 2:42). Empower youth by developing ministries in each of the four dimensions of Christian life modeled in these first Christian communities and included in the themes and components for a comprehensive ministry with adolescents. (See Acts 2:42–47.) Culturally specific youth groups and apostolic movements are privileged opportunities for ministry development. These communities welcome formation opportunities in English and/or in the native language of the young people, and seek active involvement in liturgical celebrations and prayer. Many groups and movements have a strong evangelization component and a missionary spirit to reach out to other young people. These groups see community-building as one of their most important goals and they are active advocates for young people within the parish and beyond.

Weaving a New Diverse Community

The second set of steps engages young people in intercultural relationships and in opportunities for leadership development and formation. This step also strengthens the sense of belonging to the parish community by looking at diversity as a gift and at changes generated by successful culturally specific youth ministry as a sign of growth.

4. Build relationships across cultures and ministries. Young people are willing to foster relationships across cultures and ministries by:

a) Sharing their stories, religious traditions, and cultural richness with other young people in a parish. Talking about cultural perspectives and specific issues is a powerful experience that helps overcome stereotypes by "putting a face to the race." Have experiences on spiritual reflection and formation on topics of racism, diversity, and prejudice. Promote cross-cultural communication skills and understanding.

b) Celebrating faith and life together with young people from other ministries and cultures. Participate in ethnic festivals, attend liturgy in another language. Share cultural religious feasts and traditions. Participate together at youth festivals, culturally diverse youth gatherings and conventions, service learning projects like Young Neighbors in Action, or Habitat for Humanity.

c) Networking with other youth groups and ministry efforts that may be formed among cultural/ethnic communities. Collaborate in common projects such as bicultural or multicultural liturgical celebrations and prayer opportunities. Build relationships among all young people and youth groups with a broader sense of Catholic identity and parish community. Foster the vision and the structure of one parish youth ministry with diverse youth groups, apostolic movements, and youth-oriented programs and activities.

5. Champion leadership development and formation. Young people are eager to:

a) Learn and seek opportunities for ongoing faith formation and training for ministry in English and/or in their native language. Identifying young leaders and mentoring them to achieve higher educational attainment and a solid faith formation should be a priority in youth ministry. Such formation will prepare youth to be leaders in the Church and in society.

b) Invest time, talent, and treasure in leadership development programs that are accessible and culturally relevant. Anecdotal information shows that a growing number of dioceses have staff and specific programs to assist in the formation and leadership development of young people from different cultural/ethnic and linguistic backgrounds, particularly Latinos. Young people are also eager to develop program content that is culturally appropriate and relevant to the needs of participants and to use available resources at the diocesan and parish level.

c) Be recognized and supported in their formation as full members of the parish, not only as representatives of a specific cultural group. Support involves a commitment to invest as a parish in the formation and leadership development of leaders who embody and reflect the unique ethnic characteristics of the youth groups' members or the programs' participants.

6. **View and manage crises as opportunities for growth**. Young people seek:

a) More meaningful ways to be involved in the life of the faith community. As culturally specific youth groups and ministries grow and their sense of belonging to the parish matures, expectations shift. The use of facilities, the need for more resources, and the development of specific programs or activities can be seen as too much to ask. However, if the previous five steps have been taken by the youth ministry leadership and by the parish community as a whole, the "crisis" generated by this shift in resources is viewed as a sign and an opportunity for growth that benefits the entire parish.

b) More direct support and involvement of parish staff in ministry activities. This step in the developmental process of youth ministry in culturally diverse parishes calls for parish staff to be competent culturally, to be open and able to relate to the different cultural groups, and to be a resource to them. The youth minister is not doing direct ministry in the various groups. Instead, the youth minister is a resource to the adult advisors and leadership in each one of the groups and brings them together in a well-coordinated intercultural parish youth ministry.

c) More recognition and support from the entire faith community as young Catholic leaders and full parish members. Culturally specific youth groups and apostolic movements need recognition as legitimate ministries of the parish community. The presence of the pastor and the support of the youth minister in meetings and activities of these groups strengthen the members' sense of belonging to the parish. Their presence also makes it easier for these groups and their leaders to participate at diocesan events and activities designed for young people.

Achieving Ownership and Stewardship

The third set of steps emphasizes the inclusion of young people and their families in the decision-making process of youth ministry and in the parish as a whole. Having a place at the table where decisions are made strengthens the sense of ownership and stewardship in the life and mission of the parish community.

7. Open wide the doors to the decision-making process. Young people and their families want:

a) To be recognized by parish leadership as members of the parish on equal terms. Youth also want to have structures and resources in place to generate an effective culturally specific youth ministry, not as separate structures, but as integral parts of overall youth ministry and of the parish as a whole. Ongoing consultation with leaders from cultural/ethnic communities in developing youth ministry is essential.

b) To have a place at the table where decisions are made on youth ministry among culturally diverse communities. This includes representation of young people and their families on advisory councils, the involvement of youth from different cultures on leadership teams, for young adult ministry, and in leadership positions within the parish.

c) To be an active voice on the life and direction of the faith community as a whole, and to be represented in the parish council, parish staff, and other decision-making groups within the parish and diocesan structure. Creating an intercultural youth ministry advisory council and leadership team is pivotal for the healthy development and growth of youth ministry in culturally diverse parishes and dioceses.

8. Sow and reap full ownership and stewardship. As disciples of Christ, young people from different cultures/ethnicities and their families seek:

a) To contribute time, talent, and treasure within their specific cultures and in the context of unity in diversity, which characterizes the universal Church.

b) To build a culturally diverse faith community that is their own. This understanding of cultural diversity represents a paradigm shift from being the minority group in a parish, to being members, on equal footing, of a parish that is culturally diverse.

c) To be active participants in a community of faith, in which all cultures are constantly transformed by Gospel values in order to be leaven for the reign of God in society.

9. Achieve full commitment to the life and mission of the parish. Young people and their families commit to:

a) Strengthening the unity of the parish, while honoring and embracing the diversity of each one of the cultural/ethnic groups that constitute the parish. Such commitment flows from the conviction that each culture has a piece of the Good News, which is lived and communicated through the traditions, language, ethos, cultural values, and norms of that community.

b) Being alert and ready to invite and welcome newcomers in their midst, and to providing them with the space and support they need to begin their unique journey of ecclesial integration into the one and diverse parish faith community.

c) Becoming bridge-building people by interacting and ministering with Catholics of all cultural backgrounds. Such commitment is grounded on the belief that what brings unity and strength to the Church is the Holy Spirit, not a specific culture or language. All Catholic leaders are called to go beyond their own cultures in order to become weavers of the Gospel in their culturally diverse communities.

Unity in Diversity

Adolescents in the United States today are growing up in a culturally diverse society. This reality challenges all Catholics to achieve ecclesial integration, to discover ways in which Catholic young people and communities can be one Church and yet come from diverse cultures and ethnicities.

The two-fold commitment to unity in diversity is highlighted in various pastoral statements marking the beginning of the twenty-first century. In *Renewing the Vision*, this call emphasizes the need to focus on a specialized ministry to, with, by, and for youth of particular racial and ethnic cultures and, at the same time, to promote mutual awareness and unity among all young people. To live this commitment, parishes must first take the time to know the families in their communities. Sometimes assumptions are made because of current participation. Many communities who take the time to listen and be present to youth and families from the diverse cultures within their parish experience new life as young people find the ecclesial space they need to grow in faith and to develop as members of the wider parish.

Despite the impressive development of growth of youth ministry since 1976, adolescents from ethnic communities have only benefited marginally. The unspoken assumption that they would simply assimilate into the existing mainstream parish youth group, programs, and activities proved to be incorrect. As a result, a large segment of the young diverse Catholic population has gone without appropriate pastoral attention.

On the other hand, the proliferation of culturally specific youth groups and apostolic movements within parishes is a sign of the times. Envisioning parish youth ministry as a well-coordinated network of mainstream and culturally specific youth groups and apostolic movements provides a wide enough net for a good and abundant catch.

Looking at the experience of previous generations of immigrants and the emergence of culturally specific ministries can today help point the way to the best ministering among Catholic young people from diverse cultures and ethnicities. Concepts and principles in pastoral theology and practice such as ecclesial integration, inculturation, and intercultural ministry can also provide guidance in the area of youth ministry.

The call to inculturation of the Gospel values in all cultures has direct implications for the way people relate to one another and in the way they are ministers and do ministry. Understanding that young people from each cultural/ethnic community have their own path—as individuals and as a group—empowers everyone to respect them, love them, and accompany them in their journey of faith. Understanding that the paths of all Catholic young people come together in Christ and in his vision of humanity allows everyone to be bridge-builders between them and visible signs of unity in the faith community.

Common pastoral principles and a common language in ministry development are pivotal in building an effective youth ministry that is both culturally relevant and profoundly Catholic. Knowing where one is going in ministry and having a common road map on how to get there is also essential. Moving from identity to belonging to building relationships to achieving ownership describes the journey of building up the community of faith. It is a journey that brings everyone together on equal footing and dignity. The goal is not to get there first and alone, but together and on time.

— RECOMMENDED RESOURCES —

Law, Eric. *The Wolf Shall Dwell with the Lamb*. St. Louis, MO: Chalice Press, 1993.

Law, Eric. *The Bush Was Blazing but Not Consumed*. St. Louis, MO: Chalice Press, 1996.

Law, Eric. *Inclusion: Making Room for Grace*. St. Louis, MO: Chalice Press, 2000.

Many Faces in God's House: A Catholic Vision for the Third Millennium. Washington, DC: United States Conference of Catholic Bishops, 1999, Publication #5-421. This parish guide, developed for Encuentro 2000, is an essential tool for promoting multicultural dialogue among parish members, to help everyone grow together in unity—and come to a deeper understanding of the Church's mission. The guide is divided into six three-hour sessions, providing an easy-to-follow framework for sharing experiences, reflecting on faith traditions, discussing ways of putting faith into action, and celebrating the Catholic faith as one Church.

Many Faces in God's House (video). Washington, DC: United States Conference of Catholic Bishops, 1999. This colorful and inspiring video leads viewers on a journey of discovery to the many hidden riches present within our culturally diverse communities. In on-camera interviews, parish, diocesan, and national leaders share their insights on how to bring unity out of diversity, rejoicing in our different languages and cultures yet proclaiming the same faith and one reign of God.

Pope John Paul II. *The Church in America (Ecclesia in America)*, 1999. Available through the Vatican Web site: http://www.vatican.va/holy_father/john_paul_ii/apost_exhortations/documents/hf_jp-ii_exh_22011999_ecclesia-in-america_en.html (accessed September 23, 2008). Beginning with a brief history of the events leading up to the 1997 Synod, Pope John Paul II encourages the faithful in America to experience the Lord anew. Genuine personal encounters will bring forth a renewal of the Church, for "the encounter with the living Jesus Christ is the path to conversion, communion, and solidarity."

Toward a Pastoral Approach to Culture. Pontifical Council for Culture, 1999. Available through the Vatican Web site: http://www.vatican.va/roman_curia/pontifical_councils/cultr/documents/rc_pc_pc-cultr_doc_03061999_pastoral_en.html (accessed September 23, 2008). The Pontifical Council for Culture outlines proposals for evangelization.

African American Ministry

Brothers and Sisters to Us/Nuestros Hermanos y Hermanas. Washington, DC: United States Conference of Catholic Bishops, 1979, Publication #653-0. This landmark pastoral letter promotes discussion and action against racism, "an evil which endures in our society and in our Church." The English/Spanish edition also includes *For the Love of One Another: A Special Message on the Occasion of the Tenth Anniversary of "Brothers and Sisters to Us."*

Families: Black and Catholic, Catholic and Black. Washington, DC: United States Conference of Catholic Bishops, 1985. Readings, resources, and family activities that capture the vitality of the African American Catholic community through poetry, music, and the recounting of family activities.

Keep Your Hand on the Plow: The African American Presence in the Catholic Church. Washington, DC: United States Conference of Catholic Bishops, 1996. This is a practical resource about the African American Catholic experience in the United States. Authors include the Rev. Cyprian Davis, OSB, and Bishop Curtis Guillory, SVD.

Many Rains Ago: A Historical and Theological Reflection on the Role of the Episcopate in the Evangelization of African American Catholics. Washington, DC: United States Conference of Catholic Bishops, 1990. Contains three reflections that commemorate the history and struggle of African American Catholics in the United States.

Reconciled through Christ: On Reconciliation and Greater Collaboration Between Hispanic American Catholics and African American Catholics. Washington, DC: United States Conference of Catholic Bishops. Explores the common challenges of these groups and seeks mutual reconciliation in the areas of race and language. Bilingual edition.

Asian/Pacific Ministry

Asian and Pacific Presence: Harmony in Faith. Washington, DC: United States Conference of Catholic Bishops, 2001. The Church in the United States is a Church of many races and cultures. And as this moving pastoral statement presents, the rapidly growing Asian and Pacific American communities have helped the Church shine as a sacrament of unity and universality. The work celebrates their contributions, reflects on their particular pastoral needs, and suggests helpful approaches for all to build toward a common future. Available in English, Spanish, Chinese (Mandarin) and Vietnamese.

Heras, Patricia. *Silent Sacrifices: Voices of the Filipino-American Family* (video), 2001. Available through Asian American Media: http://distribution.asianamericanmedia.org/browse/film/?i=187. A documentary directed and produced by Patricia Heras. Powerful interviews with teens, young adults, and parents about challenges of growing up/nurturing Filipino-Americans. Product of a study by Patricia Heras.

Oblate Media and Communication: Harmony in Faith (video), 2005. Available through Oblate Media and Communication: http://videoswithvalues.org/family/harmony.html. A sweeping exploration of the Asian and Pacific presence in the United States. One short segment is of Korean young adults and their struggles as second-generation, English-speaking Catholics.

Rejoicing in the Asian and Pacific Presence: Excerpts and Discussion Guide. Washington, DC: United States Conference of Catholic Bishops, 2001. Using highlights from *Asian and Pacific Presence: Harmony in Faith*, this brochure includes discussion questions that can be used during staff or council meetings, days of reflection, small faith-sharing gatherings, or retreats.

Hispanic Ministry

Cervantes, Carmen. *Prophets of Hope, Volume 1: Hispanic Young People and the Church's Response*. Winona, MN: Saint Mary's Press, 1994.

Cervantes, Carmen. *Prophets of Hope, Volume 2: Evangelization of Hispanic Young People*. Winona, MN: Saint Mary's Press, 1995.

Encuentro & Mission: A Renewed Pastoral Framework for Hispanic Ministry. Washington, DC: United States Conference of Catholic Bishops, 2002. The Hispanic presence in the Church in America has grown considerably in recent decades. In this pastoral statement, the bishops set forth the basic principles, priorities, and suggested actions for developing a truly effective ministry among Hispanics.

The Hispanic Presence in the New Evangelization in the United States/La Presencia Hispana en la Nueva Evangelización en los Estados Unidos. Washington, DC: United States Conference of Catholic Bishops, 1996, #460-0. In commemoration of the fiftieth anniversary of the establishment of a national office for ministry to Hispanics in this country, the bishops issued this publication on the Hispanic presence and the relationship between faith and culture.

Migrants and Refugees

Strangers No Longer: Together on the Journey of Hope. Washington, DC: United States Conference of Catholic Bishops, 2003. In this historic statement, the bishops of the United States and Mexico join together to examine the impact of migration on the social, political, and spiritual lives of both countries. Encouraged by the Holy Father's call for a new evangelization and greater unity between Catholics in this hemisphere, the bishops offer detailed guidance for all who minister to migrants—and concrete steps for improving pastoral experiences. The statement also offers policy recommendations to both nations that respect the dignity of the migrant.

Welcoming the Stranger Among Us: Unity in Diversity—A Statement of the U.S. Catholic Bishops. Washington, DC: United States Conference of Catholic Bishops, 2000. Designed for both ordained and lay ministers at the diocesan and parish levels, this document challenges us to prepare to receive newcomers with a genuine spirit of welcome that provides a bridge for them to cross from one culture into another. Sidebars interspersed throughout the text provide examples of successful programs throughout this country.

Welcoming the Stranger Parish Guide. Washington, DC: United States Conference of Catholic Bishops, 2000. The resources in this parish guide offer practical guidance for building more welcoming and inclusive parishes. Contains copies of published documents and related resources that can be photocopied and distributed to small groups and in other community settings.

— ENDNOTES —

1. *Renewing the Vision: A Framework for Catholic Youth Ministry.* Washington, DC: United States Conference of Catholic Bishops, 1997, p. 22.

2. *Many Faces in God's House: A Catholic Vision for the Third Millennium.* Washington, DC: United States Conference of Catholic Bishops, 1999, p. 4.

3. *Many Members, One Body.* Diocese of Galveston-Houston, 1994, p. 4

4. *Many Faces in God's House,* p. 2.

5. *Encuentro and Mission: A Renewed Pastoral Framework for Hispanic Ministry.* Washington, DC: United States Conference of Catholic Bishops, 2002, #12.

6. RTV, p. 22.

7. *Strangers No Longer: Together on the Journey of Hope.* Washington, DC: United States Conference of Catholic Bishops–Conferencia del Episcopado Mexicano, 2003, #34.

8. *Brothers and Sisters to Us.* Washington, DC: United States Conference of Catholic Bishops, 1979, p. 3.

9. *Asian and Pacific Presence: Harmony in Faith.* Washington, DC: United States Conference of Catholic Bishops, 2001, p. 5.

10. *Priest Personnel Profile and Pastoral Practices Questionnaire.* Washington, DC: Center for Applied Research in the Apostolate, July 1999, p. 12.

11. *National Pastoral Plan for Hispanic Ministry* (1988) in *Hispanic Ministry: Three Major Documents.* Washington, DC: United States Conference of Catholic Bishops, 1995, #4.

12. RTV, p. 23.

13. *Encuentro and Mission,* p. 70.

14. ibid.

15. ibid.

16. See Pope John Paul II, *Memories to Cherish.* St. Anthony Messenger. http://www.americancatholic.org/Features/JohnPaulII/6-USA-1987.asp (accessed September 23, 2008).

17. Congregation for the Clergy. *General Directory for Catechesis* (Washington, DC: United States Conference of Catholic Bishops–Libreria Editrice Vaticana, 1998), #109.

18. See GDC, #109.

19. *Go and Make Disciples*. Washington, DC: United States Conference of Catholic Bishops, 2002, p. 3.

20. *The Hispanic Presence in the New Evangelization in the United States*. Washington, DC: United States Conference of Catholic Bishops, 1996, p. 16.

21. *Many Faces*, p. 5.

22. RTV, p. 23.

23. *Many Faces*, p. 9.

24. Pope John Paul II. *The Church in America (Ecclesia in America)*. Washington, DC: United States Conference of Catholic Bishops–Libreria Editrice Vaticana, 1999), #33.

25. *On the Coming of the Third Millennium: Tertio Millennio Adveniente*. Washington, DC: United States Conference of Catholic Bishops, 1994, #45.

26. RTV, p. 34.

27. GDC, #239.

28. John Paul II. *To the Bishops, Clergy, and Lay Faithful at the Close of the Great Jubilee of the Year 2000 (Novo Millennio Ineunte)*. Rome: January 2001, #43.

29. See RTV, p. 25.

30. RTV, p. 23.

31. *A Vision of Youth Ministry*. Washington, DC: United States Conference of Catholic Bishops, 1976, pp. 6-7.

32. Hernández, Edwin, and Karen Boyd. *The State of Education Among Latino Youth in the United States*. University of Notre Dame, 2004.

33. See RTV, p. 23.

CHAPTER FIVE

Models for Effective Youth Ministry

Thomas East

Editor's Note

In this chapter, you will meet parish communities who are living the vision for Catholic youth ministry by developing eight elements that provide a variety of ways for youth and families to engage in a comprehensive approach to youth ministry. These communities are very different from each other and they each put these elements together in different ways in vibrant, engaging ministries.

How do parishes with effective youth ministry put it all together? *Renewing the Vision: A Framework for Catholic Youth Ministry* provides direction for youth ministry but does not provide one model of youth ministry that every parish should implement. Instead, parishes are encouraged to develop ministry that matches the needs and gifts of their community: "By offering this framework, we seek to provide direction to the Church's ministry and to affirm and encourage local creativity."[1] Parishes throughout the United States share a common faith and pattern for worship, but the rest of parish life is shaped by the history, context, and people of the community. Youth ministry in parishes will reflect this same diversity. There just is not one model for youth ministry that matches every parish.

Though there is not one model, there are patterns in common among parishes identified as having effective youth ministry. Two recent studies on youth ministry and faith formation came to the same conclusion in their overall finding: the life of the parish or congregation itself is the heart of faith formation for adolescents and their families.

In the *Spirit of Youth Ministry Project*, the key finding for effective faith formation of adolescents is described as "The Culture or Spirit of the Congregation":

> A "culture" seems to emerge with its pervasive and distinct "spirit" and "atmosphere" that is more powerful than its component parts. It's the combination of the core values, people, relationships, expectations, practices, and activities that seems to generate this spirit and atmosphere.[2]

These communities form youth through the life and the lived theology of the parish that is expressed through the preaching, service life, community life, and other aspects of the congregation. Families are supported in sharing faith, and youth are gathered for youth ministry activities and programs. But the heart of formation is the life of the congregation itself.

In *Effective Practices for Dynamic Youth Ministry*, this is described as becoming a "willing parish." These parishes are willing to fully engage youth within the community and surround youth with love, care, support, and challenge. In these parishes, the community is willing to entertain the change that happens when young people are involved. They embrace the energy, the questions, and the new ideas. These parishes welcome young people as full members and provide support for youth ministry. The staff and members of these communities understand youth ministry and fully expect that youth will be integrated within parish life in addition to having specific ministries available for youth and their peers.

This approach addresses one of the key weaknesses of youth ministry today: gathering youth as a youth community or youth group sometimes creates a parallel congregation. In their book, *The Godbearing Life*, Kenda Creasy Dean and Dean Foster describe this phenomenon. They describe this approach as a "One-eared Mickey Mouse model of youth ministry."[3] In the diagram you see that the youth community is next to the rest of the community but they are not really part of the larger parish. After many years of belonging to a youth group, sometimes youth have no sense of identification with the rest of the faith community. During these years, youth will have participated in separate youth service, faith learning, prayer, and worship. In many cases the ministry they experience is not connected to what the parish is experiencing at all. The young people are used to having ministry that is completely designed around their needs and interests and are often not ready to belong to a parish community that requires a sense of give and take. In one parish, the youth minister was trying to evaluate youth ministry. As she asked the young people what was going well and what needed to improve, one the youth mentioned that they were invited to be part of the parish's liturgical ministries and the adults were mean to them. The youth minister replied that this had nothing to do with youth ministry. She wanted to evaluate what was happening Sunday nights at youth group and Thursday nights for the leadership meetings. As youth minister, she really didn't have anything to do with liturgy. This story exemplifies the parallel congregation dilemma. Young people experience youth ministry as everything that happens at the parish, which is how *Renewing the Vision* describes Catholic youth ministry. Sometimes, youth ministry leaders envision the ministry in a narrow way, and this can limit the effectiveness of youth ministry in helping youth to identify with the larger parish community. As Catholics, our lives of discipleship are nourished by Eucharist, which is shared in the context of a parish as the local expression of Church. We want youth to learn how to belong to a parish and to fall in love with being part of a community that is fed by Eucharist and sent into mission. We want youth to be part of a parish community for life. This kind of identification with parish happens when youth ministry is both a gathering of youth with peers and the inclusion of youth throughout parish life.

In addition to the reliance on parish life, another common practice among parishes is a pattern of responsiveness: parish leaders know young people and become aware of their needs. Knowing youth leads to finding ways to care for them, include them in parish life, and provide responsive programs and strategies. Parish communities love the youth in their midst by including them and by providing innovative responses to their needs. There are structures that hold these initiatives together.[4] These are other common patterns that emerge from the research:

- Ministry with youth includes intentional involvement of youth in parish life as well as gatherings of youth with their peers.
- Ministry in these parishes is comprehensive; parishes do not overly rely on a "youth group only" model for providing youth ministry. Though there is often an identified youth community in the parish, youth ministry includes diverse ways for youth and their families to be involved and connected.
- The goals and components of youth ministry are provided for youth and their families through varied ways. These methods can be summarized by eight elements. The first four of these elements describe formats for gathering with youth. The last four describe connections that the parish can make.

Comprehensive Youth Ministry

Parishes with effective youth ministry provide ministry with youth that is comprehensive. This is how comprehensive youth ministry is described in *Renewing the Vision*:

> Ministry with adolescents creates flexible and adaptable program structures that address the changing needs and life situations of today's young people and their families within a particular community.[5]

There are a variety of settings and methods for reaching adolescents. These possibilities are numerous and rich with potential. Unfortunately, sometimes this variety can seem overwhelming. It is important to remember that this list is not a checklist that requires parishes to provide one of each. The role of variety in youth ministry is not intended to overwhelm leaders or parish resources. Having a variety of methods and settings means we have more ways to reach and include youth. Relying on one or two key methods is like trying to play piano using only a few of the keys. Taking advantage of all of our resources and using a variety of strategies is like playing on the whole keyboard. Youth have different needs and different starting points. Variety creates ways that youth and their families can connect and be part of the parish.

 Making the Connection

In one of the research projects explored in this chapter, parish leaders were asked this question:

What are the features or characteristics of a thriving youth ministry?

From your experience and study, how would you answer?

Youth ministry is effective when it takes these differences into account and allows young people to participate according to their interest and availability. For instance, a youth who is attending a Catholic high school may be less interested in the catechetical elements of youth ministry that might repeat the formation provided by the school. He or she might be more interested in the service programming. A young person who is already part of an intense extra-curricular involvement, like band or sports, might be less interested in the community-building events and more interested in retreats and faith-learning. A youth who is new to the area might want to take time before joining leadership projects but could appreciate having a way to meet new friends as part of a youth community.

A further benefit of varied offerings in youth ministry is that youth are more likely to be available. It is not possible to pick one time in every week that every youth is available—there are too many competing commitments in young people's lives. By having varied ways to be involved and a variety of scheduling options, every youth in the parish can find a way to participate. Youth participate according to the agenda of their heart in choosing their involvements. In this way, they are being formed for adult participation in a parish that relies upon many different ministries, service groups, and learning events.

Parishes with comprehensive youth ministry provide a variety of ministries with different levels of involvement. In each aspect of the ministry, youth are encouraged to try new involvements and to participate in youth gatherings and other parts of parish life. Comprehensive does not mean overwhelming. It does mean that youth can choose different ways to be involved and different levels of involvement. Youth can move from one involvement to another easily. Through the variety in this system, youth can find a doorway into ministry and a path for continued growth.

Group ministry has a different set of assumptions. In a parish that focuses all of its youth ministry hopes on one youth group or program, youth ministry becomes identified with that one program.

Group Ministry[6]
Group ministry begins with a group and asks people to join.

Assumes:
- that all youth needs are similar
- that all youth like to join groups
- that all youth are available at the same time
- that one or a few adults can meet the needs of the group

Comprehensive Youth Ministry[7]
Comprehensive youth ministry begins with the life of the parish and a team of adults and youth formed for ministry.

Leaders provide for a variety of ways for youth to experience ministry
- Peer gatherings
- Involvement in parish life
- Non-gathered strategies
- Family strategies

Assumes:
- that youth have different needs
- that youth like to choose how to be involved
- that youth have hectic schedules
- that youth benefit from having a variety of adults to relate to
- that many people doing a little can get a lot accomplished
- doing a little can get a lot accomplished

Comprehensive youth ministry has a different starting point and works from different assumptions. With a comprehensive approach, a leadership team begins with looking at the life of the parish and identifies ways to connect youth to parish programs and involvements. This team then identifies programs and strategies that respond to youth and promote the goals of youth ministry. This can include strategies that support families of youth. It can also include a youth community or youth group. The key difference is that one single community is not expected to fulfill all of the hoped-for outcomes of youth ministry.

Eight Elements for Dynamic Youth Ministry

Parishes with effective youth ministry develop their ministry approach using eight common elements. These elements address the goals and include the components of youth ministry. Four of these elements are formats for gathering with youth. The remaining four are connections that parishes make to young people, their families, the parish and leadership, ministry, or service roles.[8]

Formats for Gathering

The following four formats were included in the various models developed by parishes with dynamic youth ministry.

A pattern for gathering with youth on a regular basis This method of gathering with youth is often called a youth group, a youth community, or "youth night." These gatherings can be weekly, bi-weekly, or monthly. Youth and their families can count on these regularly scheduled gatherings, which work to foster a community of youth. This consistency is important because families can support this involvement and build this into the pattern for family life. These gatherings can also be a great way for youth who are new to the community to get to know youth ministry. The gatherings typically include community building, faith learning that promotes personal and spiritual growth, prayer, and informal time. Many of the components for youth ministry are addressed and included within the variety offered in these regular gatherings.

Special events and ways to gather with youth This format includes all of the gatherings that go beyond the regularly scheduled events. These events can last a few hours, a whole day, a weekend, a week, or longer. This would include social events such as a movie night, a ski-trip, or a trip to the amusement park. This also includes retreats, service experiences, trips, and participation in conferences. Day-long programs, weekend retreats, or multi-week series can address the needs of various components. These special events round out the youth ministry program and draw youth to participate in "niche" programs that appeal to varied interests. Because of the potential for extended contact time, there is a rich opportunity for deeper experiences of community.

Intentional methods for providing adolescent catechesis and faith learning Adolescent catechesis was found to be at the heart of youth ministry in parishes with effective youth ministry. These efforts included the informal teachable moments that occur when leaders and peers help connect faith to life in the midst of an experience or in response to a question that is raised. In these parishes, there were also intentional and systematic efforts to provide catechesis within youth ministry.

This occurred in three methods. In some parishes, catechesis and faith learning were infused throughout youth ministry and through youth involvement in parish life. Catechesis was part of the ongoing youth community; it was part of the way that youth were prepared for sacraments; and it was part of the way that youth were prepared for service experiences and leadership roles.

In other parishes, the systematic catechesis was provided primarily through youth participation in intergenerational faith formation events and programs provided for the whole parish community. In these communities, faith formation was provided in a multi-year curriculum that included all age groups. Some learning events included a time for the whole community to gather, learn, and pray. There was also time for age-specific groups to focus on the topic and report back to the larger community.

The third method employed by parishes in providing intentional catechesis was through distinctive religious education and sacramental preparation events. Some of these communities provided religious education in graded levels, while others provided faith sharing series and retreats that focused on catechetical topics. In all three methods, there was an emphasis on developing adolescent catechesis collaboratively among parish staff and leaders. The key to success seemed to be the intentional efforts to plan for catechesis and bring a variety of resources together.

Opportunities for youth who want to grow deeper in faith This last format focuses upon youth who are looking for ways to learn and grow in their faith in a deeper way. One of the things that we heard from youth in the interviews was their frustration when they want to learn and other youth's behavior distracts them from getting the most out of the program. By having niche programs, parishes avoid the "one size fits all" approach and allow youth who are more serious to find ways to continue their growth as young disciples. These smaller groups are often called "discipleship" groups in Protestant denominations. These niche programs also appeal to youth with different interests and levels of maturity. These are especially important for addressing the needs of juniors and seniors in high school, who sometimes do not relate to those faith learning experiences that are more geared to freshmen and sophomores. Sometimes these opportunities for deeper growth are focused on catechesis. In other cases, catechesis is combined with other components. Examples include: a six-week program designed to help older youth learn prayer forms and experience spiritual direction; a series designed to teach youth about justice, service, and advocacy; or a special program designed to teach youth to evangelize their peers.

You can see how these four formats can include a variety of the components. Community life and leadership development are often nurtured through the ongoing pattern of gathering and special events. Evangelization and catechesis occur throughout the formats. Prayer and worship is included in nearly every gathering.

Four Ways to Connect Youth to Ministry

When we think of youth ministry, we most commonly think of the big gatherings and the energy that happens when you get youth together. Gatherings are important, but ministry with youth also happens through a variety of ways to connect with youth and connect youth and their families to resources. In addition to the formats, there are also four ways to minister to youth by making connections.

Ways to connect youth to the life of the parish An essential means for ministering with youth is to connect young people to the life of the parish. We start by connecting youth to the sacraments celebrated in the parish, especially Eucharist. We can also connect youth with the faith formation, community life events, and service opportunities offered for the parish community. These connections build on the ministry that youth experience with their peers and help youth to build relationships with the parish community. Using the life of the parish means that youth ministry leaders do not have to create peer events for all of the components and goals of youth ministry. We can rely upon the parish events to serve and include youth. Sometimes it isn't automatic. Leaders need to prepare the adults who are leading different aspects of parish life so that youth are welcome and included.

Ways to connect with families of youth and to support parents We make connections for youth when we help support the family in sharing faith at home. The family is the domestic church and parents are partners in ministry with youth. Think of the impact we can have when ministry programs are understood, supported, and reinforced at home. To connect with families, we need to consider the impact of youth ministry on family life, which means that we should plan for youth ministry with families in mind. We should also communicate with parents, recognizing that they can support something when they have the information they need and they understand the vision and direction. We can also support parents with resources and helpful programs that assist them in ministering with their adolescents at home. These connections can also include occasional gatherings of families of adolescents for events such as a picnic, a volleyball tournament, or a family service event.

Ways to connect with youth through non-gathered ministry We can connect with youth by delivering ministry resources and by being present to them in their other commitments. Adult youth ministry leaders are present to youth by going to concerts, plays, and sporting events. We can also deliver ministry to youth by distributing resources as part of our ministry efforts. We make a personal connection to youth by sending birthday cards. We provide pastoral care for youth by distributing laminated cards for their wallets or purses that include a variety of emergency phone numbers and Web sites. We help youth pray by sending e-mail prayers and Scripture reflections. Non-gathered connections can be a powerful way to deliver ministry to every youth in the parish. Gathered programs can also be strengthened and extended by having non-gathered strategies that complement a gathered initiative. For instance, in a parish that is making an effort to enhance all parish liturgies for young people (a gathered program), leaders also send youth a note with ten ways to participate in liturgy (a non-gathered strategy).

Ways for youth to be involved in ministry, leadership, and service One of the best ways for youth to strengthen and solidify their faith growth is by putting their faith into action through involvement in ministry, leadership, and service. Youth are looking for a way to share their gifts and contribute to communities of which they are a part. Many parishes connect with youth by involving them as liturgical ministers or catechetical ministers—acting as aides and assistants in teaching classes with younger children. Youth can also be involved in leadership roles in the parish by participating in planning for parish events and ministries and by participating in the councils and commissions of the parish. Many youth learn to be leaders by sharing in leadership of youth ministry events with their peers. Other youth become involved in service events and in ongoing service and advocacy projects in their community. Youth learn by doing through these connections, which also help youth to become active parish members.

As you can see, these formats and connections provide a variety of ways to include the components of youth ministry and work towards the goals of empowering disciples, promoting active participation, and encouraging personal and spiritual growth. Parishes that utilize this comprehensive approach develop ministry with youth using a variety of formats and connections. Youth are drawn to participate according to their interest, through encouragement of their parents, and by invitation of their friends. Each event or strategy helps connect and invite youth to other involvements. The diagram that follows demonstrates the comprehensive approach in action.

COMPREHENSIVE YOUTH MINISTRY

*Invites youth to a community of communities
including a variety of involvements with peers
and the parish community*

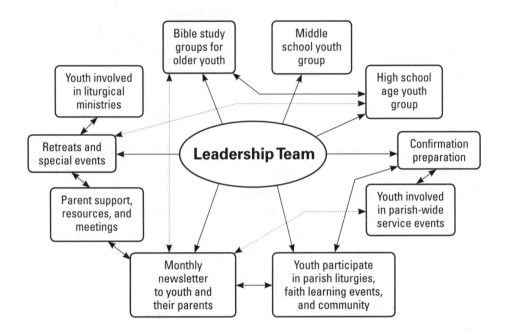

This diagram describes a parish youth ministry that includes a variety of gatherings and connections. The parish utilizes a weekly youth group for middle school and a weekly youth group for high school that feature catechetical topics twice a month. Other components are addressed on the remaining weeks. Retreats and special events complement these gatherings. Youth participate in Confirmation preparation beginning in their sophomore year. Juniors and seniors in high school who are ready for more serious faith exploration participate in the Bible study. Parents are supported in their role at home through resources provided at a parish library and through a speaker series. Special efforts are made to help youth participate in parish liturgies, faith learning events, and celebrations of the community. Ministry is delivered to youth through monthly newsletters, birthday cards, and through the caring presence of youth ministry leaders at school events.

Models for Dynamic Youth Ministry

Parishes with effective youth ministry envision and implement ministry with youth that addresses the goals and components of youth ministry using the following four formats and four connections:

Formats	*Connections*
• A regular pattern of gathering	• Connecting youth to the parish
• Special events	• Connecting with families
• Intentional adolescent catechesis	• Non-gathered ministry strategies
• Opportunities for going deeper in faith learning	• Involving youth in ongoing ministry, leadership, and service roles

Each parish accomplishes the components and goals of youth ministry by putting together a variety of initiatives using these formats and connections. Typically, each parish has one or two "anchor" gathered programs for youth. These anchors may be different for the middle school and high school age youth or there may be similar but separate strategies for these two age groups. These anchors are complemented by a variety of other gathered events and connections that involve and support youth and their families. For instance, a parish might choose to have a weekly youth program for high school age youth and one for middle school youth. Another "anchor" for this parish could be Confirmation preparation for sophomores. These anchors are complemented by seasonally offered retreats, a service learning week in the summer, a faith sharing series, community building events, and a variety of connections for youth to become involved in parish life and leadership positions. Families and youth are supported through non-gathered strategies. It is essential that there be enough flexibility in the model for youth ministry that a wide variety of youth and their families can be connected and included.

To develop a model, parish leaders consider the parish's history and listen to the youth, families, and leaders in the community. Current involvements of youth are strengthened and new ideas are explored. Eventually, a model for ministry evolves. A variety of factors influence a parish in developing a model for youth ministry. Some of the questions and considerations follow.[9]

What is the overall vibrancy of parish life? To understand the Christian message, youth need to experience a welcoming community that is continuing

Christ's mission. For some parishes, the life of the community is an obvious witness; others struggle. In developing your youth ministry model, you need to make an honest assessment of the vibrancy of parish life and its openness to youth. If the overall parish life is vibrant, with lots of opportunities for youth to experience community and join with adults and children in events and common activities, then youth ministry can provide strategic opportunities for youth to gather with each other and explore topics and activities that are particular to youth. The primary task for youth ministry in these settings is to get youth involved in the vibrant life of the parish. On the other hand, if parish life is struggling overall and there are not very many positive opportunities for youth to become involved, more intentional community building and youth peer gatherings and programs are needed. The primary task of youth ministry in these settings is to provide youth with an experience of Christian community within youth ministry, while at the same time working to help improve the vibrancy of parish life overall.

What is the racial or ethnic diversity in our parish? *Renewing the Vision* is clear in describing parish as a community of communities that allows for different groups of youth and adults to gather for ministry. A parish's model for youth ministry needs to take the cultural diversity and language needs of the community into account. In many parishes, the youth ministry model should include intentional ministry efforts for youth from particular cultures and language groups, which means that there might be many different youth communities or groups. In all parishes, the model for youth ministry should include a welcoming and inclusive environment where all youth feel welcome. Being welcome includes hospitality, but also means that young people's expression of faith finds a home within youth ministry.

How are we preparing youth for Confirmation? Many dioceses confirm youth during the high school or junior high school years. The style of the program for preparing youth for Confirmation will impact the other elements of ministry developed for high school or junior high school youth. For example, if a parish has an all encompassing two-year Confirmation preparation program for freshmen and sophomores, it is very difficult to develop the other aspects of high school youth ministry because the parish's energy, family's commitment, and youth's time are all being spent in Confirmation preparation. On the other hand, if the youth ministry includes intentional, ongoing, systematic catechesis and the Confirmation preparation is short-term and focused on preparing to receive the sacrament, there is room for the development of the remaining components and aspects of youth ministry.

What schools are youth attending in our parish community? Some parishes include youth that go to school together at the same junior high or high school. Most parishes include youth who attend many different schools. The model for youth ministry should attend to this situation and provide ways that youth from Catholic schools and public schools feel welcome and included. A key consideration is making sure that youth feel free to participate in those elements of youth ministry that they feel drawn to. A youth who attends a Catholic high school may not be interested in the catechetical elements of youth ministry but may want to participate in community events and involvement in service. The model for youth ministry should allow for this type of participation.

What distances do families travel to come to the parish? In parishes that include members that travel large distances, the model for youth ministry should include concentrated participation times. For example, instead of weekly mid-week programming in the evening, a parish might provide for monthly "retreat-style," day-long events. In parishes that are geographically closer to members, it is more convenient for youth to participate multiple times in a given week.

Is our parish mostly urban, suburban, or rural? The demographics of your community will sometimes determine an emphasis in your implementation of the goals and components for youth ministry. For instance, in some urban settings, there may be greater attention to pastoral care and family programming. In suburban parishes, there is a need for community building so that youth and families do not become lost in large congregations. In rural parishes, where youth know each other well, there can be a greater need to join with other congregations in providing events like retreats and summer trips.

The following are additional examples of parish models that are composites of many of the parishes interviewed in the study. These models can be found in a variety of settings and the descriptions are not intended to be limited to a certain area or size of parish. These descriptions are illustrations and are not prescriptive to an area; elements of these models can work anywhere. The important thing is for parishes to find and adapt the model that works for them.

Our Lady of the Lake Parish
Weekly Religious Education Program and Community Prayer

Setting: This mountain state parish is located in a suburb and has several hundred families.

Anchor Programs
The key feature of this parish is a Wednesday night program that involves youth, their families, and the whole parish community. This program begins with a meal for youth and their families. After the meal, the families and other members of the parish participate in a youth-led evening prayer service. The prayer is a modified version of evening prayer that includes a reading of the gospel for the coming Sunday liturgy. Youth preside, lead music, and serve as greeters for this prayer service. One or two youth provide a brief reflection on the gospel that they prepare by working with the pastor during the previous week. Following the evening prayer, youth participate in a community builder activity that is followed by graded level religious education for grades six through twelve. Parents and siblings of youth are free to go home after the prayer, but many parents stay and participate in special gatherings for parents that include speakers, prayer, and networking. Another anchor involvement for this parish is the many youth who are involved in liturgical ministries, leadership positions on parish committees, and ongoing service roles.

Other Gatherings and Connections
- Fall and spring retreats: day-long for middle school/weekend for high school
- Participation in leadership training week and service learning week in the summer (for older youth)
- Monthly social events
- Occasional faith sharing series on seasonal and thematic topics
- Parent resource library located in the church vestibule
- Monthly newsletter for youth and parents
- Birthday cards sent to each youth

St. Joseph the Worker Parish
Weekly Youth Night

Setting: This suburban parish is located on the West Coast and has 2,000 families.

Anchor Programs

This parish provides a weekly youth night on Tuesday nights for middle school youth and on Wednesday night for high school youth. These gatherings include a combination of catechesis, which is offered approximately every other week, along with the other components of youth ministry. Community building and prayer are a consistent part of each gathering. An important part of the weekly gathering are the announcements, which help youth to link up with parish events, family resources, special events, and other aspects of youth ministry. Another anchor program for this parish is a youth drama program. Each season, youth present a scriptural drama for the parish community. Youth prepare for these events for two months in advance. The preparation includes study of the scriptural story and a retreat to reflect on the spiritual themes.

Other Gatherings and Connections

- Retreats and faith sharing series offered for high school youth
- Middle school participation in diocesan rallies
- Confirmation preparation is a six-month process that is offered to youth who are fifteen years of age and older
- Regular involvement in parish-wide service events
- Summer participation in week-long service learning program
- Parish youth Web site that includes faith sharing "chat zones" and weekly prayer e-mails
- "Welcome to the Teenage Years" speaker series for parents

St. Theresa Parish
Small Faith Communities

Setting: This is a Midwestern parish community located in a medium sized city with 1,500 families.

Anchor Programs

High school youth are divided into groups of ten to twelve students according to grade level. These small faith communities have two "godparents" who provide weekly gatherings, which are usually located in the leaders' homes. These godparents are adult leaders who agree to work with a particular group of youth over a number of years. These gatherings are primarily focused on catechesis and evangelization. Middle school youth gather for a weekly youth night that provides religious education and community building.

Other Gatherings and Connections

- Monthly community building events for all parish youth
- Seasonal parent meetings; parents of youth in one of these small faith communities gather with each other and with the godparent leaders for networking and resource sharing
- Short-term Confirmation preparation provided in 8th grade
- Youth ministry Web site with weekly prayer e-mails sent to youth and parents
- Monthly liturgies that provide for youth involvement in planning and in the ministries; prepared by different faith groups each month
- Summer service trips and events

Holy Name Parish
Pastoral Care Responses

Setting: This parish is located in the downtown area of a large Midwestern city.

Anchor Programs

The youth ministry in this parish is focused around pastoral care for youth. There is significant gang violence and a school drop-out problem in the area. The parish has responded by obtaining funding to provide an alternative high school on the parish grounds for small numbers of youth who would otherwise not be able to attend school. The parish has also developed a "padrino" and "padrina" project, which is a foster godparent or mentor program that matches up two or three young people with two adult leaders to provide connection and guidance. There is a vibrant youth-involved liturgy each week that features a choir and band with many youth members playing a variety of instruments.

Other Gatherings and Connections

- A variety of youth communities centered around common interests
- Monthly gatherings for parents of youth with speakers and resources provided in English and Spanish
- Catechesis is provided through small groups and in family settings
- Youth employment is promoted through inter-congregational collaboration and grant funding. For instance, there is a day-care program and after-school program at the parish that employs youth and provides job training.
- Seasonal retreats

St. Columbkille Parish
Intergenerational Faith Learning

Setting: This parish is located in a mid-sized town in the Northeast.

Anchor Programs

The focus of youth ministry at St. Columbkille is the involvement of youth with the intergenerational community. The parish offers monthly intergenerational faith learning events during the school year. Youth share their gifts and leadership by helping with skits, prayer, hospitality, and leading small groups of younger children. Youth also participate in the events as part of the whole community and with each other during age specific break-out sessions.

Other Gatherings and Connections
- Youth community is developed through seasonal retreats and annual participation in week-long service learning events
- Weekly youth nights for high school and for middle school youth
- Youth involvement in parish councils, liturgical ministry, and leadership groups
- Confirmation preparation is achieved through a family-based program that is offered in the sophomore year of high school
- Youth ministry team members are intentional about participating in sports events, concerts, and plays that involve young people
- Parents of youth take advantage of a parent resource library located in the vestibule of the church

St. Thomas the Apostle Parish
Weekly Liturgy and Youth Night

Setting: This is a suburban parish located in a Southeastern state.

Anchor Programs

Each Sunday evening, there is a liturgy that includes youth involvement in planning and in the liturgical ministries. This liturgy is open to the whole parish but especially attracts youth and their families. Following the liturgy, there are gatherings for high school youth, middle school youth, and parents. In the middle school and high school "youth nights," the variety of components of youth ministry are explored and developed. The parent gatherings include prayer, informal networking, and occasional speakers.

Other Gatherings and Connections

- Monthly service events involve youth and their families
- Seasonal retreats focus on the liturgical season and connections to youth's lives
- The parish promotes participation in the National Catholic Youth Conference and brings large delegations to the diocesan youth rallies and events
- Youth and adults work together on a monthly newsletter delivered by mail and online. The newsletter features upcoming events, photos from past events, and monthly profiles of "Young Disciples" who are involved in service, ministry, and leadership roles.
- Catechesis is provided during youth nights and through retreat days and faith sharing series
- Confirmation preparation is a six-month process for sophomores and juniors that begins in December each year

St. Anthony Parish
Multiple Youth Communities

Setting: This is a large, culturally diverse parish located in a mid-sized city in the Southwestern United States.

Anchor Programs

There are a variety of youth communities at St. Anthony's that focus on the variety of language and ethnic groups within the parish: English-speaking youth group, Spanish jovenes ministry, and Vietnamese choir. Each season, these communities join together for parish-wide youth rallies that feature speakers and musicians. These events provide opportunities for the different communities to share their gifts by taking turns providing skits and leading prayer and community building events.

Other Gatherings and Connections

- Seasonal gatherings for parents of youth with speakers and resources provided in different languages
- Confirmation preparation is an eighteen month process beginning in freshman year that focuses on evangelization, catechesis, and preparation to receive the sacrament
- There is a monthly Youth Ministry Coordinating Council meeting that

brings together all of the groups and ministries that serve youth. The seasonal rallies are planned as part of these meetings.

- In the summer, there is an emphasis on youth leadership training and involvement of youth in service events
- Youth are encouraged to participate in leadership roles and liturgical ministry roles throughout parish life

St. Mary Parish
Monthly Youth Retreat Days

Setting: This parish is located in a rural community with about thirty-five adolescents between sixth and twelfth grade.

Anchor Programs

"Make the most of Sunday" is the motto for this parish, which features a day-long event for youth on the first Sunday of the month. The day begins with youth of all ages joining together for music and an opening prayer. Junior high and high school youth divide for a retreat day that includes faith learning, community building, and media and learning activities. Youth and their families join together in an evening liturgy that is followed by a meal and some type of community building event. In the summer, they show a movie outside on the parish lawn and serve popcorn and ice cream. Occasionally, the evenings will include a dance or concert.

Other Gatherings and Connections

- St. Mary's youth ministry actively connects with other congregations and parishes to provide a way for youth to be with other youth
- High school youth participate in the National Catholic Youth Conference and in an annual service learning week that joins their group with five or six other parishes
- Youth participate with the whole community in a variety of community life events
- Several times a year, different youth and their families share a meal with the parish staff, which consists of the pastor (who is also responsible for three other parishes) and a pastoral associate. This meal gathering includes shared prayer and conversation about ways to include youth in the parish.
- Every other year, youth are prepared for Confirmation through a series of retreats and through family preparation

- Youth help to organize the parish Web site, which includes photos, links to resources, family resources, and threaded conversations about faith topics that they call "Virtual Youth Group."

 ## Becoming a Responsive Parish

> Youth Ministry is the response of the Christian community to the needs of young people, and the sharing of the unique gifts of youth with the larger community.[10]

This definition of youth ministry describes a responsive relationship. The community responds to youth and includes their gifts. What this definition intentionally leaves out is the word "program." Ministry is more than a program; pastoral work with youth is not a formula. In being responsive and inclusive, parishes find ways to put together the pieces of youth ministry in a way that works for their community and achieves what they are hoping for. This way of putting things together becomes the parish model. This model grows, evolves, and changes, since this model or any one way of doing things is not the important thing. The model creates room for ministry to happen by providing a variety of ways for youth and their families to belong and connect. Over the life of a parish, there will be different leaders and many different programs and strategies. The model for the parish will grow and evolve. What remains consistent is the way the parish loves youth in Jesus' name and involves them as young disciples in the common mission of the community.

— RECOMMENDED RESOURCES —

Black, Wesley, Chap Clark, Malan Nal, and Mark Senter (general ed.). *Four Views of Youth Ministry and the Church*. Grand Rapids, MI: Zondervan Publishing, 2001.

Dean, Kenda Creasy. *Practicing Passion: Youth and the Quest for a Passionate Church*. Grand Rapids, MI: Wm. B. Eerdmans Publishing Co., 2004.

Dean, Kenda Creasy, Chap Clark, and Dave Rahn (eds.). *Starting Right: Thinking Theologically about Youth Ministry*. Grand Rapids, MI: Zondervan Publishing, 2001.

Dean, Kenda Creasy, and Ron Foster. *The Godbearing Life: The Art of Soul Tending for Youth Ministry*. Nashville: Upper Room Books, 1998.

East, Thomas. *Total Faith Initiative Coordinators Manual*. Winona, MN: Saint Mary's Press, 2004.

East, Thomas. *Effective Practices for Dynamic Youth Ministry*. Winona, MN: Saint Mary's Press, 2004.

Jones, Tony. *Postmodern Youth Ministry*. Grand Rapids, MI: Zondervan Publishing, 2001.

Lytch, Carol. *Choosing Church: What Makes a Difference for Teens*. Louisville: Westminster/John Knox Press, 2004.

Martinson, Roland. "Spirit of Youth Ministry Project." Note: This project has also been referred to as "The Exemplary Youth Ministry Project." Additional information may be found at: www.exemplaryyouthministry.org. Publications to be available in 2009.

Martineau, Mariette, Joan Weber, and Leif Kehrwald. *Intergenerational Faith Formation: All Ages Learning Together*. New London, CT: Twenty-Third Publications, 2008.

Rice, Wayne, Chap Clark, et al. *New Directions for Youth Ministry*. Loveland, CO: Group Books, 1998.

Semmel, Christina. *No Meeting Required: Strategies for Nongathered Ministry with Young People*. Winona, MN: Saint Mary's Press, 2007.

Strommen, Merton P., Karen Jones, and Dave Rahn. *Youth Ministry that Transforms*. Grand Rapids, MI: Zondervan Publishing, 2001.

Renewing the Vision: A Framework for Catholic Youth Ministry. Washington, DC: United States Conference of Catholic Bishops, 1997.

Yaconelli, Mark. *Growing Souls: Experiments in Contemplative Youth Ministry*. Grand Rapids, MI: Zondervan Publishing, 2007.

YouthWorks. Naugatuck, CT: Center for Ministry Development, 1994, 1996. (Available online through Youth Ministry Access: www.youthministryaccess.org.)

Youth Ministry Access (subscription Web site). Naugatuck, CT: Center for Ministry Development. www.youthministryaccess.org

— END NOTES —

1. *Renewing the Vision: A Framework for Catholic Youth Ministry*. Washington, DC: United States Conference of Catholic Bishops, 1997, p. 20.

2. Roberto, John. "The Spirit of Youth Ministry: Utilizing Faith Assets to Nurture Youth of Vital Faith," *Youth Ministry Access*. Naugatuck, CT: Center for Ministry Development, 2006, p. 3.

   Note: The *Spirit of Youth Ministry Project* has also been referred to as "The Exemplary Youth Ministry Project." This project is directed by Dr. Roland Martinson. Additional information may be found at: www.exemplaryyouthministry.org.

3. Dean, Kenda Creasy, and Dean Foster. *The Godbearing Life: The Art of Soul Tending in Youth Ministry*. Nashville: Upper Room Books, 1998, pp. 30-31.

4. East, Thomas. *Effective Practices for Dynamic Youth Ministry*. Winona, MN: Saint Mary's Press, 2004, pp. 10-11. Additional information about this study is also available at: cmdnet.org/symposium.

5. RTV, p. 25.

6. A similar diagram also appears in: John Roberto and Thomas East, *Guide to Youth Ministry: Leadership* (New Rochelle, NY: Don Bosco Multimedia, 1994), p. 123.

7. This diagram also appears in *Guide to Youth Ministry: Leadership*, p. 124.

8. Similar ideas are also developed in: Thomas East, et al., *Total Faith: Coordinator's Manual* (Winona, MN: Saint Mary's Press, 2004), p. 53-55.

9. Similar ideas are also developed in *Total Faith: Coordinator's Manual*, pp. 59-60.

10. *A Vision of Youth Ministry*. Washington, DC: United States Conference of Catholic Bishops, 1976, p. 6, also appears in RTV, p. 1.

Communities Nurturing Youth

One powerful image that leaders used to describe their community is a web of relationships: youth to youth, youth to adults, youth ministry leaders to parents, parents to youth, youth to the parish as a whole. Through this web, youth are served, included, and empowered.

Finding from interviews with parish teams as reported in:
Effective Practices for Dynamic Youth Ministry, p. 15

CHAPTER SIX

Building Community with Youth

Ann Marie Eckert

Editor's Note

Youth long to feel at home and accepted as part of a community. In this chapter, Ann Marie Eckert develops the theological foundations for community life and explores practical ways to build community life as we help youth belong more deeply to a peer community and the parish.

Building community life is an essential element of youth ministry. Without a sense of community and hospitality at parish and youth events, good ministry is not possible. Young people need an environment that is supportive and loving in order to hear the Good News and grow in faith. Community life focuses the attention of a parish on all the ways that its members interact with young people. As *Renewing the Vision* (RTV) states, "The ministry of community life is not only what we do (activity), but *who* we are (identity) and *how* we interact (relationships)."[1]

Community life can seem like the simplest part of ministry with youth. Get young people together, provide something fun to do, and watch the community grow. Experience shows that the organic nature of community life requires concerted attention and care.

Christian community life is not realized

spontaneously. It is necessary to educate it carefully.[2]

GENERAL DIRECTORY FOR CATECHESIS, #86A

In the *General Directory for Catechesis*, community life is described as one of the key tasks of catechesis. This statement reminds us that building community and teaching about community life needs to be an intentional part of our ministries. A community is more than a group of people who are in the same place at the same time. Ultimately, community is formed when people gather around a common purpose with common values and commit themselves to each other for this larger mission. Because we are human and we are different from each other, experiences of community will include challenges, conflicts, and growth. These aspects of our journey as a Christian community are part of the way that we realize our mission and open ourselves to each other and to the God who calls us together.

Making the Connection

Communities are a place where we learn about ourselves, others, and God.

- *In your life, what experience of community is most significant for you?*
- *What were the qualities of that community?*

This chapter will focus on ways that a parish can enhance the ministry of community life through the actions of youth ministry leaders, parish staff, and the whole Christian community.

PART I: Understanding Community

The component of community life is essential for youth ministry because community life is essential to what it means to be Christian.

> The challenge of being transformed into a holy person is not undertaken alone but within a faith community....The longing for community touches each of us at the very core of our being. It is basic to being human ..."[3]
>
> UNITED STATES CONFERENCE OF CATHOLIC BISHOPS,
> *SONS AND DAUGHTERS OF THE LIGHT:*
> *A PASTORAL PLAN FOR MINISTRY*
> *WITH YOUNG ADULTS*

> The human person needs to live in society. Society is not for him an extraneous addition but a requirement of his nature.[4]
>
> CATECHISM OF THE CATHOLIC CHURCH, #1879

God created us as social beings. Jesus commanded us to "love one another." Our experience of what it means to be Catholic is founded in community—first the community of our family, then parish, and ultimately our experience of the wider Church. Being connected to others in community goes to the very nature of who we are. "Then God said, 'Let us make humankind in our image, according to our likeness...'" (Gn 1:26). We have been formed in God's image, which is not a solitary figure, but the unity of the Father, Son, and Spirit.

> The model of the human community is the Holy Trinity: the unity of Father, Son, and Holy Spirit. The very nature of the Trinity is communal and social. "God reveals himself to us as one who is not alone, but rather as one who is relational, one who is Trinity. Therefore, we who are made in God's image share this communal, social nature."[5]
>
> NATIONAL DIRECTORY FOR CATECHESIS

We come from a Triune God and we hope to return to God in heaven—sharing in the community experience of the Trinity for all eternity. Community is our beginning and hoped-for end. In between, we form community with each other.

Throughout all time, God has been relational with his people. In the Old Testament, we hear the story of God's relationship with the Chosen People. In the New Testament, we hear the story of Jesus, the Word made Flesh—a relational God who could be seen, heard, and touched by God's people. Jesus formed the original Church community. He gathered people to himself—they spent time together, ate together, prayed together, shared the regular joys and sorrows of life, and were drawn into their mission as disciples. Our ministry is still founded on these same principles. When we gather young people together we do so with a sense of wanting to share in their life—to know what makes them happy and brings them sadness, to share a meal together, the Eucharistic meal often, and sometimes pizza, and help them know and live the Gospel message.

We know that Jesus walked with people, listened to their stories, laughed and argued, touched and healed, forgave, and did all the things that humans do in relationship to each other. But it didn't end there. Jesus gathered people to himself in order to accomplish a mission. We want to enter into relationship with young people, to create community with and among them, so that the truth we have of God's love, the truth we know about the Kingdom of God, can reach their ears and hearts.

St. Paul paints a clear and strong picture of what type of community Christians are called to.

I…urge you to live in a manner worthy of the call you have received, with all humility and gentleness, with patience, bearing with one another through love, striving to preserve the unity of the spirit through the bond of peace: one body and one Spirit, as you were also called to the one hope of your call; one Lord, one faith, one baptism; one God and Father of all, who is over all and through all and in all. (Eph 4:1-6)

Paul also reminds Christians that as followers of Jesus they are to

Love one another with mutual affection; anticipate one another in showing honor. Do not grow slack in zeal, be fervent in spirit, serve the Lord. Rejoice in hope, endure in affliction, persevere in prayer. Contribute to the needs of the holy ones, exercise hospitality. (Rom 12:10-13)

To exercise hospitality, as Paul refers to it, is a great virtue that is honored in the Catholic faith tradition. God's love comes in all persons, and so Christians welcome the strangers they meet. Hospitality is rooted in the type of environment Christians create. Genuine hospitality exists in an environment of true welcome and openness, places where people feel safe to explore their own ideas, develop meaningful relationships, find God within themselves and within others, and work together to engage in the Kingdom of God.

Ronald Rolheiser, in his book *The Holy Longing*, names community as one of the four nonnegotiable pillars of the spiritual life. Rolheiser states that

[Jesus] teaches us clearly that God calls us, not just as individuals, but as a community and that how we relate to each other is just as important religiously as how we relate to God. Or, more accurately, how we relate to each other is part of how we relate to God.[6]

Our relationships with each other are vital to our faith and friendship with our loving God. How can we claim to love a God we cannot see if we are unable to love the worshipping community around us? When Jesus was asked which of the commandments was the greatest, his answer was twofold.

Love the Lord your God with all your heart, with all your soul, with all your mind, and with all your strength. The second is this: "You shall love your neighbor as yourself." There is no other commandment greater than these. (Mk 12:30-31)

Jesus was asked which commandment was greatest—or first—yet he answered with two directives: love God and love others. These two great commandments are joined together because to love God outside of love for others is incomplete. As members of the Body of Christ, Christians are Jesus' presence here on earth in this moment. As two of our guiding documents tell us, our message is always articulated, in part, through the life of the community.

> The content of our message will be heard only when it is lived in our relationships and community life. To teach compassion, generosity, tolerance, peace, forgiveness, acceptance, and love as gospel values and to identify ourselves as Christians requires us to live these values in our interactions with young people and in our community life. God's reign was proclaimed through the relationships Jesus initiated, and it continues to be heralded every time we witness our belief in him through the relationships in our community.[7]
>
> RENEWING THE VISION: A FRAMEWORK FOR CATHOLIC YOUTH MINISTRY

> Catechesis prepares the Christian to live in community and to participate actively in the life and mission of the Church. The Second Vatican Council indicates the necessity for pastors "to form genuine Christian communities" (264) and for catechumens "[to] learn to co-operate actively in building up the Church and its work of evangelization."[8]
>
> GENERAL DIRECTORY FOR CATECHESIS, #86

It is through community that people discover their talents, form their identities, learn about God, are challenged to live according to gospel values, celebrate the joys of life, find comfort during times of trouble, and ultimately, develop into the people they are called to be.

The Journey of Community Life

Building community is more than making people feel welcome. It is a journey that builds upon hospitality, works through the deepening of relationships, and ultimately leads to sharing life and gifts. These five elements describe the practices of communities who strive to be faithful in their gospel call:

Welcome Communities are called to welcome and include others.

Respect Communities are called to respect and honor the dignity of every person as a child of God.

Value Communities are called to value each other's gifts and contributions.

Forgive Communities are called to forgive each other and work toward reconciliation of differences.

Love Communities are called to share God's love with each other and to be a sign of God's love for the world.

Developing these practices builds up the life of the community and helps the community and its members focus love and service outward, to embrace others, and serve those in need. Leading communities and facilitating authentic relationships requires time, attention, listening, and patience.

In a nation-wide study of youth ministry's most effective practices, the young people interviewed spoke about their parish as their "second home."[9] These young people were well integrated into the life of the community. They had roles of leadership at the parish—not just within youth ministry—such as altar servers, choir members, parish council members, and coffee and donut hosts. These young people received support from the parish for their summer mission trips, or applause that rained down after their youth choir sang the closing song at Mass. They worked with other parish organizations for parish-wide service projects. One young man noted that he had been a member of his parish before he was even born—his mother sang in the choir while pregnant with him. For this young man, the parishioners of his church were his extended family. These parishes demonstrated the practices of welcome, respect, value, forgiveness, and love to these young people. They supported their efforts to know and understand the faith, provided role models for how to pray, serve, and live a Christian life, and helped them as they continue to integrate the Gospel message into their everyday life.

Almost any activity within youth ministry or the parish has the potential for building community. Parishes that host Our Lady of Guadalupe celebrations that bring the whole community together provide for an appreciation of diversity. A good retreat will develop meaningful relationships, model Gospel values, and help young people nurture their faith. Some activities may have objectives that go well beyond building community, but the outcomes of these activities rely on the openness and trust that develops when people feel that they are part of a community. To be effective in our ministries, parish leaders have to be attentive to the very human need for community that all people share.

Additionally, the component of community life strives to help young people develop the skills that they will need to live in community in all areas of their life. Friendship-making skills, skills for understanding and appreciating people who are different from themselves, and skills for family communication are all a part of the mandate for this component. "Love your neighbor as yourself" helps to focus attention on both a healthy knowledge of personal strengths and weaknesses, as well as an appreciation of all people.

Atmosphere, Attitudes, and Actions

Parishes that welcome young people are generally welcoming to all—there is a sense of hospitality that permeates everything within the parish. It is from this starting point of hospitality that Christians, young and old, can develop the trust and challenge that is essential for community to exist. Young people may be considered the litmus test for community life in parishes. If youth are thriving within a community, then that parish has passed the "test of community." If young people feel alienated and unwelcome, are not included and involved in parish life, and do not have the support that community offers to live the faith fully, this experience is probably shared by many others within the parish. To avoid this pitfall, parishes can pay special attention to the type of atmosphere that the parish exudes, the attitudes of its leaders, and the way all parishioners are treated.

When a church is at its best, all the ministries of the parish, all liturgical celebrations, and all outreach done in the parish's name are encased within a strong sense of Christian community. Creating this community requires attention to three very important elements: atmosphere, attitudes, and actions. Actions are reflections of attitudes, which define the atmosphere that is created.

Actions include everything from smiling and saying "Hi," to including young people in leadership at the parish, and creating Christian communities where faith and life are shared. Actions have to match Christian values and the Gospel message preached. Authentic ministry is found in people and parishes who truly value young people and who believe that ministry to and for them is deeply rooted in the call to live out faith in the world. Actions define the type of relationships created with and between young people and things said and done which build up community within the parish and youth ministry events. Actions are the lens through which young people experience others' attitudes towards them.

Attitudes will make or break community. What is a parish's attitude towards young people? What are young people's attitudes towards the parish? In some people's experience the image that would come to mind is of a disinterested and disengaged young person sitting through (but not participating in) liturgy or a religious education class. Others might be see the image of a young person helping at a parish service project or leading a small group. Would a young person describe the parish as friendly, open, and welcoming? Would the parish describe young people in the same way?

Attitudes underlie actions and are therefore important. Young people are aware when the attitude of other youth or adults is dismissive or judging or when an attitude of acceptance and interest resides in the other youth and adults of a parish. To fully live out the Christian faith, parishioners must value all the members of the community, including the young. If young people have no great importance in a parish community, that attitude will be expressed (through time invested, money spent, openness to youth's gifts and energy, etc.) and create an atmosphere inhospitable to young people.

Atmosphere, in the earth science world, defines the very air one breathes. To visit the moon or the depths of the ocean without a lot of protective gear to make the atmosphere acceptable is impossible. For young people to feel welcomed at a parish-wide or youth ministry event, a certain atmosphere must be present. As *Renewing the Vision* says:

> Community life is nurtured when the atmosphere is welcoming, comfortable, safe, and predictable—one in which all adolescents know that their presence is welcomed, their energy is appreciated, and their contributions are valued.[10]

Perhaps the most important element of atmosphere is the feeling of safety as it is experienced by a young person. When young people show up at an event, does it feel like a safe place to them? Are they convinced that they are emotionally and physically protected from harm? Do they trust that they won't be embarrassed, talked about, or threatened in any way? If they cannot answer "yes" to the questions above, then they will not be able to relax and open up to the other people and potential opportunities that exist within a strong community. Community does not exist without trust, and trust is a slow process. As Loughlan Sofield states in the book *Building Community*, "creating a climate of trust is one of the most important tasks of any community because trust is the essential foundation and cornerstone upon which communal relations are developed."[11] An atmosphere of trust will lead to opportunities for faith sharing, personal growth, and catechesis.

Actions, attitudes, and the atmosphere in a parish have a profound impact on young people's experience of the faith community. If actions match values, and values and attitudes are deeply connected to the faith tradition and the way in which Jesus treated each person, then the atmosphere will be life-giving to young people. Creating that atmosphere is not as difficult as it may seem, but it does require paying attention, listening, and changing when necessary.

PART II: The Development of Community

Building Community within Youth Ministry Programming

A regular pattern of gathering is an element that contributes to effective youth ministry. Young people like to come together to learn, grow, discover things about themselves, and be surrounded by people that they can trust. They also need the Christian community to help them know and understand their gifts and their mission as disciples of Jesus, and to experience God more fully through faith sharing, prayer, and service.

Establishing a regular gathering for young people is important for youth ministry, and it demands special attention to the process of building community. Community does not necessarily form naturally; it most often takes time, attention, and a dedication to working through all the natural dynamics that happen when people gather. One of the assumptions that people often have about Christian communities is that they should happen automatically and be devoid of things like conflict and power-plays. Unfortunately, that is not true. Building community is often a slow and intentional process.

In his book, *Building Community in Youth Groups*, Denny Rydberg discusses five steps for building community in groups.[12] The first step involves breaking down barriers between people. Young people need to know that there is much in common between themselves and the others in a group. To create a strong community, it is important to give young people the opportunity to work together so they can find out how much alike they are to their peers. Working together can involve solving a simple puzzle, competing in a team icebreaker, or sorting clothes at the local thrift shop. Young people can talk with each other, laugh at common experiences, and gain some sense of themselves as a member of a group.

The second step in developing youth communities is to help young people open up to each other and share information about themselves. At this point in the process, the information should be non-threatening. One common mistake is to ask people to share too deeply too soon. The goal of this step is to build some trust between people. As stated earlier, trust is the cornerstone of community, and it is risky to trust another person with information about oneself.

Step two must be connected to step three—affirmation. If a young person shares a little personal information that is well received, then that young person begins to trust a group with more and more information. The opposite is also true; if shared information results in ridicule a young person will know that the group is not a safe place and will most likely shut down and cease to participate. Step three gives young people feedback that they are valued as members of a group and that what they have to share will be welcomed by others.

The fourth step is most essential if a group is to go beyond a simple level of friendship. Step four is called "stretching" because it invites a group to move beyond polite involvement in each other's lives and to tackle obstacles and difficulties together. If a group is together for an extended time (in terms of months or years or perhaps week-long events), stretching experiences may naturally arise. However, some groups build these experiences into their ministry to ensure that young people come to really rely on and trust each other.

Some common stretching experiences include group travels, rope courses, group puzzles, or simulation games. Other groups stretch by dealing with the death of a loved one, through conflicts that involve others in the group, or in situations of great stress. When a group is able to work through these hard or difficult situations, its members begin to see the strengths and weaknesses of the others and within themselves. Learning to deal with difficulties within the safety of a trusted community, young people gain an understanding of their own ability to deal with troubles outside of the group setting. They gain confidence and trust in themselves. If a group is able to survive these stretching moments, it will emerge stronger, more connected, and better able to share on a much deeper level.

This growth naturally leads to step five, which involves the opportunity to share deeply and to set group goals. This deeper sharing is now possible because the members know they can depend on each other and are confident of the trust between themselves. Within step five faith sharing can flourish. Loughlan Sofield explains it this way, "faith-sharing calls us to share with each other what it means to be a follower of Christ in the world today. Through authentic faith-sharing, we come to know and love the others in Christ whose Spirit is the bonding force of community."[13] It is also at this stage when group members can be more explicit in naming what their group goals are, and how they will live as disciples within the community.

How do these five steps get lived out within youth ministry? In a simple example, a group of young people have signed up to go on a summer mission trip. Some are "regulars" and some are new to this experience and to youth ministry in general. The young people and the accompanying adults are called together for an informational night. Besides trip details, the participants introduce themselves and engage in a few icebreakers, working together to win some friendly competitions. The leader then asks everyone to share why they are interested in going on the mission trip and one hope they have for the experience. At the following meeting, members share additional information and the leader spends a great deal of time affirming the participation of everyone in the group.

Next, the young people do a day of service at a local food pantry. During this day, some small challenges occur—including a conflict over the distribution of work and over some group decision-making that follows. By the time the team leaves for the mission trip, it has progressed to the point that the youth and adults are ready for the experience of traveling together and sharing their mission experience.

During the ten-hour van ride, more sharing happens, more affirmation is expressed, and a greater sense of community develops. After a week of stretching experiences (homesickness, reactions to witnessed poverty, changes in diet, etc.) the group returns to the parish with a tremendous level of trust.

The group then meets monthly for three months after the mission trip to continue talking about the experience and to share insights. They talk about how they have grown in faith, how they came to know Jesus in the new way through the poor, and what they discovered about themselves. Together, the members choose justice and advocacy projects to participate in during the coming year.

This group has developed a great sense of trust among its members and is a strong community. The individuals are likely to call on each other during times of joy and times of trouble, and friendships will continue to develop outside of the monthly meetings. They are likely to be a source of challenge for each other as they make decisions about how to spend their money, how often to be involved in justice activities, and how they are living by Gospel values.

The challenge for this group, as with any other, is to stay open to new people. Once true community develops, there is a natural tendency to become focused solely on the members of the community, but this is a dangerous trap. As soon as a group becomes self-serving, it begins to die. Any community, especially a Christian community, has to be focused for the benefit of others as well as self.

Using these five steps as a framework, youth ministry can promote community by ensuring that community-building is structured into all activities. As a group develops a level of trust, more sharing should be encouraged through activities and community-builders that invite participants to reveal personal information and share about faith and life issues. Affirmation must always be a part of any sharing that happens. Youth ministry leaders can find ways of creating stretching activities for a group to participate in, such as rope courses, simulation activities, service projects, retreats, and trips. These activities will help the group get to a place where deep sharing is possible. Leaders should encourage faith sharing and create opportunities for discussion, prayer, leadership, and service. Challenging group members to turn their attention towards others is essential to making sure that the community doesn't become insular.

What should we be doing to create a healthy community within youth ministry? Here are some ideas for your regular gatherings:

- Make sure someone is at the door greeting people. Too often we are running around with last minute details, and we forget to be attentive to the people walking through the door.
- Have nametags—all the time. You may not get anyone new for three weeks in a row, but if someone comes on week four and there are no nametags around, it is going to be a long night for that young person. It will also help everyone feel more comfortable, especially new volunteers, or those who are just lousy at remembering names.
- Do community builders, and make sure that they help people to get to know each other and feel comfortable. That should always be the lens through which you choose your community building activities.
- Plan for groups. Sometimes, like on a retreat, you may want the same small group to work together for the weekend so the level of sharing can grow over the course of time. At other times, you want be sure that the groupings change regularly so that people get to meet and talk to many different participants.
- Go to the next level. When group trust is high, make sure to engage participants in faith sharing and in discussions that lead to greater personal awareness.

Building Community among All Youth

Welcome and hospitality must always be extended to anyone who is new to a group. One of the fatal errors groups make is to become so consumed with the people who are already involved in the community that the group becomes closed off to "outsiders." When this happens, the group eventually disintegrates. Many youth groups will exist with great energy, enthusiasm, and a great sense of community for two to three years, only to discover that once senior members graduate, the group is left with almost no one involved. This is most likely the result of a group that paid little attention to the welcome it should have extended to "outsiders" while it was at the height of its numbers.

Beyond just making sure that people feel welcomed, it is important that leaders pay special attention to the quality of the relationships that are formed. Communities should have Gospel values as their foundation. People should be appreciated for who they are and valued for what they can offer each other. Young and old should be respected. Catholic traditions and values should be an essential element of the community's life. As *Renewing the Vision* reminds us, we cannot teach the values of our faith (forgiveness, compassion, tolerance, peace, etc.) if we do not live these values within our community life.[14]

One of the ways that we are able to create these types of communities is by recognizing that they are not formed with an unending number of people. Community can be limited by size. A sense of community at a parish is most likely achieved because an individual feels connected to a small number of other members in a positive way. This connection to a smaller community then connects them to the whole parish. One of the strongest ways to build community is to provide many different opportunities for communities to emerge—based on interests, heritage, age, and faith development. These smaller communities (Bible study group, mission trip participants, Boy Scouts) are all a part of the overall youth ministry at the parish. These different groups come together occasionally for larger events, and there are permeable boundaries between all of the smaller groupings so that young people can pick and choose how to be involved and which community or communities they are most interested in being a part of.

- Provide opportunities for a variety of communities to be formed within youth ministry and provide some ways for all youth to connect with each other over the course of the year.
- Attend to the skills of community living as part of the content in youth ministry programming by providing topics about communication, conflict resolution, cultural diversity, and peace-making.
- Continually provide ways for youth to discern their gifts and make a contribution to community life and to the larger mission of youth ministry.
- When conflicts and disagreements arise, use these opportunities to teach the values of community life. Youth will learn about community by watching the way leaders work though challenges and being part of a community that is healing and becoming whole.

Opening Wide the Doors

How do leaders ensure that hospitality is lived out in the youth ministry programs and the parish in general? Extending a personal invitation gets you started. Youth ministry needs to go out of its way to be sure that every young person is invited to participate. Developing a sense that every young person is always welcome anywhere within the programs and activities of youth ministry is worth the effort. Parishes that do this successfully seem to have a few things in common.

First and foremost, these parishes communicate regularly with all of the young people of the parish. Young people (and perhaps their parents too) receive newsletters, publicity, and invitations to be involved. They might also receive birthday cards, Christmas cards, and special blessings at Mass during exam times. Successful parishes do not assume that everyone likes to do the same thing, so they offer a great variety of opportunities to young people and value each of them equally. Someone who comes once a year to an event should be as important to a parish community as a young person who comes all the time.

Second, strong youth ministry parishes also recognize the ways in which young people are already involved in the parish community and honor all of those commitments. Involvement can include leadership for youth ministry, serving as aides and teachers in religious education programs, singing in the choir, participating in parish-wide service events, and many other activities. This is important because we don't want to focus attention only on those who participate regularly in youth ministry gatherings, but instead want to be inclusive of all the youth of the parish.

Third, these parishes recognize that cultural diversity is a great gift in our universal Catholic Church, and a key element of building community is providing opportunities for multicultural community building. One of the ways to make that happen is by providing safe ways for young people to participate in activities, which often begins by creating community within each cultural group before inviting them to come together. Sometimes, however, it is something very practical that can bring people together.

A tiny rural parish in Illinois took the time and energy to translate all of its publicity and permission slips into Spanish. Although the young people in the parish could read English, their parents could not. This parish is remarkable because there were only a few Spanish-speaking young people in the community, but the church wanted to make sure that even these young people could participate in its programs. Because of this effort the Hispanic youth of the parish began participating in youth ministry events and their unique insights and faith traditions added great depth to the whole ministry.

Fourth, parishes have an openness to young people of various abilities and disabilities. One parish in Oregon struggled each time it met to make sure that a young man with developmental disabilities was able to participate in the weekly program. Sometimes the parish was successful in helping him to participate, and sometimes the program went over his head, but he liked being there and his parents greatly appreciated the chance for their son to spend time with others his own age. Parish youth ministry should do its best to reach out to all of the young people of the parish, offering genuine welcome and hospitality—especially to those who can feel different or cast aside.

To ensure that all youth are welcome, consider the following:

- Make sure all ministry leaders work to create an atmosphere that is reflective of the Gospel values of peace, forgiveness, acceptance, and love.
- Be sure to include all the young people of the parish in your mailings and promotions. Even if a young person never comes, at least they will know that they were invited. Yearly, send out a personal invitation to youth to participate in youth ministry programs.
- Host a few "come and see" events throughout the year. Too often these are only held at the beginning of a year (end of one school year or the beginning of the next). Most people don't like joining something already in progress, and if they miss the "Welcome event" for this year, they shouldn't have to wait a whole year to feel like there is an opportunity to check things out.
- When someone comes for the first time to any event, follow-up with them. Have an adult or youth volunteer assigned to make a phone call or send an e-mail. The intention of this communication is not to make sure that they come back (become a "regular") but to make sure that they know that their presence was appreciated and to check in and make sure that they were comfortable.
- Honor and highlight youth who are involved in parish ministry through awards, bulletin boards, and newsletter articles. Honor parish youth who are achieving in other pursuits—school, theater, band, sports, etc.
- Ensure that programs are open to all youth—regardless of ability, ethnicity, language, etc. Make special arrangements as needed to include youth who can feel left out.
- Use the events of young people's lives to reach out to them. Send them birthday cards, pray for them during the petitions at Mass (before exams, or prom time, or just because), hold a dinner for graduating seniors, or a "fifth period" party after the basketball game. Sometimes we just have to step a few feet in their direction to get their attention and share with them about what is happening at church. Reaching out, even if they don't come, communicates care and a desire for a relationship.

PART III: Building Community with Youth and Their Parish

A parish in Texas suffered three great losses in one year. Within the new pastor's first year at the parish three young people died: one committed suicide, one died in a tragic accident, and a third died of a childhood disease after years of struggle. After the year was over, the pastor felt very connected to the young people of the parish because each funeral and wake affected a whole different group of young people, and he was able to walk the journey of grief and sorrow with many young people in the parish.

During his second year at the parish, the pastor took it upon himself to seek donations for a statue of St. John Bosco, the patron saint of youth. When the statue was completed, he arranged for an area of the church courtyard to be made into a special place for youth, with the statue as the centerpiece. He then invited all of the young people to come to the dedication of the St. John Bosco statue in the courtyard.

This pastor knew the important role that he could play in the lives of the youth of his parish. He also understood that he had a unique opportunity to minister to some of the young people who were not regular participants in youth ministry but who grieved the loss of their friends.

Good community involves everyone. The whole parish has the opportunity to build community with its younger members.

To invite, engage, affirm, and welcome young people, a parish can examine its current ministry efforts and recognize the ways that young people are already playing a role. By highlighting the work of those already involved in liturgical ministries, parish service, and leadership, the parish holds up to everyone the inclusion of young people in the full life of the community. Parishes can also examine their structures and policies to ensure there are no unnecessary rules keeping young people out of ministries and leadership. Parishes can intentionally include young people on committees, serve youth-friendly food at events, and make room for youthful energy within the church boundaries. Making sure that young people have access to space at the parish goes a long way towards building a healthy relationship between youth and adults.

Every parish has events throughout the year focused on helping parishioners grow in faith. Something like a parish mission is an ideal opportunity for young people to hear from the adults of the parish about the importance of faith in their lives, and for the adults to be able to hear from young people as well. It is important that these types of events be intentional in their efforts to include young people so that they are age-appropriate for young people. Usually something like a parish mission needs only a slight adjustment to be inclusive of high school youth, and perhaps a little more work to include middle school youth. This effort, however, can reap great benefits, not just for the youth but also for the whole parish, especially families with adolescents.

Youth ministry also shares the responsibility for building community between youth and the parish. In one rural parish, the youth group wanted to let the parish know that the young people valued their faith and wanted to be more a part of the parish community. To accomplish their goal, the young people committed themselves to holding the door open for parishioners who were entering Mass each week for a year. Within a few months, a wonderful sense of community had developed between these young people and the rest of the community. As winter approached, the adults were amazed that these young people continued to stand outside to welcome and open the door for them. These young people discovered a very essential truth—if you want to feel a part of the community, make yourself useful.

Another way to build community is to make sure that young people have important roles within the parish. One parish wanted young people to take on liturgical roles so they began a monthly youth Mass where all the liturgical ministers (including the choir) were youth. This helped the young people to learn the roles and provided for a good mentoring relationship to develop with older members of the parish. One month, a number of members of the "adult" choir forgot that it was the week of the youth-led Mass, and showed up to the choir loft for Mass. When they realized their mistake, they turned around to leave, but a young woman invited them to stay and sing with the youth choir. The adults did and that was the beginning of the combined adults and youth choir for the parish.

Parishes should take seriously the opportunities lying just under the surface of fundraisers and other parish events. When young people receive the support that they need (finances, prayer, advocacy) to participate fully in youth ministry events, they develop a sense of connection with the people who make these opportunities possible. Simply asking people for money (or to purchase goods) without letting them know what the funds are supporting is not as effective as offering these same supporters a glimpse into the experiences that their charity benefits. Youth ministry is learning to use opportunities such as mission trips, trips to World Youth Day or the National Catholic Youth Conference, or a myriad of other events, as community-building opportunities with the whole parish. As young people prepare for their experience and invite a parish to support them, the parish can respond with donations, prayer support, and special blessings prior to these experiences. Upon their return, the young people can publish letters in the bulletin or sponsor "supporter's dinners" to witness to what they have learned and experienced, and how they have grown in faith. Done well, these events not only serve to build community within the small group that travels together, but between the young people and many members of the broader parish community. It also provides an opportunity for young people to share their faith journey with the adults of the parish, and hopefully, for those same adults to respond in kind.

To build a stronger relationship between the parish and youth consider the following

- Change rules that limit young people's participation in parish ministries (catechetical, liturgical, leadership, etc.)
- Encourage youth to participate in parish missions, Renew groups, and other prayer and faith-sharing groups
- Involve youth in leadership roles in parish councils, commissions, and committees
- Be judicious about rules that limit young people's use of parish facilities
- Have youth-friendly food and activities available at parish-wide events
- Highlight young people who are currently involved in parish ministries and encourage all parish leaders to be open to the gift that youth could bring to ministry efforts
- Use fundraisers and other youth ministry events as opportunities for youth and the parish community to get to know each other better

PART IV: Making the Family Connection

Many parish youth ministries used to focus solely upon adolescents and did not have any connections with families of youth. Other than collecting permission slips and asking parents to chaperone big events, youth ministry seemed to ignore the fact that young people lived within families. Youth ministry is getting smarter! Parishes are increasingly honoring the importance of the domestic church and the essential role that parents have in their children's lives.

Being the parent of a teenage child is not always easy. Parents can use support to help them deal with all the new things that happen within the family when children move through adolescence. Parishes, and youth ministry, can help parents by building in opportunities for youth and their parents to continue to grow in community, and for the parents of youth to support and affirm each other. Giving parents a structured way to talk with their children—especially if the relationship they have with their children is strained because of growing independence—can be helpful. Even for parents who have very strong relationships with their children, some quiet, undivided time with their teens can be a welcomed blessing.

Parishes should consider providing a few programs each year that are aimed at parents and their teens. These programs can deal with issues such as communication skills, sexuality, decision-making, college or job preparation, or faith-sharing. Other simple strategies include inviting parents to write letters to youth who are participating in retreats, mission trips, and other faith experiences and inviting youth to write letters to parents in celebration of Mother's and Father's Days, the Feast of the Holy Family, or any other time of the year. Another option is to provide parents with information about youth ministry experiences, including some helpful hints on how to talk about the young people's experience at the youth ministry event, how to welcome a young person back from a retreat or other faith experience, and some general "how to talk to your teenager about…" information. This information could be sent to the parents in advance of the event or can be contained in a youth and family newsletter.

Helping parents to support each other is also a very important way to experience the parish community as caring about the family. One parish coordinator of youth ministry, after receiving quite a few phone calls from parents asking "What do I do about my kid?" questions, invited all the parents of teenagers who were involved in youth ministry and religious education at the parish to fill out an index card with their name and contact information. She then asked them to write on the card if they would be willing to help another family through a difficult situation that they might have personally dealt with already—such as a teenager not wanting to go to church, failing a class, staying out past curfew, or experimenting with drugs. The parish coordinator then collected cards from all the parents and told them that the next time they felt all alone in dealing with a particular issue related to their teen, they should call her. She would try to match them up with another family who could provide some insight and support. The parents used this strategy for years, and the families came to depend on each other as they shared the struggles of parenting.

Parishes can also provide Web page links to important parenting information, or list ideas to make time with teens special in the bulletin or parish Web site, or offer a lending library of parenting books and videos. When a parish is this helpful to parents—whether they are regular volunteers or Christmas and Easter Catholics—parents experience the parish as a support and help to them, which builds trust that is foundational to good community.

Parents in a parish community may know each other in a superficial way because they pick their kids up at the same places or cheer at the same ball games, but they may not have a sense of community with other parents. Parishes can provide opportunities for parents to gather to talk with each other and share their common experiences of being parents of teenagers. Once or twice a year the parish can also provide a speaker or presentation to be of assistance to parents—on parenting skills, current concerns related to youth, or spirituality for parents.

In *The National Study on Youth and Religion*, one of the key findings was that if parents of all faith traditions were religious and attended religious services, so did the vast majority of their teens.[15] If parents did not practice their faith, neither did the young people.

There are always exceptions to this finding, but it is the experience of many ministers within the Church that the apple does not fall far from the tree. Worrying about the sense of welcome and invitation a parish extends to young people is not good enough if the parish is not also reaching out to, inviting in, and welcoming their parents. Few young people will respond to the invitation to come to youth ministry if there is no sense of parish involvement within the family.

For reasons that are hard to explain, some families will not attend liturgy but will insist that their children participate in religious education. Because of this insistence on the part of the parents, the parish has an opportunity to reach out to these families. Does the parish take advantage of these moments to make the families feel welcomed, to educate them, to invite them into a fuller participation in the life of the community? Perhaps if the parish extends hospitality to these families, they might consider participating at a higher level. Too often these parents are made to feel bad about their decisions, which can make them pull further away from the Church. If parents are warmly welcomed, invited in, asked to share a glimpse of their lives, and are affirmed within this experience, they are much more likely to feel a connection to the parish. It might not bring them to church on Sunday, but perhaps if the young person is also being warmly welcomed into the parish, the young person may lead the parents and the family back to church.

Because families are so important to youth ministry, consider some of these options for developing a stronger relationship with parents of youth:

- Host programs for youth and their parents several times a year. Sometimes these programs could focus on learning, relationship-building, or prayer. Gather families of adolescents together for a service event, a picnic, or a sports event.

- Provide parents with information about the events, activities, and involvements of youth ministry. Provide resource materials that will help parents to support youth ministry activities at home.
- Create opportunities for parents to support each other through programs, small group sharing, and one-on-one relationships.
- Use Web sites, print resources, and community organizations to provide families with information and help that they might need. Consider creating a lending library of helpful books and videos.
- Use young people's involvement at the parish as an opportunity to welcome and invite parents into fuller participation in the life of the community.

Building Relationships and Witnessing Our Faith

As leaders of ministry with youth, we have the opportunity to build community within youth ministry and facilitate the building of community between youth and the other members of the parish. Good ministry happens in an atmosphere of trust, openness, and hospitality. These are the values that community building strives to engender. As the bishops of the United States wrote,

> The content of our message will be heard only when it is lived in our relationships and community life. To teach compassion, generosity, tolerance, peace, forgiveness, acceptance, and love as gospel values and to identify ourselves as Christians require us to live these values in our interactions with young people and in our community life. God's reign was proclaimed through the relationships Jesus initiated, and it continues to be heralded every time we witness our belief in him through the relationships in our community.[16]

The Catholic faith community must work at building strong relationships within youth ministry and throughout the parish. Only then can young people learn the Christian values that are taught through personal witnessing and relationships.

— RECOMMENDED RESOURCES —

Burns, Jim, Mark Simone, and Joel Lusz. *Games, Crowdbreakers, and Community Builders*. Ventura, CA: Gospel Light, 1997.

Eckert, Ann Marie. *Total Youth Ministry: Ministry Resources for Community Life*. Winona, MN: Saint Mary's Press, 2004.

Rice, Wayne. *Creative Crowdbreakers, Mixers, and Games.* Winona, MN: Saint Mary's Press, 1991.

Rydberg, Denny. *Building Community in Youth Groups.* Loveland, CO: Group Books, 1985.

Sofield, Loughlan, Rosine Hammett, and Carroll Juliano. *Building Community: Christian, Caring, Vital.* Notre Dame, IN: Ave Maria Press, 1998.

— ENDNOTES —

1. *Renewing the Vision: A Framework for Catholic Youth Ministry.* Washington, DC: United States Conference of Catholic Bishops, 1997, p. 34.

2. *General Directory for Catechesis.* Washington, DC: United States Conference of Catholic Bishops, 1997, #86a.

3. *Sons and Daughters of the Light: A Pastoral Plan for Ministry with Young Adults.* Washington, DC: United States Conference of Catholic Bishops, 1997, pp. 19-20.

4. *Catechism of the Catholic Church.* Washington, DC: Libreria Editrice Vaticana–United States Conference of Catholic Bishops, 2000, #1879.

5. *National Directory for Catechesis.* Washington, DC: United States Conference of Catholic Bishops, 2005, 168.

6. Rolheiser, Ronald. *The Holy Longing: The Search for Christian Spirituality.* New York: Doubleday, 1999, p. 68.

7. RTV, p. 34.

8. GDC, #86.

9. For more information on this study, see Thomas East, *Effective Practices for Dynamic Youth Ministry* (Winona, MN: Saint Mary's Press, 2004).

10. RTV, 34.

11. Sofield, Loughlan, Rosine Hammett, and Carroll Juliano. *Building Community: Christian, Caring, Vital.* Notre Dame, IN: Ave Maria Press, 1998, p. 51.

12. Rydberg, Denny. *Building Community in Youth Groups.* Loveland, CO: Group Books, 1985.

13. Sofield, p. 123.

14. RTV, p. 34.

15. Smith, Christian, with Melinda Lundquist Denton. *Soul Searching: The Religious and Spiritual Lives of American Teenagers.* New York: Oxford University Press, 2005, ch. 2, pp. 34-35.

16. RTV, p. 34

CHAPTER SEVEN

Connecting with Families

Leif Kehrwald

Editor's Note

There are many myths and misunderstandings about the relationship between adolescents and their families. In this chapter, Leif Kehrwald challenges these misconceptions, explores the role of family as essential to the faith growth of youth, and provides practical ways to support families as they share and grow in faith.

When I was a parish youth minister over twenty-five years ago, I was little more than a youth myself. I perceived parents and families as obstacles rather than allies in youth ministry. This meant that I viewed youth in isolation from the most important and foundational relationships in their lives. While I thought I knew a lot about those young people—they opened up to me and told me the secrets of their hearts—I realize now that I missed a key formative component for what made them tick ... or not. While not always in harmony, parent and family relationships form a foundational bedrock of identity for young people that, for the sake of their faith growth, must be nurtured during the adolescent years.

Also, since I was still young myself, their parents intimidated me. When I was put in a position of having to interact with them, I felt self-conscious and defensive.

I now know some of what the church has said all along: families are crucial for effective youth ministry. In his exhortation on the family, *Familiaris Consortio*, Pope John Paul II states, "No plan for organized pastoral work, at any level, must ever fail to take into consideration the pastoral care of the family."[1] In *Renewing the Vision*, the U.S. Catholic bishops state, "…the Church's ministry with adolescents should lead young people into a deeper faith life within their own families. In other words, ministry with adolescents should not take adolescents away from the family, but rather foster family life."[2]

God lingers in the creases and folds of ordinary family living. When we help youth and their parents interact with each other, appreciate each other, reconcile their differences, and simply enjoy each other, they can and will discover the richness of God's presence in their lives. The reverse is also true. When young people respond to God's initiative in their lives, youth ministry in the parish can and should help them communicate their discovery with parents and family members.

In their 1994 *Pastoral Message Follow the Way of Love*, the United States bishops wrote, "As Christian families, you not only belong to the Church, but your daily life is a true expression of the Church."[3] What if those of us in ministry truly believed this statement? What would our youth ministry look like if we took seriously that *daily family life* is a true expression of the Church? Our challenge in ministry is to help families recognize God's gracious presence in the ordinary—and extraordinary—events of their lives. Only then can we establish an effective partnership between the church of the parish and the church of the home.

Bring a Parent or Family with You

Before you read any further in this chapter, bring to mind a parent or family of a young person you know. Imagine that parent reading over your shoulder, perhaps pointing out key passages or disagreeing with some points. Bring that parent or family to mind and let them read this chapter with you.

Name of parent or family _____

What do you admire about this parent or family?

What struggles does this family encounter as they navigate the adolescent years?

Complete the sentence: With respect to faith and religious practice, this family…

Theological Foundation

Parents and families are crucial for effective youth ministry. While the primary focus of youth ministry is, quite naturally, on youth, if parents and families are ignored altogether, there is a significant risk of losing all benefit of that focus on youth themselves.

Making the Connection

Family life provides a home for faith and growth.

- *What is an experience of sharing faith or prayer as a family that you recall from your childhood?*

Aside from the sociological and cultural support for the above statement, there is also strong theological tradition in the Catholic Church which holds up the family as both an authentic ecclesial expression, i.e., "domestic church," and as the first and most important ecclesial influence on children and adolescents, i.e., "Parents are the primary educators in the faith."[4]

The tradition teaches that the family is a domestic church, a church of the home. "…in every Christian family the different aspects and functions of the life of the entire Church may be reflected: mission; catechesis; witness; prayer; etc. Indeed in the same way as the Church, the family 'is a place in which the Gospel is transmitted and from which it extends.'"[5]

The family is called to engage in traditional Christian practices that truly nurture the church of the home. It is in the bosom of the family that parents are "to be the first preachers of the faith for their children by word and example. They must foster the vocation which is proper to each child…."[6]

We can turn to the *National Directory for Catechesis* for further insights into the role of parents and family in the faith growth of children and youth. With respect to parents and family as "primary" this document states rather eloquently,

> The Christian family is ordinarily the first experience of the Christian community and the primary environment for growth in faith. Because it is the "church of the home" (FC #38), the family provides a unique *locus* for catechesis. It is a place in which the word of God is received and from which it is extended. With the Christian family, parents are the primary educators in the faith and 'the first heralds of the faith with regard to their children'" (LG, #11).[7]

There are two important points in this quote. First, while the Christian family is "ordinarily" the first and most influential experience of the faith for children, this is not always the case. We have all met young people who discovered God's gracious activity in their lives quite apart from parental or family influence. While this is more the exception than the rule, youth ministry must seek to help these youth remain connected with their families as an important community of faith.

Second, this quote refers to the family and the home as the place where the word is received and from *which it is extended*. This, of course, refers to the role of youth ministry in the lives of young people, i.e., *extending* the original encounter and faith influence received at home. Therefore, it also implies partnership between the home and youth ministry. This notion of partnership is explored further in this chapter.

The NDC goes on to indicate how faith is transmitted at home, in a manner that is much different from, though just as legitimate, as is done in the parish.

> Family members learn more of the Christian life by observing each other's strengths or weaknesses than by formal instruction. They learn intermittently rather than systematically, occasionally rather than in structured periods.[8]

This quote points toward a very important youth ministry task: youth ministry must purposely and proactively help youth and their families grow in faith at home, in home-grown ways. In addition to gathered programming on the parish campus, there must also be opportunities for parents and their sons and daughters to enter into conversation about the faith, engage in home ritual and prayer, and work together on works of mercy and works of justice. This task is also explored further in this chapter.

Know Them

A family perspective in youth ministry seeks to sensitize the youth minister to the realities of marriage and family life. From the statistics mentioned below, we see that today's families are not what we were raised to believe they should be. The social and cultural realities facing families today must be considered in the design and implementation of youth ministry programming.

Recently, I interviewed a parish youth minister in the Archdiocese of Boston. She had worked in the parish for a number of years, had been a parishioner there many years, and had raised her children in the parish. She knew all the young people and their families, and they all knew her. By all accounts youth ministry there flourished.

Effective ministry is all about developing relationships. For the most part, people—children, youth, and adults—grow in their relationship with Christ by growing in deeper relationship with other Christians. While some individuals recognize and respond to God's initiative in their lives outside of other human relationships, most do so in intimate connection with others. And one's relationship with God can nearly always be nurtured through relationship with other believers. This is, of course, true for parents and families just as it is true for youth. Therefore, to effectively connect with parents and families, you must know them—developmentally, statistically, institutionally, and personally. Let me explain.

Know Them Developmentally

Think about the parent or family who is "reading over your shoulder." Did you know this family five to seven years ago? How would you describe the difference between them as a childhood family and them as an adolescent family?

Just as individuals travel through developmental stages—birth, childhood, adolescence, adulthood, old age, death—families also encounter somewhat predictable tasks as they mature through their life cycle. Think about it. A young married couple spends their emotional time and energy on much different issues than new parents. Families with adolescents deal with very different concerns than new parents or parents whose children have been "launched."

Knowing the developmental tasks that adolescents encounter gives you better insight into effectively designing your youth ministry plans and programs. The same is true when you understand the developmental issues of the adolescent family!

Are the developmental tasks the same for the young person and the adolescent family? Yes and no. The adolescent family can resemble the young person as they struggle for a sense of identity, find themselves feeling self-conscious about their place in society, and vacillate between hyper-concern for the future and not being able to think about the future at all.

But the adolescent family must also wrestle with a few other tasks that are more complex. The family, as a whole, and each relationship in the family, must renegotiate rules, roles, and responsibilities, which must shift as the family matures. The children are moving toward adulthood. Boundaries must expand, yet accountability within the family, while seemingly more elusive, is also more crucial. Parental anxiety level is often higher simply because consequences for poor choices are much higher.

Now, add in one more crucial factor. In a typical adolescent family, while the children are "adolescing," the parents often find themselves on the cusp of that stage our society lovingly calls "mid-life." The issues, questions, and anxieties associated with mid-life are amazingly similar to adolescence—identity, future, personal appearance, and so on.

Due to all these factors, the adolescent family is developmentally "pregnant." Individually and as a whole family, they are laden with developmental tasks that tend to intermingle and, on occasion, clash with each other. The more we understand these issues and tasks, the more effectively we can journey with them over these hurdles by offering support, encouragement, and opportunities for mutual commiseration. When we help families deal with their issues, they become more interested in our agenda of faith formation.

When under developmental strain, parental anxiety rises, and parents sometimes respond with just the opposite of what a young person needs. For example, a young person has a growing need for expanding boundaries. Yet, in a time of stress, a parent may respond with more restrictions, fearful of the consequences from a poor choice their son or daughter may make. Or, as the young person experiences the need for deeper and more sophisticated intimacy, the parent may pull back emotionally.

When you observe behavior such as this, it's important to first attempt to interpret it as developmentally normal, giving both parents and young people the benefit of the doubt, rather than immediately presuming family dysfunction. Often, you can lower the anxiety level simply by being personally present and affirming to both youth and parents. When anxiety goes down, everyone makes better choices.

Know Them Statistically

Step back from individual families now and look at all the adolescent families involved in youth ministry or the parish. What information do you have about these families as a whole? What information do you have access to? For example,

- Do you know how many families have single-parent, blended, stepparent(s), or both parents employed outside the home?
- Do you know the ethnic background of these families: Asian, African American, Hispanic, or other?
- Do you know the sizes of these families?
- Of the youth in your program, do you know which ones are the oldest child in the family, and thus blazing new developmental territory for the family?
- Do you know which ones are younger or the youngest in the family, indicating that the family might be more concerned about "launching" than adolescence?

I could give you national statistics on these questions, and I could point you toward Web sites that provide even more information, but quite frankly, that information would be of little value to you. (If interested, though, read the article "America's Families and Living Arrangements: Population Characteristics" published by the U.S. Census Bureau and authored by Jason Fields and Lynne M. Casper. You will find the article at this link: http://www.census.gov/prod/2001pubs/p20-537.pdf.)

National figures have limited value unless you correlate them with local data. Only you can do the statistical homework that will benefit you. Gather parish census data and local or county census information—typically available on the internet through the U.S. Census Bureau (http://www.census.gov/)—and any other sources of information available to you. With this data, create a statistical portrait of adolescent families in your parish. Use the categories I've mentioned above, adding others as needed.

Once complete, gather your team of leaders to read and study the portrait. Ask yourselves what implications there are for your ministry programming. What must you do, for example, to be more sensitive to single-parent households? What must you do, for example, when you see that the vast majority of parents—moms and dads—are employed outside the home? How might you create opportunities for parent-teen interaction when family time is obviously limited?

When you ask yourselves these sorts of questions, you will soon develop a family-friendly youth ministry program.

Because of different family structures, there must be variety in the youth ministry offerings. For example, if you work with young adolescents whose parents are both employed, consider after school programming—a time when young people are often home and unsupervised.

If many of the younger teens in youth ministry are the oldest child in the family, consider offering a program for their parents. The parents can learn a bit about parenting adolescents, support one another, and generally ease their anxiety about moving into this new stage. If appropriate, consider a discussion session on divorce and "When My Parents Broke Up."

Know Them Institutionally

Again, think about that parent or family who is reading over your shoulder. How would that parent or family rate your parish and youth ministry in terms of its "family-friendliness"? Every parish must institutionalize itself in order to have the necessary organization to meet the needs of many people. Yet some programs are rigid and inflexible, allowing little room for those with out-of-the-mainstream needs and concerns. Other programs are so flexible that they lose all definition. Participants don't know where they stand with respect to the program and soon drop out.

A family-friendly ministry maintains definition, expectations, and structure but does so in a way that understands not just the needs of youth, but also the needs of the adolescents' families. In fact, a family-friendly youth ministry will build into its structure ways of reaching parents and giving them opportunities to support one another in their often difficult and confusing vocation.

A family-friendly youth ministry will also build into its structure opportunities for intergenerational learning and growth. Even though youth—and occasionally parents—say they don't really want to spend time with the other generation, when you bring them together for an intentional program of learning and growth, magic happens. Over and over, I've seen young people and parents go to a deeper level with each other in an intergenerational program than they would normally do in their routines at home.

Here's another question for that parent or family over your shoulder. How well do they know and understand your vision, goals, and strategies for youth ministry? When parents and families understand the rationale for all the things you do, they become your allies and some of your best supporters. Take the time to share with them, inform them, and raise their awareness of effective practices in youth ministry. Yes, it takes time and effort, but the partnerships you nurture will surely pay off down the line.

To keep families informed, some parishes send out an e-newsletter with all the information about the youth ministry. In addition to descriptions and schedules of activities, the newsletter has a "Parents' Corner" offering tips and insights for parents and youth. The newsletter always includes the stated philosophy and goals of the youth ministry.

Another way to stay in touch with parents is to have an "open house" session just for parents a couple of times each year. There's no need to plan a big agenda, but have nice food and drink, and create a comfortable atmosphere for parents to get to know you and each other.

Know Them Personally

In the same way that you seek to build personal relationships with youth, I encourage you to do the same with parents and families. Set a goal to make at least one personal contact with the parent(s) of each young person in youth ministry. If yours is a large youth ministry, extend the same challenge to your catechists. This simple strategy puts good will in the bank. There may come a time when you have to draw on that good will, and approach the parent about his or her adolescent's behavior or something of the sort. A previous personal encounter—even months earlier—may make all the difference.

Just as important as it is for you to know them, they need to know you personally. You are more than just a role in the parish. When parents and families get to know you as a person—becoming familiar with your gifts, strengths, and shortcomings—they will likely become your advocates. They will encourage their sons and daughters to participate in youth ministry, and they will defend your efforts with others in the parish.

Here are several practical ways to get to know parents:

- Let it be known that you will be at the back of church after Mass and would love to meet and chat with any parents of youth.
- Invite parents to come early to any youth ministry event and introduce themselves. Promise you won't make them do last minute setup, but that you will take a moment to get to know them.
- Invite yourself to a family home for supper…if it feels appropriate.

Support Them

A family perspective in youth ministry seeks to broaden the minister's perspective by viewing the individual through the lens of adolescent household life. A great deal of your success and impact on young people may depend on their experience of nurture and support at home. Youth ministry can be a catalyst for healthy family living.

A myth is something that has enough credibility to be believed, but not enough to be true. Our society perpetuates several myths about young people and their families that are easy to affirm without realizing it.

- It's a myth that the adolescent years spell trouble for the family.
- It's a myth that adolescents and parents don't know how to connect with each other.
- It's a myth that adolescents and their families cannot grow in faith together.

None of these myths is true, except to the extent that if we believe them, they become a self-fulfilling prophecy. If we expect problems from young people—or their families—they deliver. If we expect growth toward maturity, that's what they deliver instead.

Youth and their families negotiate all the tasks of adolescence with more or less the same degree of success that families in other stages deal with their tasks. In fact, in further contradiction to the myths mentioned, the parent-adolescent relationship typically remains a foundational relationship throughout adolescence. Let me explain.

Quite simply, when push comes to shove, when the chips are down, or when there's trouble in teen paradise—choose your cliché—youth turn to their parents for support and guidance far more often than they turn to their friends. According to studies conducted by Search Institute, when it comes to such things as...

- having trouble in school,
- handling one's feelings,
- drugs and alcohol,
- sex,
- feeling guilty about something,
- deciding what to do with one's life,

...young people seek a parent over a friend to talk with by at least a two-to-one margin.[9]

Does this mean that parents and adolescent don't have strained relationships? Of course, many do. Both have their own unique ways of driving each other nuts! Yet that foundational relationship remains. Problem is, when one of those issues arises, two things can happen simultaneously. 1) The young person makes a clumsy and inarticulate effort at reaching out to a parent for guidance, and that effort may go unrecognized as a plea for help. 2) The parent may be frustrated with the teen for a typical household infraction—messy room, dirty dishes, undone homework, late for curfew, you name it—and therefore is not emotionally pre-disposed to lend support and guidance.

The parent-child relationship remains foundational through the adolescent years, but often goes un-nurtured, rendering it nearly useless when an issue arises. Here is where the youth ministry program can play a role. Consider two simple strategies:

Provide tools for relationship enhancement. Through the parish bulletin, youth newsletter, take home pages, and so on, give young people and their parents practical tools to help them communicate better, understand each others' needs, and resolve conflicts. One of the most useful handouts that I give to parents and their sons and daughters as often as possible is titled *Characteristics Common Among Families Who Heal and Reconcile*:

- They recognize conflict is inevitable.
- They spend their energy seeking solutions rather than laying blame.
- They distinguish the person from than the act.
- They understand the difference between excusing and forgiving.
- They ritualize and celebrate their healing.

It doesn't take much effort to get parents and teens talking about these characteristics. What are some of your tools and strategies?

Provide structured opportunities for parents and teens to interact with each other. Recently, I met a youth minister who conducted a simple survey among youth in his parish.

He asked them two questions:

- If you could have a conversation with anyone, who would it be?
- Who do you have trouble communicating with?

The most common answer to both questions was "parents." With this data in hand, the youth minister arranged for a series of gatherings for parents and youth to talk about communication and conflict resolution. He structured the sessions so that parents and youth had plenty of interaction in peer groups, in mixed groups, and in family groups.

Gatherings and sessions like this not only lend direct support to young people and their families, but they also give those families an opportunity to develop friendships and network with each other. This can be an important catalyst in developing like-to-like ministry.

To sum up, much of your support for families will occur informally as you build relationships with them. However, in the course of a year, consider implementing one or two of the following program steps:

- Invite parents who share common concerns—such as parents of ninth graders, or parents of seniors—to gather for input and mutual support.
- Conduct a few intergenerational sessions throughout the year. Look over your curriculum and choose the topics best suited for conversation between youth and parents.
- Communicate with parents via mail and email. In addition to information about your programming, give them helpful input on parenting adolescents.
- Hold a parent appreciation night. Let them know you appreciate their efforts to raise healthy, balanced, and faithful young men and women.
- Send home discussion-starter questions whenever possible. Do what

you can to get youth and parents talking with each other about the topics youth ministry addresses.

Let Them Participate

A family perspective in youth ministry seeks to partner with parents and families for the sake of faith growth for their sons and daughters. When youth ministry effectively partners with the family, youth are much more likely to "take their faith with them" when they launch into young adulthood.

You may be thinking that this section is ill-named, and that it ought to read "How to *Get* Them to Participate." Actually, I am much more interested in parents and families participating in their adolescent's faith growth than in their participation in youth ministry. The two are closely connected, and one will likely lead to the other, but just having parents drive for retreats, bake cookies for fund raisers, and chaperone various activities does not mean those parents are necessarily actively involved in the faith growth of their adolescents.

Let me summarize some helpful research that demonstrates just how parents and families can participate in meaningful ways in the faith growth of their adolescents. Once you see this research-based information, then you can decide how to incorporate it into your plans and programs.

Years ago, I attended a "Child in Our Hands" conference conducted by the staff of the Youth and Family Institute of Augsburg College. At that conference, Dr. David Anderson talked about five key moments in ordinary family life. When families bring *intention* to these moments—as opposed to letting the moment dictate the outcome—family members will immediately like each other better and function better as a family. The five key moments are:

1. Exits and entries—leave-taking in the morning, re-entry in the evening
2. Car time
3. Meal time
4. Bed time
5. Memory making time—moments of family life that cry out to be remembered[10]

The key to these family moments is intention. When families anticipate them and plan for them, the moments become sources of strength and solidarity, rather than moments of stress and division.

Keep these five key moments in mind while I share with you some additional research. From their "Effective Christian Education Study," Search Institute concluded that there are three key activities that can encourage enduring faith in young people. When young people have the opportunity to engage in these activities, the likelihood that they will take their faith and religious practice with them when they launch into young adulthood *doubles* from among young people who do not engage in these activities. While these activities won't guarantee that youth will take their faith with them, it doubles the likelihood. The three key activities are:

1. Family faith conversation
2. Family ritual and devotion
3. Family outreach and service[11]

What's the first thing you notice about all three activities? They are rooted in the home! This is important. The research was conducted among youth and adults who were active members of their congregations. They were believers who were affiliated with their community, as opposed to those who have no affiliation or religious practice. The implication is clear: families must not only participate in the religious practice of the community through worship, faith formation, and the like, they must also attempt these three key activities at home. Even if they don't perform then well, the research indicates that the activities still have a positive impact.

When families intentionally engage in these activities, they are truly participating in the faith growth of their teens. The problem, of course, is that too many families don't know the importance of these activities, and don't know the first steps for how to engage in them.

This is where youth ministry comes in. What if you dedicated a percentage of your time and energy toward helping families understand how crucial these activities are, and gave them practical ways to engage in them? Try this exercise when your youth ministry team gathers for planning.

1. Bring to mind a variety of families of adolescents in your program. Create a short list of families that represent a variety of family forms and configurations, such as dual career, large family, small family, single-parent, and so on.
2. With this group of families in mind, brainstorm at least one idea for family faith conversation, one idea for ritual and devotion, and one idea for outreach and service—for each of the five key moments in daily family living. You should end up with a list of at least fifteen ideas.
3. Strategize the best ways to put these ideas in the hands of all families in your program and encourage them to try some of the ideas. You might create a simple handout, or you might decide to have a special session

for parents. Or you might share a few ideas at a time through the parish bulletin. Or you might try something else. What are the best strategies for you and your community?

You will surely have parents respond that they feel awkward talking about faith with their sons or daughters, or they just can't imagine doing any sort of a ritual in their home. When I hear these comments from parents, I try to reassure them with the old adage, "If it's worth doing, it's worth doing...poorly." In other words, "Just do it!" Then I follow up with examples and simple steps.

When you help families bring intention to the key moments of their lives, they become healthier families. When you empower them to engage in the three key faith activities, you give them a way to participate meaningfully in the faith growth of their young people.

Principles for Including a Family Perspective

There are a variety of channels through which God's initiative touches youth and their families, and then, in turn, the family responds and grows in faith. The following principles form a framework for your strategic response in helping families make the connection. These principles recognize the full range of faith encounters that families can have, yet offer separate "categories" from which to offer pastoral assistance and effective resources. These principles can guide you in designing youth ministry plans and programs that have the Christian vision of family life woven into them.

Intentional Parents are the first and most influential educators of their children and adolescents. Families provide the foundational setting in which a young person's faith is formed. In what ways can you communicate to parents that this principle still applies to them? What programming efforts do you employ to enhance parent-youth relationships?

Daily Life Families grow in faith when they "stop, look, and listen" in order to recognize God's gracious activity in their daily lives. As you encourage youth to develop spirituality and a prayer life, make sure that they reflect upon their experiences of home and family living, as well as all the other settings of their lives.

Wholeness and Well-being When families build healthy relationships with each other through positive interactions, sharing meals, solving conflicts, and the like, they also grow in faith together. One of the best ways to address this principle is through intergenerational programming. Bring youth, parents, and their families together occasionally. Invite them to talk about the issues that drive them apart and the things that bring them together. In an intergenerational setting, you can create an atmosphere for families to communicate with each other—perhaps even reconcile with one another—that, once done in the gathered setting, can be replicated at home.

Change While sometimes resisted, moments of change and transition in family life open windows for faith growth. When youth participate in a retreat or service week they often have profound faith encounters that change their lives. What do you do to help parents and families accept and adjust to these changes? Change, whether good or bad, always upsets the family balance. Families naturally resist change unless they are given tools and guidance for navigating those turbulent waters.

Religious Practice When families practice their faith—through conversation and discussion, ritual and celebration, outreach and service to others—they grow in faith together. Connected to your gathered programming with youth, always provide a myriad of ways for the conversations to continue at home. Give them ways to pray together and ritualize the events of their lives. When you organize service and outreach efforts for youth, design them in such a way that parents and other family members can participate.

Worship When families participate in the liturgical feasts, seasons, and rhythms of the Church, they make connections between their faith encounters and the faith life of the larger community. Faith formation of children and youth is largely ineffective if they and their families do not worship with the community. Here, we have two responsibilities: 1) continually express the expectation that worship is essential to Christian living, and 2) design liturgically sound worship experiences that engage youth and their families.

Contemporary Culture Families meet the challenges of contemporary culture by articulating their values, establishing clear priorities, and making careful decisions—all in an atmosphere of community support. Youth and their families live in a media-driven world. What can you do to help families navigate that world with a sense of integrity and values?

When parish leaders help family members, particularly adults and adolescents in the family, become familiar with and understand these seven principles, two things occur quite readily. First, they will more easily and more often recognize the "moments of meaning" that occur in their families. Second, they will have a clearer sense of how to respond to the movement of the Spirit in a way that benefits all.[12]

With these principles in mind, the parish community can continue to support the faith development of the adolescent family by implementing some of the following ideas.

- Provide resources and programs that help parents understand the dynamics of faith growth during adolescence and adulthood, and that equip them for the task of helping their sons and daughters, and each other, to grow in the Catholic faith.
- Provide resource materials for parents aimed at promoting family discussion of faith and moral issues, especially as they relate to the challenges faced by youth today.
- Organize parent-youth programs that enable family members to dialogue together about common concerns, e.g., communications, morality, sexuality, and dating.
- Provide resources and/or programs that help families with adolescents to create, revise, and celebrate a regular calendar of family rituals that reflects their family values and experiences, the practices of their family of origin, and the cultural/ethnic traditions of their extended families.
- Facilitate regular parish celebrations of milestones in the life of the family with youth, e.g., graduations from middle/junior high and high school, first jobs, getting a driver's license, birthdays and sacramental anniversaries (baptism and wedding), promotions, job changes, and family moves.
- Develop and celebrate rites of passage to mark the transition from childhood to adolescence; where appropriate, cultural celebrations such as the Orita for African American youth or Quinceañera celebrations for Hispanic families can be adopted or adapted.
- Host or find reflection/retreat experiences for family members with themes appropriate to families with adolescents organized in a variety of formats, e.g., parent-teen retreat, mother-daughter, father-son, etc.
- Model a variety of prayer formats, styles, and techniques in parish programs for young and older adolescents.
- Provide or link families to parent education programs and resources that develop an understanding of the adolescent's developmental characteristics and of the family at this stage of the family life cycle, and develop the

appropriate skills for parenting, e.g., communication, discipline, problem-solving, negotiation, etc.

- Involve parents, adolescents, and the entire family in parish-wide efforts of direct assistance to those in need and programs aimed at changing the structures that unnecessarily perpetuate the need.
- Provide opportunities for family consciousness raising and education on issues of concern both locally and globally, e.g., ecology, hunger relief, homelessness, human rights, racism, sexism, etc.

Partnership with Families

When I was a parish youth minister in the 1980s, parents were an obstacle to contend with. Twenty-five years later, today's ministry leaders must partner with parents and families for effective youth ministry. Parents *are* the primary educators of their children. They have more lasting influence over their adolescents than you do. They know their sons and daughters better than you do. You can help them make sure that their influence is positive. When you make the effort to know them, support them, and let them participate in the faith growth of their teens, that's when they become invaluable allies in your youth ministry efforts.

— RECOMMENDED RESOURCES —

Benson, Peter, et al. *What Kids Need to Succeed: Proven Practical Ways to Raise Good Kids.* Minneapolis: Free Spirit Publishing, 1998.

Brennan, Tina. *Sacred Gifts: Extraordinary Lessons from My Ordinary Teens.* Winona, MN: Saint Mary's Press, 2003.

Calderone-Stewart, Lisa-Marie. *Teens and Parents: Sessions for Growing in Faith Together.* Winona, MN: Saint Mary's Press, 2004.

A Family Perspective in Church and Society: A Manual for All Pastoral Leaders. Washington, DC: United States Conference of Catholic Bishops, 1998.

Follow the Way of Love: A Pastoral Message of the U.S. Catholic Bishops to Families. Washington, DC: United States Conference of Catholic Bishops, 1994.

Kehrwald, Leif (ed.). *Families and Faith: A Vision and Practice for Parish Ministry.* New London, CT: Twenty-Third Publications, 2006.

Kehrwald, Leif. *Youth Ministry and Parents: Secrets for a Successful Partnership.* Winona, MN: Saint Mary's Press, 2004.

Kehrwald, Leif. *Parents and Schools in Partnership: A Message for Parents on Nurturing Faith in Teens.* Winona, MN: Saint Mary's Press, 2002.

Strommen, Merton P., and Richard A Hardel. *Passing on the Faith: A Radical New Model for Youth and Family Ministry*. Winona, MN: Saint Mary's Press, 2000.

— ENDNOTES —

1. Pope John Paul II. "Apostolic Exhortation *Familiaris Consortio* of Pope John Paul II to the Episcopate, to the Clergy, and to the Faithful of the Whole Catholic Church on the Role of the Christian Family in the Modern World," #70 (November 22, 1981). See http://www.vatican.va/holy_father/john_paul_ii/apost_exhortations/documents/ hf_jp-ii_exh_19811122_familiaris-consortio_en.html#top (accessed September 31, 2005).

2. *Renewing the Vision: A Framework for Catholic Youth Ministry*, Washington, DC: United States Conference of Catholic Bishops, 1997, p. 21.

3. *Follow the Way of Love: A Pastoral Message of the U.S. Catholic Bishops to Families*. Washington, DC: United States Conference of Catholic Bishops, 1994, p. 8

4. Congregation for the Clergy, *General Directory for Catechesis*. Washington, DC: Libreria Editrice Vaticana–United States Conference of Catholic Bishops, 1998, #255.

5. Ibid.

6. Flannery, Austin, OP. *Vatican Council II: The Basic Sixteen Documents*. Northport, NY: Costello Publishing, 1996. "Dogmatic Constitution on the Church" (*Lumen Gentium*), #11.

7. *National Directory for Catechesis*. Washington, DC: United States Conference of Catholic Bishops, 2005, pp. 100-01.

8. Ibid.

9. See *Passing on the Faith* by Merton Strommen and Dick Hardel (Saint Mary's Press, 2000), pp. 48-50.

10. For more information see: Youth and Family Institute—www.youthandfamilyinstitute.org and http://www.youthandfamilyinstitute.org/conferences/cioh.asp (accessed September 8, 2005).

11. See *The Teaching Church: Moving Christian Education to Center Stage* by Eugene C. Roehlkepartain (Nashville: Abingdon Press, 1993), pp. 174-77.

12. These seven principles first appeared in *Families and Faith: A Vision and Practice for Parish Leaders*, Leif Kehrwald (ed.) (New London, CT: Twenty-Third Publications, 2006), pp. 70-71.

CHAPTER EIGHT

Connecting Youth with the Parish Community

John Roberto

Editor's Note

The parish is a rich resource for faith growth and ministry because of the intergenerational relationships and a community life that includes prayer, ritual, socials, service, and shared learning. In this chapter, John Roberto guides us through the research projects and parish experiences that focus on the role of the parish in forming faith in youth.

The parish is where the Church lives. Parishes are communities of faith, of action, and of hope. They are where the Gospel is proclaimed and celebrated, where believers are formed and sent to renew the earth. Parishes are the home of the Christian community; they are the heart of our Church. Parishes are the place where God's people meet Jesus in word and sacrament and come in touch with the source of the Church's life.[1]

The parish is where the Church lives. It is often easy to overlook the important roles of the parish community and of intergenerational relationships in ministry with young people because there is so much work to do in organizing and conducting youth programs, training leaders, and relating to and caring for young people. Yet, involving the parish community in the lives of young people and engaging young people in the life of the parish community are among the most important and difficult tasks of ministry with young people.

 ## A Growing Vision of Youth and Parish Life

In 1976, *A Vision of Youth Ministry* revitalized the Church's ministry with young people. It proposed two goals for ministry with youth. The first focused on the personal and spiritual growth of young people. The second focused on the active engagement of young people in the life of the parish community: "To draw young people to responsible participation in the life, mission, and work of the faith community."[2] This second goal challenged youth ministry and parish leaders to make young people vital members of the parish community and to provide meaningful ways to involve them in the life and mission of the parish. This goal challenges youth to live their baptismal promises and to be fully engaged in the worship, ministries, and sacramental life of the Church.

 Making the Connection

Parishes have numerous resources for sharing faith with youth.

- *What programs, events, and communities would you name as resources and assets in your parish?*

In 1997, *Renewing the Vision* expanded upon this goal. First, it emphasized that young people are "full-fledged members" of the parish community. "In parishes, young people should feel a sense of belonging and acceptance....Young people are more likely to gain a sense of identity in the community if they are regarded as full-fledged members of that community."[3]

Second, *Renewing the Vision* affirmed the insight that the parish community is richer because of the gifts and roles that young people exercise in the parish.

> In parishes, young people need to have a wide variety of opportunities to use their gifts and to express their faith through meaningful roles. They will develop a spirit of commitment within a community only through actual involvement in the many ways the Church exercises and carries out its mission.[4]

Renewing the Vision also challenged all parishes to become "youth-friendly" communities that "value young people," see them as resources, and encourage their active presence in parish life. Parish communities need to provide young people with numerous opportunities for intergenerational relationships across all ages.

Youth and the Parish Community— Mutually Reinforcing Relationships

These central insights about the importance of the parish community are reinforced by research into effective parish youth ministry. The study, *Effective Youth Ministry Practices in Catholic Parishes*, points to the necessity of "a willing parish." This study relied on interviews with youth, adult leaders, and parish staff members in Catholic parishes that were identified as providing dynamic youth ministry. In the first interview with youth, the interviewer asked the young people what a parish needed to do to be effective in youth ministry. A young woman answered that it wasn't so much what the parish does as what the parish is. The parish needs to be a "willing" parish. A parish that is willing to allow youth to be full members of the parish and to be fully integrated within parish life is a parish whose members are in relationship with the youth in their midst. These relationships change the lives of youth and bring energy and transformation to the life of the parish.[5]

The authors of the study did not find a new model for youth ministry or a single event or strategy that made the difference for parishes with effective youth ministry. What they found was a pattern of ministry with the parish at the center.

> From knowing youth, parishes responded to youth's needs and included their gifts in their community. These parishes knew young people and desired a youth ministry that was infused with the life of the parish. Parish staff and key leaders paved the way and helped the community know and appreciate their young members. Because they knew and cared about their youth, these communities were willing to respond in innovative ways. They tried new ways to involve youth in parish life and provide programs and events for youth to be with their peers. They established an ongoing peer community to help youth get to know each other better, and they opened the leadership, service, and ministry roles to youth. When planning for parish life, they thought about youth not just because they should but because they could not imagine parish life without them.[6]

Adult leaders, parish staff members, and youth interviewed in the study repeatedly described their parish as a home for youth ministry, using images like "second home," "part of the fabric," and "heart of the parish." A web of relationships grew and developed as youth grew in their ownership of the parish community and their connections with adults in the community. This web of relationships is built intentionally through concrete efforts: youth to youth, youth with adults, youth with their families, and youth with the parish community as a whole. Through this web of relationships, faith is mediated and youth are empowered as active young disciples.

Several important findings about the parish community and its relationship to youth ministry emerged from the study.

- Parish youth ministry thrives when it has the support of the whole parish. Youth feel at home in the parish and are genuinely known and liked by parish members. Youth are integrated into the full life of the parish. This involvement of youth in parish ministries and parish activities is planned for, encouraged, and affirmed. Youth share in leadership and decision-making in parish committees, ministries, and organizations. Youth have opportunities to witness to their faith with peers, children, and adults. Parish staff and leadership are supportive of youth ministry and youth involvement.[7]
- In parishes with effective youth ministry, the parish community understands and places a priority on youth ministry. Parishioners know that youth ministry is everyone's responsibility. The community desires youth ministry that is infused into parish life.[8]
- Some goals of youth ministry are best achieved when youth are involved in overall parish life, praying and working together with adults and children. Other goals are best achieved within a youth peer community where youth are relating primarily to other youth. Balancing both these dimensions is important for creating effective youth ministry.[9]

The relationship between young people and the parish community is mutually reinforcing.

> Youth, youth ministry, and the parish community all thrive when youth are connected to the parish. Youth thrive because they experience consistency between their experience of youth ministry events and parish participation, and they benefit from the relationships of an intergenerational community. Youth ministry thrives because leaders can rely upon aspects of parish life and other adults in the community to accomplish some of the goals for youth ministry. The parish community benefits because parish life is enriched by the energy, enthusiasm, and gifts of young members.[10]

Youth and Intergenerational Relationships

We live in a society defined by age segregation, in which adults and children go their separate ways. Young people experience very few settings that are truly intergenerational. The architecture and design of communities and neighbor-hoods isolate families, and virtually every program and institution is organized to meet age-specific needs at the expense of the richness of intergenerational community.

Churches, synagogues, and mosques are among the very few settings where three or more generations gather for intentional activities. Yet even in churches, young people are segregated by age from the rest of the community for most of their activities. In the typical Catholic parish today, a child can be involved in catechetical programs from first grade through high school and never have the opportunity to meet and learn with other generations in the parish communi-ty—to the detriment of the individual and the other generations.

The 2000 research study, *Grading Grown-Ups: American Adults Report on their Real Relationships with Kids* found

- There is clear evidence that young people benefit from multiple, sustained relationships with adults outside their immediate family. For example, Search Institute research has found that the more adults a young person reports that he or she can turn to, the better off that young person is. Yet just twenty-two percent of the youth surveyed reported having strong re-lationships with five or more adults other than their parents.[11]
- To grow up healthy, young people need to be surrounded, supported, and guided within a sustained network of adults in addition to their parents who choose to know, name, support, affirm, acknowledge, guide, and in-clude children and adolescents in their lives.[12]

Yet this study found that most young people lacked the sense of "connected-ness" to other generations.

Grading Grown-Ups revealed that youth and adults had shared priorities for intergenerational relationships, but these relationship-building actions were not happening often enough. A gap existed between what adults believed and what they did. Of the eighteen actions by adults that were studied, only the top three—encouraging school success, teaching respect for cultural differences, and teaching shared values—were reported to occur with any regularity. Some very important actions that adults could exercise in their relationships were not being practiced: passing down traditions, having meaningful conversations, being engaged in giv-ing and serving to help the needy, modeling giving and serving to make life fair and equal, discussing religious beliefs, and discussing personal values.[13]

The study makes clear that "forming meaningful relationships across genera-tions needs to become an expected part of everyday life. All adults need to see being engaged with kids as part of their responsibility as part of their community and this society. Children and youth need to be able to count on adults for support, guidance, and modeling."[14]

Renewing the Vision also recognizes the importance of intergenerational relationships:

> Ministry with adolescents recognizes the importance of the intergenerational faith community in sharing faith and promoting healthy growth in adolescents. Meaningful involvement in parish life and the development of intergenerational relationships provide young people with rich resources to learn the story of the Catholic faith experientially and to develop a sense of belonging to the Church. Ministry with adolescents can incorporate young people into the intergenerational opportunities already available in the parish community, identify and develop leadership opportunities in the parish for young people, and create intergenerational support networks and mentoring relationships. Age-specific programs can be transformed into intergenerational programming, and new intergenerational programs that incorporate young people can be developed.[15]

Intentionally building intergenerational relationships through ministry with youth brings a number of significant benefits to young people and the whole parish community. Features of intergenerational ministry and faith formation:

1. It is inclusive of all ages and generations, single or married, with or without children.
2. It builds community and meaningful relationships across all generations in a parish.
3. It provides a setting for each generation to share and learn from other generations (their faith, stories, wisdom, experience, and knowledge).
4. It involves the whole family in learning together and equips families with knowledge, skills, and faith-sharing activities for nurturing faith at home.
5. It provides an environment where new ways of living one's faith can be practiced.
6. It provides adult role models for children and youth.
7. It promotes understanding of shared values and a common faith.
8. It helps to overcome the age-segregated nature of our society, including parish programs.
9. It enhances people's identification with their parish and integration within the parish community.
10. It incorporates a variety of ways to learn: prayer, community building, in-

teractive and experiential presentations and activities, group discussion, and sharing.[16]

Becoming a Youth Ministry that Connects with the Whole Parish Community

Many young people are blessed with experiences of a supportive parish community and dynamic youth ministry. But this type of parish community life does not happen overnight. It comes from many years of intentional and sustained efforts to build a parish culture that values and includes young people, and a youth ministry that structures parish connections and intergenerational relationships into its vision and programming.

For this vision to become a reality, a parish needs to be intentional. Vision starts with the pastor, parish staff, and youth ministry leadership. They must all share a common ideal for youth ministry and the important role of young people in the parish community. Discussion needs to center around a careful reading and reflection on *Renewing the Vision* and move to a youth ministry vision statement for the entire parish community that becomes the foundation for action. The process culminates in an action plan with specific practices and strategies that are intentional, structured ways to create a supportive, "youth-friendly" parish community, build intergenerational relationships, and connect young people with the parish community.

This effort takes work. The challenge for youth ministry leaders is to continue to expand the scope of youth ministry—from a focus only on young people—to include ministry with the families of youth, intergenerational connections with the parish community, and relationships with all of the other religious, educational, and social organizations in the wider community. In the face of the increasing scope of youth ministry, too many parishes retreat into a youth-only focus, neglecting families and connections with the parish community.

The Importance of Leadership for Advocacy

The ministry of advocacy engages the Church to examine its priorities and practices to determine how well young people are integrated into the life, mission, and work of the Catholic community. It places adolescents and families first by analyzing every policy and program—domestic, parish-based, diocesan, and international—for its impact on adolescents and families.[17]

Advocacy means that leaders speak up for those who need support or help them to speak for themselves. In youth ministry, advocacy includes speaking up for youth and families who are in greatest need in the community. This kind of advocacy connects with justice and service efforts. Advocacy also means that a parish community considers the needs and gifts of youth and their families throughout the planning and implementation of parish life.

Sometimes advocacy happens naturally as a part of relationships among leaders. In a parish staff meeting, the youth ministry coordinator might suggest that young people assist with an upcoming parish festival. In a conversation with the pastor or the liturgy coordinator, the youth ministry coordinator may work out a way to involve adolescents in liturgical ministries. Advocacy for youth depends upon collaborative relationships, which means that youth leaders need to take the time to build trusting and mutually supportive relationships with other parish staff members and key parish leaders.

Advocacy in youth ministry also includes providing for a youth voice in the leadership groups, councils, and commissions of the parish. This might mean having two or more young people as part of a committee. When parishes involve youth on an adult board or group, the young people must be prepared and supported in this role. For some parishes and leadership groups, having a youth voice may mean identifying one or more adult members of the group to speak for the younger people. These leaders could connect with youth before and after leadership meetings to help bring youth issues into the planning for parish life.

Ideally, no one in particular needs to be a youth advocate. The whole parish community could share a common vision for youth ministry and be vested in knowing the needs and gifts of youth in the parish.

In one parish, the youth ministry coordinator worked to help the community understand youth ministry better. The coordinator and some young people developed a PowerPoint presentation with music, photos, and narration about youth and youth ministry. The leader then asked every organization in the parish to allot thirty minutes of time during a fall meeting for a brief presentation and discussion. At the end of the presentation, the youth leaders surprised the adults in these meetings when they asked, "How can youth ministry support your work in the parish?" Through these efforts, the parish grew in its ownership and vision for youth ministry.

Becoming a Willing Parish

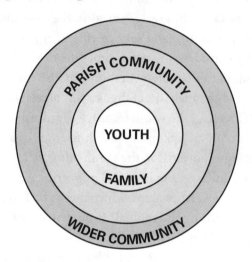

Every parish can become "a willing parish"—one that lets the young people in its midst become full members of the community, one that puts its energy and resources into developing youth ministry, one that is willing to let youth be leaders and share in ministries side by side with adults. The following approaches and strategies can start a parish on this journey, one that benefit both youth *and* the parish community.

Reflecting on Your Parish Community

Take a moment to reflect on how well your parish community connects with young people. Rate each of the nine items below from 1 (low, not part of our parish and youth ministry efforts) through 4 (high, a strong feature of our parish and youth ministry efforts). Use this simple assessment with your parish staff and your youth ministry team. Schedule time to discuss the results, reflect on the questions below, and plan for new ways your parish can connect with young people. Use the ideas in the next section to stimulate your thinking about all of the possibilities available to your parish community to connect with young people.

Connecting Youth with the Parish Community
Assessment

1	Our parish community knows and values young people, and this is communicated by parish leadership and the parish community.	**1 2 3 4**
2	Our parish community understands the vision and goals for youth ministry, knows about youth ministry programs and activities, and places a priority on ministry with young people.	**1 2 3 4**
3	Our parish invites and welcomes young people at Sunday Mass.	**1 2 3 4**
4	Our parish encourages young people to participate with other generations in parish-wide ministries and programs, and young people's involvement is planned for and affirmed.	**1 2 3 4**
5	Our parish offers intergenerational catechetical programming that connects all of the generations for learning, praying, and building relationships.	**1 2 3 4**
6	Our parish integrates young people into leadership roles such as liturgical ministers or catechists within the parish community.	**1 2 3 4**
7	Our parish involves young people in leading programs, activities, and ministries such as Stations of the Cross in Lent or a Thanksgiving food drive for the whole parish community.	**1 2 3 4**
8	Our youth ministry regularly offers youth programs that connect youth with other generations in the parish, such as youth-sponsored programs with young children or older adults.	**1 2 3 4**
9	Our youth ministry offers programming that prepares young people to participate in the life of the parish throughout the year, such as reflecting on the Sunday Lectionary readings or preparing for participation in Church Year feasts and seasons, in parish celebrations of the sacraments (e.g., Reconciliation in Advent or Lent), and in parish-wide service projects.	**1 2 3 4**

Reflection Questions

Reflect on the results of your assessment with the parish staff and youth ministry team, using questions such as the following:

► *What strengths did you identify?*

► *What areas of improvement did you identify?*

► *How "youth-friendly" is your parish community today? How connected to the parish community do you think young people feel today?*

► *What barriers do you face when it comes to connecting youth with the parish community and building intergenerational relationships?*

► *What steps can you take to overcome these barriers?*

► *What are the one or two priorities that you need to act on now?*

Strategies for Connecting Youth with the Parish Community

There is no one way to connect youth to a parish community. Every parish has its own unique identity, history, traditions, people, and geography. Customize the ideas below for your parish community. Use them to spark your own creativity. There are many ways to reach the goal of drawing "young people into responsible participation in the life, mission, and work of the Catholic faith community."[18]

Strategies are organized into five basic approaches.

- Build a youth-friendly parish culture where young people are valued and intentionally included in all of parish life.
- Infuse parish connections and intergenerational relationships and programming into existing youth programs.
- Incorporate youth into the ministries and leadership roles of the parish and community.
- Align youth programming with the life and events of the parish community.
- Create new models of intergenerational programming for all the generations of the parish community.

Approach 1

Build a youth-friendly parish culture where young people are valued and intentionally included in all of parish life.

Raise the profile of young people in the parish community by making them more visible at parish gatherings, recognizing their presence in the community, and affirming their contributions to the parish and the wider community.

Cultivate a widespread, strong expectation for engagement of the parish community with young people. Let everyone know that your parish is working to become more "youth-friendly" and that everyone has a role. Develop a consistent expectation that parishioners should be engaged positively with young people and that positive engagement is encouraged and appreciated.

Educate your parish community on the "real" picture of young people, confronting the popular stereotypes of youth in the media. Too many adults believe that young people are "aliens" from a different generation who cannot and do not want to relate to adults. Many adults believe that ado-

lescence is, by definition, a turbulent, conflict-ridden time, and that adolescents will inevitably engage in negative, dangerous behavior. Because
youth have so many problems, a lot of time and professional expertise
is necessary to make a difference in the lives of young people. Challenge
these assumptions by presenting research about and actual stories of
young people, which will help the parish community understand and become comfortable with young people.

Examine your parish's activities—from worship to catechesis to social
events—to determine if it is welcoming to all generations, especially
young people. Explore whether these activities offer opportunities for
more relationship-building across generations.

Provide opportunities for adult parishioners to reflect together on their own
relationships with young people. Identify adult's priorities for and interests in making connections.

Involve your parish community in praying for youth events, such as service
trips or retreats, and milestones such as graduations and other accomplishments. Engage young people in composing petitions to be included
in the Prayers of the Faithful.

Offer simple, one-time opportunities for adults and young people to get to
know each other. Host social events, service projects, or educational experiences. Make a concerted effort to invite people from all generations to
plan and participate in the activities.

Encourage adults of all ages to share their faith journeys, beliefs, and values
with young people. Invite young people to share their stories, too.

Link adults in the parish who have insights and life experiences on topics
such as money management, dating relationships, and vocational choices,
to a particular young person.

Through worship services, newsletters, adult education, and other venues,
urge all adults in your parish to form meaningful relationships with young
people in the neighborhood, the workplace, and in social activities—not
just in the parish.

Create communication strategies for promoting the good news about young
people and their role in the parish and wider community. For example,

> ⊳ Post a bulletin board in the vestibule with pictures and stories about in-
dividual young people who are providing service, leadership, and community involvement, notices about school achievements and events,
and pictures from youth ministry programs.

▷ Publish a quarterly youth newsletter inserted into the parish bulletin, reporting on the achievements of youth in the parish and wider community.

▷ Make presentations at the meetings of parish organizations and groups using a team of youth to explain the parish youth ministry through pictures, stories, music, and drama.

Provide community building at parish events. At the beginning of a parish mission, service day, or social function, include introductions and a brief community-building exercise. This will help youth and the adults in your community to get to know each other.

Provide youthful hospitality at parish-wide events. Create a variety of refreshments and decorations that will appeal to people of all ages, like including soda and chips along with donuts and coffee.

Approach 2

Infuse parish connections and intergenerational relationships and programming into the existing youth programs and activities.

Integrate intergenerational programs, such as quarterly intergenerational nights, into the youth program plan and calendar.

"Intergenerationalize" youth programs—take youth-only programs and redesign them to include other generations.

Structure youth programs with an intergenerational connection. For examples, create an educational program that includes interviews with parish members (or community members) of different ages or invite a panel of adults into a youth program.

Incorporate intergenerational dialogues into programming—provide opportunities for youth to access the wisdom, experience, knowledge, and interests of older adults through presentations, performances, and discussions. Provide older adults with an opportunity to be recognized and valued.

Develop mentoring relationships between youth and adults, such as prayer partners, learning-to-pray spiritual direction, service involvement, and Confirmation mentors. Mentoring programs can replace some of the parish's gathered youth programs.

Approach 3

Incorporate youth into the ministries and leadership roles of the parish and community.

Identify ways to integrate youth into leadership roles within the parish community.

> ▷ Make note of all possibilities for leadership in the ministries, programs, and activities of your parish—councils and committees, ministries and programs (liturgy, justice and service, social activities, religious education).

> ▷ Identify specific roles for adolescents, such as assistant teachers in children's religious education classes or as liturgical ministers (lectors, greeters, musicians, artists for the environment).

> ▷ Involve youth in parish committees, such as the parish council or liturgy committee—and always involve at least two young people. One young person on an adult committee can be lost or isolated. Assign an adult on the committee to support the young people by talking with them to ensure the process is going smoothly and inclusively.

> ▷ Work with parish and community leaders to connect young people to leadership roles. This approach to leadership is a great way to build mentoring relationships between adults and young people, and to utilize the gifts, talents, and energy of adolescents in the parish and community. Be sure to provide training so that young people can succeed in their new roles.

> ▷ Provide training for adults and youth on how to work with each other.

Involve youth in liturgical roles such as lectors, greeters (hospitality ministry), and musicians (voice or instruments). Identify youth who are good singers or instrumentalists (check out the school band and choir) and get them involved in music ministry. Identify artists and encourage them to use their gifts in planning the environment for various liturgical seasons. Establish an apprenticeship program and formation for youth involved in liturgical ministries.

Organize a leadership or ministry apprenticeship for youth to serve in parish and community leadership positions and committees.

Create new parish or community leadership roles that are led by young people and which draw upon some of their unique and special gifts—Web site design and maintenance, video production, drama productions, music (instrumental and voice), and art.

Create a youth program or task force to analyze youth involvement in your parish or community. Working in teams, take a month to explore the life and ministries of the parish. Create a report on youth involvement in parish life for young people, for the parish staff and leadership, and for the parish community.

Approach 4

Align youth programming with the life and events of the parish community.

Involve youth in the preparation and leadership of seasonal events (Advent-Christmas, Lent-Easter, Pentecost) or ethnic celebrations. For example, young people with dramatic and musical talent could take responsibility for preparing and presenting "Living Stations of the Cross" during Holy Week.

Prepare young people to participate in the life of the parish throughout the year by reflecting on the Sunday Lectionary readings or by preparing for participation in Church year feasts and seasons, in parish celebrations of the sacraments (e.g., Reconciliation in Advent or Lent), and in parish-wide service projects. Incorporate into catechetical programs, retreats, and other youth ministry programs, learning experiences that prepare young people to participate meaningfully in the life of the parish community. All too often, young people don't participate because they don't know how to participate. By focusing programming on upcoming parish events you can draw young people into participating more fully in the life of the parish. Parish events that can become a focus of youth ministry programming include

▷ Church year feasts and seasons, such as Advent, Christmas, Ash Wednesday, Lent, Holy Thursday, Good Friday, Easter Vigil, Pentecost, All Saints Day, and All Souls Day.

▷ Sacramental celebrations, such as parish-wide Reconciliation services in Advent or Lent.

▷ Justice and service projects of the parish community or national justice events, such as the Catholic Campaign for Human Development's Poverty Awareness Month in January or Respect Life Sunday in October.

Approach 5

Create new models of intergenerational programming for all of the generations of the parish community.

Offer intergenerational programming that connects all of the generations for learning, praying, worshipping, socializing, and serving, such as

▷ Tutoring and mentoring programs between adult and youth or youth and children, computer tutors for older adults, and justice and service projects.

▷ Music and art projects—community concerts where musicians of all ages perform together, intergenerational art exchanges or exhibits, or Advent and Lenten music festivals.

▷ Social-recreational activities, such as an intergenerational Olympics and lenten simple meals.

Offer intergenerational catechetical programs that integrate youth with other generations for learning. More and more parishes across the country are adopting an intergenerational model of learning in their catechetical efforts.[19] They are involving multiple generations in learning, praying, celebrating, and sharing faith together. Intergenerational learning helps to create a supportive faith community and provides a great way for young people to learn and share faith with all of the generations in a parish.

Intergenerational learning programs are usually two-and-a-half to three hours in length, conducted during a variety of weeknights and weekends, and are often structured around the following elements:

PART I. Gathering and Prayer

PART II. All-Ages Learning Experience
Each session may begin with the multigenerational experience of a theme that all ages share together. All-ages learning experiences equalize all ages, so that listening to music or singing, watching a dramatic presentation, making an art project, watching a video, hearing a story, participating in a ritual, and praying together allow different-aged people to participate at the same time and place in a similar manner. Learning is at a level where all may do it together. Shared experiences are absolutely critical for intergenerational learning.

PART III. In-Depth Learning Experience
Structured learning activities and discussions engage all ages in exploring the meaning of an event and theme, and develop everyone's ability to participate meaningfully in an event. An intergenerational learning program may include learning experiences for families with children (grades one to five), adolescents, and adults. Preschool children often have a separate learning group. In-depth learning experiences can be designed in one of three formats:

Age-Group Format: learning in separate, parallel groups organized by ages

Whole-Group Format: learning in small groups or table groups with the whole group assembled in one room

Learning Activity Centers Format: learning organized into intergenerational or age-appropriate activity centers

PART IV. Whole-Group Sharing Experience

The whole group re-gathers and each group briefly shares what it has learned and/or created in its In-Depth Learning Experience. Whole-group sharing provides an opportunity for each generation to teach each other, via a project or activity, a verbal summary, a symbol of learning, or a dramatic presentation. Whole-group sharing can also be conducted in intergenerational or small groups rather than in presentations to the entire group.

PART V. Sharing Learning Reflections and Home Applications

To conclude the program, participants have the opportunity to reflect on what they learned and to prepare for applying the lessons to their daily lives. This part of an intergenerational learning program is designed to prepare people to participate in the event and utilize the home activities.

PART VI. Closing Prayer Service

For more information about intergenerational learning see the books below by Roberto and Martineau and go to www.cmdnet.org.

Conclusion

Catholic youth ministry has the opportunity to make a significant contribution to the lifelong faith growth of young people. Involving young people in parish life and helping them experience the parish community as a "home" has a long-term impact on young people's future involvement as adults and provides benefits for the individual and for the whole Church.

All parish communities need to accept the challenge to embrace, engage, and empower the young people. The future of the Church depends on it.

— RECOMMENDED RESOURCES —

Benson, Peter. *All Kids Are Our Kids: What Communities Must Do to Raise Caring and Responsible Children and Adolescents.* San Francisco: Jossey-Bass, 1998.

Benson, Peter, Judy Galbraith, and Pamela Espeland. *What Kids Need to Succeed* (revised edition). Minneapolis: Free Spirit Publishing, 1998.

Dean, Kenda Creasy, and Ron Foster. *The Godbearing Life: The Art of Soul Tending for Youth Ministry.* Nashville: Upper Room Books, 1998.

East, Thomas, with Ann Marie Eckert, Dennis Kurtz, and Brian Singer-Towns. *Effective Practices for Dynamic Youth Ministry.* Winona, MN: St. Mary's Press, 2005.

Fisher, Deborah. *Working Shoulder to Shoulder: Stories of Youth-Adult Partnerships that Succeed.* Minneapolis: Search Institute, 2004.

Kimball-Baker, Kathleen. *Tag, You're It! 50 Easy Ways to Connect with Young People.* Minneapolis: Search Institute, 2003.

Martineau, Mariette, Joan Weber, and Leif Kehrwald. *Intergenerational Faith Formation: All Ages Learning Together.* New London, CT: Twenty-Third Publications, 2008.

No More Us and Them: 100 Ways to Bring Your Youth and Church Together. Loveland, CO: Group Books, 1999.

Ratliff, Mike. *Sacred Bridges: Making Lasting Connections between Older Youth and the Church.* Nashville: Abingdon Press, 2002.

Renewing the Vision: Reflections on the Social Mission of the Parish. Washington, DC: United States Conference of Catholic Bishops, 1994.

Roberto, John. "Intergenerational Learning." *Pastoral Leaders' Source Book.* Orlando: Harcourt Religion Publishers, 2004.

Roberto, John, and Mariette Martineau. *Generations of Faith Resource Manual: Lifelong Faith Formation for the Whole Parish Community.* Mystic, CT: Twenty-Third Publications, 2005.

Roehlkepartain, Eugene C. *Building Assets in Congregations: A Practical Guide for Helping Youth Grow Up Healthy.* Minneapolis: Search Institute, 1998.

Roehlkepartain, Jolene and Eugene. *Prescription for a Healthy Church: Ministry Ideas to Nurture Whole People.* Loveland, CO: Group Publishing, 2000.

Scales, Peter, Peter Benson, and Marc Mannes. *Grading Grown-Ups 2002: How Do American Kids and Adults Relate.* Minneapolis: Search Institute, 2002.

Scales, Peter, Peter Benson, and Eugene Roehlkepartain. *Grading Grown-Ups: American Adults Report on their Real Relationships with Kids.* Minneapolis: Search Institute, 2001.

Strommen, Merton, and Richard Hardel. "Congregations as Family" in *Passing on the Faith.* Winona, MN: Saint Mary's Press, 2000.

Web Resources

The Center for Ministry Development has research and resources for connecting youth to the parish and for developing intergenerational programming. Go to www.cmdnet.org.

The Search Institute has research and resources to assist with making intergenerational connections. Contact www.search-institute.org. For congregational resources go to www.search-institute.org/congregations. For articles and research reports go to www.search-institute.org/downloads.

— ENDNOTES —

1. *Communities of Salt and Light: Reflections on the Social Mission of the Parish*. Washington, DC: United States Conference of Catholic Bishops, 1994, p. 1.

2. *A Vision of Youth Ministry*. Washington, DC: United States Conference of Catholic Bishops, 1976, p. 7.

3. *Renewing the Vision: A Framework for Catholic Youth Ministry*. Washington, DC: United States Conference of Catholic Bishops, 1997, p. 13.

4. RTV, p. 13.

5. See: Thomas East, Ann Marie Eckert, Dennis Kurtz, and Brian Singer-Towns, *Effective Practices for Dynamic Youth Ministry* (Winona, MN: Saint Mary's Press, 2004), p. 9.

6. Ibid., p. 10.

7. Ibid., p. 16.

8. Ibid., p. 19.

9. Ibid., p. 19.

10. Ibid., p. 27.

11. Sacales, Peter C., Peter L. Benson, Eugene C. Roehlkepartain. *Grading Grown-Ups: American Adults Report on Their Real Relationships with Kids*. Minneapolis: Lutheran Brotherhood and Search Institute, 2001, p. 5 (accessed March 28, 2006 at www.search-institute.org/norms/2000/GradingGrown-Ups-Report.pdf).

12. Ibid., p. 49.

13. Ibid., p. ix.

14. Ibid., p. xi.

15. RTV, p. 22.

16. Roberto, John. *Becoming a Church of Lifelong Learners*. New London, CT: Twenty Third Publications, 2006, p. 86.

17. RTV, p. 27.

18. RTV, p. 11.

19. See: *Becoming a Church of Lifelong Learners*, Chapter 1, pp. 3-25.

Promoting the Personal and Spiritual Growth of Youth

The most effective catechetical programs for adolescents are integrated into a comprehensive program of pastoral ministry for youth that includes catechesis, community life, evangelization, justice and service, leadership development, pastoral care, and prayer and worship.

United States Catholic Conference of Bishops,
National Directory for Catechesis, p. 201
with reference to *Renewing the Vision*, p. 26

CHAPTER NINE

Catechesis with Youth

Tom East

Editor's Note

Like the disciples on the road to Emmaus, youth have many questions about faith and their lives. Christ walks with youth in these questions. This chapter points to the encounter with Christ as the objective of adolescent catechesis as it explores the settings, models, methods, and resources that help parishes provide transformed and transforming catechesis with youth.

> The definitive aim of catechesis is to put people not only in touch, but also in communion and intimacy, with Jesus Christ.
>
> GENERAL DIRECTORY
> FOR CATECHESIS, #80[1]

People who encounter Jesus are changed forever. When we love Jesus as our teacher and guide, we strive to know him and his ways. This is what discipleship is all about—following Jesus, learning Jesus, and allowing our lives to be fashioned to reflect the face of Christ to the world.

Starting with the "initial" conversion of a person to the Lord, moved by the Holy Spirit through the primary proclamation of the Gospel, catechesis seeks to solidify and mature this first adherence. It proposes to help those who have just converted "to know better this Jesus to whom he has entrusted himself: to know his 'mystery', the kingdom of God proclaimed by him, the requirements and comments contained in his Gospel message, and the paths that he has laid down for anyone who wishes to follow him."

GENERAL DIRECTORY FOR CATECHESIS, #80[2]

We know Jesus through our encounter with him and by learning his ways. Dr. Michael Horan explains these two kinds of knowing:

> Relational knowing includes knowing the background and facts that comprise the person's history as well as the subtleties of spirit that make this person unique in the entire world. ...While catechesis aims ultimately at a relationship, that relationship is hollow without knowledge of the background and context that shape the person's history. Knowing Christ, then, is to be steeped in two kinds of knowing.[3]

Dr. Horan goes on to describe these two kinds of knowing as the distinction between *saber* and *conocer* in the Spanish language. Both of these verbs translate as "to know," but they indicate two very different kinds of knowing. *Saber* means that one knows the facts and information. *Conocer* means that you know someone from personal encounter. Parents, pastors, bishops, youth ministry leaders, and all who love their faith and young people long for youth to encounter Christ and to know him in both senses of this word—to know him personally and to know his ways.[4]

Research in faith education also explores the relationship between religious experiences and faith learning. Carol Lytch describes this dynamic in the book that reports her research, *Choosing Church: What Makes a Difference for Teens.* Religious experience includes moments of faith connection while participating in intentional spiritual and religious programs, but it also encompasses everyday experiences that are seen in the light of faith. Lytch describes socialization as something that encompasses learning about the faith tradition and belonging to the tradition. She experienced these elements as linked in the process of faith growth:

> ... socialization conditions persons to have religious experiences by providing them with the symbols, stories, and practices to use for 'sifting' their experiences and interpreting them as religious.[5]

An experience or encounter with God's presence becomes meaningful in the life of an adolescent when it is accompanied by the "language" of faith that helps name and place the encounter into a discernible pattern and practice of faithful living. In another research interview, a young person made this same connection when she shared that she "touched the body of Christ" while helping feed the poor

Making the Connection

Beliefs and knowledge of our faith are shaped by our experience of Christ's presence.

- *What is a belief about Jesus that you hold deeply?*
- *What helped shape that belief? Who were the people and communities where you experienced that belief? What experiences or programs promoted that belief?*

at a soup kitchen. She went on to describe her longing to learn more about Catholic teachings about justice and charity as she discerned her personal mission and ministry.[6]

Youth encounter Jesus and learn his ways in communities that provide numerous ways for them to experience God's presence living among us and provide formation in the ways and teachings of the faith. Providing this kind of catechesis goes well beyond a textbook or a course of study. This kind of encounter is nourished and supported by a whole community of living faith and a comprehensive experience of ministry.

How does a community share vision, collaborate, and provide catechesis for youth and their families utilizing all of the encounters and formation that comprehensive youth ministry provides? This chapter explores this vision by examining these dynamics:

- Aims of Adolescent Catechesis
- Settings and Models
- Curriculum, Methods, and Research

Aims of Adolescent Catechesis

The following definition of catechesis was first used by Pope John Paul II in *Catechesis Tradendae* and is provided in the *Catechism of the Catholic Church*:

> Catechesis is an *education in the faith* of children, young people and adults which includes especially the teaching of Christian doctrine imparted, generally speaking, in an organic and systematic way, with a view to initiating the hearers into the fullness of Christian life.[7]

Several of the terms in this definition help us enrich our understanding of the aims for adolescent catechesis.

Education in the faith The root to the word education is *educare* which means to draw out. Faith grows as youth are drawn into sharing their experience and their hopes. Faith grows as youth are engaged in experiences within which they learn and apply their faith. To be educated in the faith means that the gift of faith, which is received from God, is nurtured and enriched as a community shares faith, teaches faith, and engages in Christian practices. This word reminds us that teaching is not telling, and learning is not listening. To educate youth in the faith, we reach their heart, expand their mind, and engage their hands in practice.

Organic To teach faith organically means that the community teaches according to its nature and throughout its life. Youth learn and grow in faith as part of their families. Youth learn through the relationships within the community. Youth grow in practice of the faith as they see faith lived in vibrant ways. These relationships grow as youth participate with the community in celebration, conversation, service, worship, and shared learning.

Systematic Catechesis includes the many informal ways that youth are immersed in faith and become engaged with faithful people. It also includes the formal ways that we share faith in a systematic way. To be systematic, we share the fullness of the treasure of our faith with people of all ages. During the adolescent years, youth should have the opportunity to grow in faith by engaging with the key faith themes that comprise our shared faith.

Initiating the hearers into the fullness of Christian life All catechesis is rooted in initiatory catechesis which continuously evangelizes, invites, engages, and renews. The aim of these efforts is to lead the faithful into greater faith understanding and practice of the faith. Youth grow in faith as they learn to bring their life to faith by using Scripture, tradition, and the community.

This type of formation occurs within a community that is practicing and growing in faith. A community of disciples and a system of experiences form youth for Christian faith: relationships between youth and their family, youth with their peers and adult leaders, youth and the parish community. These relationships are supported by the parish because of deep faith and a genuine affection for youth. These life-changing relationships are nurtured through the life of the parish including specific programs and strategies.

Adolescent catechesis sponsors youth toward faith maturity by helping them to understand and practice a living faith.[8] A mature faith is nurtured through understanding of the faith, through practice of the faith and conversion, and through participation in a life of service and ministry that helps build the Kingdom of God. The aim of faith formation for people of all ages is to inform, form, and transform persons and communities by providing an encounter with Christ and promoting discipleship.

- To inform, we nurture people's minds and hearts with knowledge of the Christian faith so that who they are and how they live is shaped and influenced by what they know.
- To form, we nurture people's identity and lifestyle as disciples of Christ.
- To transform, we promote the personal and social transformation of the world according to the Kingdom of God that Jesus preached.[9]

Empowering youth as disciples of Jesus the Christ is the overarching aim for catechesis. Adults who love youth are asking the question: How will we share a living faith with youth whom we care about? Youth are asking different questions: Who am I? Where do I belong? What will I do with my life? Where can I invest my life and energies? Where is there an adventure large enough for me to be part of? Youth are literally in the process of searching for the adventure of their life. As a Christian community, we have the opportunity and the responsibility to present the Good News and promote discipleship in Christ as this adventure.

Understood in this way, adolescent catechesis is both the intentional and informal formation of youth for Christian living that occurs in communities within relationships of trust. This formation promotes faith understanding, faith practice, conversion, service, and ministry. Catechesis that promotes vibrant faith of this kind builds on continuous evangelization and works within numerous contexts and dimensions.

Christian Faith Identity and Practices

In his classic work on adolescent development, Dr. David Elkind described the primary task of adolescence as creating an integrated sense of self-identity.[10] Without this integration, a youth's self-image is like the varied images displayed in a carnival's house of mirrors. A youth behaves one way with his or her friends, another way at school, and a different way at home with family. Faith identity is an important part of the identity that youth are forming. In fact, religious identity goes beyond the many functional identities that we live with since it is about our relationship with God our creator. John Shea describes it this way: Faith identity "points to the ultimate identity of a people, formed in living relationship with a transcendent-immanent God, who has been revealed in Jesus Christ and who continues to be present in the Church."[11]

As ministry leaders and religious educators, we sometimes worry that the youth who join us in prayer and faith sharing on Sunday act very differently at school on Wednesday. It isn't just a problem for youth; inconsistency is part of the human condition. How can we help form a faith identity in young people that they can act on and live from throughout their lives? After all, we don't want youth ministry, or participation in the parish, to be one more competing activity in young people's already busy lives. To use a computer screen as an analogy, we don't want "faith" to be just one more icon on the screen, something to click on and off. We hope that faith takes its rightful place in youth's lives. Faith is not another program or activity; faith is the operating system—it's the thing that makes everything else make sense.

For faith to become the operating system, youth must see and know people of vibrant faith. They also need to be immersed and formed in the practices of faith. Practices are things that people do. They are actions and behaviors that have values embedded within them. If you wanted to learn to be a photographer, you could read books and study photography, but to truly become a great photographer you would learn the practices of photography by spending time with a great photographer. Through this mentoring, you would learn the little things and the disciplines that make someone excellent at their craft. You would learn the practices of photography. Faith practices are like that—they are actions and behaviors we do as people of faith. Dorothy Bass describes it this way in *Way to Live: Christian Practices for Teens*: "We call these practices because they have to be practiced. Practices don't live on the pages of a book but in the bodies, hands, feet, eyes, and compassion of real people, and learning practices means doing them not just once but many times."[12] Through the *Valparaiso Project*, Bass researched the impact of engaging youth and adults in Christian practices.

> …faith formation is something that happens, when it does, in the midst of doing and being together, as adults and youth accompany one another in addressing real questions needs, and concerns.[13]

This project encourages adults and youth to identify and develop Christian practices through which individuals live the Christian life. Living practices such as hospitality, charity, and prayer deepen faith understanding. Parishes, families, and youth ministry communities form youth in the practices of faith as an integral part of faith formation.

To promote Catholic faith identity and knowledge of faith practices:

- Expose youth to people who are living the practices of faith in a vibrant way. For example, youth could learn about praying the rosary by spending time with people who make rosaries and hearing about the experiences of powerful prayer.

- Prepare youth to participate in the events of the liturgical year. To be ready for Ash Wednesday, take time in the week before to learn about the origin and symbolic meaning of ashes.
- Engage youth in the symbols, sacred art, and imagery of the Catholic faith. Our shared faith is a treasure of images that reach and teach the faithful. Take a tour of your parish' worship space and spend time with the variety of images of Jesus, the cross, and the saints. Spend time in each of the spaces identified with celebrating the sacraments such as the font, the altar, and the confessional.
- Introduce youth to devotional and contemplative prayer. Help youth to reflect on their prayer and the strengthening of faith and hunger for knowledge that flows from affective prayer. Consider practices such as *lectio divina*, adoration, and novenas.

Youth Knowledge and Practice of the Faith

Pastoral leaders and researchers are concerned about youth's faith understanding and practice, as evidenced by numerous studies, conferences, and conversations. One of the primary research studies, *The National Study on Youth and Religion*, was conducted by Christian Smith and Melinda Lundquist Denton at the University of North Carolina. The results of this study were reported in the book, *Soul Searching: The Religious and Spiritual Lives of American Teenagers*.[14]

Youth and Faith Participation

- The vast majority of American youth and parents of youth are religious and are Christian in particular.
- Though many have proposed that youth are "spiritual but not religious," youth did not identify with this statement. Most youth do not seem to seek spiritual growth outside of denominational participation.
- Most youth intend to remain practicing in the denomination in which they currently participate.
- Youth who participate in a youth group, retreat, work camp, and other parish programs have higher levels of faith understanding and practice.
- Youth who are very religious also have lower rates of at-risk behaviors and more positive family relationships.

- Some youth seem to be disenfranchised and do not participate in youth programs. This would include youth from non-practicing families and segments of the population of Hispanic youth.

Youth Beliefs

- Mainline Protestant and Catholic youth were found to be largely inarticulate in stating beliefs and doctrine when compared to conservative Christians and Mormon youth.
- Youth belief and practice mirrors the belief and practice of their parents.
- Researchers propose that for many youth and adults an alternative creed is emerging across denominations. This is not a separate religion; it is a watered down creed that inhabits most denominations. The researchers describe this belief system as "Moralistic Therapeutic Deism." In this view, an impersonal God wants us to be happy, good, nice, and fair to each other. This creed omits much of the content of traditional Christian belief.

One of the images that the researchers use to describe adolescent faith is a "mirror."

> … American youth actually share much more in common with adults than they do not share, and most American youth faithfully mirror the aspirations, lifestyles, practices, and problems of the adult world into which they are being socialized….[15]

This summary reinforces things that we know and draws attention to the challenges of faith formation in our time. If youth are mirroring the "whateverism" of their parents and the wider culture rather than embracing the deeper truths of faith, the scope of our task in faith formation is clear. The challenge goes beyond valid concerns about the formation of religious educators and ministry leaders who share faith with youth. The challenge goes far beyond the methods to use in the classroom or youth room. Our challenge is evangelizing and catechizing youth and their families in a bold and dynamic faith that is lived in an exemplary and visible way by a parish community.

Settings and Models for Adolescent Faith Formation

> Catechesis is nothing other than the process of transmitting the Gospel, as the Christian community has received it, understands it, celebrates it, lives it and communicates it in many ways.
>
> GENERAL DIRECTORY FOR CATECHESIS, #105[16]

Two recent studies on youth ministry and faith formation came to the same conclusion in their overall finding as this guiding directive from the General Directory: the life of the parish itself is the heart of faith formation for adolescents and their families. In *Effective Practices for Dynamic Youth Ministry*, this is described as becoming a "willing parish." These parishes are willing to fully engage youth within the community and surround youth with love, care, support, and challenge:

> (A community) that comes to know and treasure the youth in their midst will experience new ways of praying, celebrating, serving and learning. It is not about always letting youth have their way or about discarding the traditions of a community. But it is about letting youth have *a way to truly belong*. Youth and the community learn together and are transformed in the process.[17]

In the "Spirit of Youth Ministry Project," the key finding for effective faith formation of adolescents is described as "The Culture or Spirit of the Congregation":

> A "culture" seems to emerge with its pervasive and distinct "spirit" and "atmosphere" that is more powerful than its component parts. It's the combination of the core values, people, relationships, expectations, practices, and activities that seems to generate this spirit and atmosphere.[18]

These communities form youth through the life and the lived theology of the parish. Families are supported in sharing faith, and youth are gathered for youth ministry activities and programs. The heart of the formation is the life of the congregation itself. These communities identify and utilize the assets within their congregation to share faith with adolescents. These assets are different for each community, which creates a very positive starting point for communities seeking to enhance faith formation of adolescents:

> In an asset-building approach every parish has Faith Assets. It is only a question of how many. Congregations need to discover those that are already at work and then chart a plan for developing more assets. An asset building approach offers very tangible qualities and practices that every parish can adopt that contribute to an effective youth ministry and nurturing youth of maturing Christian faith.[19]

Within the life of the congregation, there are various ways of sharing faith. One community named a woman in the parish as a faith asset for youth because of her consistent work at a women's homeless shelter. Instead of recruiting her to become part of the youth ministry team, an adult and two youth were assigned to accompany her in her ministry for a few weeks at a time as part of the Confirmation preparation process for youth. Over the weekend they would shop for the food needed. On Tuesday afternoon, they would prepare the meal and then serve the meal together. After the meal they would stay and play cards. This sharing among the generations was intentional but was also natural as youth spent time with a disciple practicing her faith. Dorothy Bass notes that the process of sharing life among the generations benefits not only the youth, but the whole community.

> Sharing the life of faith across generational cohorts is at least as beneficial for the adults involved as it is for the youth, in part because young people sometimes articulate with great honesty concerns that are shared by the entire community. (Is this really true? How far must I go in welcoming those who are different? Is there any hope for this world? And so on.) Their energy is a gift, not a nuisance.[20]

The *Generations of Faith Project*, developed by John Roberto, was designed to explore intergenerational catechesis with people of all ages in Catholic parishes. Parishes who implemented this model found that youth grew in faith through a variety of contacts: by being part of the whole community learning faith together, by exploring faith themes with their peers and reporting to the broader community, by sharing in leadership of intergenerational learning events, by participating in the events of church life, and by continuing faith sharing at home.[21]

In *Pathways of Hope and Faith Among Hispanic Teens*, a vision for parish life is expanded in this analysis of a promising direction for ministry and catechesis with Hispanic youth and others from diverse cultural groups:

> When thinking about how to structure an appropriate youth ministry for a multicultural parish that seeks to be united in spirit and mission, enriched by its diversity, and able to inculturate the Gospel in the various ethnic and cultural milieus of the faith, the model of the church as a 'community of communities' stands out.[22]

In this model, the parish supports the development of ministries for youth from different cultural groups. Within these ministries, evangelization and catechesis can rely on the strengths and leadership within the culture. It seems natural that parishes would provide a variety of "groupings" based on need and interest. When race, language, or culture is presented as a reason for distinctive ministries, this is sometimes misunderstood as segregation or treated as some type of threat to unity. The alternative is the development of a single ministry group that leaves out many youth and families.[23]

Through a variety of lenses, this analysis points to the power of the parish in sharing faith and in empowering faith sharing in a variety of settings. An image provided in the study of *Effective Practices in Catholic Youth Ministry* seems to summarize these insights about parishes sharing faith. A web of relationships grows and develops as youth grow in their ownership of the parish community and their connections with adults in the community. This web of relationships is built intentionally through concrete efforts: youth to youth, youth with adults, youth with their families, and youth with the parish community as a whole. Through this web of relationships, faith is mediated, and youth are empowered as active young disciples.[24]

These studies reinforce what we know from a broad variety of church documents and religious education theory: the faith community is the heart of faith formation. The life of the community sponsors Christian living. The community engages and includes youth while at the same time providing faith formation for youth in age specific ways, for families at home and for youth using the broader resources in the wider community.

Adolescents often rely upon all four of these settings: parish, family, peers, and the wider community. For younger adolescents, the family remains the most important and the peer group gains in importance as a place to explore and grow in faith. Young people participate in parish life and look for consistency between the faith they learn about and the lived practice of the community. Some young adolescents who are curious about faith topics explore through wider community resources such as Internet resources or books. Many more participate in events such as conferences, retreats, or service learning programs. Older adolescents rely upon the peer setting and are able to engage in the life of the parish and use wider community resources more readily.

These four settings of faith help youth learn and integrate faith. Experiences of these settings also set youth on the course to continue their faith growth as young adults and adults.

Age-Specific Peer Group Parishes gather adolescents in peer groups to participate in youth ministry, religious education, and sacramental formation. In these peer groups, youth learn the faith in ways that connect to their development and faith maturity.

Family Families share faith through their lived practices and teachable moments of faith sharing and prayer.

Parish The life of the faith community itself forms faith in youth through worship, learning, community, and service. Adolescents strive to belong, and through their participation in the intergenerational community they learn and integrate faith.

Wider Community/Individualized Learning The wider community includes the variety of ways that youth learn and grow in faith using the resources in the wider community. This includes participation in inter-church and regional youth conferences and events. It also includes the resources for faith formation found in print media and the Internet.

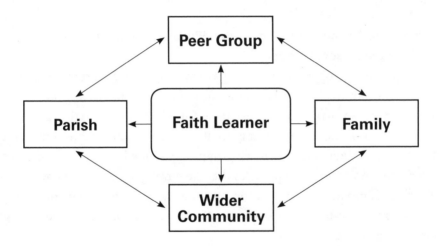

An effective model for faith formation of adolescents will take these settings into account. Typically, a parish will choose one of these settings as a foundational setting for intentional catechesis while strengthening and making connections to the other settings. For instance, a community might choose to have intentional faith formation occur primarily within the peer group and would provide support for family faith sharing, promote parish involvement, and encourage youth to learn on their own by providing resources and starting points. Another community might begin with intergenerational faith formation and complement these efforts with peer group gatherings and support for family faith sharing.

Three models emerge:

1. Intentional Catechesis Infused throughout Youth Ministry and Involvement in Parish Life

In these communities, the faith content needed by adolescents is communicated throughout the programs and strategies of youth ministry. Some themes are addressed during the weekly youth community gathering. Others are addressed within faith sharing series or retreats. Other aspects are built into experiences: youth preparing for a summer service trip experience formation in Catholic social teaching as part of their preparation. Youth who are becoming involved in worship and liturgical ministries experience formation as part of the practical preparation. The faith formation in these communities is planned and intentional though it was woven throughout the variety of gatherings and involvements.

2. Intentional Catechesis as Part of the Whole Community in an Intergenerational Model

In these parishes, people of all ages are participating in faith learning as an intergenerational community. The life of the parish becomes the starting point as the community gathers to prepare for events of church life and learn the faith in the process. Often times, these learning events begin with the whole community gathered and include time when age groups are divided for teaching and faith exploration among peers. In parishes that are employing the intergenerational model, youth ministry counts on the community to provide many of the topics for intentional catechesis. Other aspects of catechesis are addressed through other aspects of youth ministry.

3. Intentional Catechesis as a Distinct Element of Youth Ministry

In these parishes, the faith formation is a distinct element within youth ministry. Religious education classes and sacramental preparation programs are offered to youth on a regular basis. Youth who participate in these programs are encouraged to participate in other aspects of youth ministry. Some of the methods used for these elements include:

- Weekly classes that are grade level
- Sacramental preparation programs for Confirmation
- Week-long religious education programs offered in the summer
- Faith sharing series
- Home-based faith sharing programs for youth and their families

Whatever the model, effective parishes strive to provide faith formation in a way that is planned, intentional, and collaborative.

Curriculum, Methods, and Research

The word "curriculum" comes from a Latin word meaning to run a race.[25] In current use, people generally think of the curriculum as "the course to be run," which implies it is not the actual running. Since the "content" of faith education is most clearly understood as the beliefs and practices of the people, then faith formation needs to be understood as an educational ministry that is embedded in and involves the entire parish community. Therefore, the opportunities and methods for developing faith are as diverse as the community of faith itself.

This perspective significantly shifts our understanding of "curriculum." In her book, *Fashion Me a People*, Maria Harris emphasizes that "as church people we must consistently distinguish between the curriculum of education and the curriculum of schooling."[26] She suggests that "curriculum" is about the mobilizing of creative educative powers in such a way as to fashion a "People of God" through the practices of the people. This is very different from the traditional notion of curriculum as stacks of teacher guides and student textbooks.

In planning for effective faith formation of adolescents, one should consider two kinds of curriculum. The general curriculum would include the community itself, the environment and hospitality, the team of ministry leaders, and the spirit or culture of the community. The specific curriculum would include the communities, programs, and strategies directed towards adolescents and their families. This would include the variety of efforts that promote faith learning, prayer and worship, justice and service, and community life. These efforts could occur within the whole community, a community of peers, the family, or with individual youth. One way to think about this distinction is to consider the differences between non-verbal and verbal communication. General curriculum is like the non-verbal communication of a community. This communication is constantly revealing the authentic nature, message, and Word alive within the faith community. Specific curriculum is like verbal communication, which is intentional and is focused on communicating specific content and messages clearly.

There are different sources available to guide our specific curriculum with younger and older adolescents. Catechesis with younger adolescents focuses on the faith themes described in *Renewing the Vision* and is based upon the four pillars of the *Catechism of the Catholic Church.*[27] The Committee on Catechesis for the United States Catholic Bishops provides guidance in developing a curriculum to provide doctrinal formation within systematic catechesis for older adolescents through its 2008 document, *Doctrinal Elements of a Curriculum Framework for the Development of Catechetical Materials for Young People of High School Age.* The framework provides a guided journey from encounter through conversion as a disciple of Jesus Christ. This document is directed to publishers of catechetical materials and to diocesan leadership as an aid in supporting parishes and Catholic high schools in developing curriculum. The intention is to provide catechesis throughout the high school years in a way that addresses the challenges adolescents face and the questions they encounter.

> ...this framework is designed to form the content...as well as be a vehicle for growth in one's relationship with the Lord so that each may come to know him and live according to the truth he has given us.[28]

As noted in the previous treatment of the two types of knowing, catechesis includes more than the doctrinal elements. The doctrinal task of catechesis is one of the six tasks and is a central concern in helping youth know the faith and have a language for understanding and practicing faithful living. This framework can greatly enhance catechesis with youth by providing a structure for including the doctrinal elements within systematic catechesis. This content accompanies the efforts of evangelization and the broad-based ministry to youth promoted by Church leaders over the last four decades. This framework reinforces the other documents that guide catechesis and youth ministry such as *Renewing the Vision: A Framework for Catholic Youth Ministry* and the *National Directory for Catechesis,* both of which call for a renewed catechesis with youth that occurs within the goals and components of comprehensive youth ministry.[29] Together, these documents remind us that catechizing adolescents for discipleship employs a variety of contacts, methods, and experiences as part of its living curriculum of faith.

> We are moving towards a creative vision that sees all the facets of the church's life as the church curriculum, with curricular materials named simply "resources."
>
> Maria Harris, *Fashion Me a People*[30]

When the faith community claims its role as the living "curriculum" for catechesis, materials, texts, and courses take their appropriate place as resources. In planning for adolescent catechesis, a parish identifies its assets for sharing faith and follows local guidelines to name the aspect of faith that will be shared with youth within a particular season or occasion. After the theme or topics have been named, leaders can ask these questions to keep the faith of the community at the center and use resources for support:

> ▷ How will we share this aspect of our living faith with youth in our community?
> ▷ How will we use all of the resources of our community and all of the settings for catechesis?
> ▷ What resources will help us in sharing faith?

Dynamic Faith Learning

Communities that are effective in forming faith in adolescents recognize their role as faith witnesses and provide the specific curriculum for adolescent faith formation through dynamic faith learning opportunities. The following three principles summarize what we have been learning about dynamic faith learning from communities across the nation.

Effective Faith Formation helps youth enter into the experience of living faith.[31]

- Engages them *experientially*—head, heart, and lifestyles—in the learning activity, providing them with direct, first-hand experiences.
- Respects and incorporates their experience in the learning activity.
- Engages them in *real-world learning* and *application*, making the connection between learning and life, and faith and life.

This principle addresses three key aspects for utilizing experience within faith learning. First, the learning process should be experiential, allowing youth to put themselves completely into the learning process and providing youth with an experience of faith. Second, we should access the lived experience of the adolescent and help them to name and claim these experiences as they learn and grow in faith. Third, we need to help youth apply what they are learning to their everyday choices and situations. Consider these ideas:

Connect youth to adult members of the parish. Identify members of the parish who are living the faith in an exemplary way. Connect two youth to these adult mentors to accompany them in their actions on behalf of faith.

Provide affective experiences of prayer. Youth experience faith through their senses and through their experience of belonging within a community. Prayer provides a direct contact with the sacred and builds young people's relationship with God, as Father, Son, and Spirit.

Provide retreat experiences. Retreats provide an incredible opportunity for youth to experience Christ's presence within prayer, witness, community, and sacrament. The extended time of a retreat and the carefully chosen elements help youth to go deeper in their experience.

Provide opportunities for service. Experiences of service to those in need are hands-on opportunities for youth to be in touch with Christ's presence.

Effective faith formation uses a variety of methods which engage the senses.

- Incorporates a variety of *multi-sensory* methods to engage the whole person, such as art, drama, music, dance, storytelling, media, prayer, rituals.
- Engages them in *construction, discovery,* and *exploration* of the topic or concept.

This principle reminds us of the importance of engaging the senses and addressing a variety of learning styles. We are also challenged to move the faith learner from being a passive listener to being someone who is helping uncover and discover the faith content. Consider these methods for presenting and processing faith content:

Interviews

Panel Presentations

Guest Speakers

Movies / TV / Popular Songs / Story Connections

Presenting Content and Faith Sharing within Prayer

Skits / Drama / Scripture Re-Enactments

Scripture Search

Murals / Collages / Posters / Slogans

Station-Based Learning Activities

"Guided Tour" – Museum Style Presentations

Effective faith formation builds a faith learning community.

- Utilizes *collaborative* and *group-centered* formats for study, inquiry, activities, and sharing.
- Provides an environment that is characterized by warmth, trust, acceptance, and inquiry.
- Is participative and interactive, actively engaging them in the learning process.

In the *National Directory for Catechesis,* the United States Catholic bishops describe the importance of community and safety within faith formation:

[Catechesis] involves group participation in an environment that is characterized by warmth, trust, acceptance, and care, so that young people can hear and respond to God's call (fostering the freedom to search and question, to express one's own point of view, and to respond in faith to that call).[32]

Youth are naturally going to learn and grow in faith more comfortably in a community where they feel safe, accepted, and valued. This principle reminds us of the importance of building community as we promote faith learning. Consider these ideas for building a faith learning community:

Include community builders and team building activities within faith learning.

Provide opportunities for youth to share and pray for each other's concerns.

Integrate prayer throughout faith learning.

Change groupings: use dyads, triads, and different combinations of small groups to provide an opportunity for youth to get to know one another.

Go off site from the church grounds: participate together in a service project, "pilgrimage" to a place for prayer, or take a field trip to a place to experience worship, community, or service with another parish.

Research in Adolescent Catechesis and Youth Ministry

Youth ministry supports and provides catechesis for youth in a variety of ways. In the *Effective Practices for Dynamic Youth Ministry* project, parish leaders described specific ways that youth ministry leaders helped the parish community own the ministry and faith formation of youth. This same study found that parishes with effective ministry placed the catechesis and evangelization dimensions at the heart of their efforts. These communities provide systematic and intentional catechesis as well as opportunities for catechesis that are informal and integrated through ministry efforts.[33]

The *Spirit of Youth Ministry Project* described three "uniquely integrated practices" of youth ministries that demonstrated excellence in their faith formation. The first practice was a focus on families and households. The researchers in the *National Study of Youth and Religion* (NSYR) concur about the importance of this focus:

Contrary to popular misguided cultural stereotypes and frequent parental misconceptions, we believe that the evidence clearly shows that the single most important social influence on the religious and spiritual lives of adolescent is their parents.[34]

A second practice identified in the *Spirit* project described common youth ministry practices that were particularly effective in helping youth grow in faith. In a similar way, the *Effective Practices* project named five practices that had a significant impact on youth and their faith growth:

- Intentional faith formation efforts,
- Participation in extended trips such as the National Catholic Youth Conference, leadership camps, service trips, and World Youth Day,
- Participation and involvement in the ministries of liturgy,
- Participation in retreats, and
- Service involvement.[35]

The third practice found in the congregations by the *Spirit Project* is "custom designed and integrated models" of youth ministry. Communities seized opportunities that were uniquely possible in their context. One example of this was the youth leadership model employed by a rural Catholic parish that involved older youth in leadership of youth ministry and catechetical programs.[36]

In the analysis provided for the report on the Catholic results of the *National Study on Youth and Religion*, Charlotte McCorquodale identified a synergy between the various aspects of youth participation:

> …we concluded that in terms of Catholic youth who are engaged in their faith, "more equals more," meaning that when Catholic youth participate in some youth programs, they are more likely to participate in others.[37]

Within the variety of ministry methods, some research focused on specific areas to be developed. The *Youth Ministry and Spirituality Project*, led by Mark Yaconelli and Michael Hryniuk, identified specific spiritual practices as having immense potential in providing youth with religious experience that is grounded in tradition. These practices include developing a sense of Sabbath, engaging youth in contemplative prayer, teaching youth skills for discernment, and welcoming youth through profound hospitality. Underlying these individual practices is the dimension of youth apprenticeship in the Christian life.

> Young persons are attracted to and learn the faith from adults who are spiritually alive. Spirit-led ministry to youth focused on the disciplines of the spiritual life as well as the accompaniment of young people by adults who are spiritually mature can lead to a profound and sustainable relationship to Jesus Christ.[38]

One way to be intentional about connecting religious experience with socialization is to connect faith learning with other aspects of youth ministry and involvement in parish life. Using this method, youth experience formation in Christian teachings on justice before and after providing direct service. Some youth learn about worship before engaging in liturgical ministries. Other youth learn about specific faith and Scripture themes about leadership prior to becoming part of the youth ministry core team.

This method of learning matches with ideas developed by Dr. Malcolm Knowles about *androgogy*, which is his term for the teaching methodology for adults. Dr. Knowles challenges common assumptions about education:

> [Many educators believe that]...if we simply pour enough knowledge into people: 1) they will turn out to be good people, and 2) they will know how to make use of their knowledge...we must define the mission of education as to produce competent people—people who are able to apply their knowledge under changing conditions...[39]

Using the principles of androgogy, we direct learning to close the gap between what the learners now know and what they need to know in order to do what they want to be able to do. Providing connected learning motivates youth to learn the faith because there is something that they want to do to which this learning is connected. This style of faith learning also helps youth become lifelong faith learners because they see the connections between faith and action.

Michael Theisen, Director of Membership Services for the National Federation for Catholic Youth Ministry, conducted research in the Diocese of Rochester that reinforced this style of learning. In their research, they found that one of the most effective adolescent faith formation strategies was actually the Vacation Bible School program in a community that involved adolescents each year as team members. These youth learned key Scripture and faith themes each year in preparation for leading children through this week of study and celebration of faith. Many of the programs that they identified as effective had similar characteristics:

Effective Faith Formation Programs
- Creatively and fully engage young people in the learning process, often as teachers or peer leaders.
- Are intense and necessitate relationship building among the participants.
- Often offer something back to the community.
- Utilize the gifts of young people and actively involve the whole person (head, heart, and hands).[40]

To make the faith connection within a variety of experiences and involvements, Theisen suggests that parishes ask and answer key questions that keep all efforts focused on disciple making:

Five Key Questions[41]

> ▷ How is God made more visible through this (activity/program/model)?
> ▷ How will this (activity/program/model) bring young people into a deeper relationship with Jesus Christ?
> ▷ How can I more fully involve young people in this (activity/program/model)?
> ▷ How can I more fully partner with parents in this (activity/program/model)?
> ▷ How can I model and share my own faith journey through this (activity/program/model)?

Within this varied research, a pattern emerges concerning the catechetical journey of adolescents that connects religious experiences, education in the faith tradition, and growth in commitment within the faith community. These elements provide mutual support for each other as youth grow in faith in the context of community.

Movements in Fostering Faith Growth and Commitment

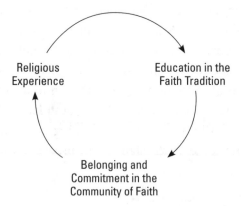

Religious Experience

Education in the Faith Tradition

Belonging and Commitment in the Community of Faith

In one example, a young person participates in a spiritual retreat and learns about practices of prayer and liturgy. These experiences lead to renewed participation in liturgy with her family and involvement in ministries of the parish, which provides for new experiences and faith learning. In another instance, a youth may experience a deepening sense of belonging through participation with their family in parish events, which leads to involvement in a youth service event that includes catechesis about Catholic social teaching.

Through the varied research projects, some common themes emerge:

- Parish communities have a profound impact on faith formation through their lived theology and their involvement of youth.
- Communities should seize opportunities to involve youth in learning Christian practices, in learning as part of the intergenerational community, and in being mentored in the spiritual life by adults of lively faith.
- Youth ministry should place evangelization and faith formation at the heart of its efforts. This priority is put into action by engaging the parish community, supporting families, and providing age-specific catechesis to youth in a variety of ways.
- Specific practices of youth ministry and religious education have special potential for helping youth grow in faith understanding and commitment. This includes connecting catechesis with ministry, leadership, and service involvements.
- One of the most vital aspects of dynamic catechesis is the vibrancy of faith held by the person who is sharing faith with youth. Special attention is needed in the formation and spiritual support of youth catechists and ministry leaders.
- Dynamic faith learning utilizes youth's experience, engages them in a learning community, and implements a variety of methods and models.

By looking at these parish practices, we see that there are many places where catechesis with adolescents is flourishing. These communities are using varied timeframes, models, resources, and opportunities to reach a variety of youth. They are also striving to make the most of each contact point with youth and their families. These concerted efforts work within an integrated vision for catechesis and pastoral ministry with youth.

Consider these ideas for enhancing catechesis for youth:

- Include catechesis within all aspects of youth ministry and with all youth communities. Begin by identifying the variety of youth communities within your parish. This might include a weekly youth group, a scouting group, a youth choir, a service group, and cultural or language-specific youth communities.
- Connect catechesis with the various ministry, leadership, and service opportunities in which youth are involved. For example, provide catechesis about ministry and liturgy with all youth involved in liturgical ministries.

Prepare youth for a service experience with catechesis about Catholic social teaching. Include catechesis as part of leadership formation for peer ministers.

- Promote "niche" opportunities for catechesis for youth with varied needs. This could include Scripture studies or discipleship groups.
- Offer seasonal programs that coincide with the liturgical year, such as an Advent retreat or a lenten faith sharing series.
- Provide catechesis in a variety of formats such as retreat models or faith sharing series.
- Connect youth to resources for catechesis in your diocese and region such as youth rallies and conventions. Take the time to have youth share with each other what they are learning and experiencing through these faith enriching experiences.

Planning for Transformed Adolescent Catechesis

Adolescents are ready and waiting to be invited to the adventure of their lifetime. The adventure of discipleship begins with the encounter with Christ. This encounter can't be programmed or scheduled, but parishes can help youth create time and space to recognize Christ in their midst. Parishes can also engage youth with a community that listens to the word and acts on it in bold and faithful ways. Amidst changing pastoral conditions and cultural transition, faith communities are finding effective ways to catechize youth. Christian Smith challenges leaders to use what we know to do the work needed with youth in our communities:

> Parents, pastors, ministers, religious educators, and congregational leaders concerned with youth need simply to *better engage and challenge* the youth already at their disposal, to work better to help make faith a more active and important part of their lives. The problem is not that youth won't come to church (most will), or that they hate church (few do), or that they don't want to listen to religious ministers or mature mentoring adults (they will and do).[42]

Communities are using varied methods to engage and challenge young people. Some of these methods are innovative while others are tried and true. The common link among these communities is the passion, zeal, and leadership demonstrated in the variety of vibrant, integrated efforts. This energy will drive continued diligence, innovation, and faithfulness, which will lead to renewed practices and examples of dynamic ministry. Through these efforts, the story of adolescent catechesis will continue to unfold as faithful disciples are compelled to share faith and live faith in ways new and old. To make this vision become a reality, parishes need to name and claim adolescent catechesis as a priority as they collaborate and plan for sharing this faith that we treasure with youth today.

> Collaboration should be the hallmark of all church work, especially among those involved in teaching others about the faith. It is so important for catechists, for teachers of the faith, to model what they teach. The purpose of catechesis is not just to pass on information about Christ, the church and the truths of our faith but to create opportunities for the learner in faith to encounter Christ and to be formed or transformed by him.
>
> Monsignor Daniel J. Kutys,
> Executive Director of the Secretariat of
> Evangelization and Catechesis,
> United Stated Conference of Catholic Bishops[43]

To get started, consult with local guidelines for catechesis and resources for adolescent faith formation. Use these resources as you gather with youth, parents, parish staff, and ministry leaders in your community to create a shared plan for adolescent catechesis.

Consider these directions:

- Assess your community.
  - ▷ Youth and Families—Who are the youth and families? How are they currently involved?
  - ▷ Strengths and Assets—What are the strengths of our community that we can share with youth?
  - ▷ Areas to Grow—What are the areas we need to grow in order to provide dynamic and effective catechesis with adolescents?
- Develop focused, innovative efforts.
  - ▷ Choose a new model or strengthen your current model for adolescent catechesis.
  - ▷ Identify your foundational setting for faith formation and complement this strategy with other offerings and support in the other settings of faith learning.
  - ▷ Utilize the assets in your community to provide new methods.
- Provide connected learning.
  - ▷ Use the calendar for the parish and youth ministry to create new opportunities for faith learning.

- Make the most of each contact.
  - ▷ Utilize the 5 key questions suggested earlier in this chapter to evaluate each gathering with youth. (See *Research in Adolescent Catechesis and Youth Ministry*.)
- Support families.
  - ▷ Provide families of youth with resources to share faith and pray at home.
- Empower people of vibrant faith to be bold, faithful, and alive in sharing faith and life with youth in the community.
  - ▷ Provide formation for religious educators and ministry leaders so that leaders are empowered to share faith effectively.

The starting point for catechesis is evangelization. What does it mean to become Good News in the lives of adolescents? Good News is not theoretical and it is not general. Good News is something specific and personal. It is something that connects with the bad news in our lives. For someone who is unemployed, Good News is the phone call from the employer offering a job. For a parent whose child is injured, Good News is the ambulance arriving to help. For someone who is hungry, good news is a bowl of food. For adolescents, the Good News of our faith will be received because it connects with their lives and their world. What are the headlines that youth carry in their hearts? Our starting point for all ministry with youth is this stance of listening and compassion for young people. As a faith community, we can listen to youth, love them, and provide witness and instruction that guides a new generation of disciples towards bold and transforming faith.

— RECOMMENDED RESOURCES —

Armstrong, Thomas. *Seven Kinds of Smart: Identifying and Developing Your Multiple Intelligences*, revised edition. New York: Plume, 1999.

Bass, Dorothy. *Practicing Our Faith*. San Francisco: Jossey-Bass, 1997.

Bass, Dorothy, and Don Richter. *Way to Live: Christian Practices for Teens*. Nashville: Upper Room Books, 2002.

Dean, Kenda Creasy, and Ron Foster. *Godbearing Life: The Art of Soul Tending for Youth Ministry*. Nashville: Upper Room Books, 1998.

East, Thomas, et al. *Effective Practices for Dynamic Youth Ministry*. Winona, MN: Saint Mary's Press, 2004.

Elkind, David. *All Grown Up and No Place to Go: Teenagers in Crisis*. Reading, MA: Addison-Wesley Publishing Company, 1984.

Foster, Charles. *Educating Parishes*. Nashville: Abingdon Press, 1994.

Groome, Thomas. *Christian Religious Education*. San Francisco: Harper & Row, 1980.

Gross, Ronald. *Peak Learning*. New York: Tarcher/Putnam, 1991.

Harris, Maria. *Fashion Me a People: Curriculum in the Church*. Louisville: Westminster/John Knox Press, 1989.

Kehrwald, Leif. *Youth Ministry and Parents: Secrets for a Successful Partnership*. Winona, MN: Saint Mary's Press, 2004.

Kehrwald, Leif (ed.). *Families and Faith: A Vision and Practice for Parish Leaders*. New London, CT: Twenty-Third Publications, 2006.

Lytch, Carol E. *Choosing Church: What Makes a Difference for Teens*. Louisville: Westminster John Knox Press, 2004.

Martineau, Mariette, Joan Weber, and Leif Kehrwald. *Intergenerational Faith Formation: All Ages Learning Together*. New London, CT: Twenty-Third Publications, 2008.

Mercadante, Frank. *Make It Real: A Practical Resource for Teen-Friendly Evangelization*. Winona, MN: Saint Mary's Press, 2004.

Partnership for Adolescent Catechesis, Source Book on Adolescent Catechesis: Volume 1. Washington, DC: Partnership for Adolescent Catechesis, 2008.

Schultz, Thom and Joani. *The Dirt on Learning*. Loveland, CO: Group Books, 1999.

Smith, Christian, and Melinda Lundquist Denton. *Soul Searching: The Religious and Spiritual Lives of American Teenagers*. New York: Oxford University Press, 2005.

Smith, Timothy. *The Seven Cries of Today's Teens: Hear Their Hearts Make the Connection*. Nashville: Integrity Publishers, 2003.

Strommen, Merton P., and Richard A. Hardel. *Passing on the Faith: A Radical New Model for Youth and Family Ministry*. Winona, MN: Saint Mary's Press, 2000.

Sweet, Leonard. *Post-Modern Pilgrims: First-Century Passion for the 21st-Century World*. Nashville: Broadman and Holman Publishers, 2000.

Yaconelli, Mark. *Growing Souls: Experiments in Contemplative Youth Ministry*. Grand Rapids, MI: Zondervan, 2007.

Web Resources

Youth Ministry Access (subscription Web site). Naugatuck, CT: Center for Ministry Development. www.youthministryaccess.org

Call to Discipleship (subscription Web site). Orlando, FL: Houghton Mifflin Harcourt Religion Publishers. www.calltodiscipleship.com

— ENDNOTES —

1. Congregation for the Clergy, *General Directory for Catechesis*. Washington, DC: United States Conference of Catholic Bishops, 1997, #80.

2. Ibid.

3. Horan, Michael, Ph.D. "Adolescent Catechesis: An Unfinished Agenda," *Source Book on Adolescent Catechesis: Volume 1*. Washington, DC: Partnership for Adolescent Catechesis, 2008, p. 56.

4. See also: Maura Hagarty, Ph.D., "What the Church Has Been Telling Us about Adolescent Catechesis," and Daniel S. Mulhall, "What the New *National Directory for Catechesis* Says about Adolescent Catechesis," which are also contained in *Source Book on Adolesent Catechesis: Volume 1*.

5. Lytch, Carol. *Choosing Church: What Makes a Difference for Teens*. Louisville: Westminster/John Knox Press, 2004, p. 62.

6. See: Thomas East, *Effective Practices for Dynamic Youth Ministry* (Winona, MN: Saint Mary's Press, 2004), pp. 51-53 for a discussion of service in the life of adolescents.

7. *Catechism of the Catholic Church*. Washington, DC: United States Conference of Catholic Bishops–Libreria Editrice Vaticana, 1994), #5, quoting *Catechesis Tradendae*, (Pope John Paul II, 1979), #18.

8. See: *The Challenge of Adolescent Catechesis: Maturing in Faith* (Washington, DC: National Federation for Catholic Youth Ministry, 1986), p. 8.

9. Adapted from Thomas Groome, "Of Silver Jubilees and the Ground Gained," *PACE 25*, January 1996, pp. 13-20.

10. Elkind, David. *All Grown Up and No Place to Go: Teenagers in Crisis*. Reading, MA: Addison-Wesley Publishing Company, 1984, p. 5.

11. Shea, John. "Perspectives on Catholic Identity–Article 1: Catholic Identity and Its Carriers." Naugatuck, CT: Center for Ministry Development, 1989, Occasional Paper #29, p. 2.

12. Bass, Dorothy C., and Don C. Richter, *Way to Live: Christian Practices for Teens*. Nashville: Upper Room Books, 2002, p. 9.

13. Quotation is drawn from report submitted by Dorothy Bass for the "Consultation on the Christian Formation of Youth, Lilly Endowment, Inc." (Indianapolis, November 7-8, 2006), p. 17. See also: *Way to Live: Christian Practices for Teens*.

14. See: Christian Smith and Melinda Lundquist Denton, *Soul Searching: The Religious and Spiritual Lives of American Teenagers* (New York: Oxford University Press, 2005). See also: Web site for the National Study on Youth and Religion: www.youthandreligion.org, and Hispanic Catholic Data Report—Youth Ministry and the Socioreligious Lives of White and Hispanic Catholic Teens in the U.S. (Stockton, CA: Instituto Fe y Vida, 2006) www.feyvida.org.

15. Smith, p. 191.

16. GDC, #105.

17. EPDYM, p. 10.

18. Roberto, John. "The Spirit of Youth Ministry: Utilizing Faith Assets to Nurture Youth of Vital Faith," *Youth Ministry Access Journal* (Naugatuck, CT: Center for Ministry Development, 2006), p. 3.
> Note: The *Spirit of Youth Ministry Project* is directed by Dr. Roland Martinson. Additional information may be found at: www.exemplaryyouthministry.org.

19. Ibid., p. 4.

20. Quotation is drawn from report submitted by Dorothy Bass for the "Consultation on the Christian Formation of Youth, Lilly Endowment Inc." (Indianapolis, November 7-8, 2006), p. 17. See also: *Way to Live: Christian Practices for Teens.*

21. See: John Roberto, *Becoming a Church of Lifelong Learners* (New London, CT: Twenty-Third Publications, 2006).

22. Johnson-Mondragon, Ken (ed.). *Pathways of Hope and Faith Among Hispanic Teens: Pastoral and Strategies Inspired by the National Study of Youth and Religion.* Stockton, CA: Instituto Fe y Vida, 2007, p. 345.

23. Ibid., pp. 332-37.

24. EPDYM, p. 32. A diagram identifying the cycle of deepening relationships is available on p. 11.

25. For historical development and understanding of curriculum, see: Maria Harris, *Fashion Me a People* (Louisville: Westminster/John Knox Press, 1989), Chapter 3, pp. 55-72.

26. Harris, p. 64.

27. For a list of Young Adolescent Faith Themes, see: *Renewing the Vision: A Framework for Catholic Youth Ministry* (Washington, DC: United States Conference of Catholic Bishops, 1997), pp. 31-32.

28. Committee on Evangelization and Catechesis. *Doctrinal Elements of a Curriculum Framework for the Development of Catechetical Materials for Young People of High School Age* (Washington, DC: United States Conference of Catholic Bishops, 2008), p. 1.

29. See: *Renewing the Vision*, p. 10 and pp. 28-31. See also: *National Directory for Catechesis* (Washington, DC: United States Conference of Catholic Bishops, 2005), pp. 199-202.

30. Harris, p. 18.

31. These principles were developed from findings about effective learning from the *Generations of Faith Project* (Naugatuck, CT: Center for Ministry Development, 2006) by Leif Kehrwald, Mariette Martineau, John Roberto, and Joan Weber. See: www.cmdnet.org.

32. NDC, p. 201.

33. EPDYM, p. 44.

34. Smith, p. 261.

35. EPDYM, pp. 43-56.

36. See: Roberto, *Spirit of Youth Ministry*, p. 3.

37. McCorquodale, Charlotte. "Identifying the Essential Questions for Successful Ministry with Catholic Youth," *Seminary Journal*, Volume Thirteen, Number Two, Fall 2007 (Washington, DC: National Catholic Education Association), p. 11.

38. Quotation is drawn from report submitted by Michael Hryniuk for the "Consultation on the Christian Formation of Youth, Lily Endowment, Inc." (Indianapolis, November 7-8, 2006), p. 50. See also: Mark Yaconelli, *Growing Souls: Experiments in Contemplative Youth Ministry* (Grand Rapids, MI: Zondervan, 2007). This insight about the vibrancy of adult faith is echoed in the *Effective Practices* research. See: *Effective Practices*, p. 44, 64-65, and 74-75.

39. Knowles, Malcolm S. *The Modern Practice of Adult Education: From Pedagogy to Androgogy.* Englewood Cliffs, NJ: Cambridge Adult Education, 1988, pp. 18-19.

40. Theisen, Michael. "Adolescent Catechesis Today: On the Road to Transformation," *Source Book*, p. 26.

41. Theisen, p. 24.

42. Quotation is drawn from report submitted by Christian Smith for the "Consultation on the Christian Formation of Youth, Lily Endowment, Inc." (Indianapolis, November 7-8, 2006), p. 84.

43. Kutys, Daniel J. "Fostering Collaboration Means Fostering Community," *Catechetical Leader*, May/June 2008. Washington, DC: National Conference of Catechetical Leaders, p. 5.

CHAPTER TEN

Evangelization of Youth

Mariette Martineau

Editor's Note

What does it mean to become Good News in the lives of adolescents today?

Mariette Martineau guides us to consider this question as we plan for the various dimensions of evangelization with youth.

Fifty years ago in the church world, the term "evangelization" was not used in the everyday language of a pastor, church worker, or parish volunteer. "Evangelization" is now probably one of the most talked-about words in the Church. The vocabulary now includes pre-evangelized, newly evangelized, ongoing evangelization, initial evangelization, re-evangelized, gospeled, ungospeled, churched, and unchurched.

Evangelizing "means bringing the Good News into all the strata of humanity, and through its influence transforming humanity from within and making it new."[1] This definition comes from *On Evangelization in the Modern World* (*Evangelii Nuntiandi*), written by Pope Paul VI in 1975 as one of the foundational documents on evangelization for today's Church after the Second Vatican Council. In this description, we are reminded that evangelization is not a state to be achieved but a process of being invited into relationship with Jesus so that throughout one's life the Good News is able to *form* and *transform* people into his living witnesses.

Evangelization with young people is bringing the Good News of the Gospel into their lives, that they may celebrate and treasure the God who has given them life and that they may be transformed to be life-givers through the power of Jesus and the Holy Spirit in today's world. This evangelization is not simply a verbal proclamation of the Good News but the "proclamation of Christ and his Gospel by word and the testimony of life."[2]

The starting point for the ministry of evangelization with young people is

> Our recognition of the presence of God already in young people, their experiences, their families, and their culture....Through the Incarnation of God in Jesus, Christians are convinced that God is present within and through all of creation, and, in a special way, within humanity. Evangelization, therefore, enables young people to uncover and name the experience of a God already active and present in their lives. This provides an openness to the gift of the Good News of Jesus Christ.[3]

Young people are living in a specific time and place that holds many challenges for evangelization. The *National Directory for Catechesis*, names the following challenges:[4]

- a frantic pace of life that inhibits participation in church offerings
- materialism and consumerism being the true "gods"
- a great gap between rich and poor, which calls evangelizers to put the needs of the poor and vulnerable first
- the gap between faith and practice—Catholic in name but not in value or practice
- the independent thinking and problem solving skills being nurtured in young people today, which, though positive in itself, makes them "more critically minded in their learning styles than ever before."
- the information revolution, which lays upon educators and formators the challenge to be "entertaining"
- utilizing new technologies to proclaim the Gospel
- religious indifference, ambiguity, and the growth of sects, cults, and New Age spirituality

These challenges should not scare us or overwhelm us, but motivate us further to proclaim the Good News of Jesus to all young people, especially to those who are lost and are seeking meaning and purpose. As the *National Directory for Catechesis* states, "Every culture needs to be transformed by Gospel values because the Gospel always demands a conversion of attitudes and practices wherever it is preached. Cultures must often be purified and restored in Christ."[5] In true Catholic authenticity, we celebrate the presence of God that is there while illuminating the darkness that still seeks to be transformed with the light of Christ.

 **Making the Connection**

"How beautiful are the feet of those who bring good news!"
ROMANS 10:15

This passage reminds us to be grateful for the people who evangelize us.

- *When you were an adolescent, who shared the Good News of faith with you?*

What Does Evangelization Look Like and Include?

Evangelization is the energizing core of all ministry with adolescents. All of the relationships, ministry components, and programs of comprehensive ministry with adolescents must proclaim the Good News. They must invite young people into a deeper relationship with the Lord Jesus and empower them to live as his disciples.[6] All programs and strategies are called to root young people in the community of the Holy Trinity, that they may live out their call to be God's children as disciples of Jesus Christ with the strength and grace of the Holy Spirit. As the document *Go and Make Disciples* says in paragraph one, "Jesus set the world on fire, and that blaze goes on even today."[7] How is this "blaze" nurtured through youth ministry?

The ministry of evangelization, as defined in *Renewing the Vision* (RTV), includes the actions of:

- Sharing the Good News of the Reign of God
- Inviting young people to hear about the Word made flesh
- Being living witnesses to the Reign of God that has become realized in and through Jesus[8]

Go and Make Disciples says there are two elements at work in evangelization: Witness, which is the simple living of the faith, and sharing, which is spreading the Good News of Jesus in an explicit way.[9]

Each of these actions integrates three important dimensions. First, evangelization is about sharing faith. It is about sharing the story of the Good News of Jesus and sharing his centrality to the Catholic faith. It is not merely knowledge about Jesus, it is sharing the story of one's personal relationship with Jesus and of the community's relationship with the risen Lord. Evangelization is about engaging young people in the story of the Catholic Church, through the Church's narrative of sacrament, Scripture, service, worship, and community. Evangelization is sharing the story of faith in Jesus and his faith in people. As the way, the truth, and the life, Jesus enables all to see for themselves the "grandeur for which they are made, [for unless people realize that] they cannot reach fulfillment and their lives will be incomplete."[10] Jesus believes in our ability, as created in the image and likeness of God, to be God's goodness and presence in our world.

Second, evangelization is about being faithful to the person of Jesus Christ—all of who he is and what his kingdom of love, hope, and justice is all about. "All evangelizing activity is understood as promoting communion with Jesus Christ."[11] Catholics do not fabricate an image of Jesus for the world or choose the aspects of the Good News that they like most; they root themselves in faithful discernment of the Gospels and Church teachings in order to be honest in sharing Jesus with young people. Through the universal church, the diocesan church, and the local parish community, communion with Jesus Christ is proclaimed, lived, taught, and witnessed to through the daily practice of discipleship. This discipleship includes living one's life modeled on Jesus, and calling others to do the same.

Third, evangelization is about being faithful to the traditions and teachings of the Church. Individuals evangelize in a specific context and from a specific faith perspective, which means we are evangelizing youth from a Catholic understanding of mission and Christology. In *Evangeli Nuntiandi*, the Church has clearly stated that "the task of evangelizing all people constitutes the essential mission of the Church...she exists in order to evangelize."[12] Therefore all that she teaches and does is to evangelize.

At the heart of proclaiming the Good News of Jesus Christ and inviting others into relationship with him is conversion. As evangelizers we are called to conversion, called to continually examine our lives and to change what needs changing in order to be authentic disciples of Jesus Christ. As *Go and Make Disciples* says, "Conversion is the change of our lives that comes about through the power of the Holy Spirit. All who accept the Gospel undergo change as we continually put on the mind of Christ by rejecting sin and becoming more faithful disciples in the Church. Unless we undergo conversion, we have not truly accepted the Gospel."[13] Our role as evangelizers includes supporting and challenging others to the ongoing conversion that the Gospel through the Spirit calls us to. Conversion, like evangelization, is both initial—the initial conversion one experiences when opening one's heart to Christ, and ongoing—the ongoing change and metanoia that a disciple is called to in faithful relationship to Jesus Christ. "Faith is a gift, destined to grow in the heart of believers. Adhering to Jesus Christ, in fact sets in motion a process of continuing conversion, which lasts for the whole of life."[14]

Initial conversion for some is dramatic, like St. Paul who was knocked from his horse when he encountered Christ on the road to Damascus. Initial conversion for most is gradual over many months or years, and often occurs in relationship with someone who has a significant presence in their life—a good friend, a spouse, a church community that offers assistance in time of need, and so on. It is important to remember when evangelizing young people that conversion does not happen in the same time frame and experience for each person, but rather through the grace of the Holy Spirit, whose means and timing are not in our control. As *Go and Make Disciples* says so pointedly, "Without the Holy Spirit, evangelization simply cannot occur."[15] We are responsible for creating an environment where conversion might take place, but the act of conversion is through the power of Father, Son, and Spirit.

Ongoing conversion is possible when one remains connected to a faith community and participates in Eucharist, Reconciliation, and other sacraments as called by the Holy Spirit. Ongoing conversion happens through regular participation in formation and catechesis, prayer and acts of justice, and through retreats, missions, and special events such as World Youth Day and national or diocesan youth events. "The spirit of conversion, highlighted in the liturgy and particularly in the Rite of Christian Initiation of Adults, should radiate through the actions of all Catholics so that the call to conversion is experienced and celebrated as a part of our way of life."[16]

Conversion is not forced, but is a free choice, celebrating the gift of freedom that God placed in the hearts of all people. We as evangelizers are called to trust in God's initiative in inviting people into relationship, and to remember that we are servants of God "proclaiming an eternally faithful God."[17] Conversion is not only individual but communal. "Our relationship with Jesus is found in our relationship with the community of Jesus—the Church. The way to Christ is through the community in which he lives…Jesus is present and among his disciples, the People of God."[18]

Evangelization and the Settings for Youth Ministry

Family

Youth ministers sometimes succumb to the myth that teenagers want to spend as little time with their families as possible. Sociological studies say otherwise. In his 2002 study, Reginald Bibby notes that "during this time in their lives when conflict with parents is widely regarded as both inevitable and pervasive, a majority of young people nonetheless say that family life is very important to them and that they are receiving a high level of enjoyment from their mothers and fathers, siblings and grandparents."[19]

Evangelization with young people includes intentional strategies and programs to reach the home in which they live. Strategies include options such as

- Occasionally inviting teens and their parents to a gathered evangelization session together
- Keeping parents informed about the details of retreat ministry and other programs that are nurturing the faith of their children
- Providing parents with tools and resources to help faith be a part of their home life like meal prayers, discussion starters, and contemporary Christian music
- Offering opportunities for parents to learn more about the faith development needs and challenges of young people

Young people also serve as evangelizers in their homes. They carry into the home their stories and experiences of faith, they initiate prayer and faith-sharing, and through their example of living the Gospel they challenge family members to do the same. Together youth and their families live their faith and evangelize their friends, family, and neighbors.

Parish

The reality of most parish communities is that they are better at maintaining parish life than they are at thinking and acting in an evangelizing manner. When adults evangelize youth, they are also inviting them to join the community. Christians do not act alone; they are people who commit together to be the Body of Christ in the world. Evangelization in youth ministry is vitally connected to a parish's understanding of itself as a whole community that is called to evangelize not only youth, but all its members.

As it says in the document by the United States Conference of Catholic Bishops, *Go and Make Disciples,*

An evangelizing spirit will touch every dimension of Catholic parish life. Welcome, acceptance, the invitation to conversion and renewal, and reconciliation and peace, beginning with our worship, must characterize the whole tenor of our parishes. Every element of the parish must respond to the evangelical imperative—priests and religious, lay persons, staff, ministers, organizations, social clubs, parochial schools, and parish religious education programs. Otherwise, evangelization will be something a few people in the parish see as their ministry—rather than the reason for the parish's existence and the objective of every ministry in the parish.[20]

Parishes that take evangelization seriously are parishes where young people are involved in leadership roles and are visible in the faith community—leading music, welcoming people to liturgy, and so on. These parishes notice and welcome young people in their midst, taking time to get to know their names, needs, and gifts. These parishes do not isolate young people into youth groups or youth-only liturgies, but integrate young people into all aspects of parish life. Successful parishes invest time and finances in youth ministry and in training young people to be leaders in the Church today. These parishes are willing to change and proclaim the Gospel to young people in words and images that are relevant to today's youth. Parishes that take evangelization seriously are parishes where people of all ages—including youth—feel welcomed, challenged, affirmed, and included.

Parish membership is not a one-way relationship; it is not just about what the parish can do for young people, but also about the gifts and resources that young people have to share with their parish community. As members of our parish community, young people are to be challenged to be responsible disciples, to be leaders, servers, evangelizers for all they come in contact with. They are to be called to a "living, fruitful confession of faith."[21]

The Wider Community—Resources for Evangelization

As outreach is a critical part of evangelization, collaborative efforts with other churches and youth-serving organizations is important. Not only does outreach offer great witness to the power of Christians working united in a common effort, but it offers more chances to reach youth with the Good News.

Parishes can collaborate with other churches in joint program offerings. "The Holy Spirit, through the ecumenical movement, is calling churches and ecclesial communities into ever-deeper communion through dialogue and cooperation."[22] The Alpha Course for youth is one such example. Alpha is an ecumenical evangelization program that looks at different issues having to do with Christianity, such as who Jesus is, what faith is all about, why people pray, and how God speaks to people today. For more info see www.alphana.org, which includes information on using Alpha in a Catholic context. Other ideas include hosting contemporary Christian music concerts, service projects, retreats, working together with community organizations to reach at-risk youth and to deal with unique local youth issues that need advocacy, and drop-in centers where churches could create weekly schedules so drop-in space is open every day but each church is only responsible for one day of the week.

Collaboration with other churches and youth-serving agencies—including schools—can be as simple as sharing calendars and as involved as working together on joint projects.

Celebrations such as parades and homecomings are good ways to advertise youth friendliness to the community by involving young people in the creation and staffing of a parade float, a food booth, a talent show, and so on. Evangelization also takes place when a young person or adult is commissioned by the parish to carry the community's Christian views to local youth recreation boards, student councils, etc.

The wider community context also includes youth and youth inclusive programs on the diocesan level such as retreats, mission trips, leadership camps, and so on. It also includes the universal church context and central events such as World Youth Day on a national and international level, diocesan youth exchange programs, pilgrimages, and other diocesan-sponsored youth events.

Implications for Youth Ministry

> All ministry with adolescents must be directed toward presenting young people with the Good News of Jesus Christ and inviting and challenging them to become his disciples.
>
> RENEWING THE VISION[23]

Simply put, evangelization is the underlying goal of all youth ministry efforts. It is the core purpose and reason for every program, activity, or strategy undertaken by a parish.

Consider the relationship of evangelization to the components of youth ministry. (See RTV, pages 26-48 for an explanation of the components.) Through the ministry of Advocacy, leaders work to make sure that the needs of all young people are met. This occurs because something or someone is violating Jesus' principle of the fullness of life for all people. The components of Catechesis and evangelization are intimately linked, because catechesis is a "moment" within Evangelization. Catechesis deepens one's understanding of Jesus and his Church, and through that process evangelizes young people into a deeper relationship with him. The ministry of Community Life evangelizes young people by connecting them in meaningful and challenging ways to the Church community and to relationships with others who will support them on their journey with Christ. People who look at the world through Jesus' eyes are called to respond through Justice and Service, which in turn renews their relationship with Christ by being blessed to meet him in the poor and suffering of the world. Being baptized in Christ, Christians are called to be his hands, hearts, and body in the world as they empower young people and others in the ministry of leadership development.

Through the ministry of Pastoral Care Catholics bring the Good News to the sometimes-perceived "bad news" in the lives of youth as they deal with the natural challenges of maturing and life. Prayer and Worship challenges leaders to remain focused on what is important—intimate communion with Jesus—as everyone shares the riches and power of the spiritual traditions and journeys with young people and their families. Ministry with young people begins and ends with Jesus. Evangelization is core to everything that a parish does in actualizing its ministry with young people.

Sharing Faith with Youth: Strategies

The Gospel's message is too powerful and deep to be contained within one strategy or medium. Youth leaders are called to be creative and imaginative with the tools and strategies in the parish's evangelization plan for youth.

Non-Programmatic Opportunities

There are many ways to evangelize youth that don't require the leadership to gather with them. Leaders can share faith with youth in an indirect manner through the use of Web, print, or other media.

Before undertaking any of these strategies it is important to be aware of the safety guidelines issued by the diocese or parish. Initially, some safety guidelines can seem as though they are obstacles to nurturing healthy relationships with young people. These safety parameters are designed to keep youth safe and to make sure that the Gospel can continually be proclaimed. Look at them through the lens of evangelization. For instance, if parents need to be included in all communication with their adolescent children, there is an opportunity for the parents to be evangelized and informed about what the parish community is offering its young people.

At this moment in history, technology provides Catholic leaders with a new world of possible means for communication that have incredible power and potential to share the Good News. What tools and resources can youth leaders use to reach today's young people in a media and style that are comfortable to them?

Web sites

A parish or parish youth ministry Web site provides a cyberspace bulletin board that not only can post things in an efficient manner but can be interactive as well! Just imagine the possibilities a Web site offers as part of an evangelization strategy.

1. Prayer A virtual prayer room can be created that enables young people to post their prayer intentions for all to join in supporting them. Seeing others seek help from God and Jesus in times of trial and joy is evangelization.

2. Scripture Link the parish Web site to a site that offers the Sunday readings and reflections, or to a site that offers Catholic reflections on the readings. *Disciples Now*, a Catholic Web site for teenagers, offers reflections on the Sunday readings written for teenagers.[24] Engage the young people in the parish in evangelizing others by inviting them to write and post their own reflections that the leader edits and posts on the Web site.

3. Music Offer a song of the week that speaks of Jesus' love for his people. Two Web sites provided by Catholic organizations could be of assistance here: spiritandsong.com offers a wide selection of contemporary Catholic music, and cornerstonemedia.org provides suggestions for ways to use popular music with teenagers. Have a conversation with the music leaders in your parish community to include songs from the hymnal that the parish uses, perhaps made into a CD by the parish music team.

4. Announcements of Upcoming Events Provide announcements of upcoming events and programs for youth and their families provided by youth ministry, the parish, and the wider community. Include the opportunity to appreciate the evangelizing presence of Christ at Eucharistic devotions and adoration, Bible studies, Liturgy of the Hours, prayer groups, prayer experiences, and so on.

5. Faith Testimonies Post young people's reflections on living their faith in today's world.

6. Seasonal Prayers, Reflections, and Rituals Make the parish Web site the virtual place to "be" as the Church year unfolds, providing young people with prayers, stories, reflections, and simple rituals to enable them to participate fully in the Church season.

Newsletters

Newsletters are a common tool to stay in touch with the young people of the parish. Whether an e-newsletter or an actual paper newsletter, this medium can disseminate many of the ideas described under the previous section on Web sites, without ever creating a Web site.

E-Mail and "Snail"-Mail Postcards Short e-mail messages that do not list recipient e-mail addresses or "snail"-mail postcards are good tools. Use them to invite young people to upcoming events or to return to a program if they have been absent for a while, to let them know to check out something new on the Web site or that are being prayed for, to offer greetings of thanks or birthday or congratulations, and so on. Do not minister exclusively to young people with e-mail access; note on information forms who needs the information on a regular basis with regular "snail"-mail.

Retreats

Youth retreats have a unique ability to touch the hearts of young people. Retreat experiences help build communities of faith, help youth grow closer to God, and draw them back into active involvement in parish life. Simply put, retreats have the power to change the lives of young people, calling them more deeply into discipleship.[25]

Those who have experienced retreats as young people and who have facilitated retreats with and for young people know the power that they have to invite all in attendance into a deeper relationship with Jesus. Retreats that are facilitated with honesty and with respect for healthy principles—balance of activities, recreation, food, adequate sleep, safe environment—need to be part of every parish's evangelization ministry with youth. An excellent way to learn about designing or planning youth retreats is to participate in a youth retreat being facilitated by an experienced parish with a good reputation for effective retreat ministry. Many dioceses host diocesan youth retreats or have teams of young people trained and able to facilitate a retreat for any parish. Contact the local youth ministry office to see what retreat programs are available and for support, training, and resources. Also see the bibliography at the end of this chapter for some recommended retreat ministry resources. Some principles to keep in mind when planning a retreat:

- Leaders need to have a profound respect for the dignity of each person and the individuality of each person's journey. Faith-sharing and retreat-witnessing from a variety of youth and adults with different journeys help retreatants to know that God reaches everyone in a multitude of ways.
- The heart of an evangelization retreat—like the heart of evangelization—is Jesus, with Scripture and Church teachings as the guide. Christians speak as loudly through their actions as through their words. Hospitality and helping everyone to feel comfortable and welcome are critical in retreat ministry.
- Youth retreats prepare the retreatants to return to their everyday lived experience, bringing with them their learning from the retreat. Communication with parents about what has taken place on the retreat, complete with ideas for how parents can help the young people live out their renewed commitments, is an important aspect of effective and healthy retreat ministry.
- Retreat ministry stays relevant, connecting the Good News to current events and issues currently impacting on the lives of teens and broader contemporary issues.

Gathered Evangelization Programs

Part of evangelization is hosting gathered programs where youth explore the person of Jesus Christ in greater depth and nurture the intimate communion all people are called to have with him.

Principles

Evangelization happens when the word of Jesus speaks to people's hearts and minds. Needing no trickery or manipulation, evangelization can happen only when people accept the Gospel freely, as the "good news" it is meant to be, because of the power of the gospel message and the accompanying grace of God.[26]

Gathered evangelization sessions share many of the same principles about retreats that were mentioned previously. In addition to those ideas, gathered evangelization sessions should

- Happen in a comfortable place, where young people will feel at home in talking about their faith. Some young people may even be more comfortable in gathering at a non-church place such as the back room of a restaurant.
- Be well prepared. A dry run/rehearsal should take place before presenting the session to a gathering of young people. The dry run should include imagining how the young people might respond to the faith-sharing or questions being asked of them, in order to ensure that the questions are the right ones and have been written in the right way.
- Be rooted in prayer. "Without prayer, the Good News of Jesus Christ cannot be understood, spread, or accepted. These goals [of evangelization] can be accomplished only by opening our hearts to God, who gives to his children everything they seek ..."[27]

The central principle of a gathered evangelization session is respect—Catholics are called to evangelize like Jesus did. He proclaimed the Good News, he challenged his listeners, he listened to their stories, but he never judged them. A listening, respectful tone is critical in evangelization. Jesus makes it clear when we are not responding as we ought, but is not judgmental in his response. He calls humanity to be uncomfortable and give beyond what is thought possible in their response to God's invitation to serve.

Formats for Facilitating Evangelization Programs

Before designing an evangelization session, the leader must choose a central aspect of the life of Jesus to be explored and a relevant Scripture passage to ground that aspect in the Gospels. A gathered evangelization session contains the following elements:

Welcome and Greeting of Participants The welcome includes both an individual welcome to each young person to the gathering as they arrive, as well as a welcome to the whole group to formally start the session.

Community-Building These are intentional activities to help everyone "arrive"— to enable them to become comfortable with one another and open to the created program through a sense of trust. Activities such as ice breakers, music, and games help people to feel comfortable at the session.

Ritual or Prayer Experience Depending on the design of the evening or the comfortableness of the gathered group, pray together as a community using Scripture that is directly connected to the faith-sharing to come, a ritual action connected to the evening's focus, and music. Use a pattern for prayer—such as gather, listen, respond, and go forth. When using this pattern, choose elements of prayer for the first movement of prayer, which is "gather." Choose Scripture or other readings for the second movement, which is "listen." Select ways that those who are gathered can respond in prayer during the third movement, which is "respond." Finally, select the concluding elements of prayer that send the participants from the prayer to continue the work of the prayer. This is the final movement, which is "go forth." Clips from contemporary films and symbols can also be part of the opening prayer experience.

Proclamation and Faith-Sharing Proclaim the Scripture and provide a brief faith-sharing presentation connected to the evening's evangelization focus, that includes a story from the speaker's life. Faith-sharing needs to be intimately connected to the Scripture passage chosen as the heart of the evangelization focus. The faith-sharers use personal stories and other examples to illustrate what they have learned about Jesus and how the session's Scripture passage has helped them to understand their experience and lead them into deeper relationship with Jesus.

Group Faith-Sharing Opportunity exists for those in attendance to integrate the message about Jesus they have heard. Playing a piece of music that connects to the evangelization focus is one way to allow young people to take some personal reflection time before moving into a structured activity or group faith-sharing. Group discussion, storytelling among participants, quiet reflection time, or artistic responses are good ways to facilitate faith-sharing and integration of the Gospel message.

Closing Close the evangelization session with a prayer connected to the Scripture passage or a symbol that connects back to the opening prayer experience. Challenge the young people, gathering together some of the ideas that they have, to go forth and live out their relationship with Jesus. Serve refreshments and allow time for the young people to informally be with one another.

Outreach with Youth

> We are engaged in a noble, sacred task whose boundaries are as wide as the world and whose purpose is nothing less than the glory of God. We must remember that it is the tradition of our faith that God's Spirit is not confined to the Church but roams the world and its peoples breathing where it will. The arena of mission is not simply the Church but the world itself.[28]

Outreach is one of the three evangelization components in youth ministry. Catholics are called to do outreach through existing gathered programs and to do outreach in the broader community with young people whose presence does not yet grace existing programs. Young people have a variety of entry points through which they make contact with the parish communities; each of these contacts is an opportunity for evangelization.

Young People in Contact with the Parish Community
One entry point is sacramental preparation, when young people come to communities seeking confirmation preparation or through the Rite of Christian Initiation. Many young people still seem to surface from nowhere when a parish offers preparation for Confirmation. How is the parish designing its sacramental preparations to really help young people experience Christ both in the preparation and in the celebration itself? Does it offer faithful companions for confirmation candidates to journey with; does it help them prayerfully discern God's call in their life as they seek confirmation?

Young people have contact with parish communities through funerals of older generations or immediate family members, weddings and wedding anniversaries, Sunday liturgies, and seasonal liturgies like Ash Wednesday and Easter Sunday. Does the parish make special efforts to reach out to unknown young people at these times? Does it offer them resources to understand what is taking place at these liturgies?

Weekly Sunday Eucharist is a time when some young people make regular or semi-regular contact with their parish communities. In many parishes, these young people are not spoken to and are not personally invited to participate in or share their gifts in the parish's youth ministry plans. Their names, passions, and interests are unknown; so is their location on their faith journeys. Does the parish have a plan in place to personally welcome each young person when they arrive in the parish complex? Are there hospitality ministers who remember the names of these young people and who intentionally seek them out at Eucharist, asking them about their week, and their activities?

Young people make contact with their faith communities through justice and service projects and activities, leadership training (including preparation for liturgical ministry), personal crises, and sporting programs. Is every point of contact with young people an opportunity to witness through hospitality the hope and joy of being a disciple of Jesus? Every time a young person makes contact with a parish community is an opportunity to offer the individual—through word and action—an experience of Jesus.

Outreach to Youth Not Connected to Parish Communities

> Evangelization loses much of its force and effectiveness if it does not take into consideration the actual people to whom it is addressed, if it does not use their language, their signs and symbols, if it does not answer the questions they ask, and if it does not have an impact on their concrete life.[29]

Outreach to young people needs to go where they are, sometimes physically and sometimes by addressing contemporary issues from their world. What are some ways to be present in the lives of youth? The central question a parish needs to ask itself as it thinks about doing intentional outreach with the youth of the area is, "Where are they? Where do they hang out?"

The parish can organize itself to be present in the good and not-so-good places where young people are. Adult leaders can attend youth sporting events, arrange to help out in the coaching of local sports teams, go to their concerts, affirm them in their places of employment, and work with other churches to be a presence at local high schools and youth centers. Parish leaders can be present to those in legal troubles by being a place where the young people can serve their community service hours or by being part of regular outreach to juvenile justice centers. When their parents are ill or hospitalized, youth can be connected to local hospital ministries. Parishes can work with local community organizations to understand what the critical needs are for young people in the area and then line up the resources to help address those needs, like drop-in sports programs or after-school place to hang out and receive food and homework help.

Parish communities can be present to young people by being attentive to the questions and issues that surface in the lives of youth. Parishes can work with other churches to offer prayer services in relation to current crises like war and natural disasters, advocate for young people when budget cuts affect their schools and recreational centers, and provide support and resources to them as they address local justice needs and social issues.

The heart of outreach is a gift that Jesus offered this world—presence. How are parishes present to young people wherever they are and whatever they are facing?

Outreach With Youth—Remembering the Family Connection

Leaders in ministry need to consider the home and the family as an integral component of the ministry plan. Outreach strategies with young people are always filtered through the lens of the home to which they are returning. How will this strategy impact their families? What tools, resources, and support might help families evangelize and support one another?

First of all, parents and guardians are not just an "add-on" audience to evangelization plans but a key aspect of them. With their support, parish leaders are able to share the Good News with young people in a manner that enables a whole household to newly embrace the Good News. In ministry with youth, youth leaders are part of the "team" of an evangelizing parish, and are therefore called to work with other parish ministry areas so that the faith life of parents is intentionally nurtured. Together with other parish ministries, youth leaders can see every contact point with parents as an opportunity to affirm them in their role and to answer their central questions: Is my child normal? What can you do to help me be the best parent I can be? How does faith fit in to the daily realities of our lives?

For example, when a parish's confirmation program gathers parents—with or without the confirmation candidates—the meeting is an opportunity to deepen their faith as adults and as parents. Many of the parents of today's teenagers themselves are disconnected from the Church and lack foundational understanding of basic Church practices and teachings, and are in need of an invitation to deepen their own relationship with Christ so that they may journey in faith with their children.

Witnesses of Faith

Youth are not merely the recipients of the Good News but are also carriers of this message to their peers and to the world. Young people witnessing to young people and others is one of the most powerful ways for the Good News to be shared. What can parish leadership do to support young people to be evangelizers?

- Offer resources and programming that challenge and deepen young people's relationship with Jesus Christ.
- Organize prayer partners or adult mentors to journey with them.
- Offer them leadership opportunities that nurture and challenge their faith—retreat ministry, liturgical ministry, ministry with younger children, and vacation Bible camps.
- Provide them with opportunities to be involved in local or national justice and service projects. Arrange for them to gather with other young people at youth rallies, diocesan youth congresses, and World Youth Day events.

Young people need tools to evangelize their peers and others. One tool that they need is a foundational understanding of how to read the Good News and how to access good Catholic reflections on it. A second tool is the guidance to reflect on their lives as Christians, for it is often in hindsight when, pondering what is taking place in their lives, they recognize Christ's presence in their lives. Ongoing faith formation and catechesis deepens the young people's understanding of their Catholic identity and how Catholics live and understand the Good News in today's world. A fourth tool is a practical one. How does one talk about Jesus with somebody? Where does one start to tell the story? Youth leaders can provide young people with the skills and confidence they need to be faith witnesses, through mentoring and evangelization training programs.

Adults also need preparation to evangelize to and with young people. As the *Catechism of the Catholic Church* says, each believer is "a link in the great chain of believers."[30] Adults serve as links between young people and the Good News, helping them to find their way to Jesus. Adults need the tools listed for youth in the preceding paragraph, but they also need a solid understanding of the stages of faith for youth, clarity about being an adult faith-sharer in the life of youth, tools and support to reflect on their journey with Christ so that they may share it with others, and support to be healthy and integrated witnesses of the Good News.

Community of Faith: A Parish's Call to Witness the Good News to Youth

"The fruits of evangelization are changed lives and a changed world" (*Go and Make Disciples*, #18). Parishes offer young people the hope of the risen Lord that continues to transform their lives and the world. Young people need to see the impact of the Good News on their lives, and come to understand that the choices and decisions in every area of life are made through the lens of faith. Through the witness of the community, may young people see the Good News as a challenging and life-giving way of life, and join us in the mission to "make disciples of all nations" (Mt 28:19).

— RESOURCES FOR EVANGELIZING YOUTH —

Church Documents

Catechism of the Catholic Church. Washington, DC: United States Conference of Catholic Bishops–Libreria Editrice Vaticana, 1994.

Congregation for the Clergy. *General Directory for Catechesis.* Washington, DC: United States Conference of Catholic Bishops, 1997.

Department of Education. *Sowing Seeds: Notes and Comments on the General Directory for Catechesis.* Washington, DC: United States Conference of Catholic Bishops, 2000.

Go and Make Disciples: A National Plan and Strategy for Catholic Evangelization in the United States. Washington, DC: United States Conference of Catholic Bishops, 1993.

John Paul II. *On Catechesis in Our Time* (*Catechesi Tradendae*). Washington, DC: United States Conference of Catholic Bishops, 1979.

Pope Paul VI. *On Evangelization in the Modern World* (*Evangelii Nuntiandi*). Washington, DC: United States Conference of Catholic Bishops, 1975.

Renewing the Vision: A Framework for Catholic Youth Ministry. Washington, DC: United States Conference of Catholic Bishops, 1997.

Sharing the Light of Faith. Washington, DC: United States Conference of Catholic Bishops, 1979.

Recommended Resources

Boyack, Kenneth (ed.). *The New Catholic Evangelization.* New York: Paulist Press, 1992.

The Challenge of Catholic Youth Evangelization: Called to Be Witnesses and Storytellers. Washington, DC: National Federation for Catholic Youth Ministry, 1993.

DeSiano, Frank. *The Evangelizing Catholic: A Practical Handbook for Reaching Out.* New York: Paulist Press, 1998.

DeSiano, Frank. *Sowing New Seed: Directions for Evangelization Today.* New York: Paulist Press, 1994.

DeSiano, Frank, and Kenneth Boyack. *Creating the Evangelizing Parish*. New York: Paulist Press, 1993.

Dean, Kenda Creasy, and Ron Foster. *Godbearing Life: The Art of Soul Tending for Youth Ministry*. Nashville: Upper Room Books, 1998.

Garlinski, Michelle, Mariette Martineau, and Dean Woodbeck. *Total Youth Ministry: Ministry Resources for Evangelization*. Winona, MN: Saint Mary's Press, 2004.

Greeley, Andrew, and Mary Greeley Durkin. *An Epidemic of Joy: Stories in the Spirit of Jesus*. Chicago: ACTA, 1999.

Hawkowski, Maryann. *Getaways with God: Youth Retreats for Any Schedule*. Winona, MN: Saint Mary's Press, 2003.

McCarty, Robert J. *Meeting the Challenge: Resources for Catholic Youth Evangelization*. Winona, MN: Saint Mary's Press, 1993.

McKinnon, Greg. *The Bottom Line: How to Help Youth Become Disciples*. (*Skillabilities for Youth Ministry*) Nashville: Abingdon Press, 1998.

Mercadante, Frank. *Make It Real: A Practical Resource for Teen-Friendly Evangelization*. Winona, MN: Saint Mary's Press, 2004.

No More Us and Them: 100 Ways to Bring Your Youth and Church Together. Loveland, CO: Group Books, 2000.

Ponsetto, Daniel. *Walking Together: Outreach and Evangelization Resources for Youth Ministry*. Winona, MN: Saint Mary's Press, 1995.

Reaching Kids Most Youth Ministries Miss. Loveland, CO: Group Books, 2000.

Shea, John. *Elijah at the Wedding Feast and Other Tales*. Chicago: ACTA, 1999.

Shea, John. *Gospel Light: Jesus Stories for Spiritual Consciousness*. New York: Crossroad Publishing, 1998.

Shea, John. *The Legend of the Bells and Other Tales*. Chicago: ACTA, 1996.

— ENDNOTES —

1. Paul VI. *On Evangelization in the Modern World* (*Evangelii Nuntiandi*). Washington, DC: United States Conference of Catholic Bishops–Libreria Editrice Vaticana, 1975, #18.

2. *Catechism of the Catholic Church*. Washington, DC: United States Conference of Catholic Bishops–Libreria Editrice Vaticana, 1994, #905, citing Second Vatican Ecumenical Council, *Dogmatic Constitution on the Church* (*Lumen Gentium*) (November 21, 1964), 35§1, §2.

3. *The Challenge of Catholic Youth Evangelization: Called to Be Witnesses and Storytellers*. Washington, DC: National Federation for Catholic Youth Ministry, 1993), #7-8.

4. *National Directory for Catechesis*, p. 12-17.

5. NDC, #21A, p. 63.

6. *Renewing the Vision: A Framework for Catholic Youth Ministry*. Washington, DC: United States Conference of Catholic Bishops, 1997, p. 36.

7. *Go and Make Disciples: A National Plan and Strategy for Catholic Evangelization in the United States* (Washington, DC: United States Conference of Catholic Bishops, 1993, #1.

8. RTV, p. 37.

9. *Go and Make Disciples*, #36.

10. Ibid., #31.

11. Congregation for the Clergy, *General Directory for Catechesis*. Washington, DC: United States Conference of Catholic Bishops, 1997), #80.

12. *On Evangelization in the Modern World*, #14.

13. *Go and Make Disciples*, #12.

14. GDC, #56.

15. *Go and Make Disciples*, #34.

16. Ibid., #85.

17. Ibid., #20.

18. Ibid., #26.

19. Bibby, Reginald. *Canada's Teens: Yesterday, Today, and Tomorrow*. Toronto: Stoddart, 1991, p. 55.

20. *Go and Make Disciples*, #85.

21. GDC, #82.

22. *Go and Make Disciples*, #42.

23. RTV, p. 10 (italics original).

24. See: www.disciplesnow.com/celebrate/index.cfm (accessed September 30, 2008).

25. East, Tom, et al. *Effective Practices for Dynamic Youth Ministry*. Winona, MN: Saint Mary's Press, 2004, p. 49.

26. *Go and Make Disciples*, #19.

27. Ibid., #81.

28. Secretariat for Evangelization. *Ministry through the Lens of Evangelization: The Gospel and the Call to Mission*. Washington, DC: United States Conference of Catholic Bishops, 2004, p. 151-152.

29. EN, #63.

30. *Catechism of the Catholic Church*, #166.

CHAPTER ELEVEN

Justice and Service

Sean T. Lansing

Editor's Note

Parish communities help youth connect faith to life when they engage the idealism of youth and connect their energies to provide service, and work for justice. In this chapter, Sean Lansing leads us to explore the dimensions of justice rooted in Scripture and faith teachings. He guides us to consider practical methods for educating youth in justice, engaging them in service, and leading them to become advocates for those in need.

The ministry of justice and service nurtures in young people a social consciousness and a commitment to a life of justice and service rooted in their faith in Jesus Christ, in the Scriptures, and in Catholic social teaching; empowers young people to work for justice by concrete efforts to address the causes of human suffering; and infuses the concepts of justice, peace, and human dignity into all ministry efforts.

UNITED STATES CONFERENCE OF
CATHOLIC BISHOPS,
*RENEWING THE VISION:
A FRAMEWORK FOR CATHOLIC
YOUTH MINISTRY*[1]

This description of the ministry of justice and service from *Renewing the Vision* paints a beautiful picture of socially conscious youth working regularly to alleviate injustice in the world. Their actions are born from their unwavering commitment to Christ and are supported and strengthened by a parish youth ministry that has the Church's rich Catholic social teaching at the heart of all ministry efforts. Maybe all youth ministries are not exactly what *Renewing the Vision* describes, but is the vision even possible?

The answer is yes! This chapter will explore the component of justice and service in youth ministry and uncover concrete ways for making this component of the vision for Catholic youth ministry a reality in the community. To that end, this chapter focuses on what the church means by justice, practical ways to infuse justice education into youth ministry efforts, and ways to engage youth in service that challenges their perspective and informs their spirituality.

 Making the Connection

Youth make an amazing difference when we awaken their passion for justice.

- *What areas of need and injustice in our world do you experience youth to be concerned about?*

What Is Justice?

> The concerns for non-violence, sustainable development, justice and peace, and care for our environment are of vital importance for humanity. They cannot, however, be understood apart from a profound reflection upon the innate dignity of every human life from conception to natural death: a dignity conferred by God himself and thus inviolable.
>
> BENEDICT XVI, WORLD YOUTH DAY, JULY 17, 2008[2]

What is justice? The question seems simple enough, but there has been volumes written to capture the fullness of the word's meaning. Ask this question of a group of adolescents (or adults for that matter) and the myriad responses will range from the strictly legal to the altruistic.

The *Catechism of the Catholic Church* defines justice as "the moral virtue that consists in the constant and firm will to give their due to God and neighbor."[3]

Giving our due to God is called the virtue of religion. Giving what is due to our neighbor is the virtue of justice.

Three Forms of Justice

The Catholic tradition identifies three forms of justice: commutative, distributive, and contributive or social.[4] Commutative justice refers to agreements or contracts between private individuals or private groups. Commutative justice demands that these agreements honor and respect the dignity of both individuals or groups entering into the agreement. In other words, tradition expects that agreements and contracts be fair and equitable. Both sides must enter freely into agreements and neither side may break the agreement in a casual way or for personal gain. To force individuals or parties into an agreement is a violation of commutative justice. Catholic social tradition argues that one violation of commutative justice occurs when a worker is forced to take a job at an insufficient wage because the alternative is no wage at all.[5] The primary values that commutative justice invokes are the dignity of each person, fidelity to one's word, and a sense of working together for mutual benefit (interdependence).

Distributive justice is the just relationship between society and the individuals and groups that make up society. Society, or those institutions and structures that govern society, have a responsibility to maintain the common good and ensure that all people have a share in public goods, such as the benefits of a productive economy and the fruits of the earth, including security, food, and water. Distributive justice demands that everyone, including children, the elderly, and the infirmed, receive public goods even if they cannot help provide them. This is because sharing in the goods of the earth and of the community does not need to be earned; rather, it is a right because of the dignity inherent in all people. Distributive justice also demands that these public goods be distributed in a way that supports the common good.[6]

Contributive justice, often called social justice, speaks to the relationship individuals and groups have with society. Contributive justice is an obligation to contribute to society and to aid in creating just systems and institutions to provide for the common good. Contributive justice means that contributions may not be fair or equal; everyone is obligated to contribute to society as their gifts allow. This is an easy concept for youth ministers to grasp. When young people stop coming to gathered youth ministry programs, the leadership can often invite them back by reminding them that the programs are not the same without them. The young people's contribution to the group helps make programming better. This illustrates what contributive justice is all about. Great youth ministry happens when individuals use their gifts, talents, and resources contribute to the whole; a just world requires the gifts, talents, and resources of individuals and groups to work for the common good.

A Biblical Perspective of Justice

The three modes of justice begin to tease out the underlying values that shape Catholic social thought, but as a people of the Word, Catholics also need to understand what Scripture has to teach about justice. John R. Donohue, S.J. describes the biblical perspective on justice as being faithful to the demands of a relationship.[7] This perspective captures the practicality with which Scripture approaches justice.

The United States bishops, in *Economic Justice for All* articulate seven biblical perspectives that offer a foundation for reflecting on social justice. They are:

Created in God's Image[8] Human beings are created in God's image. Therefore, every human being has a fundamental dignity that cannot be taken away and must be protected.

A People of the Covenant[9] God liberated the Israelites from slavery and created a covenant with them. The prophets taught that this covenant was broken when the people worshipped false gods and when they failed to hear the cry of the poor and oppressed.

The Reign of God and Justice[10] Jesus proclaimed the reign of God that calls us to transform the world, living a life marked by loving God, loving your neighbor as yourself, and feeding the hungry, caring for the sick, welcoming the stranger, clothing the naked, and visiting the imprisoned.

Called to be Disciples in Community[11] We see in the New Testament that Jesus' disciples formed communities to support and sustain each other in their discipleship, which includes imitating Christ's openness to the will of God and being in service of others. It also means following the way of the cross, being willing to enter into the mystery of Jesus' death and resurrection.

Poverty, Riches, and the Challenge of Discipleship[12] This theme, especially evident in Luke's gospel, teaches about the challenge that wealth brings to living a Christian life. From the prophets to the Beatitudes, Christians are called to take the side of the poor and detach ourselves from hoarding riches.

A Community of Hope[13] Being new creations in Christ, working to bring justice and peace to this world gives witness to the belief that God's love is active in this world. God's love and saving action in this world sustain us with hope and faith for a world marked by love.

A Living Tradition[14] A contemporary look at today's social issues is not informed by Scripture alone, but also by the living tradition of the Catholic faith. Following the example of Catholic communities throughout history, communities today are called to live this biblical tradition of justice in today's world.

> **These two passages exemplify the scriptural call to justice:**
>
> *Your cereal offerings I will not accept, nor consider your stall-fed peace offerings. Away with your noisy songs! I will not listen to the melodies of your harps. But if you would offer me holocausts, then let justice surge like water, and goodness like an unfailing stream.*
>
> AMOS 5:21-24
>
> *The Spirit of the Lord is upon me, because he has anointed me to bring glad tidings to the poor. He has sent me to proclaim liberty to captives and recovery of sight to the blind, to let the oppressed go free, and to proclaim a year acceptable to the Lord.*
>
> LUKE 4:16-19

Rather than speak abstractly about justice, Scripture explains what it means to do justice. The prophets remind the people of the Covenant that it is in remembering the poor, the naked, and the outcast that God sees a sign of faithfulness (Is 58:6-9, Dt 24:17-22). Worship and acts of piety are empty if those who worship do not care for the poor in their midst (Am 5:21-24; 8:4-7). Jesus affirms this biblical preference for the poor and the outcast by proclaiming as his mission the preaching of the Good News to the oppressed, the imprisoned, and the poor (Lk 4:16-18). Scripture is filled with over two thousand references to the poor and the outcast, calling Christians into relationship with their brothers and sisters so that they can authentically live out their relationship with God.

What is justice? What does God demand of us? The bottom line is that being a person of justice means entering into a relationship with people who have been cast aside, who are poor, who struggle, whom society and its structures and institutions deem worthless. It is letting these relationships shape how people discover and protect the dignity of every one of their brothers and sisters. These relationships will require the risk of standing up to unjust systems, the risk of being in relationships with people who are different, the risk of being unpopular. It may even require a change of lifestyle and a change for whom and with whom one prays. This is the challenge of the Gospel, this is the worthy adventure God calls for and into which he invites young people.

The Role of Justice in Youth Ministry

The challenge of the Gospel entails all that an adventure does: risk, sacrifice, danger, and reward. Why engage young people in political issues instead of just "sticking to" issues of faith? The answer is quite simple: Catholics cannot enter into the Gospel as they understand it without grappling with issues of justice and injustice in the world.

The bishops teach about this relationship between the Gospel and justice in many documents, and they challenge youth ministers to see this relationship as well. In *Renewing the Vision: A Framework for Catholic Youth Ministry*, the bishops name justice and service as one of the eight components of youth ministry. Clearly, ministry efforts with young people must equip them to see how Gospel values are relevant to the world.

In 1971, a few years after the Second Vatican Council, the Church's bishops gathered together for a World Synod and produced a document called *Justice in the World*. In this document, the bishops said many challenging things about the call to be people of justice. One of the most profound statements was that being involved in acts of justice was a "constitutive dimension of preaching the Gospel."[15] Justice is an integral part of spreading the Gospel: no justice, no Gospel. No one would argue that youth ministries should not include the Gospel.

The bishops of the United States say it just as clearly: "The Church teaches that social justice is an integral part of evangelization, a constitutive dimension of preaching the Gospel, and an essential part of the Church's mission."[16] As we preach the Gospel and invite youth to be part of the Church's mission, we must engage youth in social justice.

Amy tolerated her confirmation preparation program. She dutifully attended everything she was required to. Although she was always present, her body language and especially her piercing stare during presentations made it clear that she would rather have been anywhere else. A guest speaker came to the program, talked about faith and service, and ended the evening by inviting anyone interested to come to a week-long service trip in the summer. Amy signed up to go on the trip. Amy came home changed. She joined the youth ministry leadership team and spoke excitedly about her experience of service and how it made her faith come alive. When she went to college, she helped her new parish start a summer service trip experience for their young people. She was invited to live out the mission of the Church, and it was a conversion experience that had a profound impact on her.

Inviting young people to work for justice can be an opportunity for conversion, a conversion for which they are hungry. In *The Challenge of Catholic Youth Evangelization: Called to Be Witnesses and Storytellers*, the National Federation for Catholic Youth Ministry writes that one of the five hungers of youth is the hunger for justice.[17] Today's generation of youth certainly embody this hunger, which is only deepened by immediate access to information about the world that continually reminds them that the world is not fair. Contemporary research indicates that this generation— sometimes called the millennial generation—has a deep desire for connectedness that goes beyond comfortable and familiar relationships.[18] The Gospel invites people into deeper relationships that stretch them beyond themselves and calls them to greater solidarity; youth ministry efforts must do the same.

Love, A Starting Point for Justice

In the Christian framework, our desire for justice is rooted in love—primarily through the love that God has for us. Pope Benedict XVI, in *Deus Caritas Est*, writes about how it is impossible to separate our love of God from our love of neighbor.

> No longer is it a question, then, of a "commandment" imposed from without and a calling for the impossible, but rather of a freely-bestowed experience of love from within, a love which by its very nature must then be shared with others.[19]

Youth ministry efforts help youth share this love and learn to live a life of justice by inviting them into a relationship with people who are outside of their own comfort zone. It is in these relationships that they will be transformed. Why? Relationships reveal the dignity inherent in each human person. Everyone becomes opened to the ways that they are similar instead of living within the barriers that separate them from each other. Relationships invite people to live in solidarity with their brothers and sisters who are marginalized. When social problems like poverty, homelessness, and war become the problems of real people, those in relationships cannot help caring and wanting to make a difference.

Entering into relationships is facilitated by good justice education. Some young people went to do service in a men's homeless shelter. The vast majority of men being served by this shelter were African Americans. When the youth came back from the service event and were asked what they had learned, one young man raised his hand and said, "I learned that most homeless people are African American men." What was especially striking about the young man's answer was that he was African American himself. This illustrates the importance of not just doing service, but being engaged in justice education. If the young man had been involved in justice education, he would have spent some time looking at the issue of homelessness and he would have learned that the majority of people who are homeless today in America are children. He would have also been given the tools to ask the question, "Why are the majority of homeless men at this shelter African American?" By not giving him the tools and the context he needed, his conclusions were drawn from assumptions and stereotypes, which never allow for authentic learning or authentic relationships.

Educating Youth for Justice

The goal of justice education is to equip young people with the ability to think critically about contemporary social issues and to understand what values their faith brings to the experience. Justice education is essential to comprehensive youth ministry for two important reasons. First, justice education engages young people in Catholic social teaching. Second, it shatters stereotypes and assumptions about contemporary social issues and gives young people the skills to analyze social issues and learn about their realities.

How is justice education done? The pastoral circle in Illustration #1 provides an accessible method and is the kind of tool that works well in the flexible and adaptive climate of youth ministry.[20] The pastoral circle has four movements: involvement, exploration, reflection, and action.

Together they provide a practical and comprehensive approach to justice education with youth.

Illustration #1

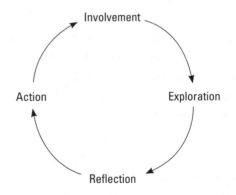

Involvement Involvement is the movement of the pastoral circle in which the issue moves from the abstract to the real. This movement takes youth out of their regular patterns of thinking and feeling into broader social issues. Involvement gives participants a reason to care about an issue and a motivation to learn more. Involvement can spring from a personal experience or the lived experience of the group. If the faith community exists in a neighborhood that is deteriorating from a variety of different economic forces, then it is already involved. Many times, however, involvement will come from some type of contrived activity to "hook" youth into the journey of the pastoral circle. An involvement activity can be anything that makes the issue more real: speakers sharing their stories, simulation games that illustrate a particular scenario of injustice, songs or movies, anything that draws participants into the reality of a justice issue and moves them to want to learn more about the issue.

Exploration Sometimes called social analysis, exploration is the next movement of the pastoral circle. Two things should be accomplished during exploration. The primary goal is to take a broader look at the social issues they have become involved with and uncover the social structures, connections, and dynamics at work. Youth are invited to look past their immediate experience without letting it be definitive. In other words, if one's only experience of a homeless person is someone "hustling money" for alcohol, that experience alone cannot decide that the solution to homelessness is alcohol addiction counseling. Rather, exploration allows for moving beyond that experience and asking the questions that give a clear and accurate picture of the social issue. In exploration, the primary goal is to find out the "who, what, where, and why" of the situation.

Looking at homelessness again, the first questions to ask are, "Who is homeless? What are the demographics of homelessness in my community? Why are people homeless? What are the economic forces at work? What are the obstacles to ending homelessness?" Exploration is the hardest movement of the pastoral circle for youth ministry folks, partly because it feels a lot more like sociology then ministry. Yet it is an essential part of justice education because it is within this movement that stereotypes are shattered, myths are debunked, and young people begin to understand the problem in ways that allow them to find real solutions. For example, exploring homelessness would uncover the fact that thirty-nine percent of homeless people in the United States are children under the age of eighteen, although the image that comes to mind when one thinks of a homeless person is almost never a child.[21]

The second goal of exploration is to give participants the tools to continue to do exploration regularly. These tools are the ability to think critically about justice issues, to ask the questions necessary to discover the reality of a situation, and to develop the habit of looking at a situation from its many different levels, including the structural level. This is essential. The call of the Gospel requires Christians to fight against injustice. The only way to do that is systemically. Therefore, young people must be helped to develop the habit of analyzing the injustices of the world from a systemic viewpoint.

Reflection The third movement of the pastoral circle is reflection. Reflection attempts to answer the question, "What does the Catholic faith have to say about this issue?" Youth ministries are not just social service agencies; the motivation for creating a just world comes from a deep conviction of faith. It is in the reflection movement that young people enter more deeply into the values that will inform the actions they take, delving into Scripture and Catholic social teaching and examining the current work that the Church is doing on each issue.

Reflection brings youth ministers back into comfortable territory. This is what they do—share the faith and break open Scripture and Tradition in ways that are meaningful and relevant to the issues that young people face in their lives. Reflection is the catechetical moment of the pastoral circle. Reflection is an opportunity for the Word of God and the Tradition of the Church to transform the hearts of young people.

Scripture—both Old and New Testament—is filled with challenges to be more just and to develop a clearer sense of God's justice. Young people deserve a scriptural literacy that includes God's vision of justice; educating for justice demands it as well. There are many creative ways to break open Scripture with youth and an abundance of creative ideas and resources to use. For example, parishes could provide a Bible study using the *lectio divina* method for Scripture reflection, or youth could work together in a group to re-write a passage in a contemporary context.[22] Take advantage of these techniques and use resources from the Catholic Campaign for Human Development and Catholic Relief Services for Scripture guides on Old and New Testament passages with justice themes.

Key sources for reflection are the social encyclicals, papal letters, synod statements, bishops' statements, and letters written by the bishops' conferences of a particular country, such as the United States Conference of Catholic Bishops. These documents discuss specific issues in light of their current contexts. For example, *Strangers No Longer: Together on the Journey of Hope*, a pastoral letter written collaboratively by the bishops of Mexico and the bishops of the United States, applies the justice tradition of the Church to the issue of immigration, particularly across the Mexico-United States border, as it exists in the context of 2003.

In a pastoral circle process, reflection provides the opportunity to familiarize young people with the documents of Catholic social teaching when the issues they are studying warrant it. There is almost always a church document, that addresses each issue of justice. These documents teach how the values of the Gospel apply to a specific issue in a specific historical context. As we engage youth in understanding these documents of Catholic social teaching, it is important to expose young people to the values that underlie these teachings of the Church. The United States Conference of Catholic Bishops articulates a framework for these values with the seven themes of Catholic social teaching. These themes are:

- The life and dignity of the human person
- The call to family, community, and participation
- Rights and responsibilities
- The preferential option (commitment) to the poor and vulnerable
- The dignity of work and the rights of workers
- Solidarity
- Care for God's creation[23]

Knowing and understanding these seven themes gives young people a starting point for thinking critically about what the Catholic faith has to say about a given situation before even looking at a document. Giving young people an opportunity to learn Catholic social teaching is inviting them into a deeper understanding of how the Gospel values apply to contemporary situations. It affirms their Baptism by giving them the ability to enter the Tradition of their faith and exposes them to a faith that is relevant, contemporary, and stands up for something in the world.

Action The last movement of the pastoral circle is action, which is what it is all about. The pastoral circle (or any other justice education method) should ultimately lead to action. Action, when informed by exploration and reflection, is effective because it is rooted in the reality of the situation and informed by the values of faith. Not only is there an opportunity to do something that can bring about meaningful change, but those doing the action are changed as well.

It is evident at this point in the pastoral circle that the issues are complex and one simple action will not solve the social problem. If it did, all the issues of injustice would be solved by now. Complexity can breed a sense of hopelessness because of the overwhelming nature of the problem. The complexity of the issues provides the opportunity for a variety of different action responses. This is a good time to ask young people what God-given gifts they have that can be a part of the solution. A variety of different action responses may result. Let the age of the group help dictate the action response. With younger adolescents, plan something as a big group; let older adolescents explore where God is calling them to respond in the situation.

Action takes on many different forms and may not always provide direct service to the "victims" of injustice. Appropriate action responses include

- Committing to behavior changes (e.g., only drinking fair-trade coffee after learning about unjust wages paid to coffee farmers)
- Praying differently (who for and who with?)
- Deciding to learn more about the situation
- Joining a group that does advocacy
- Beginning to discern how God may be calling one to work for justice in this area as a personal vocation

The pastoral circle is a great tool for justice education because it allows intentional programming and the kind of flexibility that good youth ministry requires. The pastoral circle process can be done in three or four weekly sessions, as a weekend retreat, or even as a week-long service experience. Use different movements of the pastoral circle to include some of the different settings of youth ministry. For example, the findings of an exploration exercise might provide an opportunity to share the learning with the whole community. As a part of reflection, send home family activities so the whole family can engage with Catholic social teaching. Be creative and utilize all of the settings of a comprehensive vision of youth ministry.

A word of caution is appropriate when engaging youth in social justice. One of the challenges of doing justice and service with young people is that sometimes parents get uneasy, especially if they feel their political stance is being challenged. To help this situation always communicate with parents so that they know what their young people are learning, and always be true to the teaching of the Church. Doing justice education is not the time to convince young people of a personal political viewpoint. Rather, introduce them to the moral framework that the Church teaches and help them to form their own conscience. Stay away from attacking or endorsing politicians and political parties and stay focused on the issues themselves. This is the approach of the Church.

Involving Youth in Service and Advocacy

In understanding the dimensions of justice, consider the two feet of justice. The first foot provides direct service to those in need, which is an essential part of living out the faith and meeting the greatest needs. The second foot is advocacy for social change. Advocacy includes all of the ways toward changing the structures and institutions that are unjust. Injustice is often discovered through good exploration. Without advocacy, the faithful can never move forward, since both feet need to be moving in order to get somewhere. This next section looks at strategies for doing effective service with young people and at ways to empower youth for advocacy.

Illustration #2: The Two Feet of Christian Service[24]

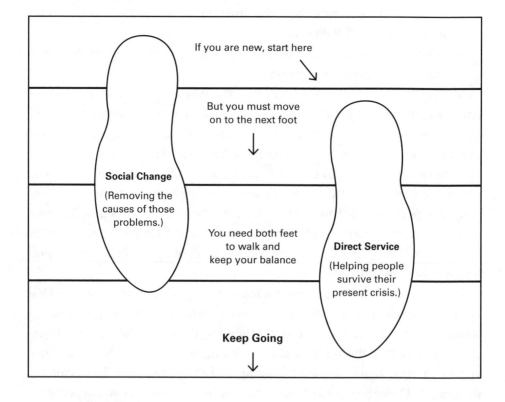

Involving Youth in Service

It is impractical for all service done in youth ministry to happen in the context of the pastoral circle. However, all service should involve three key elements: preparing, engaging and reflecting.

Preparing Good preparation is the key to a successful service experience. Preparing includes getting youth ready for the experience, but it also means checking everything out in advance. For example, when using a service agency, visit the agency ahead of time, find out what their experience of youth volunteers has been in the past, and make sure that there is enough work to do (often volunteer coordinators underestimate the energy of young people eager to do service).

Spend time preparing the young people for their service experience as well. If the service they will do requires skills, train them. Whenever possible, use the pastoral circle process. If this process is impractical, make sure young people are given good background information about the service they are going to do. For example, a youth ministry group doing service for a local housing initiative helped rehabilitate homes that had been condemned and turned them into livable places for low-income people to purchase and own. The group was excited because the members anticipated working with a family who would be moving into the house. The young people never met the family, a potential disappointment that could have soured the group's experience. However, because of their preparation the young people knew why they were there and what their work was going to accomplish for the overall mission of the housing initiative. They accepted that their personal hopes were not met because they knew why they were there.

Another important piece of good preparation is to help young people enter into a sense of solidarity by challenging and preparing them to be in right relationship with those whom they are serving. Challenge young people to recognize the dignity of the people they are serving and to avoid the temptation of feeling above them. Performing service does not make super Christians, it merely begins to authenticate baptism.

Engaging When engaging youth in service, it is important to have a servant's attitude. The attitude that one brings to service is just as important as the act of service itself. Sometimes, those who perform acts of service are just as concerned about what they will get out of the experience and how it will make them feel. Sometimes the motivation is to have a sense of accomplishing something or being on the receiving end of someone's gratitude. These are natural, but if they are the dominant motivation, then it is fair to ask whose needs are really being met by performing this service. It is important to root service in love and in a sense of responsibility to relationships with all of our brothers and sisters.

It is also important to have strong adult leaders who are engaged in the service with young people. A shared experience of service allows adults and youth to learn and grow in their understanding of discipleship together.

Reflecting Reflecting on the experience can be a small group process that involves journaling and discussion or discovering where everyone saw God in their experience. This discussion can be a formal process or a simple conversation engaged in while eating pizza after their work is completed. Use pastoral judgment to decide which approach is appropriate, but always do reflection. Reflection concretizes learning, provides the faith perspective on the service, and allows the group members to learn from each other.

Involving Youth in Advocacy

Advocacy is the logical "next step" after good exploration and reflection. Understanding the structural and institutional connections to issues of injustice compels people to change the system itself. Is it possible with youth? Absolutely!

Good advocacy starts with two things: knowledge of the problem being addressed, and knowledge of the systems of influence to change the situation. These systems include understanding how a bill gets turned into law, learning at which points in the process advocacy will have the greatest impact, and knowing who has the greatest influence over an unjust situation. For example, influencing big buyers (like universities) not to buy sweatshop-produced clothing could make a big impact on manufacturers' decisions to use sweatshops.

Some simple strategies to prepare young people for advocacy may be to provide good justice education and to teach young people about the systems of influence. Being blessed to have a participatory government, young Americans need to understand the political system so that they can enter into it and influence real change. Youth also need to become informed on the issues that Congress are going to discuss. Youth ministers should use these issues when planning justice education sessions.

An additional strategy is to provide young people with resources—especially Web resources—they can use to stay informed about issues important to them, and to provide youth with the Scripture and Catholic social teaching they need to help them understand the issues through the values of the faith.

Real and permanent change can only happen when social structures themselves are changed. Christians cannot avoid doing advocacy. Advocacy can be done with young people, and when done well, it gives witness to the reality that real change is possible. It provides youth and the whole community with a sense of empowerment and hope. Advocacy helps the community to be the voice for the voiceless in society.

Advocacy as a Component of Youth Ministry

Advocacy is not only a part of good justice education with young people, it is also one of the eight components of a comprehensive vision of youth ministry. *Renewing the Vision* says this about advocacy:

> Poor, vulnerable, and at-risk adolescents have first claim on our common efforts. The ministry of advocacy struggles against economic and social forces that threaten adolescents and family life, such as poverty, unemployment, lack of access to affordable health care, lack of decent housing, and discrimination. The ministry of advocacy supports policies and programs that support and empower adolescents and their families and works to overcome poverty, provide decent jobs, and promote equal opportunity. In all advocacy efforts we must remember to focus on adolescents and families with the greatest need. This is the "option for the poor" in action.[25]

If youth ministries are committed to doing justice and service well, advocacy must permeate all youth ministry efforts. A preferential option for the poor and vulnerable cannot be taught if youth ministry is not reaching out to the young people and their families in the faith communities that live on society's margins. Young people cannot be empowered to advocate for structural change if the youth leadership is not willing to look at the structures of its own ministries in light of the Gospel vision of justice. The component of advocacy in a comprehensive youth ministry reminds everyone of this responsibility and calls them to be a voice for young people so that they may live out their full membership in their faith communities. It also calls everyone to be that same voice in their communities, helping them be safe places for young people to learn and grow. This advocacy always starts with the most vulnerable, the most at-risk in the communities.

Putting It All Together

The introductory image was one of socially conscious youth fighting injustice because of their unwavering commitment to Christ. The young people are supported and strengthened by a parish youth ministry that has the Church's rich Catholic social teaching at the heart of all ministry efforts. Here are some practical examples of the ways to integrate justice into the life of youth ministry:

- Include topics of justice in regular youth ministry gatherings.
- Invite speakers who are involved in justice work locally or globally to share their faith and insights with youth.
- Include Catholic social teaching when planning for adolescent catechesis. Catholic social teaching should be included as a unit or topic but should also be integrated within other topics.
- Include justice education as a part of confirmation preparation programs.
- Model just living as a youth community. When purchasing products like t-shirts, make the effort and extra expense to be sure that they are not produced using sweatshop labor. Take the time to let youth know why you make these choices.
- Model stewardship for creation by recycling, reusing, and avoiding wasteful conveniences like paper plates and plastic silverware during youth events.
- Practice peace-making by using non-violent communication skills for resolving conflicts.
- Send youth on a service learning trip like Young Neighbors in Action.
- Provide monthly or seasonal service events that include preparation and reflection.
- Provide retreats on justice education and formation for justice spirituality that include the pastoral circle process.
- Identify ongoing service commitments in which youth and their families could be involved.
- Participate in advocacy events such as the Walk for Hunger, Walk for Life, or peace prayer vigils.
- Have a regular spot in the bulletin or on the parish Web site where young people share with the parish what they have learned about particular justice issues throughout the year.
- Teach peace-making skills and take the time to pray for peace in the community and throughout the world.
- As a youth ministry community, take leadership of involving the parish community in advocacy for justice issues. Involve youth and adults in identifying issues to advocate for justice locally, nationally, and globally. Provide information about issues in the bulletin, on the parish Web site, and through gatherings.

- Make prayer in the youth ministry community includes issues of justice.
- Involve a group of youth and adults who will write prayers of the faithful (intentions) that address justice and faith issues in the community and throughout the world.
- Gather with juniors and seniors to explore the connections between justice and career and educational choices.
- Gather with youth who are turning eighteen to provide formation about what it means to be a just and informed voter. Use this opportunity to register youth and their families to vote.
- Find ways to support families to do justice education. Send home family packets with information on an issue. Include the issue, some background reading, and some discussion questions for parents to have good conversations with their child.
- Plan service projects for the whole family, or invite families to projects that already exist. One parish youth ministry regularly helps prepare a Christmas dinner with the Salvation Army, a tough service project that included a lot of work and early morning hours, all on Christmas Eve morning! One year the parish invited families to be a part of it and now it has become a holiday tradition for many parish families.
- Have a parent enrichment night during one of the regular youth gatherings and focus on a spirituality of justice.

Conclusion

Catholic social teaching helps to answer the question, "How do I live the values of the Gospel in the contemporary world?" Ministries to young people help them answer this question when justice is infused into all ministry efforts. We invite young people into the adventure of living the Gospel and being disciples of Jesus Christ by providing intentional justice education, by providing opportunities for service and advocacy, and by modeling the values of justice. Today's young people are ready for that invitation.

— RECOMMENDED RESOURCES —

Ballenger, Barbara. *Prayer Without Borders: Celebrating Global Wisdom*. Baltimore: Catholic Relief Services, 2004.

Bright, Thomas, et. al. *Total Youth Ministry: Resources for Justice and Service*. Winona, MN: Saint Mary's Press, 2004.

Burghardt, Walter J. *Justice: A Global Adventure*. Maryknoll, NY: Orbis Books, 2004.

Himes, OFM, Kenneth R. *Responses to 101 Questions on Catholic Social Teaching*. Mahwah, NJ: Paulist Press, 2001.

Holland, Joe, and Fr. Peter Henriot, SJ. *Social Analysis: Linking Faith and Justice*. Maryknoll, NY: Orbis Books, 1983.

Kammer, SJ, Fred. *Salted with Fire: Spirituality for the Faithjustice Journey*. Mahwah, NJ: Paulist Press, 1995.

Korgen, Jeffry Odell. *My Lord and My God: Engaging Catholics in Social Ministry*. Mahwah, NJ: Paulist Press, 2007.

Massaro, SJ, Thomas. *Living Justice: Catholic Social Teaching in Action*. Franklin, WI: Sheed and Ward, 2000.

McKenna, Kevin. *A Concise Guide to Catholic Social Teaching*. Notre Dame, IN: Ave Maria Press, 2002.

Roundtable Association of Diocesan Action Directors. *Living God's Justice: Reflections and Prayers*. Cincinnati: St. Anthony Messenger Press, 2006.

Documents from the United States Conference of Catholic Bishops

Everyday Christianity: To Hunger and Thirst for Justice, 1991.

Economic Justice for All: Pastoral Letter of Catholic Social Teaching and the U.S. Economy, 1986.

A Place at the Table: A Catholic Recommitment to Overcome Poverty and to Respect the Dignity of all God's Children, 2002.

Sharing Catholic Social Teaching: Challenges and Directions, 1998.

— ENDNOTES —

1. *Renewing the Vision: A Framework for Catholic Youth Ministry* (Washington, DC: United States Conference of Catholic Bishops, 1997), p. 38.

2. Benedict XVI. "Welcoming Celebration by the Young People Address of His Holiness Benedict XVI." Vatican Web site: http://www.vatican.va/holy_father/benedict_xvi/speeches/2008/july/documents/hf_ben-xvi_spe_20080717_barangaroo_en.html (accessed September 24, 2008).

3. *Catechism of the Catholic Church*. Washington, DC: United States Conference of Catholic Bishops, 2000, #1807.

4. Komonchak, Joseph, Mary Collins, and Dermot A. Lake (eds.). *The New Dictionary of Theology*. Collegeville, MN: Liturgical Press, 1991, p. 550-51.

5. Burghardt, SJ, Walter J. *Justice: A Global Adventure.* Maryknoll: Orbis Books, 2004, p. 5-6.

6. NDT, p. 551.

7. Donohue, John R. "Biblical Perspectives on Justice" in Thomas Bright and John Roberto (eds.), *Access Guide to Youth Ministry: Justice.* New Rochelle: Don Bosco Multimedia, 1990, p. 30.

8. *Economic Justice for All.* Washington, DC: United States Conference of Catholic Bishops, 1986, #31-34.

9. Ibid., #34-40.

10. Ibid., #41-44.

11. Ibid., #45-47.

12. Ibid., #48-52.

13. Ibid., #53-55.

14. Ibid., #56-60.

15. World Synod of Bishops, *Justice in the World,* #6, in David J. O'Brien and Thomas A. Shannon (eds.). *Catholic Social Teaching: The Documentary Heritage.* Maryknoll, NY: Orbis Books, 1992, p. 289.

16. *Communities of Salt and Light: Reflections on the Social Mission of the Parish.* Washington, DC: United States Conference of Catholic Bishops, 1994, p. 3.

17. *The Challenge of Catholic Youth Evangelization: Called to Be Witnesses and Storytellers.* Washington, DC: National Federation for Catholic Youth Ministry, 1993, p. 5-6.

18. Sweet, Leonard. *Soul Tsunami: Sink or Swim in the New Millennial Culture.* Grand Rapids, MI: Zondervan, 1999, p. 221.

19. Pope Benedict XVI. *Deus Caritas Est.* Washington, DC: United States Conference of Catholic Bishops, 2005, #18.

20. *Access Guide,* p. 157. See also Joseph Holland and Fr. Peter Henriot, SJ, and their book *Social Analysis: Linking Faith and Justice* (Maryknoll: Orbis Books, 1983).

21. From the *National Coalition for the Homeless* Web site: http://www.nationalhomeless.org/publications/facts/Whois.pdf (accessed September 23, 2008).

22. *Lectio Divina,* literally divine or holy reading, is an ancient form of praying Scriptures by reading a certain passage in four different ways: 1) listening; 2) meditation; 3) prayer; and 4) contemplation. For more on the *lectio divina* process see M. Basil Pennington, *Lectio Divina: Renewing the Ancient Practice of Praying the Scriptures* (New York: Crossroad Publishing, 1998).

23. *Sharing Catholic Social Teaching: Challenges and Directions* (Washington DC: United States Conference of Catholic Bishops, 1998), p. 4-6.

24. *Access Guide,* p. 178.

25. RTV, p. 27.

CHAPTER TWELVE

Pastoral Care with Youth

Carolyn Coll, RSM

Editor's Note

Youth and families need the attention and support of caring adults and communities. In this chapter, Carolyn Coll helps us consider the role that Pastoral Care plays in youth ministry and parish life. She encourages leaders to examine their own needs as they work with youth and plan for providing pastoral support.

Pastoral care is woven within the variety of connections, communities, and involvements that include youth and their families. Through caring relationships, youth experience ministry that promotes prevention of crises and attends to crisis situations. These elements of ministry are brought together into a holistic response to adolescents and their families. The emphasis is focused on relationships. The whole community is involved as we discover the most effective ways to work together and share resources in the development of healthy adolescents.

Context for Pastoral Care

A variety of converging forces are making the need for effective pastoral care even more urgent and central within youth ministry. In the past, young parents could rely on the support of nearby family. As our society became more mobile, we saw the breakdown of extended family support, community support, and neighborhoods. The work force also had become insensitive to the needs of parents and especially to the needs of single parents, who were a growing segment of our society. Finally, one of the last places of safety for young people fell victim to the times. Schools had once been a place of unquestioned safety but now we could no longer rely on that. Metal detectors and school safety officers were fast becoming the norm. Gangs were growing in great numbers. No one was immune—not the city, the suburbs, or the rural areas.

The world of the young is not as simple as it had been. Divorce is on the rise, access to drugs and alcohol is abundant, and AIDS is in the news. Sexual activity, teen pregnancy, and sexual abuse are growing concerns. Some believe these are not new problems but simply more visible problems. Whatever one believes, the world is changing and it is not always youth-friendly. It is becoming a much more complex and difficult place for adolescents to grow up in. The media is also playing a much more influential role in the life of adolescents. Family stress is on the rise. Many parents are overwhelmed and distracted. Many are unsure of their role as parents. Many families are looking to the Church for guidance in this time of turmoil. All of this calls for a broader understanding of what pastoral care needs to be today and how we are being called to respond in this changing world.

Another challenge that we face today is that many of our young people lack the necessary life skills to help them in the future. For some, these skills are the difference between success and failure, or between healthy life choices and at-risk behavior. We can no longer presume that our youth have the basic social and communication skills to succeed in life. We must intentionally include instruction in these skills in all that we do with our youth.

Though there are particular challenges and opportunities today for youth, the need to care for young people has always been part of ministry and outreach. Pastoral care can be traced back to biblical times but it is in the twentieth-century that it took on a theological dimension in the works of Seward Hiltner and others.

 Making the Connection

Caring adults and communities can make a world of difference for young people by providing an "echo" or support with parents.

- *Besides your parents, what adults provided you with care and support during your adolescent years?*

> An approach that integrates the shepherding perspective of Hiltner with later developments in pastoral care and counseling suggests that six dimensions (healing, reconciling, sustaining, confronting, guiding, and informing) are woven together in the care and counseling approach to crisis.[1]

Pastoral care, as a response to crisis, may reflect any of the above dimensions. This shepherding approach serves to assist those individuals facing a crisis of any kind with a sense of being listened to and cared for in a way that is modeled after the ministry of Jesus in the Scriptures.

Pastoral care can be of an informal nature, such as over pizza during youth night, or it can utilize a more formal approach, such as a scheduled meeting or talk session. It may also be proactive—recognition of pastoral care issues of a developmental nature, such as life skills, that need to be addressed with the group as a whole. Pastoral care provides prevention programs for youth and families, cares for those in crisis, and provides guidance during times of decisions and moral choices.

> The ministry of pastoral care is a compassionate presence in imitation of Jesus' care of people, especially those who were hurting and in need. The ministry of pastoral care involves promoting positive adolescent and family development through a variety of positive (preventive) strategies; caring for adolescents and families in crisis through support, counseling, and referral to appropriate community agencies; providing guidance as young people face life decisions and make moral choices; and challenging systems that are obstacles to positive development (advocacy).
>
> *Renewing the Vision: A Framework for Catholic Youth Ministry*[2]

Five important principles of pastoral care are presented within this chapter.[3]

1. Pastoral care is not counseling. Youth ministers, by the nature of their ministry, are called to be pastoral care agents but only those who are professionally trained can be counselors. Pastoral care does require sound theological principles with good interpersonal skills and other qualities that will be discussed later in the chapter.

2. Pastoral care is not limited to crisis situations. Pastoral care is, and should be, proactive rather than reactive. It continues to challenge those in ministry with youth to help adolescents and their families to navigate the adolescent years as smoothly as possible.

3. Pastoral Care is a Community Responsibility. Within our own communities, there are times when we must work together for the needs of youth. Other times require us to move beyond the boundaries of our own parish and school to local, diocesan, state, and even national venues to speak for the needs of those to whom we minister. It requires pulling down walls between us to build collaboration in our parishes, diocese, local organizations, and wherever else it is needed.

4. Pastoral Care Promotes the Life Skills Necessary for Youth to Prepare for the Future. In my work with those just entering college, I have met many who have been prepared for the academics but lack the necessary life skills to navigate the stresses and difficulties that often arise in college. Without these skills, many will not survive or succeed in the world they are entering.

5. Pastoral Care Must Address the Needs of Families Experiencing Stress. One doesn't have to go far to see that the family structures and systems as we knew them have changed and continue to do so. Robert J. Hater, PH.D, speaks to the changing world of the Catholic family. "Families rely on the church for more than instruction."[4] He goes on to say that families seek other forms of help from their parishes during times of stress or brokenness, and that it requires competent ministers to reach out to these families. The Church should provide a place for them to come and explore these issues in a caring environment.

Youth Ministers, Youth, and Pastoral Care

Renewing the Vision describes the scope of pastoral care within youth ministry: "The ministry of pastoral care is a compassionate presence in imitation of Jesus' care of people, especially those who were hurting and in need."[5] If one were to reflect on the Gospels, we would see just how broad and challenging this can be.

In talking about the meaning of pastoral care, it is important to understand several basic principles. First, pastoral care is something all of us as youth leaders and volunteers are called to do. In fact, it is the earliest form of ministry in the Church. All one would need to do is read the Gospels to see how Jesus teaches us by his healing works, his compassionate care, and his ability to listen and walk with those in need. It involves the ability to be a non-anxious presence— listening, providing compassionate confrontation when necessary, and always willing to assist in finding the necessary resources when appropriate. Charles Shelton reminds us that we are called to be care agents and not counselors. As youth leaders, we recognize our limitations but are prepared to assist youth and families in finding what they might need.[6]

We must be knowledgeable of the resources available in our parishes, dioceses, and local communities to support families in need—resources such as counseling centers, social service agencies, emergency hotlines, and other services. Pastoral care is not limited to crisis situations. Instead it is about being proactive rather then reactive. Sometimes we will meet some who are at risk and we must be prepared to offer the guidance and the skills necessary during this critical time in their lives. However, most of us will spend our time helping young people to navigate the waters and waves of life, not the hurricanes. For most it will be navigation of normal developmental ups and downs and family stresses.

Pastoral Care within Youth Ministry

Pastoral care has always been an integral part of Catholic youth ministry. In 1993, Sharon Reed wrote an article in *Pastoral Care: Guides to Youth Ministry*. In this article she stated, "Over the years in youth ministry, one of the most valuable documents I ever read was *A Vision of Youth Ministry*. I found this vision to be quite expansive, forward-looking, idealistic yet grounded, and quite radical in its challenge."[7] Youth ministry was to foster the whole person while providing for their spiritual growth and calling them into participation in the life, mission, and works of the Church. She went on to say that this meant youth ministry needed to be grounded in Scripture and Gospel values and oriented to persons much in the same way as Jesus carried out his ministry. Thus it called for people over institutions and relationships over programs.

We need to adopt a more pastoral approach in our work with youth. Reed defined a pastoral approach as "an on-going process of caring deeply and confronting honestly, of meeting people where they are and showing them the rich possibilities of human wholeness. It is the call for adolescents to believe in themselves because someone else already believes in them."[8] This pastoral approach set the tone for the 1997 document, *Renewing the Vision: A Framework for Catholic Youth Ministry*.[9] This new document brought the insights of the original *A Vision of Youth Ministry* statement and added the lessons we had learned in twenty years of implementing this vision with youth. *Renewing the Vision* challenged us to teach as Jesus taught using the Emmaus journey as the backdrop (see Luke 24:13-35). After his resurrection, Jesus comes upon two of his disciples and he walks with them as they talk about their experiences with Jesus, but they do not recognize him until they sit down and break bread together. As in the story, we are called to walk with Jesus and share his Word that others might come to recognize Christ in us. Through this, they might also come to recognize Christ in themselves and in their lives. This vision calls us to be pastoral and to reach out to all of our youth and to their families.

In the old model of serving youth through Catholic Schools, CCD (religious education programs), and CYO (youth groups and clubs), we had become accustomed to being compartmentalized into separate and unrelated programs. In *Renewing the Vision*, we are challenged to let go of these old boundaries, set aside any differences and work together. It was not a call to throw out what had been, or to fix it, but rather to go deeper while renewing our commitment to young people in a clear and concise way. It was a call to a pastoral care approach. Pastoral care was not something new—it had always been part of the Church's ministry. Reed noted that, in essence, youth ministry was synonymous with pastoral care. No longer did we look at youth as isolated individuals. We realized that we were not the only influence touching their lives. From a systems perspective, the world of influence upon our youth had grown very large.[10] We need to understand what that means and how we can help. If they are going to grow in faith and come to know Christ in a deep and personal way, we have to help them navigate the world around them with all its pulling and distractions. Pastoral care is not an optional part of ministry—it is an important ingredient in what we are about as a Church. We have to encourage youth to test their skills and abilities while we provide the necessary care, reach out to them, support, guide, invite, and transform.

Over the years of youth ministry, it became clear that this work is not the sole responsibility of the youth ministry leader or their volunteers—rather it is the responsibility of the entire community. We must all work together in collaboration to assist young people to grow to their fullest potential while providing for their safety needs.

Families with Adolescents

While these changes have been taking place, the United States Conference of Catholic Bishops has challenged pastoral leaders to minister more directly to the needs of the family. In *A Family Perspective*, the bishops offered us new foundational concepts and a guiding paradigm that served to broaden our approach to families as well as our understanding of the challenges and difficulties faced by them as we entered into the end of the twentieth century. The times were calling for new strategies and approaches. We read:

> A family perspective is a guiding vision for planning, implementing, and evaluating programs, ministries, and policies in a parish, school, or any other church institution. It is an example of a systems view of reality. It functions in two related ways. First, it views individuals in the context of their family and other social relationships. Second, it uses family relationships as a criterion to assess the impact of programs, ministries, and policies.[11]

Human beings are shaped by their families. We see this evidenced in the different patterns of family interaction. One family may have a largely non-verbal and non-confrontational pattern of interaction. Another may be very interactive in their verbal and confrontational style. In family systems theory, we believe that families consist of individuals whose interactions make up the system. Virginia Satir, a family systems theorist, used a mobile as the image of the family system. When you bump or pull on one piece of the mobile, it affects all the pieces. "The impact reverberates throughout the entire system. After a few moments, the mobile comes back to its resting place. For a family, a 'bump' to one person that reverberates throughout is actually a sign of health. Adolescence is filled with bumps like accomplishments, disappointments, emotional outbursts, highs, and lows."[12] Sometimes these bumps are a source of great stress. We know that the greater the stress, the more difficult it is for a family to bounce back. While we cannot solve the problem for either our youth or their families, we can help by our willingness to journey with them, to be a non-anxious presence, and to be bearers of hope.[13]

Pastoral care needs to address the challenges and stresses that many families are experiencing by using this family systems approach. We cannot help the young person in isolation of the family when the family unit is in turmoil or crisis. Rather, we must address the immediate stressors that they may be experiencing before healing and reconciliation can occur. This requires that we familiarize ourselves with the family life cycle and the normal stressors vs. those that put a family at risk.

To respond to these challenges, pastoral care for youth and their families needs to be integrated throughout a parish's ministry with youth. It will also need to have direction, resources, and leadership so that it can help a parish community surround youth with the love and care that they need.

The Tripod of Pastoral Care

To present a vision of a way to understand our response to this challenge, I would like to use the image of the tripod. My favorite pastime is taking pictures, but sometimes, when I am trying to take that "perfect picture," I can see the lens of my camera shaking very slightly. I have said to myself, if I only had a tripod on which to put my camera, I could take a better picture. The same is true in pastoral care. What we need is a tripod that can help us sharpen our vision and our ability to be effective pastoral care agents. There are three different, yet interdependent, legs to this tripod. By relying on the strength of each of these important dimensions of pastoral care, we provide an integrated approach to this component of youth ministry.

1. *Promotion/Prevention:* provide the ministry leader with tactics to promote healthy development in our youth and their families.
2. *Care in Crisis:* give ministry leaders the strategies necessary to respond through direct assistance to both youth and families in crisis.
3. *Advocacy:* provide ministry leaders with tools to both engage and challenge all systems, whether they are in our parish, diocese, or in local or national government, in order to promote the needs of youth and families.

The legs of this tripod are the foundation for pastoral care. Together they help us to develop a holistic approach to providing youth and their families with the skills and resources to succeed.

Promotion and Prevention

With the release of *What Kids Need to Succeed: Proven Practical Ways to Raise Good Kids* in 1998, Peter L. Benson, Judy Galbraith, and Pamela Espeland presented an understanding of the needs of young people and a positive tool for helping them on the road to healthy adulthood. They suggest that there are 40 developmental assets that children need in order to succeed in life. Developmental assets are the building blocks that young people need for healthy development. The asset approach comprises internal and external asset areas. The internal asset areas are commitment to learning, positive values, social competencies, and positive identity. The external asset areas are support, empowerment, constructive use of time, and boundaries and expectations. The asset approach indicates that young people need these assets if they are to succeed.

Further, there is positive correlation between the number of developmental assets a youth possesses and his or her probability of success in life. So important were these findings that they have become foundational to all we do in ministry with youth. This research outlines both those things that young people need to develop for themselves and what a healthy community must provide. It causes all of us to pause and reflect on the role that all of us must play if we want our youth to succeed. It is not an individual, parent, congregation, or community alone that makes the difference but rather all of us together that can make positive change in the culture in which the young are living. It calls for strong adult role models. It also requires a change in attitude—from seeing the worst in our youth to seeing the best, from being reactive to their problems to being responsive to their needs. The challenge for all us, whatever our role, is to work towards helping young people on the road to adulthood.

The asset approach provides us with the tools necessary to be asset builders as a way of raising healthy youth.[14] It is a broad plan for what we, the adult community—parents, church members, local and national government—can contribute to the health and well being of the youth of our communities. The asset approach offers a new tool with which to build our ministry with youth. We have arrived at a new clarity and a deeper understanding and appreciation for where we had been and where we are to go if we are to impact the lives of youth and their families in the coming twenty-first century. Pastoral care is no longer a hidden component or something we did occasionally. Rather it is seen as integral to all we do in youth ministry.

Care in Crisis

When youth or their family are in crisis, our primary response is to refer them to crisis agencies and counselors that can provide the professional support needed. I believe one of the most difficult parts of working with youth is knowing when we are in over our heads and need more professional expertise. This can be a difficult question for anyone to answer since some crises that adolescents or their families experience may fall into the area of normal developmental or adolescent issues. Perhaps the best way for pastoral care ministers to know when to refer to a professional is to ask several questions.

1. How upsetting, painful, or hurtful is the experience to the adolescent?
2. Is the problem getting worse? If so, how do you know?
3. What are the issues, as described by the young person, that are causing the concern? It is important to be as specific as possible and to describe the issue in terms of their actions.
4. How serious would you say the young person is? Use a scale of one to five, with five being high and based on what you identified so far.

5. Does the young person have supports or the necessary personal resources? The more supports accessible in terms of peer relationships or personal gifts/life skills, the greater the young person's ability to navigate the crisis. The fewer resources available, the more difficulty they will have.
6. Are the problems increasing?
7. Looking ahead, what will the adolescent's situation look like six months or a year from now without some form of intervention? It may even be an important question to pose to the young person.
8. What makes this situation different from others in similar situations you have encountered in the past?
9. What do others say on your team?[15]

A good rule of thumb for determining the need for intervention is the degree of distress that the adolescent is experiencing. The greater the stress, the higher the risk and the need for intervention. Also, the same questions and principles may be used when working with a family in need of referral. To be ready for this part of our ministry, we should know the resources in our area and have a list of agencies and individuals to whom we can refer. We should also be aware of the reporting procedures in our state and our diocese in cases when the crisis situation could include abuse, suicide, or potential acts of self-harm or violence. Youth ministry leaders should involve another pastoral minister (such as the pastor or another staff member) during these situations for additional support in the process. Because these situations can be new to a leader and the consequences can seem overwhelming, it is important that the youth ministry leader assess his or her vicarious anxiety in the situation. As leaders, we should be aware that sometimes our own judgment gets clouded by our personal anxiety.

Finally, whenever we encounter a situation that makes us uncomfortable, we need to trust our instincts and not be afraid to refer. Knowing our limits is an important part of serving others. It does not mean that we forget about the youths in crisis but rather that we enter into a relationship of companionship with them through prayer, personal contact, and support in conjunction with a counseling professional. Always this is done with the least intrusion and the greatest respect for their privacy.

Advocacy

"The ministry of advocacy engages the Church to examine its priorities and practices to determine how well young people are integrated into the life, mission, and work of the Catholic Community."[16] As youth leaders and volunteers, it becomes our mission to engage our parish leaders and membership in dialogue regarding how effective we are in carrying out this challenge as laid out by the bishops. It is not enough to rely on our own occasional visibility with the youth to meet this challenge. Rather, we must be intentional in our development of the gifts and talents of our youth. They become active participants in the life of the faith community rather than the passive recipient of our occasional life together.

Advocacy looks at the adolescent, not in isolation, but as a member of a family. It looks at the impact the many different entities that touch their lives have on them, either directly or indirectly. "It places adolescents and families first by analyzing every policy and program—domestic, parish-based, diocesan and international—for its impact on adolescents and families."[17] As advocates, we are challenged to speak out rather than stand on the fringes. Advocacy requires being informed and knowledgeable about policies, programs, health care issues, etc., that affect both the adolescent and their family. Thus, in many instances, advocacy affects the quality of life for both adolescents and their families.

To be an advocate for youth and families, we begin by examining the practices of the parish to see how the community life, worship, and programs of the community support or hinder pastoral care with adolescents. For example, we advocate that programs for faith formation of youth and children be sensitive to a variety of family situations when scheduling meetings and events so that some families don't feel left out or neglected. We advocate that pastoral care resources for youth and families be included in a parish library and become part of a parish family festival. After looking at our own parish efforts, we join with others in the community to advocate for the pastoral care of youth and families. By joining together, we can help address situations of violence in our community, lack of services or gaps in educational access.

An Integrated Approach

If you are like me and wear glasses then you know that there are times when it is necessary to get your eyes checked. On occasion, you might discover that your eyes have changed a little or maybe you need new lenses. In an integrated approach, one must use a new lens to look at what we have done, are doing, and will do. The lens is called pastoral care. An integrated approach to pastoral care calls us to integrate caring ministries throughout youth ministry.

In order to develop a program, we must come to know our young people, their families, our communities, and our parish to see clearly the needs of those we serve and the ways we might assist. Once we have accomplished that, we then need to discover the most effective way to accomplish our goal of integrating pastoral care into what we have already planned—through collaboration with another, creating a program that fits our needs, or by using an already existing program.

Pastoral care is not about a new program so much as it is a plan to be more intentional in how we reach out in this ministry of care to the adolescents we serve, their families, and their many different needs. It is learning to respond to the difficulties encountered in the everyday life events of the adolescents and families we encounter on a daily basis while still accomplishing the goal of youth ministry as outlined in *Renewing the Vision*.

Connecting with Youth and their Families As we focus on the needs and concerns of adolescents, it is easy at times to forget that they belong to a family. Certainly, there is an energy we receive from working with adolescents and their families. It can be very rewarding and can even serve to enrich the faith life of the family. We read in *Renewing the Vision*, "Their growth in faith and active participation in parish life can encourage the entire family to make the Catholic faith central in their lives."[18] Along with enriching the faith life of the family, we are also challenged to strengthen family life by providing opportunities for reconciliation and programs that improve family skills such as communications, decision-making, and problem-solving.

Connecting with the Parish "The parish community has a special role in promoting participation in the life, mission, and work of the faith community."[19] "In parishes, young people should feel a sense of belonging and acceptance as full-fledged members of the community."[20] Being treated as full-fledged members fosters a sense of identity for young people. While programs appropriate to the developmental and faith needs of the adolescent are essential, so is the development of their various gifts and talents. Such opportunities strengthen the relationship of the young person to the community while bringing a new vitality and energy to parish life.

Connecting with the Wider Community Another aspect of the parish's commitment to youth is concern for the wider community. Through the ministry of advocacy and by collaboration with the various faith traditions, public schools, youth serving agencies, and other community organizations, parishes have opportunities to reach high risk youth while fostering healthy adolescent development and healthy communities. This also creates opportunities to share resources and co-sponsor programs.

Integrating Pastoral Care within Youth Ministry

As noted earlier, pastoral care requires examination and evaluation of our foundations. We need to look at how we are to carry out this important task in our ministry. Many times, when we hear about the needs of young people, we feel overwhelmed. But we must remember that we are not called to throw away everything we have done and create something completely new. Rather, it is about affirming what we are doing and building on it. We have to evaluate what we are doing to determine where we are already succeeding and where the holes are. We must be able to look into the community and recognize where others are filling those gaps for us. Sharon Reed states that there are four strategies that one may use in developing an integrated approach to pastoral care: 1) integrating pastoral care into an existing youth program, 2) incorporating a family perspective into pastoral care programming, 3) utilizing and collaborating with existing pastoral care programs and resources, and 4) designing new pastoral care programming.[21]

Integrating Pastoral Care into an Existing Youth Program Integrating a pastoral care response into existing programming involves being aware of what is already happening and how it can be enhanced by introducing a new activity, by using new program resources, or by networking with parish or community leaders and resources. It encourages us to look for opportunities for pastoral care and to bring them to the attention of others.

There are several strategies that enable us to carry out this approach. These include partnering with parents and families, promoting positive values in all programming, and providing meaningful service involvement.

Incorporating a Family Perspective into Pastoral Care Programming In my work in the parish, one of the pleas I have heard from families is to be sensitive to family time. More recently, we have heard a great deal about family catechesis and intergenerational programming. Part of the task of pastoral care is to support and work to strengthen the family unit. This requires sensitivity to the cultural and structural diversities of families within our communities. There are many ways to incorporate a family perspective into programs. Providing a resource library for families, offering parent education as well as family involvement in a current program, and creating in-home resources and activities are just a few ways to do this.

Utilizing and Collaborating with Existing Pastoral Care Programs and Resources In the past, I felt I had to always create my own programs. After investing a great deal of time and effort, I often discovered that another youth minister or church already had something very similar. Many times I struggled to put together a program on an important topic only to find that there was someone within my own community who had the expertise and the experience to do what I was trying to do. By utilizing what is already in existence and/or collaborating on devising new programs, we free ourselves to address areas of more immediate concern. This approach requires us to take the time to investigate what is already happening, what resources are already available, or what is already being offered in the local community, school, or another church. In an effort to offer the most to our young people and their families, we need to work with other community organizations in our efforts to promote healthy adolescent development while taking advantage of the wealth of ideas, programs, and possibilities available through collaboration.

Designing New Pastoral Care Programming Sometimes, situations arise where there may be nothing that meets the need at hand. When an unmet need or gap arises, we may have to design our own program. Let me share an example. A while back, I met a youth minister whose parish had experienced a terrible tragedy. Three of their young people were murdered in a robbery. It had devastated the parish and the youth. What was available at that time seemed so inadequate for the gravity of the situation. The youth minister needed something very specific that reflected her community and their needs. She was at something of a loss.

After attending the Pastoral Care course (in the Certificate in Youth Ministry Studies Program), she developed a program that reflected the unique needs of her community. She did not create this program in a vacuum. She took the best of what was available and added to it according to what she needed. She utilized materials from other programs and called in experts from other areas. Through this integration, she developed what I believe was an excellent and well executed program that responded to the crisis.

These approaches and strategies afford us several avenues for providing pastoral care to a much broader audience without undue stress to the youth minister. Using them, we can increase our effectiveness as well as our circle of influence.

Knowing Our Limits as Pastoral Caregivers

If we are to be truly pastoral in our approach to youth and their families, it means that those of us in ministry to youth need to ask ourselves some very difficult questions. In *Pastoral Counseling of Adolescents and Young Adults,* Charles Shelton, S.J. presents a guideline of what we need to ask ourselves if we are to bring a healthy adult presence to the youth we serve.[22]

1. Reflect on what it means to be a "healthy adult."
2. Ask yourself to what extent you have been able to forgive your own parents.
3. Ask yourself how you deal with loss.
4. Have healthy relationships.
5. Find time for solitude.
6. Maintain adequate boundaries.
7. Realize and accept the fact that you cannot save every adolescent.
8. Focus on the experience of gratitude and cultivate a sense of being grateful.
9. Remember that ministering to youth does not mean you are expected to do everything right.
10. Maintain a sense of integrity.

These guidelines have been fundamental in my work with youth leaders as I train them to understand and develop the pastoral care aspects of their ministry. Let me take a moment to elaborate on each of these guidelines.

Reflect on what it means to be a "healthy adult." As role models for youth, it is important that we examine our motivations and expectations as we enter into this important ministry. We should ask ourselves, "Am I doing this for the right reasons?" In other words, am I responding as the result of a call? Is my desire to serve the result of my prayer and reflection or is it part of an unmet need that I hope will be fulfilled by what I am doing? That is not to say that these reasons do not play a role but they must never supersede the needs of the youth we serve. A desire to meet their needs should be foremost in our minds and hearts. This ministry requires persons who are committed to the Gospel and to the tenets of our Catholic faith.

Ask yourself to what extent you have been able to forgive your own parents. Important to any work we do with young people is how we have or have not resolved issues from our own past, especially related to our family. If we have not taken time to address concerns that are not resolved, we run the risk of our issues becoming intertwined with our ministry. How often have we been in a situation where we find ourselves drawing comparisons between the situation and our own past? These comparisons are rarely useful as each situation and person is unique. In working with youth and their families, we risk making decisions based on our past. Thus, transference, the process in which our emotions associated with a parent or sibling are unconsciously passed to another, becomes a real pitfall that we must consciously avoid.

Ask yourself how you deal with "loss." When we speak of loss, we are not only referring to the death of a loved one. Losses can also come in the form of a lost job, a parent's separation or divorce, or a friend that moves away. We also experience frequent smaller losses such as a disappointment, a bad grade, etc. Our small daily concerns prepare us to handle the larger losses when they come, as they always do. Loss is difficult for everyone. The real test is how we deal with it. Our losses can make us stronger. We can grow from the experience and learn to help ourselves and others through the losses to come. Or we can get bogged down in our misfortunes and fail to move on. How we deal with our losses can mean the difference between becoming a bitter person or a better person.

Have healthy relationships. When we turn on the TV, listen to the music of young people, or read anything about the relationship patterns of adolescents today, it is easy to see the urgency in this statement. As I mentioned earlier, positive role models are an essential external asset for young people. These positive role models are often in short supply. We are called to model positive relationships for our youth. It is not enough to talk about our values. We must model them.

Find time for solitude. One of the things I have seen in my work in ministry is the neglect of our spiritual and creative selves. Time and again, we read in Scripture how Jesus withdrew to pray, yet we often feel we can keep going without those moments of peace and reflection. Reflection helps us to keep life in balance—especially when we have to juggle many different roles at one time. I also believe that unless we take time to reflect and pray, we are in danger of leaving out the most important aspect of our pastoral ministry, Jesus Christ. I am reminded of a story I heard years ago about a soldier during WWII who found a bombed out church. In it he saw a crucifix on which Jesus was missing his arms and legs. Seeing this, the soldier realized that he was called to be Christ's arms and legs...and so are we. Yet if we are to walk with Christ, we must be quiet occasionally so we can hear where he wants us to go.

Maintain adequate boundaries. In youth ministry, we often feel that we should be available to our youth twenty-four hours a day. I have learned that this is not always healthy for the minister or for the young people served. Boundaries are important to healthy development and serve to help young people develop realistic expectations of the relationships in their lives. Maintaining boundaries also reminds us that we do, and should, have lives outside our ministry.

Realize and accept the fact that you cannot save every adolescent. As caregivers, we are called to walk with, to guide, to lovingly confront, and to let go. One of the most difficult things for a parent to accept is that sometimes children make poor choices. In our ministry we often have the same problem. As youth ministers, we may not agree with some of the choices youth make. We can guide and we can suggest but there is a time when we must step back and leave the rest to God.

Focus on the experiences of gratitude and cultivate a sense of being grateful. I believe this is another way of saying the glass is half full rather than half empty. For many young people, this is a difficult task when they live in a world that teaches them you must have your needs met. We must help them grow in gratitude for what they have rather than allowing them to focus on what they do not have. This can only help them to be at peace with themselves as adults.

Remember that ministering to youth does not mean you are expected to do everything right. I don't think there is anything more freeing than knowing this. It is essential to admit your fallibility to them and to yourself, and then to move on. Young people appreciate and respect an adult who can admit when something is not right or can say "I'm sorry." If we want our young people to be willing to admit their own mistakes, we must be willing to admit ours.

Maintain a sense of integrity. Young people listen more to our actions then to our words. What made Jesus so believable was that his words and actions matched. In fact, his actions spoke louder. This should be our model.

These are important ideas for us to internalize if we are going to help promote healthy adolescent development and prevent unhealthy behavior. In order to recognize issues in our youth we must first begin with ourselves.

Conclusion

Pastoral care includes specific and intentional efforts to minister with youth. It is also a lens with which we view all aspects of our ministry with youth and their families. It is an integrated approach that can lead to an ever-expanding circle of collaboration while increasing the involvement of the parish and local community. Through the different approaches and strategies, pastoral care enables us to provide for the diversity of needs and challenges our youth and families face on a daily basis.

At the same time, pastoral care recognizes and affirms the importance of the youth minister. It emphasizes that we must first look to our own wholeness to ensure that we bring the needed skills to the table. Pastoral care begins with us and with our families.

The asset approach gives us the building blocks for proactive and concrete foundations that lead to healthy adolescent development. This approach recognizes and affirms the role of the youth minister and the power of many. We do not minister to our youth alone. We minister to them as a part of our community. The quality of the relationships fostered within the faith community plays a key role in asset building for our youth.

Finally, if we are to be true pastoral care givers, we must develop our skills and talents as well as our spirituality. We are to be instruments of promotion and prevention. We are to provide care in crisis. We are continually challenged by the gospels to be the voice to the voiceless. For we are always reminded that it is in God's time that healing and reconciliation can occur.

— RECOMMENDED RESOURCES —

Ayer, Jane E. *Guided Meditations for Ordinary Times: Courage, Loss, Gratitude, and Needs*. Winona, MN: Saint Mary's Press, 1998.

Benson, Peter L., Peter Benson, Judy Galbraith, and Pamela Espeland. *What Kids Need to Succeed: Proven Practical Ways to Raise Good Kids*. Minneapolis: Free Spirit Publishing, 1998.

Giannetti, Charlene C., and Margaret Sagarese. *The Roller Coaster Years: Raising Your Child through the Maddening Yet Magical Middle School Years*. New York: Broadway Books, 1997.

Goodwin, Carole. *Family Ideas for Ministry with Young Teens*. Winona, MN: Saint Mary's Press, 2004.

Kehrwald, Leif. *Parents and Schools in Partnership: A Message for Parents on Nurturing Faith in Teens*. Winona, MN: Saint Mary's Press, 2002.

Kehrwald, Leif. *Youth Ministry and Parents*. Winona, MN: Saint Mary's Press, 2004.

Kielbasa, Marilyn. *Total Youth Ministry: Ministry Resources for Pastoral Care*. Winona, MN: Saint Mary's Press, 2004.

Pike, Maggie. *The Power of Discernment: Helping Your Teen Hear God's Voice Within*. Winona, MN: Saint Mary's Press, 2003.

Renewing the Vision: A Framework for Catholic Youth Ministry. Washington, DC: United States Conference of Catholic Bishops, 1997.

Shelton, Charles M. *Pastoral Counseling with Adolescents and Young Adults*. New York: Crossroads, 1995.

Strommen, Merton P., and Richard A. Hardel. *Passing on the Faith: A Radical New Model for Youth and Family Ministry*. Winona, MN: Saint Mary's Press, 2000.

A Vision of Youth Ministry. Washington, DC: United States Conference of Catholic Bishops, 1986.

— ENDNOTES —

1. Rowatt, G. Wade. "Theological Foundations of Pastoral Care" in *Guides to Youth Ministry: Pastoral Care*, ed. Sharon Reed (New Rochelle, NY: Don Bosco Multimedia, 1993), pp. 3-11.

2. *Renewing the Vision: A Framework for Catholic Youth Ministry*. Washington, DC: United States Conference of Catholic Bishops, 1997, p. 42.

3. Adapted from: Sharon Reed, *YouthWorks*, Section 13: Pastoral Care–Introduction (Naugatuck, CT: Center for Ministry Development, 1994). Similar information also appears in: Marilyn Kielbasa, *Total Youth Ministry: Resources for Pastoral Care* (Winona, MN: Saint Mary's Press, 2004), pp. 21-23.

4. Hater, R.J. *The Catholic Family in a Changing World*. Orlando, FL: Harcourt Religious Publishers, 2005, p. 102.

5. RTV, p. 42.

6. Shelton, Charles M. *Pastoral Counseling with Adolescents and Young Adults*. New York: Crossroads, 1995, pp. 9-14.

7. "Youth Ministry and Pastoral Care" in *Guides to Youth Ministry: Pastoral Care*, p. 146.

8. Reed, p. 149.

9. See: RTV.

10. Reed, p. 147.

11. Summary of: *A Family Perspective in Church and Society*, provided by the Secretariat for Family, Laity, Women and Youth. Available online at: www.usccb.org/laity/marriage/family.shtml (accessed March 28, 2006).

12. Kehrwald, Leif. *Youth Ministry and Parents.* Winona, MN: Saint Mary's Press, 2004, p. 64.

13. See: Peter L. Benson, Peter Benson, Judy Galbraith, and Pamela Espeland, *What Kids Need to Succeed: Proven Practical Ways to Raise Good Kids* (Minneapolis: Free Spirit Publishing), 1998.

14. Ibid.

15. Shelton, pp. 79-80.

16. RTV, p. 27.

17. Ibid.

18. RTV, p. 12.

19. RTV, p. 13.

20. Ibid.

21. "Strategies for Effective Pastoral Care" in *Guides to Youth Ministry: Pastoral Care,* pp. 168-79.

22. Shelton, pp. 9-14.

CHAPTER THIRTEEN

Prayer and Worship with Youth

Thomas East

Editor's Note

How can we help youth participate fully in the Liturgy of the Eucharist? How do we create and sustain prayerful youth ministry? This chapter explores these questions by going to the heart of prayer—our relationship with our loving God. This includes practical strategies and resources that support youth participation in prayer and worship.

People in love make signs of love, not only to express their love but also to deepen it. Love never expressed dies. Christians' love for Christ and for one another and Christians' faith in Christ and in one another must be expressed in the signs and symbols of celebration or they will die.

MUSIC IN CATHOLIC WORSHIP:
THE THEOLOGY OF WORSHIP, #4[1]

Our prayer and participation in worship expresses and deepens our relationship with our loving God. Youth are at a time in their life when they are very focused on relationships. They are learning about friendships and community. They are widening their sphere of relationships. As youth ministry leaders, we have a profound opportunity to invite youth to deeper prayer and participation in the worship community. We help youth to find a way to pray, a time to pray, a place to pray, and a community with whom to pray.

In *Renewing the Vision: A Framework for Catholic Youth Ministry*, the dimensions of this relationship are described.

> The ministry of prayer and worship celebrates and deepens young people's relationship with Jesus Christ through the bestowal of grace, communal prayer, and liturgical experiences; it awakens their awareness of the spirit at work in their lives; it incorporates young people more fully into the sacramental life of the Church, especially eucharist; it nurtures the personal prayer life of young people; and it fosters family rituals and prayer.[2]

 **Making the Connection**

Prayer is central to our relationship with God and with the community of faith.

- *How would you define prayer?*
- *What helps you pray?*
- *What hinders you or distracts you from prayer?*

It is clear from this statement that prayer is God's initiative. We are reminded that God is already walking with youth on their journey. The relationship between God and youth is not something we create. All of us exist in God's love and care; our invitation to youth to join in prayer helps them to become awake to this truth. Through prayer and participation in liturgy and the sacraments, young people develop their relationship with God. Prayer also leads youth to a greater sense of personal integrity and wholeness. They come to rely upon their faith and their connection to God through prayer as they make their choices and find their way.

This passage from *Renewing the Vision* reminds us that there are many different dimensions to our ministry of prayer and worship with youth. This chapter addresses the following areas:

- Promoting youth participation in the Liturgy of the Eucharist
- Encouraging youth participation in the sacraments
- Involving youth in communal prayer
- Nurturing the personal prayer life of youth
- Fostering family rituals and prayer
- Developing prayerful youth ministry

Promoting Youth Participation in the Liturgy of the Eucharist

The Church earnestly desires that all the faithful be led to the full, conscious, and active participation in liturgical celebrations called for by the very nature of the liturgy. Such participation by the Christian people ... is their right and duty by reason of their baptism.

CONSTITUTION ON THE SACRED LITURGY, #14[3]

Many different groups of people have joined in voicing their concerns and their hopes about youth participation in liturgy. Many parents are concerned for their teenage children; they know that their faith has been a treasure in their own lives and they fear that youth will lose their faith because young people often experience liturgy as boring. Pastors, parish staff, and youth ministry leaders are looking for new ways to encourage youth participation. Young people are also concerned about participation—many long to belong and want to be engaged in vibrant worship.

To participate fully, youth need to feel welcome in the community and at its celebration of liturgy. They also need to be prepared and open to participation. Promoting participation is not something that can be achieved through a "quick-fix" solution. Being ready to participate fully requires a concerted effort from parents of youth, the youth ministry program, and young people themselves. Parents support youth participation by sharing faith at home and modeling active participation. A parish's youth ministry builds toward youth participation in liturgy by helping youth to prepare for liturgy and by being connected with the liturgical year. Youth participation in liturgy builds their personal prayer life and their experience of family prayer. If we are not bringing our personal prayer lives to liturgy, the expression of communal prayer can feel awkward and forced.

Building youth participation also needs the effort of the parish community, whose welcome, encouragement, and willingness to engage youth make a critical difference. To encourage participation, we need to look at these three aspects:

- How do we prepare youth to participate in liturgy?
- How do we prepare liturgies for youth involvement?
- How do we prepare the community for youth participation?

Preparing Youth for Liturgy

The Liturgy of the Eucharist is the central prayer of our faith. It is also described as the source and summit of our lives as Christians.[4] It is not surprising that this prayer, which has such an important place in our faith life, is rich in its complexity. It requires some practice to know how to participate in it fully. In fact, we could compare participation in the liturgy to participation in a marathon. Like a marathon, the liturgy requires a variety of disciplines, understandings, and attitudes. To help youth participate, it is helpful to look at the dimensions of participation.

Youth can participate in liturgy fully, actively, and consciously when…

- they bring their personal prayer life to our shared prayer.
- they feel welcomed and at home in the worshipping community.
- they are comfortable singing our prayer.
- they know how to join in our shared prayers.
- they express their prayer in their posture and gestures.
- they know how to hear the Word of God and live it in their lives.
- they are comfortable praying with silence.
- they are familiar with symbols and rituals.
- they know, love, and are challenged to live the Eucharist.
- they understand the call to continue the liturgy beyond the dismissal through lives of service and faithfulness.[5]

By looking at these aspects of participation, we can plan for ways to help youth participate more fully.

For instance, within our youth ministry efforts, we can help youth to pray as a community and we can give them skills and new ways to pray as individuals. All experiences of prayer help youth participate in liturgy better. The National Federation for Catholic Youth Ministry describes this relationship in their document *From Age to Age: The Challenge of Worship with Adolescents*: "The symbols and rituals of liturgy become more meaningful for youth when they draw from their experiences of private prayer."[6]

We can also help youth to become comfortable with some of the elements of liturgy by having these elements become part of our youth ministry gatherings. Introduce silence as a part of the way that you pray and gather. Use symbols as part of the way youth learn and share. Have youth create and participate in rituals as part of prayer with the youth community. Include faith sharing about the Scriptures as a way to help youth learn to listen to the word. Help youth sing at liturgy by having music and singing within all youth ministry events.

Another way to prepare youth for liturgy is to bring the readings for the coming Sunday into the youth gatherings in the previous week. Some youth ministry communities use the Gospel of the coming Sunday as the focus for prayer for their meeting during the week. Other youth communities have learned to pray the readings using *lectio divina*, an ancient prayer form of listening to and applying Scriptures to one's life. by reading a certain passage in four different ways: 1) listening, 2) meditation, 3) prayer, and 4) contemplation.[7] For more on the *lectio divina* process see M. Basil Pennington, *Lectio Divina: Renewing the Ancient Practice of Praying the Scriptures* (New York: Crossroad Publishing, 1998).

An important aspect of encouraging youth participation is to help parents in their role of guiding youth. Many parents struggle to find effective ways of encouraging their teenage children to attend Mass. When you gather with parents, offer these suggestions for supporting youth participation:

- Attend liturgy together as a family. Parents, let your children know that this is what we do as a family. Attending Mass on Sunday is part of who we are.

- Tell your children your feelings about liturgy and the reasons why their participation is important to you. Take the time to talk about the importance of Eucharist in your life and the real presence of Christ that you receive through participation in liturgy. Share your values and why you believe participation in Mass is central in your life.

- Make going to Mass an occasion—go to breakfast afterwards or join in a special family activity.

- Let youth sit with their friends during Mass if they want to. Being part of a community means that there are people we look forward to being with. This is true for young people as well.

- Plan for time together as a family following liturgy. This will give you an opportunity to continue the conversation about faith and life.

- Be careful about complaining about the parish, your pastor, the homily, the music, or other aspects of the liturgy and parish community. It is normal to talk about things with each other as adults, but youth can misinterpret such concerns and critique as negativism and become discouraged about being part of the community.

- Make it personal by asking the young person to go to Mass as a gift to you. Sometimes parents just cannot convince young people they should participate for their own good; however, a parent can let youth know what it means to them to be there together.[8]

As youth ministry leaders, we can provide intentional preparation for youth so that they understand what they are celebrating. Parishes can prepare youth for the different aspects of liturgy within weekly meetings, retreats, and other gathered programs. One parish provided a retreat for youth that was entirely on the theme of liturgy. On Friday night they gathered as a community and provided some community building, and then they talked about the gathering rites within liturgy. On Saturday they spent time learning about the Old Testament, the Psalms, the Letters, and the Gospels. Then they talked about the readings in liturgy. Saturday night focused on the Last Supper and the institution of the Eucharist. Following that, the community discussed the liturgy of the Eucharist and the way that we pray during this time of Mass. Sunday was about the dismissal: what does it mean to be sent in service and mission? They reviewed the ways to participate in liturgy, including an icebreaker called "Catholic Calisthenics" that playfully reminded youth of the various postures of liturgy. Following this exercise, they talked about the meaning of the different postures and gestures. They also presented the responses and talked about the scriptural origins of liturgical prayers. The retreat ended with a celebration of liturgy that brought the whole experience together.

Youth want to join us in prayer; we can help by preparing them. Helping youth to be comfortable with the symbols and movements of liturgy is highlighted as an important element within the document of the National Federation for Catholic Youth Ministry, *From Age to Age: The Challenge of Worship with Adolescents*: "A specific objective of intentional catechesis for liturgy is to assist teens through reflection and sharing in exploring how liturgical symbols and rituals celebrate their experiences of God and life events."[9]

Preparing Liturgies for Youth

In talking about youth and liturgy, it is important to address the issue of special Masses for youth. The liturgical norms instruct communities not to provide special liturgies that separate one part of the community on a regular basis. The intention of these norms is to promote a sense of unity among the parish community in its expression of its highest prayer at liturgy. In many ways, the situation of youth and liturgy is not that different than the situation of the family meal. We know the power that comes from breaking bread as a family, yet, many youth don't experience sitting around the table with their family for a shared meal. Meals are often "on the go" or eaten in front of the television. The family meal is something that needs to be intentional. It is an expression of the relationships among and between family members. A youth minister was visiting with a recently divorced friend whose teenage daughter was at home. The mom invited the friend to stay for dinner and called upstairs to her daughter to ask if she would join them. The daughter answered back that she would eat in her room. This had been her pattern for most meals since the divorce. This concerned the youth minister. Youth eating separately from the family is something that can and should happen on occasion. For instance, a young person may have friends over and eat pizza with them while watching a movie. As a pattern, eating away from the family could weaken and ultimately break the family relationships. Forcing a child to eat with the family by itself won't resolve the situation—the whole relationship needs to be nurtured and healed. A shared meal is a part of that, but so is the entire home environment and the development of trusting, caring relationships.

In the example of the meal, the issue wasn't about fixing the daughter's favorite foods or using special china. The issue was about the relationship. To encourage youth participation in liturgy, parish leaders and parents need to help youth develop relationships of trust within the community. We also need to help youth develop their relationship with their loving God as young disciples. Our hope as a parish is that youth would learn how to be disciples that are nourished at the Eucharistic table for life, as members of a parish community. Parishes should avoid choosing to implement a "youth Mass" as a quick fix for a situation that is much more complex than this seemingly simple solution. An important concern about youth-only liturgies is the long-term effects—what happens to a youth after several years of participating in liturgies that were completely geared around their needs and style? How ready are these youth to participate as part of a parish liturgy that by its nature engages the whole community?

Some parishes address these concerns by developing regularly scheduled liturgies, weekly or monthly, that are prepared with the whole community in mind but include youth in specific leadership and ministry roles. These Masses utilize youth gifts and inevitably include a youthful style and energy, but retain the focus as a parish liturgy.[10]

All liturgies that include young people should engage their energies and encourage their participation. In the *From Age to Age* document, four elements of liturgy preparation are highlighted as being essential for engaging youth:

Effective Preaching

"**Vibrant Worship Includes Effective Preaching of the Word.** Quality preaching is the number one issue named by youth when they are asked what makes liturgy meaningful. They regularly mention storytelling and the use of examples that relate to their own situation in life as effective techniques for preaching."[11]

Music and Song

"**Vibrant Worship Has a Youthful Spirit in Music and Song.**" This principle has several dimensions:

Include youthful music: "…The music of the young brings freshness and variety to our current musical genres and can infuse sacred music with energy and vitality."[12]

Introduce youth to sacred music: "We have a responsibility to invite youth to appreciate a variety of traditional and contemporary liturgical music styles."[13]

The style of the musical expression is important: "[Young people] respond as much to the way the music is performed and styled as they do the actual melodies and texts. When music is played with enthusiasm, a variety of instrumentation, and an upbeat pace, they are more likely to participate."[14]

Dynamic Symbols and Actions

"**Vibrant Worship Incorporates Visually Dynamic Symbols and Actions.** The liturgy and sacraments depend upon 'signs perceptible to the senses.' We have an obligation to assess how 'perceptible' our preparation of the symbols and symbolic actions of the liturgy are."[15] "[Youth] become bored when the visual nature of the rites is weak."[16]

Interactive and Communal Dimension

"**Vibrant Worship Has an Interactive and Communal Dimension**…As we develop our approach to liturgy as a celebration of the whole community—rather than a time for collective, individual devotion and prayer—we will assist youth in entering into the experience of liturgy. Teens want to belong. They want to feel welcomed. They are very sensitive to the hospitality displayed at liturgy."[17]

There are occasions when youth will experience liturgy that is prepared primarily for them. It is important that these liturgies be celebrated in an exemplary way that will help youth experience the fullness of participation and increase their engagement with the whole community in Sunday liturgies on a regular basis.

"**Celebrate Liturgies at Youth Events Well.** Liturgies celebrated primarily for and with adolescents occur within the context of retreats, days of reflection, or other youth events in the parish, diocese, or region. These events provide an opportunity to pay greater attention to the life experiences and issues young people bring to worship."[18] Another important element of preparing liturgies for youth is the opportunity to involve and apprentice youth in the liturgical ministries. In a recent study of effective practices in Catholic youth ministry, youth and parish staff members highlighted the involvement of youth in liturgical ministries as a source of revitalization for the whole community:

[Parishes with effective youth ministry] also actively include youth in liturgical ministries. This is seen as a tremendous value to the parish community. Youth bring energy, needed skills, and their powerful presence to the parish's liturgical life. Liturgical involvement helps young people grow in confidence, in faith, and in developing their gifts.[19]

Preparing the Community for Youth Participation

Pastoral and liturgical leaders need to provide a welcome and safe environment in which teens can offer their gifts and enthusiasm.[20]

Youth want to be essential to our community. At a recent workshop, young people were asked what they needed in order to participate in their parish liturgy more fully. The workshop leader expected the usual answers: youthful music, dynamic homilies, or having youth involved in the liturgies. One young woman raised her hand and stated clearly her need to be essential: "What I need is to know that someone would notice if I wasn't there." She was speaking a truth about youth involvement. Youth are essential to many of the commitments they make to their schools, their workplaces, and their homes. They desire to be essential in our communities as we pray, as we share our lives, and as we serve others in God's name.

By their baptism, youth have a right and responsibility to participate in liturgy. When youth are not present, we are diminished as a community and deprived of the gifts that they bring. As leaders in ministry with youth, we can help youth to take their place in the worshipping community by becoming advocates and bridge builders. We need to help youth to understand the adult community and to know how to be respectful as they take their place in the worship community.

We also build bridges by helping the parish community as a whole become ready for active youth participation. Any parent of a teenager will tell you that youth participation is not a quiet thing. That isn't to say that youth will inevitably be disrespectful in liturgy. When youth participate, they want to bring not just their prayerful presence but all of their gifts. They have ideas to share; they have musical skills and artistic talents. Accepting youth at worship is part of a larger process of becoming a youth friendly parish.[21]

Sometimes members of a parish can express their concern for young people in ways that don't encourage youth participation. Consider this scenario: a young person who has dyed her hair blue and pierced her ears multiple times comes to Mass. When this youth enters a typical parish, there will be adult members whose concern comes out as a scowl and judgmental stare. Do we want to welcome this young person to our weekly worship? Perhaps the externals of their appearance are just that and they have no deeper meaning or cause for concern. Alternatively, the young person's appearance might be a sign of larger rebellion and unrest within the youth. In either case, don't we want them to be with us? As youth ministry leaders, we need to help parish communities learn how to love the young people in their midst. This includes helping a community to understand young people and to reclaim their identity as an evangelizing and welcoming community.

Nurturing Youth Participation in the Sacraments

Sacraments are powerful moments of connection with the risen Christ. Sacraments are also the way we pray as Catholics. Youth long for this connection and need the peace, healing, and strength that they can receive through participation in the sacraments and through the understanding of this vital aspect of our Catholic faith. In addition to promoting participation in the liturgy of the Eucharist, parish communities should seek to promote the active participation of youth in the sacramental life of the community.

Youth will approach the sacraments of initiation from a variety of perspectives. Some youth who are already members of the community will attend Baptisms or First Communion celebrations for their siblings, cousins, or the children of friends. Other youth, who are not initiated, may be waiting for an invitation to participate in Christian initiation. Many parishes regularly have special processes for teens who are preparing for initiation and reception into full communion. These young catechumens provide a witness to the meaning of Baptism. Some youth may be asked to become a godparent. All of these opportunities are teachable moments in the lives of young disciples. Each sacramental celebration in the parish should be planned with youth in mind and with special consideration going to youth who may have been away from active church participation.

In many dioceses throughout the United States, Confirmation is celebrated in the adolescent years. Preparation for this important sacrament should work hand in hand with other aspects of youth ministry so that youth are initiated into an active youth community within a welcoming parish. Confirmation also presents a wonderful time to help youth to take their place in ministry, leadership, and service roles throughout the parish. One parish makes this connection by asking the leaders of ministry groups in the parish to greet and invite youth to join their ministry as the newly confirmed youth process to the parish hall following Confirmation.

As older youth begin to consider life choices and discernment about vocation, parish communities can provide catechesis about the sacraments of marriage and holy orders at the service of communion. One effective method for opening up these sacraments would be having speakers witness to their lives as married people and as priests and deacons. As youth become more involved in parish life and form relationships with married and ordained members, the informal friendships and witness of their lives will provide a lived explanation of the celebration of these sacraments.

It is important to help youth to experience the sacraments of healing by providing ways for young people to experience Reconciliation and by providing for those who need the sacrament of Anointing of the Sick. Many youth do not take advantage of the peace and grace within reconciliation; we can help them to be comfortable with this sacrament by preparing them for participation and by encouraging their participation in Reconciliation within a wider parish celebration or in a reconciliation service provided specifically for adolescents. For youth to participate in reconciliation, they need clear information about when and how to participate. Many youth also need assurance about the privacy they will experience. Youth should also be aware of the power of the sacrament of Anointing of the Sick; youth who are experiencing serious illness or who are undergoing major surgery can contact a priest to receive this sacrament. Youth who are overcoming drug addictions and other dangerous patterns in their life may also be eligible to experience the peace of this sacrament.[22]

The Role of Prayer in Youth Ministry

The *Catechism of the Catholic Church* defines prayer as God's Gift, as Covenant, and as Communion:[23]

> The wonder of prayer is this gift of God, a God who "thirsts that we may thirst for him." (#2560)

> It is the human heart that prays. This heart is our "hidden center, beyond the grasp of our reason and of others; only the Spirit of God can fathom the human heart and know it fully...it is the place of truth...it is the place of encounter, because as image of God we live in relation; it is the place of covenant." (#2563)

> [Prayer is] the habit of being in the presence of the thrice-holy God and in communion with him. (#2565)

As we can see through these definitions, the role of prayer in youth ministry goes beyond a method for opening and closing gatherings. Prayer celebrates our relationship with our loving God. This relationship is at the heart of why we gather and why we are committed to each other.

To nurture prayer in the lives of youth and in our life as a community, we offer youth a time to pray, a place to pray, and a way to pray. We provide a time to pray by designating specific times within youth ministry for prayer. Sometimes these can take the form of an opening or closing prayer, but in other occasions prayer will be provided throughout a gathering. Sometimes our shared prayer will be a brief spoken blessing or intention. On other occasions, it will be a prayer service within a gathering. On some occasions, prayer is the reason for the gathering. We provide a place to pray by creating a prayerful environment. Sometimes this means that we transition to prayer by moving to a space that we have prepared for prayer or to a dedicated worship space. Other times, we transform our learning and community-building space into prayer space. Both methods speak a truth about prayer. By moving to prayer, we acknowledge that prayer is something about which we should be intentional. It helps to be in an environment that promotes reflection and focuses on the purpose of prayer. By transforming space used for other purposes, we acknowledge that holiness is all around us. All parts of our gathering can be prayerful if we keep our hearts focused on God and revere the holiness within our brothers and sisters. When provided with enough structure and guidance for prayer, youth feel invited to pray within the community. Sometimes the way to pray will be through silence or by listening to music. On other occasions, the way to pray will include the use of specific prayer forms or styles. The key is to invite, to guide, and to lead prayer so that we create an environment where youth can commune with their creator in the context of a community.

Providing Youth with Experiences of Communal Prayer

Communal prayer experiences are powerful parts of youth ministry and often provide youth with an encounter with God through community that nourishes their lives and their relationship with God, self, and others. In preparing communal prayer with and for youth, keep these aspects in mind:

- Follow a pattern for prayer that helps youth to make a connection between communal prayers and the central prayer of our faith, which is liturgy. One pattern for prayer is: Gather, Listen, Respond, and Go Forth.

- ▷ *Gather* We transition to become a community of prayer by gathering. This element can include an opening song, shared prayer, simple ritual or gesture, and brief faith sharing.
- ▷ *Listen* We listen to God's word of wisdom spoken to our lives today. This element should include a reading from Scripture and could also include readings from other sources. Drama, music, faith sharing, and meditation can also be utilized.
- ▷ *Respond* We respond to God's word by placing ourselves in prayer. This often includes spoken prayer petitions, ritual movement, opportunities for reflection, and prayer with symbols. It is essential that the community has a way to respond in order to fully participate in prayer.
- ▷ *Go Forth* Prayer concludes and we transition to continue our lives as disciples. This element can include blessing prayers, music, gesture, prayer with symbols, and shared prayer.

- Provide a variety of prayer experiences that will attend to the variety of youth in our community. Sometimes, the prayer style of the youth ministry leader becomes the prayer style for the whole of youth ministry. Like adults, youth are attracted to many different styles and types of prayers. If we limit prayer to one style or form, some youth will be left out or, worse yet, they can feel as though there is something wrong with them because they don't get it. We should think of prayer as a banquet and provide many different ways for youth to pray: pray with psalms, pray the Liturgy of the Hours, pray with meditation, pray with spontaneous prayers, pray with written prayers, pray with music, pray with song, pray with silence, pray with movement, pray with gesture, pray with symbols, pray with litanies, pray with nature, pray with Scripture, and pray with faith sharing.

- Pray with the symbols, songs, and spirit of the many cultures that comprise our Church. Catholic means universal, which means that we pray in union with our brothers and sisters throughout the world. We can enrich the prayer of our youth community by including written prayers, songs, symbols, language, art, and prayer forms from many cultures. This is especially important in communities with diverse cultural groups. In these communities, we have a special obligation and opportunity to affirm the values and symbols of the young people who are gathered—youth and adults need to feel that they are "at home" in our shared prayer, which means that they can bring their gift and experience God as he has been revealed to people of many cultures.

- Connect prayer to lived faith. Our communal prayer should lead to conversion and Christian practice. Our work in ministry, service, and leadership is nurtured by prayer and sacraments. Prepare prayer in a way that helps youth to connect their shared prayer with their work for justice and service to those in need. Youth should also feel guided and strengthened by prayer for leading lives marked by personal morality and holiness.

Nurturing the Personal Prayer Life of Youth

Prayer is a touchstone and a treasure in our lives. Part of the task of youth ministry is to help youth to nurture their personal prayer lives so that they can turn to God in their joys and their sorrows, in the moments of solitude, and in the midst of a crowd. We nurture the personal prayer lives of youth by teaching about prayer and prayer forms. We also help youth experience a variety of ways to pray individually. This includes helping youth to value and understand the prayer traditions of the Catholic faith, which include traditional composed prayers, meditation, praying with Scriptures, praying with psalms, the Liturgy of the Hours, rosaries, novenas, and praying with the communion of saints. Consider these ideas:

- Provide a retreat day that introduces youth to a variety of prayer forms.
- Introduce youth to a prayer form such as praying the rosary by identifying people who can powerfully pray with that form to young people. Gather youth to experience the faith witness of two or three members of the parish that share a passion for a prayer form.
- Provide spiritual mentoring for youth by having adults trained to help youth in their prayer life. Provide input on prayer forms and then provide times for youth to meet with prayer mentors.

Fostering Family Prayer and Home Rituals

The simple fact of gathering all family members around the table in and of itself is holy. A lighted candle stands in the center of the table, and the family joins hands (or doesn't). Disregarding feelings of embarrassment, they lift their voices in simple song. Traditional and/or spontaneous prayers hover over the mashed potatoes and the cries of [a] cranky infant or child. The family meal may be the scene of chaos, but it can be easily ritualized all the same. This is good; this is sacred; this is holy.[24]

Youth develop the habit of praying and participating in sacraments when they experience the "echo" that comes from seeing the connections between home church and the wider church community. We can help youth develop their prayer life and strengthen their participation in sacraments by helping families to pray together as a family at home and within the occasions of family life. One parish encouraged family prayer by having the young adolescents provide an Advent prayer service for families that included distribution of Advent wreaths and a prayer booklet created by the young adolescents. Another community gathered families of adolescents together for a retreat day to share prayer styles and ideas for family prayer. A family prayer and faith sharing library was created in one parish and housed in the vestibule of the church. This library was created through donations from parish members who were invited to choose a resource from the "wish list" and dedicate the book, video, DVD, CD or cassette tape to a family member who had shared faith with them. As you can see, parishes find different responses to the opportunity for supporting families of adolescents in praying at home.

Other Aspects of Prayerful Youth Ministry

Developing prayerful youth ministry goes beyond specific programs or strategies. Prayerful youth ministry is a context from which all ministry flows. Consider these additional elements:

Occasions for prayer in youth ministry. Part of having prayerful youth ministry is recognizing the natural moments for prayer throughout our ministry. When Joslyn sprains her ankle while playing volleyball, it is natural for us to contact parents and make arrangements to take her to seek medical care. It should be natural for us to also pause and pray with Joslyn as a community. Another occasion for prayer would be a brief blessing before the bus leaves for the retreat center. This kind of prayer leadership requires mindfulness and readiness so that we can lead the community to prayer.

Praying for youth in the community. This includes times that we pray with youth and times that we pray for the youth of our parish. In the midst of a pastoral conversation with a young person, we can ask if they would like us to pray with them about their concerns. We can ask youth for their prayer intentions and keep these in our prayers. As youth ministry leaders, we can also develop the habit of calling to mind the youth in our community as we pray.

Praying as a youth ministry team. Team prayer is a powerful witness to our trust and humility in ministry. As youth ministry leaders, we need to pray for strength and guidance in our important task. Our shared prayer communicates our trust in God and our awareness that our ministry is not about connecting youth to youth ministry leaders, it is about connecting youth to Christ.

Conclusion

All of the efforts of youth ministry are geared towards helping youth to grow in their relationship with their loving God. This relationship is nurtured and developed through shared prayer. Youth are encouraged to lead faithful and holy lives as disciples who are nourished by their participation in liturgy, sacraments, and our shared prayer as a community. This happens throughout the settings of youth ministry. Youth are encouraged to pray in the youth setting through a variety of youth ministry programs and strategies. They are also encouraged through the care and guidance of caring, prayerful youth ministry leaders. Families share the love of God with youth through shared prayer and family rituals. The parish community provides a rich context for encouraging youth participation, especially through the inclusion of youth in liturgy and the celebrations of the liturgical year. The wider community is a place where youth will experience prayer with the larger Church at youth retreats, rallies, and conferences.

Throughout the variety of components, programs, strategies, and gatherings of youth ministry, we have an incredible opportunity to invite youth to experience the peace, challenge, and wholeness that comes from living a life of prayer. Youth will grow in their relationship with God through personal prayer and communal prayer, through liturgies and blessings, through family prayer, and through prayer with the parish. Youth will join their hearts and voices with ours as we pray in ways that are old and new, treasured and innovative, bold and gentle, and energetic and calming. As youth ministry leaders, let us be guided by the Spirit to help create an environment where youth can be awake and present to the voice of the God who loves them completely.

— RECOMMENDED RESOURCES —

Ayer, Jane E. *Guided Meditations for Ordinary Time: Courage, Loss, Gratitude, and Needs.* Winona, MN: Saint Mary's Press, 1998, includes cassette. (Note: There are twelve books in this series on a variety of topics.)

Brown, Therese. *Catechetical Sessions on Liturgy and the Sacraments.* Winona, MN: Saint Mary's Press, 2004.

Carotta, Michael. *Sometimes We Dance, Sometimes We Wrestle: Embracing Spiritual Growth of Adolescents*. Orlando, FL: Harcourt Religion Publishers, 2002.

Calderone-Stewart, Lisa-Marie. *Prayer Works for Teens, Book 1*. Winona, MN: Saint Mary's Press, 1997. (There are four volumes in this series.)

Calderone-Stewart, Lisa-Marie. *Touch the Word: Lectionary-Based Prayer Reflections*. Winona, MN: Saint Mary's Press, 1996.

Chesto, Kathleen. *Family Prayer for Family Times: Traditions, Celebrations, and Rituals*. Mystic, CT: Twenty-Third Publications, 1996.

Cornerstone Media. *Scripture Themes and Popular Music* (2 CDs and Leader's Book) and *Stations of the Cross and Themes of Holy Week*, (2 CDs and Leader's Book), available through www.cornerstonemedia.org; also distributed by Saint Mary's Press.

Delgatto, Laurie, and Mary Shrader. *Total Catechesis: Catechetical Sessions on Christian Prayer*. Winona, MN: Saint Mary's Press, 2004.

Dues, Greg. *Searching for Faith: Prayer Experiences for Teen Assemblies and Retreats*. Mystic, CT: Twenty-Third Publications, 1993.

Dues, Greg. *Seasonal Prayer Services for Teenagers*. Mystic, CT: Twenty-Third Publications, 1991.

East, Thomas. *Total Youth Ministry: Ministry Resources for Prayer and Worship*, Winona, MN: Saint Mary's Press, 2004.

Fleming, Austin. *Preparing for Liturgy: A Theology and Spirituality* (revised edition). Chicago: Liturgical Training Publications, 1997.

Francis, Mark R. *Shape a Circle Ever Wider: Liturgical Inculturation in the United States*. Chicago: Liturgy Training Press, 2000.

Haas, David. *Prayers Before an Awesome God: The Psalms for Teenagers*. Winona, MN: Saint Mary's Press, 1998.

Haas, David, and Victoria M. Tufano. *Music and the Mass: A Practical Guide for Ministers of Music*. Chicago: Liturgical Training Publications, 1998.

Hakowski, Maryann. *Sharing the Sunday Scriptures with Youth* (Cycle A, B, or C). Winona, MN: Saint Mary's Press, 1998.

Huck, Gabriel. *Liturgy with Style and Grace* (revised edition). Chicago: Liturgical Training Publications, 1999.

Hughes, Kathleen. "Lay Presiding: The Art of Leading Prayer," in *American Essays in Liturgy*. Collegeville, MN: Liturgical Press, 1988.

Kielbasa, Marilyn. *Prayer: Celebrating and Reflecting with Girls*. Winona, MN: Saint Mary's Press, 2002.

Koch, Carl (ed.). *Dreams Alive: Prayers by Teenagers*. Winona, MN: Saint Mary's Press, 1991. (Note: There are several other books in this series that are collections of prayers written by youth.)

Koch, Carl. *Send Your Spirit: Praying for Our Teens.* Winona, MN: Saint Mary's Press, 1999.

The Liturgy Documents: A Parish Resource, Volume 1. Chicago: Liturgy Training Publications, 1991.

Regan, S. Kevin. *Teen Prayer Services: 20 Themes for Reflection.* Mystic, CT: Twenty-Third Publications, 1992.

Richstatter, OFM, Thomas. *Liturgy and Worship: A Course on Prayer and Sacraments* (for adolescents). New York: William H. Sadlier, Inc., 1997.

Singer-Towns, Brian (general ed.). *Vibrant Worship with Youth: Keys to Implementing From Age to Age: The Challenge of Worship with Adolescents.* Winona, MN: Saint Mary's Press, 2000.

Spirit and Song: A Seeker's Guide for Liturgy and Prayer. Portland, OR: Oregon Catholic Press, 1999. (This is a hymnal for prayer and liturgy with youth and young adults.)

Tirabassi, Maren C., and Kathy Wonson Eddy. *Gifts of Many Cultures: Worship Resources for the Global Community.* Cleveland: United Church Press, 1995.

Warren, Michael. *Faith, Culture, and the Worshipping Community.* New York: Paulist Press, 1989.

Yaconelli, Mark. *Growing Souls: Experiments in Contemplative Youth Ministry,* Grand Rapids, MI: Zondervan Books/Youth Specialties, 2007.

Web site

Center for Liturgy at Saint Louis University has a free online resource that includes commentary, spirituality articles, reflections written by youth and young adults, and prayers. http://liturgy.slu.edu

— ENDNOTES —

1. *Music in Catholic Worship: The Theology of Worship*, #4.

2. *Renewing the Vision: A Framework for Catholic Youth Ministry*. Washington, DC: United States Conference of Catholic Bishops, 1997, p. 44.

3. *Constitution on the Sacred Liturgy*, #14.

4. CSL, #10.

5. Similar ideas were also expressed in: Thomas East, *Total Youth Ministry: Resources for Prayer and Worship* (Winona, MN: Saint Mary's Press, 2004), p. 29.

6. National Federation for Catholic Youth Ministry. *From Age to Age: The Challenge of Youth Worship*. Winona, MN: Saint Mary's Press, 1997, #58.

7. For more on the *lectio divina* process see: M. Basil Pennington, *Lectio Divina: Re-*

newing the Ancient Practice of Praying the Scriptures (New York: Crossroad Publishing, 1998).

8. These ideas are adapted from: *Total Youth Ministry: Resources for Prayer and Worship*, pp. 30-31.

9. *From Age to Age*, #39.

10. See: *From Age to Age*, #94.

11. *From Age to Age*, #61.

12. Ibid., #64.

13. Ibid., #66.

14. Ibid., #67.

15. Ibid., #68.

16. Ibid., #69.

17. Ibid., #72.

18. Ibid., #90.

19. East, Thomas. *Effective Practices for Dynamic Youth Ministry*. Winona, MN: Saint Mary's Press, 2004, p. 48.

20. *From Age to Age*, #84.

21. See: RTV, pp. 11-12.

22. See "Chapter 8: Pastoral Care of the Sick" in *Saying Amen: A Mystagogy of Sacrament* by Kathleen Hughes. Chicago: Liturgy Training Publications, 1999, for a greater explanation and guidance in use of the sacrament of anointing.

23. *Catechism of the Catholic Church*, #2560, 2563, 2565.

24. Roberto, John. *Family Rituals and Celebrations* (Chapter 1 by Mitch Findley). New Rochelle, NY: Don Bosco Multimedia, 1992, p. 4.

Leadership and Planning for Youth Ministry

The multifaceted nature of youth ministry requires a process of collaboration among all persons involved in it, rather than fragmentation or competition....Part of the vision of youth ministry is to present to youth the richness of the person of Christ, which perhaps exceeds the ability of one person to capture, but which might be effected by the collective ministry of the many persons who make up the Church.

United States Conference of Catholic Bishops,
A Vision of Youth Ministry, p. 11

CHAPTER FOURTEEN

Youth Ministry Leadership

Ann Marie Eckert

Editor's Note

Leadership makes youth ministry happen. Involving youth and adults in leadership also propels faith growth and a sense of ownership in the community. In this chapter, Ann Marie Eckert helps us consider Jesus as our model for leadership as she explores the roles for leadership in youth ministry, and the practical processes and resources for empowering youth and adults as leaders for ministry.

The ministry of leadership development *calls forth*, *affirms*, and *empowers* the diverse gifts, talents, and abilities of adults and young people in our faith communities for comprehensive ministry with adolescents. Leadership roles in adolescent ministry are key. Leaders must be trained and encouraged.

RENEWING THE VISION:
A FRAMEWORK FOR CATHOLIC
YOUTH MINISTRY
[ORIGINAL ITALICS][1]

Youth ministry happens because of leadership. Without leadership, there is no one to gather young people, no one to lay out a plan for sharing the Catholic faith, no one to design programs, or to accompany youth on mission trips, to send out a newsletter or design a Web site, and no one to include youth in parish ministries. Many parishes, full of well-meaning adults and talented youth, fail to live up to their potential because of leadership issues—

not enough people involved, lack of support from parish leadership, poor training and resources, the inability to collaborate, and countless other issues. This chapter will explore the ministry of leadership as it pertains to pastors, parish staff, youth ministry coordinators, adult volunteers, and youth. Every parish has the gifts necessary to minister to their adolescents. Parishes that fail to create a leadership system usually over-rely on a few committed leaders and consequently often fall short in their youth ministry efforts.

 ## Jesus as Leader

In the miracle of Jesus' feeding of the five thousand (Mt 14:13-21), one of the central elements of the story is that Jesus did not act alone. He used the gifts that were already present within the gathered masses, and invited them to share from their abundance. In reflecting on this reading, Parker Palmer states, "He acted in concert with others and evoked the abundance of community."[2] Palmer goes on to speak of Jesus' leadership:

> Jesus exercises the only kind of leadership that can evoke authentic community—a leadership that risks failure (and even crucifixion) by making space for other people to act. When a leader takes up all the space and preempts all the action, he or she may make something happen, but that something is not community. Nor is it abundance, because the leader is only one person and that one person's resources invariably run out. But when a leader is willing to trust the abundance that people have and can generate together, willing to take the risk of inviting people to share from that abundance, then and only then may true community emerge.[3]

If young people are to understand what it means to be gifted by God, to be called to share those gifts in service to others, and to live in community, then they will learn from the ways in which they experience Church. Youth ministry should communicate in word and action to young people and larger parish communities that we are so abundantly blessed by our God. When a few lead-

 Making the Connection

One definition of a leader is someone who makes a difference for good. Over our lifetimes, each of us exercises leadership in a variety of roles.

- *What leadership roles have been important in your life experience?*
- *What personal gifts do you bring to leadership?*

ers have to do everything, when those leaders are stressed and running low, and when only those individuals' gifts are made known to youth, young people will not come to know the abundance of gifts within the community nor what true community looks and feels like.

The call to community for the good of all must be taken very seriously if youth ministry efforts are to be an authentic witness to Jesus' life and ministry. Jesus, God's own son, did not act alone. He purposefully invited others to share in his ministry, invested time and energy into building up his team of disciples, engaged others who had gifts to share, and constantly found ways to involve people in his work. What better example exists?[4]

No matter how a parish is staffed, there are many members of each community who are ready and willing to become outstanding youth ministry leaders. But for that to happen, the parish must invest in these ministers as Jesus invested in the disciples. Close attention to the life of Jesus shows that Jesus created a whole leadership system in order to accomplish his mission. His system included the Twelve Apostles, who received significant training and formation, other leaders who contributed in important ways to his overall mission, and lots of people who shared what they had seen and heard and who brought others to Jesus. This is the model that helped Jesus accomplish his goal of sharing the Good News, and this is the same model that will help a parish to provide effective youth ministry.

Beyond Jesus' leadership example, there are other sources of wisdom within our Church tradition. Embedded in Scripture and Church teaching is the understanding that all Christians have gifts for ministry and that there is mutuality to those gifts—complementary gifts, given by the Holy Spirit, for the common good of all.

> Through the sacraments of Baptism, Confirmation, and Eucharist, every Christian is called to participate actively and co-responsibly in the Church's mission of salvation in the world. Moreover, in those same sacraments, the Holy Spirit pours out gifts which make it possible for every Christian man and woman to assume different ministries and forms of service that complement one another and are for the good of all.[5]

Catholics believe that every person, regardless of age, ability, style, gender, or race, has gifts that can contribute to the common good.

In a parish in Omaha lives a young boy with Down syndrome, a developmental disability. His gift to the parish is made evident each week at Mass. He loves being at church—he loves seeing the people, giving a hug at the sign of peace, and putting his money in the basket. It is impossible to sit anywhere near this young man and not smile and be drawn into his exuberance for liturgy.

Part of the mystery of God's great love is that he made each person with gifts to share. St. Paul helps explain this abundance of gifts when he speaks of the Christian community as being the Body of Christ. Paul says that every part of the body is important and that all parts must work together. No part of the body is more important, and no part can say to the rest, "I don't need you." (See 1 Corinthians 12:12–26.)

Effective youth ministry learns to use the gifts of the community to minister to all of the young people of the parish. Ministry leaders embrace the giftedness of both youth and adults, and involve them in the parish and youth ministry in a variety of ways. No one person is assumed to have all the gifts for ministry, and all people are invited to contribute to the overall ministry in whatever way they can.

This call to follow Jesus' leadership example and embrace the gifts of the community is challenging and rewarding. It is a model that makes vibrant ministry possible. Leadership for youth ministry must be taken seriously and intentionally implemented. Developing a leadership system includes inviting leaders, training, supporting, providing resources, and mentoring. Like Jesus' life example, it will take years to develop a system to sustain a mission of such great importance, but sharing the Good News with young people is worth the effort.

The Importance of Leadership

Effective leadership is essential to making good things happen at the parish. In the book *Good to Great*, author Jim Collins studied companies that went from being good to great in their particular field.[5] Collins found that one of the key factors in moving a company forward was not so much having the right plan, but having the right people.

> When we began the research project, we expected to find that the first step to taking a company from good to great would be to set a new direction, a new vision and strategy for the company, and then to get people committed and aligned behind that new direction. We found something quite the opposite. The executives who ignited the transformations from good to great.... first got the right people on the bus (and the wrong people off the bus) and then figured out where to drive it. They said, in essence, "Look, I don't really know where we should take this bus. But I know this much: If

we get the right people on the bus, the right people in the right seats, and the wrong people off the bus, then we'll figure out how to take it someplace great."[6]

Getting the right people involved in youth ministry can make all the difference. Do the people in leadership of youth ministry genuinely love young people? Are the leaders committed to their specific roles within the ministry? Is there energy and enthusiasm for the overall ministry effort? Without the right people in the right roles, it is hard to achieve dynamic ministry.

In the *Good to Great* study, Collins did not find that one leader made the difference; it was a team effort. Research showed that success did not come from having one excellent leader who did everything—quite the opposite. Great companies were run by leaders who recognized the importance of building up a team of strong people. Companies that were run by "geniuses" were successful only for the period of time that the strong leader was at the helm. After that, they fell apart.[7]

The same is true for ministry. Parishes need to bring in leaders for youth ministry who can build a strong team and animate the work of the parish as it ministers to its youth. Parishes make a mistake when they try to hire a youth minister solely based upon his or her ability to work directly with youth, without also considering their ability to gather a team and organize a ministry.

This situation can become the "guru" ministry model, which is often unsuccessful. A parish hires someone who is great at working directly with youth, but who has little talent for assembling a team. The parish is happy because the youth seem well taken care of by this one guru, but as soon as the guru leaves, the parish is back at square one. And too often, the parish begins a search process for a new "guru," and the cycle continues.

If a parish believes that hiring one person to work directly with young people is what "hiring a youth minister" means, it is setting itself up for failure. Youth ministry includes all the ways the Church reaches out to the young people of the parish and includes them in the life of the faith community. Clearly, it takes more than a few adult and youth leaders to live out that vision. If every young person of the parish (all 25, or 250, or 2,500) is to experience the church's ministry to them, no one program will work, and no one person can do the job. Since there are a variety of programs, events, and strategies that are needed, it also stands to reason that the parish will need many different types of leaders to support the variety of ways that the parish will minister to youth. (See Chapter 5 for additional information about models for providing youth ministry.) *Renewing the Vision* states clearly,

> This approach involves a wide diversity of adult and youth leaders in a variety of roles. Many will be involved in direct ministry with adolescents; others will provide support services and yet others will link the ministry effort to the resources of the broader community.[8]

Effective Practices for Dynamic Youth Ministry is a research study that interviewed parishes that went from good to great in youth ministry. One of the key findings within this research was the importance of creating a team of people to move the ministry forward. In the words of one of the parish staff members who was interviewed:

> A great gift for a youth minister, or anybody in a leadership position, is knowing that you cannot do it all by yourself, and it is very important for you to surround yourself with good people—adults and youth.[9]

Youth ministry cannot be the work of any one individual. Parishes with effective youth ministry assemble a team of other ministers who each add their particular gifts to the overall effectiveness of the ministry.

Leadership Roles for Youth Ministry

Parishes that are committed to ministering with their young people engage a variety of people in different roles. Pastors, parish staffs, parish leaders, and the whole community have an important role to play in youth ministry. There are also specific leadership roles in youth ministry to help the entire process work together. *Renewing the Vision* suggests the following roles:

Coordinator of Youth Ministry. This person's job is truly coordinating. The coordinator ensures that the parish, staff, ministry leaders, and youth ministry volunteers are all working in concert with each other for the good of youth. The coordinator is also the primary person to advocate for youth when necessary.

A coordinating team, made up of youth and adults, works directly with the coordinator. This team's job is to plan for youth ministry programs, find ways for young people to be infused into parish ministries, identify resources, and help to find, train, and support volunteer leaders for youth ministry.

Program leaders. Program leaders are utilized to run specific youth ministry programs. For instance, there may be a program team for the Confirmation retreat that includes an overall retreat coordinator, and a variety of adults and youth in leadership roles. Program leaders may take on multiple roles in youth ministry and become "core" leadership people, or they might help with one or two events a year.

Support staff. Many people are very happy to produce newsletters, enter data, buy food, or handle some behind-the-scenes details. Engaging people in supportive roles gives the opportunity to people with different gifts to shine and it frees the "up-front" volunteers from lots of organizational work that might over-stress them.[10]

Many different gifts are needed in all the opportunities for both youth and adults to be involved in leadership. Youth ministry thrives when the work is not all left to a small handful of people, but there is an even more important reason to engage a variety of leaders: young people need the opportunity to meet many different Catholic Christians so that they have many different role models. Each person who volunteers in youth ministry has the opportunity to touch the life of a young person in a unique way. *Renewing the Vision* quotes from the original youth ministry document, *A Vision of Youth Ministry*, to explain this point.

> Part of the vision of youth ministry is to present to youth the richness of the person of Christ, which perhaps exceeds the ability of one person to capture, but which might be effected by the collective ministry of the many persons who make up the Church.[11]

The roles within youth ministry provide an opportunity for a diverse group of adults and youth to present the "richness of the person of Christ" to young people.

The Coordinator of Youth Ministry

Every parish needs someone to coordinate youth ministry, although this position is not always salaried. The role is essential because the coordinator has primary responsibility for planning, administration, developing a leadership system, and advocating for youth. Each of these roles benefits the parish in unique ways.

- Planning (in collaboration with the coordinating team) ensures a well-rounded and solid youth ministry effort.
- Administration ensures the safety of the young people and volunteers and provides the information the youth and their families need for participation.

- Developing a leadership system ensures that the abundance of the community is poured out in service to young people.
- Advocacy ensures that young people are represented and heard within the parish and the wider community and that young people are fully engaged in all the ministries of the parish.

If no one serves in this role, it is too easy for many of these tasks to go undone. Too often the role of coordinator is given to someone who is already highly invested in a specific program within youth ministry, or in many of them. The problem with this solution is that the role of coordinator calls for some very specific actions and skills—skills which are not always the interest of an adult who is used to working directly with youth. Even when a parish hires someone to be the coordinator, the new employee may not embrace the above outlined roles if he or she is used to spending all the time directly engaged in youth ministry programming. Planning and administration take time, energy, and lots of paperwork. Creating a leadership team demands skills in training and mentoring, as well as the ability to invite others into leadership. Advocacy demands that the coordinator be available for staff meetings and parish leadership gatherings. Additionally, the coordinator has to have skills at coordinating—bringing people together to engage in youth ministry. The coordinator will work with all the other people serving in leadership roles in youth ministry—the coordinating team, the program leaders, and the support staff—and will help the parish leaders and the whole community to embrace youth.

Being a good organizer is a part of the job, but coordinators of youth ministry also breathe life into youth ministry. At the national symposium on effective youth ministry practices held in 2002 in Omaha, Nebraska, the parish coordinators used the term "animators" to best describe their role within the parish. They were not necessarily in charge of every event, but they did more than just coordinate the parish's youth ministry. They animated it by providing the direction, support, energy, and spirit to make programs run successfully and to make young people feel a part of the overall parish life.

The personality of the coordinator is very important. The youth ministry efforts of the parish are enhanced by the coordinator's personal gifts, spirituality, strong vision and leadership skills, and his or her ability to engage the gifts of the community. Those coordinators who show a genuine love of and appreciation for young people are always highly valued by the parishes in which they work. In *Effective Practices for Dynamic Youth Ministry*, the study finds that coordinators of youth ministry are valued, in part, because they are

- Healthy and well-balanced
- Dedicated and enthusiastic
- Good communicators
- Approachable
- Trustworthy
- A team player within the parish[12]

The coordinator of youth ministry engages the parish in setting the direction and vision for youth ministry in the faith community. Although *Renewing the Vision* sets the overall framework for youth ministry, each parish community utilizes its particular strengths and gifts in living out that vision. The coordinator is the person who helps the parish to name its vision, and then helps to bring that vision to life.

The coordinator works with the coordinating team to develop a leadership system for youth ministry. Together, these leaders invite, train, and mentor youth and adults within youth ministry. The coordinator of youth ministry should never be considered a parish's only "youth minister."

When the coordinator spends the majority of time ministering directly with young people two negative things happen. Young people only meet this one person and can come to believe that no one else in the parish cares. The youth end up thinking, "It is a good thing our youth minister likes us, because no one else does." The other risk is that a coordinator who spends all the time with youth never has the time to really train and mentor others. Effective coordinators know they have to create time to engage others' gifts within the ministry and to provide the support and training necessary for others to succeed.

To be effective in diverse parishes, coordinators must be able to minister within diverse cultural settings. Too often, youth ministry programs attract the majority culture within the parish community, leaving those who do not belong to that culture with little or no way to be involved. Coordinators need to develop skills for working with people of different cultures, and learn how to best minister to the many cultures represented within their parish. This challenge continues to be an area for growth among youth ministry professionals and volunteers alike.

If a parish has the resources to hire a coordinator of youth ministry, or if it is going to appoint a volunteer to serve in this role, the parish should pay attention to the following:

- Does the individual see his or her role as coordinating and animating? If the person is only interested in working with youth and seems to lack the ability or confidence to invite and train others for youth ministry, this should be a concern.

- Does the individual have a clear sense of youth ministry as integrated within the life of the parish community? Youth ministry will be at its strongest when youth are involved in all parish ministries. Can this individual help to make this vision a reality?
- Does the individual have a vibrant faith life? Can they share their faith journey and the teachings of the Church with passion?
- Does the individual have strong leadership skills—good communication, the ability to collaborate, good planning and administration skills?
- Does the individual cherish and love young people? Does he or she have the personal characteristics to be successful?
- Is the individual trained? If not, is he or she committed to learning more about the ministry and the skills required by this leadership role?

One of the key responsibilities of the coordinator is to lead the coordinating team to accomplishing their tasks.

Coordinating Team

The coordinating team is made up of youth and adults who are involved in the parish and should have between six to twelve members. At least half of the group should be adults. This group's job is to plan for the youth ministry programs and strategies of the parish. Not all members of this team are necessarily involved in hands-on work with youth. The group represents a diversity of ages, marital statuses, and experiences within the parish. The team should be prepared for its leadership role, which includes planning, involving other leaders, advocating, and identifying resources.

One parish located in a rural area has a very strong coordinating team. The members meet in the summer for a day of training about youth ministry to learn how to do effective seasonal planning. Once a month they meet to plan the youth ministry calendar and to work on inviting other adults to be involved as program leaders. When the coordinator needed some help in convincing the pastor to make a change at the parish for the good of youth, the coordinating team was a great resource. One member had served as parish council president and another had chaired a building campaign. Most importantly, both were parishioners, not paid staff. The pastor listened to these two individuals and made the requested change.

To create a good team it is important to look for individuals with the following skills:

- Ability to commit to training and meetings for at least a year, perhaps two or three
- Strong planning skills and the ability to see the big picture
- Concern for all the young people of the parish, not just those involved in a specific program within the overall youth ministry effort
- Representative of a specific group within the parish (teenagers, young married couples, seniors, etc). The team should be as diverse as possible to bring great creativity and depth to the team.
- Connections to groups and individuals within the parish that enable the coordinating team to be good at identifying resources and people who can help with youth ministry programs

Program Leaders

There are a variety of ways that parishes structure youth ministry (see Chapter 5 for ideas), but every parish relies of programs and activities to accomplish their goals. These programs and activities need leaders. These leaders are youth and adults who do direct ministry with young people. The leaders plan the specifics of the programs, whereas the coordinating team does macro planning (such as scheduling a retreat focused on Jesus in March). The program leaders for such a retreat would do the micro planning—developing the retreat outline, assigning tasks, training the team, or creating publicity.

Program leaders are people who might minister on a weekly basis at the Sunday night youth gathering, or they might be brought in to help with a specific program throughout the year. When a parish thinks broadly about program leaders, it can see all sorts of ways to involve youth and adults in leadership roles. For example, there may be a team of people who work on the March retreat referenced above. One or two people will serve as the retreat leaders, a few youth and adults will be invited to give a witness talk, other youth and adults will be asked to be small group facilitators and activity leaders, one or two adults will manage the kitchen, and a small group of youth will help to feed everyone for the weekend. This retreat is able to happen because there are a variety of people with various gifts who are all brought together to make the retreat program a success. A whole different team of adults and youth (with very different gifts) might coordinate the open gym night at the parish. Still a whole different collection of people might lead the Boy Scout troop.

Using this model will involve a great number of leaders throughout the year, freeing people to volunteer for what they are most interested in, and letting people use their specific interests and gifts to determine how they will participate. If an individual is passionate about justice, she can accompany young people to the soup kitchen or on the summer mission trip, but she does not have to go to the amusement park. If someone is a great coordinator, he can help to run the spaghetti dinner fundraiser, but he need not be good at sharing his faith as a catechetical leader. The more people who are involved as program leaders, the better. Although it is important to have some consistency in leadership— regular volunteers who know young people by name and can bridge the gap from one activity to the next—it is also important to have a variety of leaders who will share their unique personality and faith journey with the young people and who can bring their best efforts to a program or project that they have passion about.

Support Staff

One of the least utilized roles within youth ministry is that of support people. There are many people in a parish who would prefer not to be actively engaged in direct work with youth, but who are still willing to help. These people might gratefully volunteer to help design publicity, enter information in the database, shop for snacks, update the Web site, or collect permission slips.

One coordinator, after years of unsuccessfully trying to manage the finances and budget for youth ministry (not her gift!) finally asked an accountant to help. The accountant was more than happy to use his training and expertise, and his work freed the coordinator to attend to things at which she excelled.

To get people to help with support staff roles, just ask. People are often more willing to do these clerical jobs because they are less threatening. Sometimes these roles serve as an "entry-level" opportunity for someone who later becomes a vital program leader within youth ministry.

Adult and Youth Leaders In Youth Ministry

Adults Have a Huge Impact on Youth

The success of youth ministry is often tied very directly to the quality of the adults who are working with the young people. Ask a young person if he likes his religious education class, and you will probably find out whether or not he feels valued by the catechist. Ask another teenager why she goes to youth group, and you will probably hear about an adult (or two) who has made her feel welcomed and important. Young people need strong, faithful, and genuine adults within their lives. When a parish is able to attract these types of people to the ministry, they are almost always successful. In the *Effective Practices for Dynamic Youth Ministry* book, a young person said this about the adult leaders in the parish:

> They have such a commitment to you. They have a job and have a life and have their own children. They have their own life and then they are committed to you. It is a great comfort.[13]

This teenager communicated well what young people are looking for from adults—someone who can connect with them, who truly values them, who believes in their goodness, who shares their faith through example and conversation, and who is able to give enough of his or her time to demonstrate these attributes. Every parish has these types of adults within the community. The challenge is to name them, call these individuals forward, and then give them the training, support, and opportunity they need to shine.

Youth Leaders Are Essential

All young people have the ability to be leaders, especially if the definition of leadership is "making a difference for good." Every young person in the parish should be invited to make a difference for good in his or her own particular way. This might mean serving on a committee or retreat team, or chairing an event. Some youth prefer upfront leadership roles while others prefer to be good listeners to peers in need, volunteers in the community, or aides in religious education classes. Each of these roles is meaningful, helpful, and important. Young people should be encouraged to use their particular gifts for the good of the community, their families, and the parish.

Young people should have a meaningful role within the leadership structures of parish youth ministry. No one can speak for the specific needs of young people in the parish better than young people themselves. Listen to young people, hear their struggles (with faith, life, school, relationships), and tap into their dreams. The more young people directly communicate with parish leadership, the better ministry efforts will be. However, it should never be young people's responsibility to create youth ministry for their peers on their own without adult leaders. Young people should be partners in youth ministry, not left to their own efforts. They need adults to work with them—sometimes to mentor, sometimes to companion, and other times to lead.

It is also important for young people to play an active role within the parish community. When the parish's ministries are open to young people, each individual can choose the opportunities that most appeal to him or her. Within the context of the whole parish, there are also great opportunities within youth ministry programs for young people to develop their gifts and talents: leading small groups, giving presentations or witness talks, leading activities, playing music, being a prayer leader, modeling behavior, and facilitating meetings are just a few of the many ways that young people can grow through youth ministry involvement.

When parishes invest in their youth, these young leaders take on a huge responsibility within parish programs. They become the backbone of the parish youth ministry, and often emerge as leaders within other parish structures. In order for this to happen, however, it is important that someone (the coordinator, the program leaders, the coordinating team, or the parish staff/leaders) take the time to help develop the skills that young people need for leadership. This is most often done through one-on-one mentoring, group interaction and feedback, and parish and diocesan training programs.

Involving young people in leadership can have a profound effect on both the parish and the young people. In her book, *Changing Lives: Transformational Ministry and Today's Teens*, Lisa-Marie Calderone-Stewart talks about five layers of leadership for youth:

- Teenagers can be Church leaders now
- Teenagers can inspire other teenagers to become leaders
- When teenagers are given leadership roles, they want to contribute
- Being a leader helps a teenager develop ownership for learning more and for passing on the faith
- More teen Church leaders today could mean more adult Church leaders tomorrow[14]

As Calderone-Stewart states, the more often young people were given meaningful roles within the parish and Church, the more they found ways to contribute. Young people have many gifts to share, but the ways they are currently being asked to share may need to be examined more closely. The less one asks of young people (or anyone), the less they will give. When young people are given meaningful ways to contribute, they most often rise to the occasion.

Parish Leadership for Youth Ministry

Many people assume that "youth ministry" refers to the specific programs that gather young people together at the parish. However, youth ministry also includes the ways that a parish includes young people in the life the parish community. In order for youth ministry to be most effective, it must be infused within parish life.

This infusion has direct implications for the leadership structures of the parish. When parishes take youth ministry seriously, everyone at the parish has a role to play. Parishes with effective youth ministry understand that the parish staff and leadership minister to youth within their regular responsibilities. In the national *Effective Practices for Dynamic Youth Ministry* study, parish leadership plays an essential role in the effectiveness of youth ministry efforts.

> In parishes with effective youth ministry, the parish staff and leaders support each other and work collaboratively. The boundaries between ministries are permeable, that is, ministries overlap and staff are not rigid or protective about their ministerial areas of responsibility.[15]

These parish leaders make it easy for the youth ministry leaders to include young people within the life of the parish because every staff member is a part of the youth ministry team, and every parish organization or ministry sees young people as gift and contributors.

Although parish structures vary widely throughout the country and within every diocese, there are some common expectations for parish leaders, which need to be met if parishes are to have a strong, healthy youth ministry.

Pastors Provide Support and Supervision

In *Effective Practices for Dynamic Youth Ministry,* Tom East reports on the findings of a research project that sought to find the practices of parishes with effective youth ministry. Among the many findings was that "pastor support for youth ministry is crucial."[16] Pastors have a unique role to play within the leadership system of the parish because they set the tone for the parish. If their support for youth ministry is not clear, it is easy for the ministries and ministers at a parish to undervalue their young people.

This support for youth ministry consists of providing personnel for youth ministry (as paid or volunteer staff, or as an additional responsibility for a staff person), including young people within the leadership and ministerial opportunities of the parish, and ensuring that there are resources (budget, space, and people) to minister to the young people of the parish. Pastors are typically the supervisors for youth ministry leaders. Often this means that a pastor is the direct supervisor for a paid or volunteer coordinator of youth ministry, but this role also has larger implications. If young people are not allowed to sing in the "adult" choir because a music director doesn't like working with youth, this becomes a supervision issue for a pastor. If youth ministry is shut out of using the best space of a parish (a new parish community room, for instance), this also is a leadership issue for a pastor. Pastors have to keep an eye on what is best for all the people of the parish community, and this must include the children and youth.

Pastors also need to have some way of connecting to the young people of the parish. Pastors do not necessarily need to be at every youth event—which is probably not practical or desirable for most pastors—but young people should have some opportunities throughout the year to talk with, listen to, and come to know the pastor of their parish. Pastors who are most successful at this are the ones who partner with youth ministry leaders to find appropriate and easy ways to be involved.

Pastors can show their support for youth ministry in a variety of ways. Here are some practical ideas:

- Once or twice a year a pastor can be invited to an "ask the pastor" night with the youth of the parish. This question-and-answer session can build a solid relationship between youth and pastor. Other options are to arrange for the pastor to teach a class, go on a service project, say Mass for the confirmation retreat, or otherwise participate in a few youth activities throughout the year.
- Pastors should be attentive to the young people with whom they regularly come in contact—altar servers and other liturgical ministers, and youth who are involved in parish activities and leadership roles (parish council, youth ministry council, etc.)
- Pastors can use homilies and other opportunities to talk about young people—either addressing specific life concerns or highlighting something that youth of the parish are doing. Pastors should take care to address positive things about youth in addition to sharing concerns or challenges in homilies and talks.
- Pastors should ensure that youth ministry has an active voice in the leadership structures of the parish. Youth ministry should be represented on the parish council, and youth should have roles within other leadership structures at the parish.
- Pastors should oversee the supervision of youth ministry staff and the hiring or selection process for a coordinator of youth ministry. Sometimes the pastor is not the direct supervisor. However, it is essential that the coor-

dinator of youth ministry (volunteer or paid) has a staff member of the parish who is responsible for supervision and support. If the pastor is not the supervisor, he can make sure this support is in place.

Pastors should ensure there are adequate resources available to youth ministry. These resources should include a budget for materials and program resources, perhaps a salary for staff, availability of space within the parish buildings, and a dedication to training and support for those who work with youth.

Pastors do not work alone, so it is also important that all parish staff and volunteer leaders are ready and willing to help in youth ministry efforts.

Parish staff and leaders are collaborators in youth ministry efforts

Sometimes when people hear "everyone has a role to play in youth ministry," they fear that they are being asked to "take a turn" at running a youth group or chaperoning an event. But this is not what is being requested! Parish staff and leaders should minister to young people through the ministries and work they are already doing. How can a parish staff person or parish volunteer leader engage young people within their programs, utilize the gifts of youth to enhance their efforts, or support youth ministry programs or specific youth through their resources, time, or talents?

For a parish to have strong youth ministry, the parish staff and leaders must be supportive of youth ministry in concrete, observable ways. Parish staffs and leaders must collaborate together on projects, be willing to make a special effort to include youth in their ministry efforts, and welcome, smile at, and befriend young people of the parish whenever possible. Parish staffs and leaders need to trust each others' gifts, rely on each others' programs, and work together to provide strong ministry for all of the people of the parish.

In parishes with vibrant youth ministry, young people do much more than baby-sit or set up tables for the parish picnic. In strong communities, youth are liturgical ministers, religious education teachers and aides, and members of parish leadership teams. The young people help with parish service projects and share leadership in events provided for the whole parish. When parish leaders gather to plan a yearly parish mission, young people's needs are considered; youth may also be part of the planning group. Great youth ministry happens at parishes that know how to work together and how to value the giftedness each leader brings to the effort.

How do parish leaders become effective ministers to youth? Here are some simple starting points:

Parish staff and organizations/ministries can spend some time learning more about adolescence and youth ministry. In one parish, the staff studied *Renewing the Vision* over the course of a few months. For thirty minutes at each staff meeting, the members learned more about the goals, settings, and components of comprehensive youth ministry, and were engaged in conversation about how they could help in living out this vision. In another parish, the youth ministry leaders met with each parish organization for about an hour to talk about what youth ministry was currently doing, ask about how they could work together, and find out what ideas or suggestions the organizations had.

Parish staff and councils can work to assess their current efforts in the area of youth ministry and then make strategic changes to current policies, staffing, and leadership for youth ministry. For example, if an assessment indicates that very few young people are involved in parish liturgical ministries, work to invite, train, and schedule young people into those liturgical roles. One parish accomplished this by having the young people take all the liturgical roles during one Mass a month for a year. The parish started a youth choir that sang at the Mass, and had youth ushers, lectors, Eucharistic ministers, and altar servers. In this particular parish, a few members of the adult choir showed up to sing on the day that the youth were scheduled, so the adults were invited to sing with the youth that week. The youth and adults began to sing together each week, bringing new life and leadership to both choirs.

Parishes can make sure that leadership structures are open and inviting to youth. In one parish, the council decided to invite youth ministry to send two representatives to attend the council meeting each month. This sounded like a good step, but no one ever welcomed the young people to the parish council, introduced the young people to the other members, or helped them to understand the way the meetings worked. Even worse, the council never invited the young people to share their thoughts or opinions unless they directly related to youth ministry. After three months, the young people stopped showing up because they thought it was a waste of their time to attend as there was no good way for them to participate. Involving youth on the council was a good idea, but someone needed to set this idea up for success. When the council recognized the situation, several members met with the youth and developed a plan for including their ideas in a more effective way.

Collaboration is key to helping young people be involved in many different ways. Parish staff who work well together can easily involve youth in many different programs and efforts. One parish has many young people involved in leadership within its catechetical programs because the coordinator for children's catechesis works hand-in-hand with the coordinator for youth ministry to ensure this involvement. At the same parish, the justice and service coordinator and the coordinator of youth ministry plan the summer mission trip together.

Youth ministry has to work to educate parish organizations about ways to involve young people. A youth ministry coordinator was asked by the parish service team to have some young people come and help with the sorting of food from the Thanksgiving food drive. At nine o'clock on a Saturday morning (not a young person's favorite time), ten young people showed up to the parish center to help with the sorting, only to be told "We don't need you anymore." To make sure something like that didn't happen again, the following year the coordinator of youth ministry met with the service team to talk about youth ministry and why the young people needed their example and experience. The coordinator then had members of the service team talk with the young people about their ministry and the people who would be receiving the food. By working together and sharing information, a great collaboration was formed.

Parish staff members should relate to youth as they would to anyone else. A parish liturgy coordinator knew a young man who played saxophone in the parish choir. The coordinator thought the boy had really grown into the role to the point of "praying the saxophone," not just playing it. The coordinator made a point of stopping the youth and sharing her insight with him after Mass. The boy got tears in his eyes because he had felt the power of his prayer as well. One of the signs of strength in this parish is that the liturgist didn't tell the youth ministry leader, who then told the young person—the liturgist herself was in direct relationship with the young person. Young people can be treated as "one of the crowd" and invited in, supported, challenged, and praised in the same way as adults. Although youth might need additional support and preparation to be involved in parish ministry, supporting youth is something that many people in the parish can and should do to help young people feel valued and welcomed.

Mobilizing the Parish Community

Youth ministry thrives when leaders invest time and develop a way for many people to participate by adding their own special gifts to the effort. Some people may have one specific event to which they devote their time. Others may help occasionally when there is a need. Others are weekly or monthly volunteers—the cornerstone of most youth ministry programs. There are still others who support youth ministry with money, resources, or prayer.

A youth ministry leader might be asking, "How do I get these volunteers?"[17] People are often reluctant to volunteer because previous experiences have been poor. Marlene Wilson, in her book *How to Mobilize Church Volunteers*, speaks about the reasons why so few people are involved in Church ministry:

- Most volunteer ministry jobs in the Church are not clearly defined
- Tradition often squelches new and creative ideas and approaches
- Time and talent sheets have helped officially reject people's gifts every year (This happens when people mark the box on the new parishioner packet, or sign up at Stewardship Sunday, or fill out the time and talent survey, and then never get called.)
- Clergy and lay leaders alike are often very poor delegators
- The jobs to be filled often receive more attention than those filling them
- It is often difficult for members to describe
  - ▷ What they are good at
  - ▷ What they are tired of doing
  - ▷ What they don't like to do
  - ▷ What they want to learn
  - ▷ Where they are being led to grow
  - ▷ When they need a sabbatical[18]

For each of those concerns, there is a solution. A parish community can tap into the existing potential and uncover the abundance lying near the surface of the parish. This effort, however, will take some new ways of acting, new ways of thinking, and a community-wide leadership effort to be successful.

A better question and a better starting point might be "How do I help people understand their own giftedness and create opportunities for those people to live out their baptismal call?" This question helps find an abundance of ministers by focusing on how to empower parish members to respond to the great gift of God's love in their lives. Marlene Wilson rightly states that "the pews are filled with potential unrealized and energy untapped."[19]

Inviting, Training, and Supporting Leaders

An essential element of a good leadership system within a parish is the ability of the coordinator and the coordinating team to find, train, and support volunteer leaders, both youth and adults. Developing this system will yield confident, prepared leaders for youth ministry for years to come.

Inviting

Successful recruitment begins well before a leader approaches a potential volunteer. Prior to inviting anyone, leaders need to know what kind of help, what gifts, and what time commitment is necessary. To capture that information, write job descriptions. Write lots of them! Job descriptions should include a clear description of tasks, expectations, and support provided. When creating these descriptions, break big jobs down into manageable parts. People are much more apt to say yes to a little job than a big one. Writing down what is expected of people gives them the opportunity to see if they have the skills, interests, and time for the job.

If there is training needed for the role, be clear about how that will happen. The more people know about what they are being asked to do, the easier it will be for them to say "yes." Imagine being asked, "Will you volunteer within youth ministry?" This is a vague question that may strike fear in people's hearts. However, "Can you come with the young people to the soup kitchen next month?" is not as intimidating.

It is important to recognize that adults who are volunteering within ministry for roles that will involve them directly with youth must be screened and must complete the Protecting God's Children diocesan requirements, which include a background check and training. (Consult the diocesan office for specific information.)

It is also very important to be selective in who works with children and youth. Although this can seem like a burden when inviting adults to volunteer, it need not be. Protecting the safety and well-being of children is always a priority, and screening ensures not only that the adults who work with youth are not a danger to them, but also that the adults have training on how to spot unhealthy and unsafe behaviors by other adults.

To invite leaders, consider the following:

- Ask people for recommendations. Youth know family members and neighbors that they connect with. Parish staff have a sense of who has

SMALL GROUP FACILITATOR

Program: Fall Retreat

Responsibilities: Leader Tasks to be Performed
- Serve as a small group leader for 6-8 youth, ensuring that all youth have a chance to share and experience a supportive community
- Engage in the activities, games, and prayer experiences of the retreat
- When appropriate, share your own faith journey with youth.

Qualifications: Abilities Needed
- Deep love and appreciation for youth
- Good facilitation skills
- Strong faith life
- Willingness to get to know youth and be present to their experiences

Length of Commitment:
Retreat is first weekend in November. There are two preparation meetings (2nd and 4th Tuesdays in October) and one evaluation meeting (3rd Tuesday in November)

Training Required:
Training will be provided at the preparation meetings. You will have the opportunity to learn more about the overall goals of the retreat and to learn skills and good practices for small group facilitation.

Responsible to: Retreat Team Leader

Supervision/Support:
The retreat team leader is responsible for providing you with the training and support you will need to do a good job. The retreat team leader will meet with you individually during the retreat for support, and provide feedback to you during the evaluation meeting.

Benefits of the Position to the Leader:
Opportunity to know young people and hear more about their personal faith journey. A chance for you to be a part of a retreat and reflect on your own faith journey. Opportunity to relate to other adults and youth leaders in the program.

worked well in the past with youth, and adults have lots of connections to tap in to.

- Invite people personally. Few people will volunteer because of something in the bulletin. Best results occur by calling people by name and inviting them into a specific volunteer role.
- Place information in the bulletin, newsletters, and on bulletin boards. Although people aren't likely to initiate a call, at least when they are called, they will know that someone in the parish is looking for help.
- Help adults and youth to see the value in a volunteer opportunity. Too often, we make the job sounds miserable and then people are asked to volunteer: "I am so sorry to have to ask, but we just need one more volunteer to come to the amusement park. I know it will be a long day and you have other things you would rather do, but we really need you." Instead, name what they will experience, learn, and enjoy: "We are going to have a great day at the amusement park and we would love to have you join us. I know you love roller coasters and we have some kids who do too. I know that the young people would love to meet you, and you will love our kids. They are a great bunch."
- Be on the lookout for people's gifts and talents, and invite them to volunteer in jobs that are a perfect match. If someone returns home from college after four years in college theater, tap them to run the Passion Play next year.

Training

Once people get involved, it is essential to help them succeed. The quickest way to lose volunteers is to ask them to do something for which they are ill-equipped. Every person, regardless of role, needs some level of orientation. For example, adults who are chaperoning a dance need to gather ten minutes prior to the start of the dance to meet with the leader. The leader lets the adults know what is expected—what is appropriate behavior, what doors need to be watched, how often the bathrooms should be checked, the rules related to coming and going, etc. On the other hand, volunteers who will be catechists for the year might need a day-long orientation in order to get the basic information they need for their role. No one should ever be asked to give their time without receiving the orientation they will need to be effective.

Additional training is often necessary beyond orientation. Many people can learn "on the job" as long as intentional direction, support, and feedback is provided. When someone is new to youth ministry or to a particular role, it is essential to give them feedback—both positive comments and helpful hints—so they continue to grow in the role. Successful parishes often create a climate of constant feedback, in which every program is evaluated and every person hears of successes and mistakes within a loving and supportive community.

Specific training for a role can also be critical—people will need to learn skills for working with small groups, for giving a witness talk, or for planning prayer. It is important to remember that this is not just training of adults and youth for a job, but also for a ministry. Volunteer leaders will need opportunities to talk about faith, to learn about the Church, and to grow spiritually.

Take advantage of diocesan and national training programs. Build training into planning meetings. Provide access to online or video training so that people can prepare in their own time. Provide print resources that will further explain what is expected of people. Not every job needs the same level of training, but everyone can grow through training.

Supporting

Everyone needs and appreciates support and supervision. Support can mean affirmation, gifts, public recognition, and thank-you notes, or being engaged in people's lives and sharing their struggles, joys, and heartaches. Most people will stay involved in volunteer work if they feel that they are making a difference *and* that they belong to a community which values them.

Parishes are very creative in ways to provide support. One parish sent a free pizza certificate to the houses of all the volunteers who were working the weekend retreat. For those who had left spouses and kids at home, the certificate was a thank-you to the family for "lending out" the parent working the retreat. For single people, it was a welcomed "Sunday night dinner" after being away from home all weekend. Support can mean providing babysitting for parents of young children, prayer cards in times of heartache, and thank you notes that name the specific gifts of the volunteer.

Inviting, training, and supporting leaders is one of the key roles of the coordinator and the coordinating team. It takes intentional work, but it is well worth the effort. In the words of a coordinator,

> We made a concerted effort about a year and a half ago to really put money
> and time into forming volunteers. That would be a huge focus for us. It made
> a whole lot of difference.[20]

Supervision literally means to "vision with." Sometimes organizers are afraid to supervise volunteers because they don't want to criticize helpers or scare them away. Supervising is providing feedback and communicating expectations. Typically, this means catching volunteers in the act of doing something right and letting them know what they did and why it worked so well. Correction or redirection of a volunteer's work is sometimes necessary. Communicating the value of work lets volunteers know that it matters how they do their job. People want to be part of a team that has high standards; this does not necessitate becoming picky or overly critical. Everyone learns from constructive criticism and affirmation. Volunteers in youth ministry deserve feedback and mentoring.

One of the best ways to support a volunteer is to walk the journey with them from novice to confident leader. When a volunteer begins a new ministry, be very clear and directive about how they can help. As they gain experience, provide coaching for them as they take greater leadership roles. Eventually the volunteers may be ready to lead on their own with little support.[21] This attention to supervision and support can make all the difference in a parish.

Growing Leadership

Growing leadership for youth ministry takes attention and time. It begins with parish leaders—pastors, staffs, councils, and coordinators of youth ministry—who are willing to take a careful look at the parish as it is and see opportunities for youth within the parish. Leadership extends to those adults of the parish who are willing to take on some role within youth ministry, and includes young people who are ready and willing to use their gifts and talents within youth ministry and the parish.

To grow in this area, it is important to start with an assessment of the current leadership system:

- Does the parish have someone who is coordinating youth ministry efforts? Are there people who help with these tasks, a coordinating team?
- Are there a variety of different adults and youth involved in leadership?
- Is orientation, training, and support provided to leaders?
- Are roles within the parish open to youth—liturgical, leadership, service, ministry?
- How well does the staff work together? How well do parish organizations interact with youth? Are there places where greater collaboration is possible?
- Are there clearly defined roles with written job descriptions?

For parishes that want to move in the directions outlined here, consider the following:

- How can the parish get the right people into the right roles? Who will make those assessments and work on recruiting the people most wanted? Someone with authority—a pastor, staff member, coordinator—needs to take the lead on making sure that the right people are in place.
- How will youth ministry be connected to the parish staff—as a full-time employee, a part-time responsibility within a larger job, a part-time employee, a volunteer? Youth ministry should not be disconnected from parish leadership, so make arrangements to ensure that someone on staff is connected to the youth ministry leaders.
- Are there ways that the parish staff and key leaders will need to change in order to make the parish more open to the leadership potential of youth? How can youth play a more vital and energizing role? After an honest look at the parish, there may be many ways in which youth are excluded from participation and full membership within the community. Find where the parish is falling short and make changes.
- Does the parish need to be educated on the value of team ministry? How can individuals within the parish be helped to value the role they could play within youth ministry? Consider a ministry Sunday that really focuses on each individual's gifts. Begin to talk more overtly about youth ministry as a parish ministry. Invite lots of new people to be involved.
- What type of training needs to be provided to key leaders and occasional volunteers? What resources would make the job easier for volunteers? Talk to the diocesan office and find out what is locally available. Purchase resources so that volunteers can spend their time preparing for, instead of designing, programs. Create a plan for training your volunteers.
- How will youth be encouraged to use their gifts within the parish and youth ministry? What type(s) of training will they receive? Use local and national training programs and print resources to train youth for leadership. Highlight youth for the gifts they already have, and help the parish to recognize their contributions through awards, announcements, and blessings.

Each parish will experience its own highlights and face its own difficulties in creating a strong leadership system for youth ministry. It might take years to feel confident in handing this important ministry over to people who initially seem ill-prepared. But every parish has the gifts necessary to minister to youth, and every parish should take the opportunity to create a system for leadership that will give youth a strong and vibrant youth ministry. Every parish can create many opportunities for youth to use their gifts. With this strong foundation, youth ministry and parish life can grow and flourish for coming generations.

— RECOMMENDED RESOURCES —

Blanchard, Ken, John P. Carlos, and Alan Randolph. *The Three Keys to Empowerment: Release the Power Within People for Astonishing Results.* San Francisco: Berrett-Koehler Publishers, 1999.

Buckingham, Marcus, and Donald O. Clifton, Ph.D. *Now, Discover Your Strengths.* New York: Free Press, 2001.

Calderone-Stewart, Lisa-Marie. *Changing Lives: Transformational Ministry and Today's Teens.* Dayton, OH: Pflaum Publishing Group, 2004.

Collins, Jim. *Good to Great.* New York: HarperCollins Publishers, Inc., 2001.

Doohan, Leonard. *Spiritual Leadership: The Quest for Integrity.* Mahwah, NJ: Paulist Press, 2007.

East, Thomas, Ann Marie Eckert, Leif Kehrwald, Brian Singer-Towns, and Cheryl Tholcke. *Total Youth Ministry: Coordinators Manual.* Winona, MN: Saint Mary's Press, 2004.

East, Thomas, Ann Marie Eckert, Dennis Kurtz, and Brian Singer-Towns. *Effective Practices for Dynamic Youth Ministry.* Winona, MN: Saint Mary's Press, 2004.

Eckert, Ann Marie, with Maria Sanchez-Keane. *Total Youth Ministry: Ministry Resources for Youth Leadership Development.* Winona, MN: Saint Mary's Press, 2004.

Hiesberger, Jean Marie. *Fostering Leadership Skills in Ministry: A Parish Handbook.* Liguori, MO: Liguori, 2003.

Lay Ecclesial Ministry: The State of the Questions. Washington, DC: United States Conference of Catholic Bishops, 1999.

Rath, Tom. *Strengths Finder 2.0.* New York: Gallup Press, 2007.

Renewing the Vision: A Framework for Catholic Youth Ministry. Washington, DC: United States Conference of Catholic Bishops, 1997.

Trumbaurer, Jean Morris. *Created and Called: Discovering Our Gifts for Abundant Living.* Minneapolis: Augsburg Fortress, 1998.

Trumbaurer, Jean Morris. *Sharing the Ministry: A Practical Guide for Transforming Volunteers into Ministers.* Minneapolis: Augsburg Fortress, 1998.

Wilson, Marlene. *How to Mobilize Church Volunteers.* Minneapolis: Augsburg Fortress, 1983.

— ENDNOTES —

1. *Renewing the Vision: A Framework for Catholic Youth Ministry.* Washington, DC: United States Conference of Catholic Bishops, 1997, p. 40.

2. Palmer, Parker J. *The Active Life: Wisdom for Work, Creativity, and Caring.* San Francisco: Harper Collins, 1990, p. 136.

3. Ibid, p. 138.

4. These two paragraphs also appear in: Ann Marie Eckert, "It Takes a Team!" *Youth Ministry Access* (Naugatuck, CT: Center for Ministry Development, 2005), www.youthministryaccess.org, p. 2.

5. *Called and Gifted for the Third Millennium.* Washington, DC: United States Conference of Catholic Bishops, 1995, p. 15.

6. Collins, James C. *Good to Great: Why Some Companies Make the Leap—and Others Don't.* New York: HarperBusiness, 2001, p. 41.

7. Collins, pp. 45-46.

8. RTV, p. 40.

9. East, Thomas. *Effective Practices for Dynamic Youth Ministry.* Winona, MN: Saint Mary's, 2004, p. 59.

10. RTV, p. 41.

11. RTV, citing *A Vision of Youth Ministry* (Washington, DC: United States Conference of Catholic Bishops, 1976), p. 24.

12. EPDYM, p. 60.

13. EPDYM, p. 64.

14. Calderone-Stewart, Lisa-Marie. *Changing Lives: Transformational Ministry and Today's Teens.* Dayton: Pflaum, 2004, pp. 24-27.

15. EPDYM, p. 22.

16. EPDYM, p. 21.

17. Adapted from Ann Marie Eckert, "It Takes a Team!" *Youth Ministry Access*, pp. 2-3.

18. Wilson, Marlene. *How to Mobilize Church Volunteers.* Minneapolis: Augsburg Fortress, 1983, p. 22.

19. Ibid., p. 21.

20. EPDYM, p. 67.

21. For more information about empowering leadership, see: Ken Blanchard, John P. Carlos, and Alan Randolph, *The Three Keys to Empowerment: Release the Power Within People for Astonishing Results* (San Francisco: Berrett-Koehler Publishers, 2001).

CHAPTER FIFTEEN

Planning and Visioning for Youth Ministry

Thomas East

Editor's Note

"If we can dream it, we can do it, together."[1]

These inspirational words remind us that the first step in making something happen is to imagine and envision the new desired reality. Next, we develop a plan to use everyone's gifts to make it happen. This chapter explores the process for shaping a vision and crafting a plan for youth ministry to make our hopes come alive.

I love it when a plan comes together. There are times when everything connects. What you hope for comes to fruition when people work together to make something happen. In youth ministry, visioning and planning happens continuously as the ministry develops and grows. Though it is not everyone's favorite part of the ministry and it is not the most glamorous part, successful leaders and communities know that a clear vision and good planning make a huge difference.

This is probably easiest to see when examining some common reasons why youth ministry efforts fail. Sometimes, communities with high hopes and good intentions for youth ministry experience disappointment. These are some of the common problems encountered by parishes:

Lack of common vision and clear purpose Have you ever tried to paddle a canoe across the lake with a whole group of people? The canoe goes quickly and smoothly when all of the oars are in the water, in synch with each other, and going in the same direction. Imagine twelve sets of oars splashing about the water at all different times, some going forward and some going backward. In all of this commotion, the unstable canoe is spinning and just waiting to tip over. That is what it is like when a parish is unclear about what they are trying to achieve in youth ministry. For example, in one parish, some of the parish leaders and some parents of youth decided that all the youth need is education in the faith. They wanted to plan a lecture series for youth and get rid of all of the other elements of youth ministry. The youth ministry team, other parents, and many youth wanted to continue to provide their traditional elements of youth ministry, which emphasized community building, service, and worship. The current youth ministry elements were effective and well attended. The youth ministry could have benefited by more intentional faith learning. This could have been a good dialogue, but unfortunately, leaders in the parish did not know how to listen to each other and develop a ministry for the parish that reflects the principles of youth ministry. The bickering and divisive behavior exhausted the leader's enthusiasm and the parish's resources for youth ministry.

Isolation and lack of support Studies of effective youth ministry are clear: youth ministry thrives with the support of the whole parish. Without this support, youth ministry can become an isolated program supported by a few leaders that is tangential to the parish community as a whole. Youth ministry needs a variety of levels of support throughout the parish system, among youth and their parents, and within the community. This support will help the resources to come together in a way that helps the ministry overcome obstacles and challenges.

No plan Sometimes planning for youth ministry goes something like this. The youth minister usually does is it all. When he or she becomes overwhelmed, they "delegate" part of the ministry that they understand the least and are most burdened by. This part of the ministry is unloaded (at the last minute) to sympathetic, already overworked volunteers in the parish who cannot say no. These volunteers struggle and sometimes fail at their task, which just proves to the youth minister that they "really do have to do everything themselves." It doesn't have to be this way. When parishes set aside time for planning and engage members of the community in creating the plan, these parishes discover that they do have the resources they need to pull together dynamic, effective, and engaging youth ministry. There needs to be a clear plan for how people and resources will come together to make a plan happen in a timely way.

Ministry that is stuck Parish leaders can become attached to the way that they do youth ministry even when it isn't working. Sometimes, leaders fail to keep the main thing the main thing; they hold on to a particular program, model, or strategy too long. The Good News of our faith is constant, but the way that we will engage and involve young people in this Good News must continue to grow and develop. This means that leaders need to constantly evaluate how they are doing ministry and propose changes and refinements that will help the ministry reach young disciples.

Failure to anticipate resistance Sometimes parish leaders know that a change is needed and understand the right new direction, yet still fail to make the ministry work. This can happen when leaders are naive to the resistance they will encounter from a community that does not want to change or does not know how to change. A parish is a system; systems tend to continue doing things the way they have always done them. There is built-in momentum for a parish to continue current practices even when they aren't working. As Arthur W. Jones stated, "All organizations are perfectly aligned to get the results they get."[2] If we want different results, we need to align ourselves differently. This means change, and for some, change is painful. To be successful, leaders must expect resistance and must plan for the change process simultaneously to planning new initiatives. This is part of how we get all of those oars in the water going in the same direction.

Planning for youth ministry can help a parish develop a common vision and clear purpose. A sound plan can help build support for youth ministry throughout the parish and the community. It can create a clear plan in which many people can successfully execute their part. It can help parishes get "un-stuck" and move ahead to new, exciting ways of ministering with youth.

Good Planning Builds Your Capacity for Good Ministry

Sometimes, experiences of planning, organizing, and decision-making are tedious and end up going nowhere. This may lead us to the question: "Why plan?" We conclude that we should "Just get in there and work and make it happen because that's what leaders do." There's truth in this statement: ministry does happen because of hard work and because leaders act to make things happen.

For many, a huge part of effective leadership for youth ministry is intuition and instinct. As leaders in youth ministry, we know how to spin on a dime and plan tonight's youth night at the last minute. We know how to wade into a youth gathering and just make it work. But after a while, we come to realize that the youth need more than we can give them alone and that we need to increase our capacity for ministry. We want to find more ways to connect with youth and their families. We reach the limits of just working harder. To increase our parish's capacity for ministry, we need to envision and plan for ministry in a more intentional way. We move

Making the Connection

There is a special energy in a team when a plan comes together.

- *When have you been part of a team that accomplished something important to you?*
- *How did you work together to make it happen?*
- *What were the qualities of that team?*

beyond our instinct and involve others in creating ministry efforts that are beyond what we could imagine on our own. We name the tasks needed to complete a project in a way in which everyone can find a way to help. The situation is similar to Grandma's incredible spaghetti sauce. There comes a time when we want to learn how to make this sauce that Grandma puts together by heart by throwing in a little of this and a lot of that at just the right time. At some point, we need to watch Grandma and slow her down enough that we can write down the steps of the recipe. That way, more people can help make the sauce and we can share the recipe with other family members. Youth ministry is like that great sauce. If we have been putting it together on instinct, we need to slow down, involve others and take the time to vision and plan. That way, lots of people can join in the ministry and find their way to help.

I recently helped my middle school daughter's band transport instruments to the elementary school for a concert. I wasn't required to come to a meeting for this task, I was just asked to show up. Twelve parents with vehicles showed up to the school twenty minutes before the buses were to leave with the students. The band director came out to each vehicle as it arrived and decided which instruments we would carry. He gave us a sheet of paper on which he had written the kind of instruments that were to go into our car and an assigned vehicle number. We taped this sheet to the inside of a window visible to the outside. He told the youth to put their instrument into the vehicle assigned to their instrument and then remember the vehicle number so they could retrieve their instrument quickly when they arrived at the school. I helped youth load the instruments, joined in a caravan to the school and helped youth find their instrument upon arrival. I stayed for the concert, reversed the process when it was over and went home. This was a successful plan and I felt good about volunteering. I was asked to do something I could do and I wasn't required to spend a lot of extraneous time in meetings or decision-making.

This could have gone another way. If the band director had not had a plan, we would have arrived at the school needing to figure it out. We would have spent a lot of time trying to fit instruments into cars (loading and reloading, no doubt) and the young people would have had trouble knowing where their instruments were upon arrival (after all, minivans and SUVs begin to look alike after a while.) We would have wasted a lot of time and energy. A simple plan eliminates a lot of mess and makes any job easier. What we were being asked to do was simple and had been done before. It didn't need our best creativity, just cheerful coopera- tion (and safe driving). If the same band director wanted to plan a weekend trip for the band, he would gather a small group of parents to create a plan for the trip. The plan they would develop would include many more people to make it happen. Given the band director's style, everyone would show up and know how to do the task for which they were assigned.

This story demonstrates some principles to keep in mind. Good planning can save time and energy because we can anticipate what needs to happen when. That allows us to involve others in the project. We don't need to go overboard or expend all of our energy in plans and reports. Planning is functional—we should plan something just enough to make it clear so that everyone can join in and do their piece of the plan. When we want to accomplish a plan that takes creativity and new thinking, we need to involve people at the beginning and use a process that helps us capture and retain the creativity of the group. A good plan shouldn't slow us down and need not overcomplicate things, but it can multiply our ministry efforts because a good plan makes room for lots of people to participate and share in the work. It also anticipates the kind of support and cooperation needed to make it happen.

Effective Planning Steps

David Allen is a productivity specialist who works with businesses, corporations, and non-profit agencies to help them realize their objectives. He believes in the unlimited potential of human beings and their ability to create fantastic ideas, solve problems, and make unbelievable things happen. When these things don't happen, it is because we are stuck; stuck in patterns that are not productive and stuck in isolation from the resources that would help us solve our problems. He helps people get unstuck. His approach to planning is to use the natural way our brains plan to help us plan projects big and small. When we want to do something fun on a Friday night, we naturally think about what we're hoping for. We envision what it will be like to be with friends and we start thinking about the possible ways to get together. These hopes become a plan when we take the first step. We call to see if we can get reservations to the restaurant we want to go to or we check to see if the movie we want to see is showing or we call our friends to see what they want to do. The rest comes naturally.

In this simple process, you will find the elements of successful planning. According to Allen, we define the purpose and principles (why we want to go out). We envision the outcome (what it will be like to be together). We brainstorm options (Movies or dinner? Video or movie theater?). We organize (I'll start by calling Mike and Jane to see if they are available) and we identify the next actions (go online and get tickets for the 9 PM show). When we're planning something simple we don't think about these things. When we're planning for youth ministry, we need to. Sometimes, planning does not seem natural or easy because we get stuck. We start by trying to name the "good idea." We assume that everyone will support the good idea without taking the time to get them on board. We ask people to do parts of the plan without naming the principles that should guide the plan. Then we're surprised when the outcomes are different than we hoped.[3]

To be successful, planning for youth ministry should include these essential steps:[4]

- Name your purpose and vision
- Identify resources and partners
- Create a plan
- Build support
- Implement and refine
- Learn from experience

Naming Your Vision and Purpose

Why do you want to do your vision and purpose? Why is it important? What will happen if you do this? What will be lost if you don't? These are basic questions that are addressed when a team names the vision and purpose for their ministry. Asking the "why" questions has a variety of benefits:

It defines success. When you answer why you are doing something, you name what you are hoping for in explicit language. This way, you can evaluate and know when you are achieving your hopes. It will be hard to get anyone's support without a clear sense of why this is worth the effort, resources, and time.

It creates decision making criteria. Knowing why we are doing something helps us to know how to make key decisions about the project. If we are stuck between hard choices about a project, our clear statement of purpose will help us decide which choice preserves our hopes.

It aligns resources. Knowing why helps us "keep the main thing the main thing" and prioritizes our use of resources.

It clarifies focus. When we are in the midst of the project and it seems harder than we thought, a clear purpose can help us keep the team focused and remind us of the reason we are working so hard.

It expands options. When we are clear on the "why" of a project, we naturally expand our thinking about how to make the desired results happen. Allen describes it this way, "When people write out their purpose for a project in my seminars, they often claim it's like a fresh breeze blowing through their mind, clarifying their vision of what they're doing."[5]

Along with naming our vision, we also name our principles. We don't always think about the values and standards we have for a project until we experience a time when these principles are compromised. Inherent to the vision are certain standards that we expect will be part of what people will experience as a benefit of our ministry effort. Allen suggests that one way to think about your principles is to complete this sentence: "I would give others totally free rein to do this as long as they... —What?"[6] For example, if we are planning a retreat, we might name that we would give people free rein to plan the prayers as long as they connected to the theme, involved the whole community, and included dynamic music and readings. If we name the policies or the things that need to be true about the ministry, we are naming the principles that we hope will guide the entire project. This will also help us to trust other people to implement ministry in accordance with explicit principles.

Another part of naming our vision is to envision the outcomes. What will people experience when this ministry is implemented? What will it be like when youth and their families participate in this event or use these resources? Envisioning the future is a powerful planning tool. This exercise aligns our energy in the direction of the outcomes we are hoping for. This also helps us to begin envisioning the way we can accomplish our project. Allen suggests three basic steps for envisioning outcomes:

1. View the project from beyond the completion date.
2. Envision 'WILD SUCCESS' ! (Suspend "Yeah, but…").
3. Capture features, aspects, qualities you imagine in place.[7]

The results of this exercise are that you can give people a preview of the new place they will get to if they invest their energy, time, and resources in your plan. The energy that is created when you name your vision and purpose gets others on board with the vision and sustains the team in implementing the plan in a way that matches your values and hopes.

To name your vision and purpose:
- *Describe what you are trying to achieve and why it is important.*
- *Name the principles which should guide the project.*
- *Envision the outcomes that will result from implementation.*

Identify Resources and Partners

The movie *Apollo XIII* tells the story of how NASA rescued three astronauts during a failed moon exploration mission. The director of the operation for NASA names the purpose of their mission and draws a line on the chalkboard from a figure of the space module to the earth. "We have to figure out a way to get these men, in this module, to land on earth safely. Failure is not an option." Later in the movie, we see the engineers who designed the spacecraft trying to figure out a way to make the filters in the rocket module fit the filtering system in the lunar module. They have to make a square filter fit into a round hole. They begin their planning by pouring out a box of materials that represent everything the astronauts have available to them in their module.

Planning for youth ministry is like Apollo XIII; we have to start by naming our purpose and vision. Failure is not an option! Then we identify the resources and partners we have available to help us make the plan happen. In the case of parish youth ministry, resources will include financial resources, facilities, and resource materials like books, magazines, and Web sites that help us plan. People are also resources—parishioners with knowledge and skills who can help in our efforts. Sometimes, when we take the time to name our potential resources, we are surprised by the possibilities.

Partners are people who share our concern and our sense of urgency in accomplishing this mission. Anyone who agrees to the importance of our vision and purpose can be a partner in this project to some degree. Some partners will collaborate and help make the project happen. Others will lend their prayerful and public support for the project.

Partners could include other ministries or organizations in the parish or in the community. When we ask the question: "Who else would care about whether or not this happens?" we identify potential partners who could share our vision.

To identify resources and partners:
- *Name all of the resources available for the project.*
- *Identify partners who could support the effort.*

Create a Plan

How will we achieve what we hope for? How can we create a strategy or plan that will create the outcomes that we have envisioned? When we create a plan, we get practical and create a way to realize our dreams. One way to think about this part of the planning is to consider this image: our vision and purpose describe the island that we want to get to; our partners will accompany us on this journey, and our resources are our luggage. A creative plan is the bridge that gets us from where we are to where we want to be. This plan will include the main idea of the program or strategy. It also includes a description of the component parts of a plan, the sequence of steps, and the priorities to be maintained in implementation. The plan should be just detailed enough to provide clarity about the leadership steps and tasks.

Once the "what" and "why" (envisioning the outcome) have been named, ideas can be generated for the "how." To create an innovative and responsive plan, it often takes the creativity and shared wisdom of a team of people. One way to help unleash the creativity of a group is to engage in brainstorming. When an individual or a group brainstorms options, they are collecting new ideas in random order. This process generates new ideas, old ideas, big ideas, little ideas, good ideas, and not-so-good ideas. After the ideas are collected, they are compared with the purpose and outcomes. One or several that match well are chosen for implementation. Often this happens internally—in solving a problem we consider options and choose the one that feels right.

The key to brainstorming is to keep the ideas flowing, which means that we should instruct the group not to judge, debate, evaluate, or critique ideas until the end of the brainstorming time. This will keep a group from censoring ideas with phrases like, "that will never work," "we tried that once," or "that's not the way we do things." Refraining from judgment can be hard but it is the only way to maintain the energy. Team members can be assured that all ideas will later be compared to the defined purpose, principles, and vision.

This can be a helpful process even when you are planning something on your own. A scrap of paper and five minutes of permission to just write down new ideas can save an hour of trying to make something work.

After you have brainstormed and chosen options, it is good idea to begin planning some of the details. Some basic questions to address would include:

> ▷ What is the plan or strategy?
> ▷ When will the program be held or the strategy be implemented?
> ▷ Where will this happen?
> ▷ Do we need facilities?
> ▷ Who will be invited to participate?
> ▷ What will the plan include?
> ▷ What is an outline of the plan or strategy?
> ▷ What supplies are needed?
> ▷ How will we publicize?
> ▷ Who will help lead?
> ▷ Which of our partners can be part of this?

After you have named the plan and the pieces of the program or strategy, the next step is to name the various steps of the project and divide up the work.

The steps to the plan can be put into a sequence so that each piece of the plan comes together at the right time. For each step, name the task, the date by which it needs to be accomplished, and the leader or leaders responsible. With this information, your plan is getting close to being ready for implementation.

To create a plan:
- *Brainstorm options.*
- *Name the project's priorities, components, and sequencing.*
- *Identify who is going to do **what** by **when**.*

Plan for Support

Support can make or break our ministry plans. There are a variety of sources of support to consider. First, any plan or strategy designed for youth must have the support of youth and their families. A successful plan will involve adolescents and their parents from the early planning stages all the way through to implementation and evaluation. Input from these "stakeholders" in the ministry can help shape ministry efforts and provide valuable information about interests, availability, and competing events. In many parishes, youth and families have been on a roller coaster ride with youth ministry efforts that have risen and fallen with rotating leaders. To win their confidence back, we need to listen. We also need to share the ideas about new events and strategies with enthusiasm. We need to sell youth and families on the ideas and gain their support.

In addition to youth and families, an effective plan also needs support from the gatekeepers, which would include a variety of parish staff members and leaders. A gatekeeper is anyone, with an official or unofficial position, whose support can help make the event or strategy happen. These leaders often control the financial resources, the facilities, and the permission or the legitimacy that fledgling plans need to succeed. It is smart to involve these leaders in the planning and to work to get their support for ministry plans.

For example, let's say you are concerned about youth participation in liturgy and you are creating a plan to promote more active participation. You would want to meet with youth to find out more about their current experience of liturgy. You would also meet with the parents of youth to hear more about their concerns and hopes. This would help to shape your plan and could help create expectations and enthusiasm for new efforts. In your planning, you might have identified the director of religious education as a partner in these efforts. As the planning moves along and you begin to identify specific strategies, it becomes clear that the music director, the liturgist, and the sacristan are gatekeepers. In your community, you didn't see these leaders as partners in the project, but you now realize that you will need their support to implement your project, so you take the time to share information and incorporate their ideas and concerns into your planning.

As you are planning to build ownership and support, it is wise to realize the potential resistance you might experience if you are planning something that will change existing programs and patterns. As leaders, we might assume that everyone will be grateful when we provide something new or improve an existing program. We might be caught off guard when people resist the new ideas and sometimes actively work against our initiatives. John P. Kotter is the author of *Leading Change*, which describes step-by-step methods for helping make a change in a business, community, or organization. He suggests some ideas to keep in mind when planning for change:

- You need to lead change by planning for ways to address resistance right from the beginning of your initiative. Assume that people will have concerns and try to address these concerns with clear answers and a strong vision.
- If your change is significant, it is wise to involve leaders in your community that have enough authority to help the change be implemented. Create a team that includes gatekeepers and people of influence at the parish.
- To justify a change, you need to create a sense of urgency. You address these questions: Why is this new initiative needed? How will this help young people and their families? Change always involves risk and cost; you can plant the seeds for the new ideas by helping people to clearly see the need for the change.
- You need to make a case for the change you are proposing and communicate the purpose of your initiative throughout your community and its leaders. You should be able to articulate what you are doing and why in a brief statement or announcement so that people can understand and support the new ideas. Don't be afraid of over-communicating—it takes a while for new concepts to be understood.
- Create short-term wins, which could be small elements of the change that can be implemented right away and can be a visible way for people to see the benefits of the change. Be sure to take the time to publicly celebrate

these small "wins" as a way of helping the community to see the potential for bigger projects.[8]

To plan for support:
- *Be intentional about involving youth and their parents (stakeholders) from the beginning of the planning.*
- *Work to gain support for the project from parish staff and leaders (gatekeepers).*
- *Anticipate and plan for resistance to new program initiatives.*

Implement and Refine According to Your Principles

If you have ever been on a cross-country car trip, you will be familiar with the idea of "refining" your plan as you go. You might have made careful decisions about which roads to take and how far to go only to find that construction work and traffic jams send you in new directions. As you implement the plan for your project, you will be continuously making refinements to the plan. Because of your careful work in naming your purpose, principles, and envisioned outcome, these refinements are all made in conjunction with your vision. If all of the leaders share the vision and integrate the principles, refinements and adjustments can be made throughout the project as the team learns more about how to make this project fly. Sometimes, refinement is needed because new opportunities come along that make the project bigger and potentially more helpful. Sometimes, unforeseen challenges and resistance make the project harder than you thought it would be. Some leaders become frustrated when plans are adjusted, as though this means that the plans failed. Youth ministry requires flexibility; a plan is a good plan if it gets us where we need to go. We should expect that there will be shifts and changes as we go. This requires us to be open to the Spirit!

To implement and refine your project:
- *Remember the vision and principles that guide the project.*
- *Share the vision and principles with all of the team so that implementation matches with your hopes.*
- *Be ready to be flexible to seize new opportunities and address unforeseen challenges.*

Learn from Experience: Evaluation

Once we find ourselves in the place that we have been dreaming of, we will want to remember how we got there! We learn from our experience when we take the time to evaluate our plans. Through evaluation, we can see how the plan matched up with our stated purpose, vision, and outcomes.

There are different dimensions to evaluation. One source of evaluation should be the people who participate in the program or who benefit from the implemented strategy. Evaluation is always about listening; we need to be humble leaders who will accept praise and criticism of the efforts that we've planned. We can evaluate by meeting with youth and their families, by using written evaluations during an event, by following up with e-mail questionnaires, or by some combination of these methods.

It is also a good idea to ask for evaluation from collaborators, partners, and supporters of the project. This could include a variety of parish staff members and parish leaders. We want to find out more about their experience of the project. This input can help refine future planning.

A third source of evaluation is the team who implemented the project. From their perspective, how did the project go? What were the strengths and weaknesses? How did we meet our hoped-for outcomes? Where did we fall short? What did we learn in the process? We also want to evaluate the process of planning and implementing the project. As for team members, was their time used well? Were they prepared? How efficient and effective was the planning process? How did we treat each other as team members? What do we want to do differently next time?

The evaluations of the project should be collected and used by leaders to implement future and similar projects. The only way to learn from our experience is to take the time to listen and use the input we receive.

To learn from our experience:
- *Ask participants or those who used the resources of the project to evaluate the effectiveness of the project.*
- *Evaluate the project outcomes with partners, collaborators, and supporters.*
- *Evaluate the project with team members to determine the project's effectiveness and to learn about ways to improve the process of planning and implementing.*
- *Record and use the evaluation input in future projects.*

Applying the Planning Steps to an Event or Strategy

These planning steps can be used to plan for your overall ministry or for an individual event, program, or strategy. To use these planning steps, you begin by identifying what you want to do and why. Usually this starts with a sense that something is missing that needs to happen. Through our observation of youth, our conversations with young people, or the news we hear of events at other parishes, we become aware that our community needs something new to happen. As an illustration, let's explore what it would take to make a retreat come together for freshmen youth in your parish community. By talking to eighth graders and freshmen, you became aware of distinctive spiritual and support needs that freshmen face as they begin high school. In networking with other parish leaders, you hear about retreats that are designed for freshmen. To make this plan come together, you gather with others who could help make it happen and who you think would also be excited about this event, such as the youth ministry coordinator, the director of religious education, and some of the high school youth ministry volunteers.

At an initial meeting, you share the reason why you think this event would be important. You make your interests and your concerns come alive and share your commitment to help this happen. After some discussion, the group begins to name the purpose and vision for the event: this will be a "welcome young disciples" retreat that will help youth address the personal and spiritual issues of transition to high school and the changes they are experiencing as freshmen. This will also address changes in their family and skills for communication with parents. Hospitality and respect for retreat participants are named as two of the values that will guide this program (Name Your Vision and Purpose). The group identifies resources like books, Web sites, and leaders at nearby parishes with similar experiences. Nearby retreat facilities are located. The idea of potential partners is discussed. This leads to an idea of joining with two or three nearby parishes.

Eventually, the group decides to focus on youth within your parish to promote a sense of identity. High school juniors and seniors will be recruited to help plan and implement the retreat. The parish music director will be asked to join the retreat and help with music and worship (Identify Partners and Resources). You brainstorm themes and topics for the retreat to outline a tentative plan and schedule. Your team takes the time to identify and divide the tasks of the retreat. Each task is given a "complete by" date so that the plan can move ahead (Create a Plan). You gather with parents of eighth graders and you meet with eighth graders to tell them about the retreat plan for the fall. You also meet with the parish liturgist to plan for ways to include prayer about the retreat in the Sunday liturgies (Build Support). As you continue your plan, you change facilities because of concerns that have been raised about cost. You also involve more leaders in helping when you become aware of the interest in the retreat. As team leader, you meet with the retreat team to review the themes and prepare for the retreat details (Refine and Implement).

During the retreat, you plan for youth to complete a simple evaluation card. You also create a series of evaluation questions to ask youth participants and their parents in a simple phone interview. After compiling this information, you meet with the team to celebrate your work together on the retreat and to share the results of the evaluation. You take the time to evaluate the retreat with the team and you evaluate the process of planning to identify ways that the team could have been more efficient or prepared. You identify that the retreat could have been shorter to accommodate the freshmen's increased homework load. Team members ask for more training in leading small groups and encouraging good behavior of youth in future events. You thank the team members and record the plans and evaluation for future events (Learn from Experience).

Planning for Youth Ministry that is Built to Last

An important way to build a youth ministry that lives beyond a particular leader or team is to involve the parish in long-range planning. Jim Collins and Jerry Porras provide a schema for this type of planning in their book *Built to Last*, which is based on a research project about successful corporations. Collins and Porras make a distinction between clock building and time telling. A time teller reads the signs of the times and knows how to respond. He or she may be a charismatic leader who could be successful for a period of time because they can tell the time—they can read the signs of the current situation and respond effectively. However, these leaders don't invest in sharing this vision with the rest of the organization. A clock builder helps the whole organization know the time. They share the vision and build this competence and understanding throughout the organization. Through this effort, clock builders build organizations that outlast their tenure and excel over time. The corporations they studied were successful because they had this type of empowering and generous leadership.[9] Through their interviews and research, they also discovered that companies that remain successful have an identified core ideology that is made up of two parts: core values, which name the essential values or principles that guide every aspect of the organization's work, and core purpose, which is the reason why the organization exists. Organizations that name and live by their core ideology are able to sustain themselves over time because they continue to adapt to new circumstances while remaining true to their essential mission. Because they have named the things that should never change, they are free to change everything else. Sometimes organizations are out of alignment, which means that parts of the organization are aligned in a way that works contrary to the core ideology. Effective leaders take the time to name and correct these misalignments.[10]

The essence of *Built to Last* applies to parishes and ministries as well. By sharing the vision of youth ministry throughout our community, we help build a ministry that will outlast a particular leader or group of leaders. We are able to impact the culture and processes of the parish community. By naming the core values and purpose for our ministry, we can identify those things that will always be true about the ministry and give ourselves permission to innovate, adapt, change, and abandon the strategies, programs, and events that we use as long as we remain faithful to our core. By looking closely at our current youth ministry efforts, we can identify places where what we say does not match what we do—where we are out of alignment with our core ideology. The process of determining our alignment helps us to make sure that the experience of youth ministry throughout the parish matches our core values and purpose. This helps us to address the inconsistencies that youth sometimes experience between some youth ministry involvements and some ways that they are treated within their participation in parish life.

To engage your community in this kind of planning, gather a group of leaders that embody the essence of youth ministry in your community (including some gatekeepers and people of influence). Lead this group through the following steps.

1. Take the time to study and reflect upon *Renewing the Vision: A Framework for Catholic Youth Ministry.*
2. Introduce the concepts of core values and core purpose to your team using the insights and examples from *Built to Last,* chapter 11.

   "**Core values** are the organization's essential and enduring tenets—a small set of timeless principles that require no external justification; they have intrinsic value and importance to those inside the organization."[11]

   "**Core purpose**, the second component of core ideology, is the organization's fundamental reason for being. ... An effective purpose reflects the importance people attach to the company's work—it taps their idealistic motivations … it captures the soul of the organization … it is like a guiding star on the horizon—forever pursued, but never reached."[12]

3. Identify the core values of youth ministry in your community (narrow this list to three to seven key ideas).

4. Identify the core purpose of youth ministry in your community (this should be a statement that identifies the essence of the ministry).

5. Introduce the concept of alignment from *Built to Last*, chapter 11.

   "**Creating alignment** … requires two key processes: 1) developing new alignments to preserve the core and stimulate progress, and 2) eliminating misalignments—those that drive the organization away from the core ideology…."[13]

6. Take the time to evaluate how well your parish community is aligned with your core values and core purpose. Address these questions:

   ▷ What can we add to our youth ministry to better preserve our core values and core purpose and stimulate action? (Make two or three specific recommendations for new initiatives.)

   ▷ What should we eliminate from our youth ministry that's currently driving us away from our core values and core purpose? (Make two or three specific recommendations for changes or actions.)

Planning in Context for a Year or a Season at a Time

Travel is amazing when you have a wonderful host. Because they know you, your host considers what you would enjoy when planning for your visit. Because they know the area that you are visiting, they know how to connect you with places to see and experience. Planning for a year or season of youth ministry can be similar to being a good host; we plan better when we know young people and we know what is happening with their families, the parish, and the wider community. We take the real lives of youth and their families into consideration as we plan for ways to connect youth with the events, celebrations, and seasons of our parish, the Church year, and the community in which we live. Some of the events and strategies within youth ministry, like trips and retreats, require us to plan a year or more in advance. This allows time for fund raising, facilities planning, and team development. Many youth ministry teams plan most of their schedule a season at a time, working one season ahead of the one they are implementing. For instance, a parish could plan for three months of programming within each season, fall, winter, spring, and summer. In early September, the team will plan and develop their calendars for the winter season. While implementing the fall events in September, October, and November, the leadership team is completing the detailed plans and is inviting and preparing leaders for the events and strategies of the winter season, which will include December, January, and February. Working ahead in this way allows leaders the opportunity to publicize upcoming events and prepare leaders for their roles.

To plan for a season of ministry, consider these steps:

1. Gather information

You will need good information to make an effective plan. To avoid competing with schools, be sure to get the calendars for the Catholic, private, and public schools that youth attend. You will also need the calendar for parish events and the schedule for the liturgical year for the season in which you are working. If you have recently completed an evaluation of your ministry, a needs assessment process, or long range planning, be sure to have that information available to the team as you plan.

2. Consider the Context of the Season

To be a good host, we need to think about youth and their families as we develop a plan and calendars for the season. Use newsprint to collect the ideas from the team as you identify the context of the season by reflecting on these questions:

In the Lives of Youth What is happening in the lives of youth during this season? What are the stresses they might experience? What kinds of things are they experiencing in school? What events will they be paying attention to and attending? What is their energy level? Is this a season in which youth will be very focused on jobs?

In the Lives of Families of Youth What is happening in the lives of our families of youth in this season? What is happening for parents? What are the likely stresses? What is the energy level for families? What events or activities will be competing for family attention and time?

In the Life of our Parish Community What is happening in our parish community during this season? What is happening in the liturgical year? What parish traditions, events, and programs are scheduled during this season?

In the Life of our Wider Community What is happening in our wider community during this season? What is being emphasized in popular culture? What local traditions, events, and programs are scheduled during this season? How is the weather likely to affect our ministry this season?

3. *Identify Potential Opportunities and Conflicts*

This information will really help you make connections for youth and their families for the season that you are planning. Some of the events or issues present terrific opportunities for youth ministry to make a connection. For instance, during September, parents of incoming freshmen may be a bit nervous about how to support their young person in making this transition to high school. This could be an opportunity for a gathering of parents to share resources. Liturgical year events provide wonderful opportunities for helping youth to learn the faith and prepare for upcoming feasts and celebrations. Other events should be avoided when we are scheduling so that we don't compete for youth and family time. For example, Homecoming weekend would not be a good time for our fall retreat. Finals week for high school students would not be a good time to schedule a big fundraiser at the parish. However, it might be a great time to send home "study bags" to all the students.

Ask the team to identify the connections you collected from the previous questions and identify potential opportunities to connect and potential conflicts within this information. Consider these questions:

- In looking over the "context" of this season, what does this tell us about how we should plan?
- What opportunities are there to connect with youth and their families?
- What events represent a potential conflict? What should we avoid?

It is also a good idea at this point to post a list of those events, programs, and strategies that are already planned. You can start with ongoing programs, such as a youth community that meets weekly. You may also have extended events or special occasions that are planned a year in advance. For instance, you may have already decided to provide a retreat this season and Confirmation may already be scheduled.

With this information in hand, the team is ready to brainstorm new ideas for your continuing programs, new events, gatherings, programs, and strategies. You can feel more confident in your plans because you invested the time to think about the season and its connections for youth and their families.[14]

Creating Vibrant Ministry with Youth

"Then afterward I will pour out my spirit upon all mankind. Your sons and daughters shall prophesy, your old men shall dream dreams, your young men shall see visions...."

JOEL 3:1 (NAB)

God assures us that the Spirit will guide our efforts of creating vibrant ministry with youth. Disciples, young and old, will dream together and envision a ministry that helps youth to find their way in faith. To be effective in making our visions and dreams of ministry come to fruition, we need to trust and rely on this guidance.

We also need to be leaders with a passion for youth ministry. Communities are waiting for someone who can tell them with conviction that youth ministry can and will work in their parish. Passion makes a plan come together. It inspires others to join in the effort. People want to be part of something big and exciting. It makes resources become available. Leaders with confidence in a new plan can overcome the skepticism and resistance of a community that has been disappointed before. Most of all, passion for youth ministry makes youth want to come and see. Will this really be different? Youth and their families in our parishes are awaiting leaders with vision and passion who will use all of their resources to plan for ministry that serves and connects youth to our living faith.

— RECOMMENDED RESOURCES —

Allen, David. *Getting Things Done: The Art of Stress-Free Productivity*, New York: Penguin Books, 2001.

Bossidy, Larry, and Charan, Ram. *Execution: The Discipline of Getting Things Done*. New York: Crown Business Books, 2002.

Collins, James C., and Jerry I. Porras. *Built to Last: Successful Habits of Visionary Companies*, New York: Harper Collins, 1997.

East, Thomas. *Total Faith Initiative Coordinators Manual*. Winona, MN: Saint Mary's Press, 2004.

East, Thomas, et. al. *Effective Practices for Dynamic Youth Ministry*. Winona, MN: Saint Mary's Press, 2004.

Kotter, John P. *Leading Change*. Boston: Harvard Business School Press, 1996.

Renewing the Vision: A Framework for Catholic Youth Ministry. Washington, DC: United States Conference of Catholic Bishops, 1997.

Renew items at: www.
rockfordpubliclibrary.org

Item ID: 31112016992915
Title: Game of my life,
Chicago White Sox :
memorable st
Date due: 9/16/2019,23:59

Total checkouts for session:
1
Total checkouts:1

Do you know that by
borrowing from RPL today
you just saved: $24.95